fatoz

교양 영어

English
of
Culture

著者: 이 홍 구 (李 鴻 玖)
서울대학교 사범대학 영어교육과
서울대학교 대학원 영문학과
West Virginia University 영문학과

fatoz 교양 영어 (1st edition)
초판 1 쇄: 2015 년 11 월 10 일
Copyright ⓒ 2015 by Baron English Publishers

Printed in the Republic of Korea
ISBN 978-89-951232-1-8   53740

바른영어사 (신고번호: 제 2015-000009 호)
주소: 경기도 양평군 옥천면 아신리 상곡길 21
교재주문: 010-5136-9737 대표전화:031-773-2251

책 머리에

Shoot for the moon.
Even if you miss,
You will land among the stars.

영어 공부의 필요성은 새삼 말할 필요가 없겠지요. 외국인들과의 의사소통을 위해서는 물론이거니와 동서고금의 고전들을 읽는 독서 행위를 위해서도 절대 필요한 것이 외국어 공부랍니다. 영어 하나만이라도 제대로 익히면 웬만한 교양인이 되는 데 별 무리가 없을 것입니다. 하지만 외국어 공부는 기억력이 왕성할 때 하지 않으면 제대로 하기가 거의 불가능할지도 모릅니다. 많은 사람들의 경우에는 고등학교 시절의 영어 실력이 평생의 영어 실력이 된다고 해도 지나친 말은 아닐 것입니다.

영어를 잘 구사하기 위해서는 많이 듣고, 말하고, 읽고, 써야 함은 물론입니다. 그리고 무엇보다도 중요한 것이 빠르고 정확한 글읽기 입니다. 탄탄한 문법 지식과 풍부한 어휘력에 기초한 속독력이 영어 공부와 교양 독서의 관건이라 할 수 있습니다. 좋은 글과 문장들을 많이 접하면서 착실하게 꾸준히 익히는 수 밖에 없겠지요. "배움에는 王道가 없다(There is no royal road to learning.)"는 말이 있지요. 특히 외국어 공부는 더욱 그러합니다. 영어 공부에 지름길이 있다는 말은 크게 믿을 게 못됩니다.

이 책은 기본적으로 중급 정도의 영어 실력을 갖춘 학생들을 염두에 두고서 기획한 것입니다. 여러분이 더 높은 수준으로 도약하여 영어의 최고봉을 향해 나아감에 이 책이 적지 않은 도움이 되었으면 합니다. 부지런히 갈고 닦아서 영어라는 연장을 잘 다룰 수 있기를 바랍니다. 아울러 우리 모두 자유와 정의의 큰길에 앞장서 나아가는 용기 있는 민주 시민이요, 관용과 아량을 베풀 수 있는 "인간적인, 너무나도 인간적인" 세계 시민이 되었으면 합니다. 여러분의 건투를 빕니다.

Do your best,
for today will soon be tomorrow,
and tomorrow will soon be forever.

Contents

명작 감상

Unit 1 품사

1. 명사(noun)

1) cat, book; Paul, Korea; truth, beauty; water, coffee; family, police

2) dog*s*, bus*es*, cit*ies*, lea*ves*; feet, oxen, dice, media; fish, salmon, deer, sheep

3) a *cup* of coffee, two *glasses* of water, a *pound* of sugar, a *piece* of furniture

2. 대명사(pronoun)

1) I, you, they; myself, himself, themselves; one, some; who, what; mine, yours

2) *I* want something new. This is *my* friend. She likes *me*. This is *mine*.

3. 동사(verb)

1) "be"동사: I *am* a student. *Are* you a student? They *are not* students.

2) "have"동사: I *have* a car. He *has not* a car. She *doesn't have* a car.

3) 일반 동사: He *works* hard. She *does not work* hard. *Did* they *work* hard?

4. 형용사(adjective)

1) She is *beautiful*. She was a *beautiful* woman.

2) He is *alone*. She fell *asleep*. They look *alike*. We are *afraid* of the snake.

3) the rich, the poor, the young; the true, the good, the beautiful

5. 부사(adverb)

1) The dog runs *fast*. It's *too* expensive for me to buy. He likes her *very* much.

2) easily, carefully; badly, lately, nearly; seldom, hardly, scarcely, rarely

6. 전치사(preposition)

in, on, at, to, of, by, for, with, from, into, out of, beside, behind, instead of

7. 접속사(conjunction)

and, but, or, so, for; as, when, while, because, if, unless, (al)though, even if, as if, as soon as; not only ~ but (also) ~, either ~ or ~, neither ~ nor ~

8. 감탄사(interjection)

ah, eh, oh, lo, alas, ouch, crikey, God!, Jesus!, Heavens!, Wonderful!

[필수 문법] 품사(parts of speech)

* 문장을 구성하는 최소 단위인 개개의 낱말들을 그 기능별로 분류한 것.

* 문장이라는 완제품의 조립/생산에 동원되는 8 가지의 기능적 부품들(parts).

1. 명사: 세상 삼라만상의 이름을 지칭하는 낱말.

   1) 종류: 보통 명사, 고유 명사, 추상 명사, 물질 명사, 집합 명사 등이 있다.

   2) 복수형: 단수형에 "~(e)s"를 붙임; 불규칙형 (foot, ox, die, medium); 단수/복수 동일형

    *복수형이 되면 뜻이 달라지는 명사: arms (무기), pains (수고), goods (상품), glasses (안경)

   3) 물질 명사: 수량을 나타낼 때는 특정 단위를 도입함: a *loaf* of bread, two *sheets* of paper

2. 대명사: 이미 언급된 명사의 반복 사용을 피하기 위해, 그 명사를 대신해서 쓰이는 낱말.

   1) 인칭 대명사, 재귀 대명사, 부정 대명사, 의문 대명사, 소유 대명사 등이 있다.

   2) 인칭 대명사의 격변화: 주격(~는/가), 소유격(~의), 목적격(~을/에게), 소유대명사(~의 것):

   I my me mine; you your you yours; he his him his, she her her hers,
   it its it - ; we our us ours; you your you yours; they their them theirs

3. 동사: 사람이나 사물의 행위, 동작, 상태를 나타내는 낱말.

   1) "be" 동사: "~이다" 또는 "~에 있다"는 뜻: He *is* smart. Where *are* you? I *am* here.

   2) "have" 동사: 미국 영어에서는 대체로 일반 동사로 봄: *Do* you *have* a car? I *don't have* a car.

   3) 일반 동사: 부정문/의문문의 경우, 조동사 "do/does/did"를 도입: When *did* you do it?

4. 형용사: 사람/사물의 모양/상태를 나타내는 낱말: 술어 동사와 함께 서술부(predicate)를
   구성하는 "서술적" 기능을 갖거나, 뒤에 오는 명사를 수식하는 "한정적" 기능을 갖는다.

   1) 대부분의 형용사: 문장의 서술적 기능과 (명사를 수식하는) 한정적 기능 모두를 갖는다.

   2) 철자가 "a"로 시작되는 형용사: 서술적 기능은 갖지만, 대체로 한정적 기능은 못 가짐.

   3) 형용사 앞에 정관사 "the"를 붙이면, 흔히 복수 보통 명사나 단수 추상 명사가 된다:
    (부자들/빈자들/젊은이들; 진/선/미) *the accused (피고), the deceased (고인)

5. 부사: 동사나 형용사나 (또 다른) 부사를 수식하는 기능을 하는 낱말.

   1) "fast"는 동사 "run"을, "too"는 형용사 "expensive"를, "very"는 부사 "much"를 수식함.

   2) 형용사의 말미에 "~ly"를 붙이면 흔히 부사가 됨; "몹시, 최근에(recently), 거의(almost)";
   부정("not")의 의미를 담고 있는 부사들 대부분은 "거의/좀처럼 ~않다"의 뜻을 가짐.

6. 전치사: 명사/대명사 앞에 놓여서, 앞뒤의 낱말/어구를 서로 연결하는 기능을 하는 낱말.

7. 접속사: 등위 접속사, 종속 접속사, 상관 접속사: 앞뒤의 낱말/어구/어절을 연결하는 기능.

8. 감탄사: 기쁨/슬픔/놀람/고통/후회 등의 갑작스러운 격한 짧은 감정 표현을 위한 낱말.

[문법 연습 A] 잘못된 부분을 고치세요.

1. We had stayed up lately drinking whiskey.

2. They wanted many advices on how to do it.

3. Most of the people can neither read or write.

4. Is there new anything in today's newspaper?

5. The committee was divided in their opinions.

6. He didn't know her family was all early risers.

7. The police is looking for a tall, middle-aged man.

8. She couldn't hardly understand what he was saying.

9. The nurse was kind itself to the patients of the ward.

10. The space shuttle was launched to carry alive animals.

11. Neither of the three sisters wants to get married to him.

[문법 연습 B] 밑줄 친 낱말의 품사는?

1. He is nothing <u>but</u> a mere opportunist.

2. It was the <u>very</u> book I was looking for.

3. I know all of you <u>long</u> to see her again.

4. There's nothing <u>like</u> a good cup of coffee

5. You were there quite a <u>while</u>, weren't you?

6. I still enjoyed the week <u>despite</u> the weather.

7. There was always some question <u>regarding</u> education.

8. I've been running <u>about</u> all morning trying to find you.

9. There is, <u>however</u>, another thing you have to remember.

10. You may understand that we learn <u>much</u> from experience.

11. <u>Once</u> the sun had set, the air in the valley turned very cold.

12. He's tall <u>enough</u> to change the bulb without getting on a chair.

13. She remained silent, <u>for</u> her heart was heavy and her spirits low.

14. Flattered <u>as</u> I was by his attention, I knew he wasn't the man for me.

[실전 문법 A] 각 문항의 바른 문장은?

1. 1) Nile River is longest in the world.

   2) The Nile is longest river in the world.

   3) Nile River is the longest in the world.

   4) The Nile is the longest river in the world.

   5) The Nile River is a longest river in the world.

2. 1) Cattle was sold for next to nothing last year.

   2) They used to sit up lately at night on weekends.

   3) We have only a two-weeks vacation during the year.

   4) The jury were different in their opinions on the accused.

   5) There was wonderful something in the story of her dream.

3. 1) The children never have seen such a funny sight.

   2) They were very busy to answer the phones in the office.

   3) This software is for computers running on Windows 7 or later.

   4) There are many alone people living in apartments in urban area.

   5) I was standing just nearly enough to hear what they were saying.

[실전 문법 B] 각 문장의 빈칸에 알맞은 것은?

1. Do you have to buy _____ for the new house?

   1) many new furniture   2) much new furniture

   3) many new furnitures   4) much new furnitures

2. The epic appealed to my dramatic instinct, and excited _____ in me.

   1) poetry   2) a poem

   3) a poet   4) the poet

3. I know you are busy, but I have a matter _____ to discuss with you.

   1) very important   2) much importance

   3) of vital importance   4) with much importance

   5) for the great importance

[필수 어휘 A] 밑줄 친 부분의 뜻은?

1. His failure <u>was due to</u> his ignorance.　　＿＿＿＿＿＿＿＿＿＿

2. The committee <u>is due to</u> meet tonight.　　＿＿＿＿＿＿＿＿＿＿

3. He <u>is likely to</u> be still in love with her.　　＿＿＿＿＿＿＿＿＿＿

4. They <u>are anxious to</u> please their guests.　　＿＿＿＿＿＿＿＿＿＿

5. The poison <u>is capable of</u> causing death.　　＿＿＿＿＿＿＿＿＿＿

6. I <u>am</u> well <u>aware of</u> the dangers we face.　　＿＿＿＿＿＿＿＿＿＿

7. She <u>was forced to</u> take part in the crime.　　＿＿＿＿＿＿＿＿＿＿

8. He <u>is inclined to</u> be somewhat domineering.　　＿＿＿＿＿＿＿＿＿＿

9. He seems to <u>be acquainted with</u> my brother.　　＿＿＿＿＿＿＿＿＿＿

10. This kind of shoe <u>is apt to</u> slip on wet ground.　　＿＿＿＿＿＿＿＿＿＿

11. We <u>are supposed to</u> wear a seat belt in the car.　　＿＿＿＿＿＿＿＿＿＿

12. They <u>were</u> still <u>willing to</u> die for their country.　　＿＿＿＿＿＿＿＿＿＿

13. The actress <u>was reluctant to</u> be photographed.　　＿＿＿＿＿＿＿＿＿＿

[필수 어휘 B] 밑줄 친 부분의 뜻은?

1. The prices <u>are subject to</u> change.　　＿＿＿＿＿＿＿＿＿＿

2. We <u>are</u> all <u>gifted with</u> conscience.　　＿＿＿＿＿＿＿＿＿＿

3. Children <u>are prone to</u> colds in winter.　　＿＿＿＿＿＿＿＿＿＿

4. My friend <u>was involved in</u> the robbery.　　＿＿＿＿＿＿＿＿＿＿

5. Your problems <u>are</u> very <u>similar to</u> mine.　　＿＿＿＿＿＿＿＿＿＿

6. They <u>were</u> seriously <u>exposed to</u> radiation.　　＿＿＿＿＿＿＿＿＿＿

7. We <u>are</u> fully <u>convinced of</u> your innocence.　　＿＿＿＿＿＿＿＿＿＿

8. I <u>was</u> utterly <u>absorbed in</u> what I was doing.　　＿＿＿＿＿＿＿＿＿＿

9. She <u>is</u> not <u>suited for</u> the role of motherhood.　　＿＿＿＿＿＿＿＿＿＿

10. They <u>are preoccupied with</u> their final exams.　　＿＿＿＿＿＿＿＿＿＿

11. We <u>are opposed to</u> the use of nuclear weapons.　　＿＿＿＿＿＿＿＿＿＿

12. I <u>am grateful</u> to you <u>for</u> all you've done for me.　　＿＿＿＿＿＿＿＿＿＿

13. He <u>is indebted to</u> his parents for all he has today.　　＿＿＿＿＿＿＿＿＿＿

[구문 연습] 다음 문장을 우리말로 옮기세요.

1. Narcissus, wearied with hunting in the heat of the day, lay down here: for he was attracted by the beauty of the place, and by the spring. While he sought to quench his thirst, another thirst grew in him, and as he drank, he was enchanted by the beautiful reflection that he saw.

2. He fell in love with an insubstantial hope, mistaking a mere shadow for a real body. As golden wax melts with gentle heat, as morning frosts are thawed by the warmth of the sun, so he was worn and wasted away with love, and slowly consumed by its fire.

3. Nothing remained of that body which Echo once had loved. His sisters mourned for him, and cut off their hair in tribute to their brother, but his body was nowhere to be found. Instead of his corpse, they discovered a flower with a circle of white petals round a yellow center.

[작문 연습] 다음 문장을 영어로 옮기세요.

1. 나의 취미는 낚시, 등산, 음악 감상, 그리고 기타 연주이다.

2. 저희에게 물 한 잔, 커피 두 잔, 맥주 세 병 갖다 주시겠습니까?

3. 그녀는 음악과 미술뿐만 아니라 문학과 철학에도 흥미를 느꼈다.

4. 오늘날 거의 모든 생활 영역에서 새 것이 낡은 것을 몰아내는 것 같다.

5. 정부 당국은 가난하고 소외된 이들을 돌볼 준비가 되어있어야만 한다.

[실전 독해 A]   각 문항의 물음에 답하세요.

1.   One of the questions often asked in a Reading Comprehension test is about the main idea of the passage. The main idea is the most important idea in the passage or what the passage is about. The main idea is more _____ than the subordinate ideas or supporting details in the passage. The main idea may be the first or the last sentence in the paragraph, but this is not always the case. If the main idea of the passage is not clear, combine the main points of each paragraph to find the main idea. The main idea should relate to the entire passage and not to just one part of it. Also, the main idea should not be so _____ that it goes beyond the passage.

> Q. 빈칸에 공통으로 들어갈 낱말은?
>   1) formal   2) general   3) compact
>   4) accurate   5) effective

2.   Why do you read light materials so slowly? Are you afraid that you will "miss something" or "lose comprehension" if you skip a few words? Your old habits can slow you down unnecessarily. The paradoxical truth is that when reading material is fairly easy, your comprehension actually drops if you read it too slowly. Many studies have shown that average readers can double their rate in general reading with no loss of basic comprehension. And if you are ready to venture into rapid reading, you must be prepared to use your eyes efficiently. Use soft focus as you read. Don't peer tensely at the words. Relax your eye muscles and face muscles. Look slightly above the line of print, and let your eyes "float" down the page. Try to read the lines, not each letter and word. As you concentrate on the ideas on a page rather than on each word, your brain will become more alert and active. In fact, comprehension often improves because you are reading fast enough to see the materials as a whole and to focus on the content.

> Q. 이 글의 내용과 일치하지 않는 것은?
>   1) 속독을 위해서는 낡은 독서 습관을 고쳐야 한다.
>   2) 빨리 읽어도 글의 이해력이 떨어지는 것은 아니다.
>   3) 독서에서 중요한 것은 빠르고도 정확한 글읽기이다.
>   4) 빨리 읽는 것이 글의 전체적인 내용 파악에 유리하다.
>   5) 속독할 때는 긴장을 풀고 눈을 효율적으로 사용해야 한다.

3. ¹⁾Children seem to be always getting into trouble, but someday parents will look back upon all this and laugh. ²⁾No mother or father wants to be the parent of a brat; parents everywhere try to control their children's behavior. ³⁾Some parents spank their children, and other parents won't let their children watch TV or eat dessert. ⁴⁾In Korea or Japan, parents often send their children outside when they misbehave and tell them they can't come into the house. ⁵⁾In the United States, parents do just the opposite: they send their children to their bedrooms and tell them they can't go outside.

   Q. 1)～5)의 문장 중 글의 흐름에 맞지 않는 것은?

4. Picasso shocked the most adventurous artists when he painted the work, *The Ladies of Avignon*. He was searching for new ways to paint and was inspired by several African artworks, including the masks made by the Fang people, and the brass figures made by the Bakota people. When Picasso saw the African works, he realized that African artists had their own standards for art that were very different from European ideas of realistic beauty. African works seemed to Picasso more direct and powerful than European works, and they gave him new ways to think about art. The African artworks Picasso saw were _____ images of the human face. Picasso decided to experiment with ways of showing human features based on African styles of representation. Like the faces in the African works, Picasso's faces in *The Ladies of Avignon* have triangular noses, long ovals for faces, and dashes for mouths. Because Picasso's figures looked to European artists as though they were made up of cubes and triangles, this style came to be known as cubism.

   Q 1. 빈칸에 알맞은 낱말은?
       1) abstract   2) modern   3) primitive
       4) traditional   5) conspicuous

   2. 이 글의 주제는?
       1) Picasso's new conception of art
       2) Picasso's tastes in African works
       3) The origin and development of cubism
       4) *The Ladies of Avignon* as a masterpiece
       5) The effect of African artworks on Picasso

[실전 독해 B] 각 문항의 물음에 답하세요.

1. Some thieves, on breaking into a house, found nothing in it but a cock, which they picked up and took away. They were about to sacrifice it, when it begged to be spared on the plea that it rendered men a useful service by waking them before daybreak to start their work. "All the more reason for killing you," was the reply, "for by waking them you stop us from stealing.

> Q. 이 글의 제목으로 적절한 것은?
>   1) A Good Reason   2) A Useful Service
>   3) An Absurd Opinion   4) A Poor Excuse for Theft
>   5) A Different Point of View

2. Americans are fascinated by their own love of shopping. This does not make them unique. ① It's just that they have more to buy than most other people on the planet. It's also an affirmation of faith in their country, its prosperity and limitless bounty. ② They have shops the way that lesser countries have statues. When the superlative Union Station was rebuilt in Washington, what did they choose to stuff it with? ③ They are the first thing many visitors see when they arrive in the nation's capital, proud symbols of America's majesty. The Capitol is what you see next. ④ Food stores are among the glories of America. The most stupendous grocery I have ever seen was the Safeway in Page, Arizona. Page is a small town in the middle of the desert. ⑤ America is the only country in the world where desert dwellers believe they have the right to live precisely as if they inhabited the center of a large temperate city.

> Q 1. ①~⑤중 다음 문장이 삽입되기에 적절한 곳은?
>   *Dozens of shops, of course.*
>
> 2. 이 글의 제목으로 적절한 것은?
>   1) The Union Station   2) Food Stores in America
>   3) The American Faith   4) Shops as American Symbols
>   5) Americans' Love of Shopping

3. ①We're waiting for a _____ to come from Germany. ②He came from a remote _____ of China. ③Accountants now play a very active _____ in the shaping of international business. ④They will be taking _____ in the discussions, along with many other organizations. ⑤We live in a society which is in large _____ determined by the underlying structure of our ethical beliefs.

Q. ①~⑤의 문장의 빈칸에 공통으로 들어갈 낱말은?

4. High school students who took a public speaking class had to give a speech. One student chose as her topic euthanasia—the painless killing of people who are incurably sick. After she gave her speech, one student said to another, "Her speech was interesting. But she didn't say anything about teenagers in countries like China, Korea or Japan." The student thought the topic of the speech was not "Euthanasia" but "_____."

Q. 빈칸에 들어갈 적절한 말은?
   1) Eurasia   2) Europeans
   3) Eastern countries   4) Youth in Asia
   5) The death of Asian teenagers

5. Antarctica is the most isolated place on earth. Every year, scientists from all over the world travel there to work in conditions of extreme cold, a)with temperatures reaching minus 100 degrees Fahrenheit. b)In addition to being cold, the atmosphere is extremely dry and windy. Between February and October each year c)it gets very cold that parts of the continent are inaccessible. Around the middle of the continent, near the South Pole Station, the cold weather causes plane fuel to change consistency, d)making impossible for aircraft to land. Between February and October, thus, the team of researchers at the station must live together in isolation.

Q. 밑줄 친 a)~d)중 어법에 맞지 않은 것은?
   1) a, b   2) c, d   3) b, c
   4) b, d   5) a, d

[명작 감상]　　　Nathaniel Hawthorne (1804 ~ 1864)
　　　　　　　　The Great Stone Face 『큰 바위 얼굴』

One afternoon, when the sun was going down, a mother and her little boy sat at the door of their cottage, talking about the Great Stone Face. They had but to lift their eyes, and there it was plainly to be seen, though miles away, with the sunshine brightening all its features....

The Great Stone Face, then, was a work of Nature in her mood of majestic playfulness. It was formed on the perpendicular side of a mountain by some immense rocks, which had been thrown together in such a position as, when viewed at a proper distance, precisely to resemble the features of the human countenance. It seemed as if an enormous giant or a Titan had sculptured his own likeness on the precipice. There was the broad arch of the forehead, a hundred feet in height; the nose, with its long bridge; the vast lips, which, if they could have spoken, would have rolled their thunder accents from one end of the valley to the other.

It was a happy lot for children to grow up to manhood or womanhood with the Great Stone Face before their eyes, for all the features were noble, and the expression was at once grand and sweet, as if it were the glow of a vast, warm heart, that embraced all mankind in its affections, and had room for more. It was an education only to look at it. According to the belief of many people, the valley owed much of its fertility to this benign aspect that was continually beaming over it, illuminating the clouds, and infusing its tenderness into the sunshine....

And Ernest never forgot the story his mother told him. It was always in his mind, whenever he looked upon the Great Stone Face. He spent his childhood in the log-cottage where he was born, and was dutiful to his mother, and helpful to her in many things, assisting her much with his little hands, and more with his loving heart. In this manner, from a happy yet often pensive child, he grew up to be a mild, quiet, unobtrusive boy, and sun-browned with labour in the fields, but with more intelligence brightening his aspect than is seen in many lads who had been taught at famous schools. Yet Ernest had had no teacher, save only that the Great Stone Face became one to him.

---

* Youth is the opportunity to do something and to be somebody.
　젊음은 의미 있는 일을 하고 의미 있는 사람이 될 기회다.

[학인 학습] 다음 문장을 우리말로 옮기세요.

1. Many studies have shown that average readers can double their rate in general reading with no loss of basic comprehension.

2. They were about to sacrifice it, when it begged to be spared on the plea that it rendered men a useful service by waking them before daybreak to start their work.

3. America is the only country in the world where desert dwellers believe they have the right to live precisely as if they inhabited the center of a large temperate city.

4. It was formed on the perpendicular side of a mountain by some immense rocks, which had been thrown together in such a position as, when viewed at a proper distance, precisely to resemble the features of the human countenance.

5. According to the belief of many people, the valley owed much of its fertility to this benign aspect that was continually beaming over it, illuminating the clouds, and infusing its tenderness into the sunshine.

[words & phrases]

A1: reading comprehension 독해, subordinate 종속적인, combine 결합하다, relate to ~에 관련되다
A2: skip 건너뛰다, paradox 역설, efficient 효율적인, float 떠다니다, alert 방심 않는, content 내용
A3: get into trouble 말썽을 일으키다, brat 개구쟁이, behavior 행동/행위, spank 찰싹 때리다/갈기다,
A4: inspire 고취하다/고무하다, mask 탈/가면, brass 놋쇠, experiment 실험(하다), represent 묘사하다,
　　oval 계란형, be made up of ~으로 구성되어 있다, cube 정육면체, triangle 삼각형, cubism 입체파
B1: but ~외에는, be about to(do) 막 ~하려고 하다, sacrifice 희생(하다), plea 탄원/간청, 변명/핑계
B2: fascinate 매혹시키다, affirm 긍정하다, prosper 번영하다, bounty 하사품/축하금, statue 상/조상,
　　stuff 채워 넣다, Capitiol 의사당, stupendous 굉장한, inhabit 거주하다, temperate 온화한/온대의
B3: accountant 회계사, play a part in ~에 역할을 하다, shape 모양/형성하다, ethics 윤리/윤리학
B4: give a speech 연설하다, euthanasia 안락사, incurable 치료할 수 없는, not A but B (A가 아니라 B)
B5: Antarctica 남극 대륙, isolate 고립시키다, in addition to ~외에도, access 접근, consistency 농도/밀도
C1: cottage 오두막, perpendicular 수직의, countenance 용모/안색, sculpture 조각(하다), precipice 절벽,
　　lot 운/운명, embrace 포옹(포용)하다, affection 애정, owe 빚지다, fertile 비옥한, benign 자애로운,
　　pensive 생각에 잠긴, obtrusive 주제넘은/거슬리는, lad 소년, save ~을 제외하고는

[실력 점검 A] 다음 각 동사의 우리말 뜻을 쓰세요.

1. owe: 2. skip: 3. mourn:

4. float: 5. cause: 6. enchant:

7. crush: 8. reflect: 9. interrupt:

10. inherit: 11. isolate: 12. multiply:

13. submit: 14. interpret: 15. establish:

16. quench: 17. reproach: 18. dominate:

19. represent: 20. comprehend:

[실력 점검 B] 각 항목에 대응하는 영어 단어를 찾아 쓰세요.

보기 crop, reward, coward, weapon, fatigue, peasant, sacrifice, originality, proverb, tolerance, commodity, stable, divine, fragile, prevalent, instructive, fossil, accessible, substantial, transparent

1. 상품: 2. 화석: 3. 무기:

4. 희생: 5. 속담: 6. 피로:

7. 관용: 8. 보답: 9. 농부:

10. 농작물: 11. 겁쟁이: 12. 독창성:

13. 신성한: 14. 투명한: 15. 상당한:

16. 안정된: 17. 교훈적인: 18. 풍미하는:

19. 부서지기 쉬운: 20. 접근하기 쉬운:

[실력 점검 C] 빈칸에 알맞은 낱말은 쓰세요.

1. What is a good man _____ a bad man's teacher?

 What is a bad man _____ a good man's job?

2. Thieves and burglars try to find a house _____ the people are _____ vacation and not likely to return soon. They do this by looking for houses _____ no lights _____ in the evening. When mail and newspaper are piled _____, they can tell that the people have been _____ for days.

명시 감상

Once Only

Gary Snyder

almost at the equator

almost at the equinox

exactly at midnight

from a ship

the full

moon

in the center of the sky.

* equator 적도, the spring(=vernal) equinox 춘분, the autumnal equinox 추분, midnight 자정, the full moon 보름달

Unit 2   주어

A. 주어의 유형

1) *One* must do one's best. *They* speak English in Canada.

2) *Curry and rice* is one of my favorite foods.

3) *The rich* are not always happier than the poor.

4) *Reading a good book* is like making a good friend.

5) *To keep early hours* is a good habit of life.

6) *That smoking causes cancer* is already known.

7) *How we should live* is an important moral question.

B. 가주어/진주어

1) *It* is no use *crying over spilt milk.*

2) *It* is necessary *to help poor people around us.*

3) *It* is important *for you to be present at the meeting.*

4) *It* is not always true *that slow and steady wins the race.*

5) *It* doesn't matter *who will win the race tomorrow.*

C. 비인칭 주어

1) What time is *it*? *It*'s five to ten. *It*'s a quarter past ten.

2) *It*'s raining. *It*'s getting dark. *It*'s cold and windy today.

3) What day of the week is *it* (today)? *It*'s Wednesday.

4) What day of the month is *it* (today)? *It*'s April the first.

5) How far is *it* (from here) to your school? *It*'s ten minutes' walk.

6) How is *it* going (with you)? *It*'s all finished between us.

D. 형식 주어

1) *There* is *someone* at the door. *There* were *many plants* in her house.

2) *It* was Peter *that* I happened to see in the library yesterday.

   It was in the library *that* I happened to see Peter yesterday.

E. 주어의 생략

1) Sit down. Be seated, please. Don't buy that stuff.

2) Thank you. Nice to meet you. See you tomorrow.

   Seems you're tired. Serve you right! Why reproach him?

[필수 문법] 주어(subject)

* 문장의 술어 동사가 나타내는 행위, 동작, 상태의 주체.
* 문장의 술어 동사와의 사이에 인칭 및 수의 일치를 보인다.
* 명사, 대명사, 명사구, 명사절, 전성명사 등이 주어가 될 수 있다.

A. 주어의 유형

  1) 일반 주어: one, we, you, they: *We* have much rain in summer.

  2) 명사/대명사: *John* is very smart. *The computer* is now a necessity of life.

  3) 전성 명사/명사구: *Slow and steady* wins the race.

  4) 동명사: *Keeping a diary in English* is a good way to improve your English.

  5) 부정사: *Early to bed and early to rise* makes a man healthy and wealthy.

  6) that-절: *That slow and steady wins race* is not always true

  7) 기타 명사절: *Where the treasure is buried* is still a mystery.

B. 가주어/진주어

  예문의 "it"는 모두 가주어: 뒷부분에 있는 명사구/명사절이 진주어.

  1) It ~ ...ing ~ : *It* is important *making good friends*.

  2) It ~ to ~ : *It* is not easy *to keep a diary every day*.

  3) It ~ for ~ to ~ : *It* seems impossible *for him to finish the work in a week*.

  4) It ~ that ~ : *It* is already known *that smoking causes lung cancer*.

  5) It ~ 기타 명사절: *It* makes no difference *whether we believe in God or not*.

C. 비인칭 주어

  예문의 "it"는 모두 비인칭 주어: 시간/날씨/요일/날짜/거리/사정(상황) 등을 나타냄.

  What time is *it*? *It* was Sunday and 10 o'clock in the morning. Is *it* Friday, the thirteenth?

  How long does *it* take to get to Boston? *It* is all over with him.(그는 이제 끝장이다.)

D. 형식 주어

  1) 예문의 "there"는 형식상의 주어: 내용상의 주어는 각각 *someone, many plants*.

    There was *nobody* there. There can be *no doubt* about it. There lived *an old man* there.

  2) 예문의 "it"는 강조 구문(it is ~ that ~)의 형식 주어: 예문에서 강조되고 있는 부분은

    각각 *Peter, in the library*: "내가 어제 우연히 만난 것은 피터/도서관에서였다."

E. 주어의 생략

  1) 명령문에서는 대체로 주어 "You (will)"이 생략된다: Open the door, will you?

  2) 구어체의 평이한 말투에서는 흔히 주어/(동사)가 생략된다:

    (It's) nice to see you. (I'm) pleased to meet you. (I'll) see you tomorrow.

    Why (do you) reproach him? (It) serves you right! (꼴 좋다, 고소하다!)

[문법 연습 A] 잘못된 부분을 고치세요.

1. It is you that is to blame for the accident.

2. Ten years were a long time for her to wait.

3. If she will come tomorrow is still uncertain.

4. All work and no play make Jack a dull boy.

5. You are necessary to learn a foreign language.

6. A good set of encyclopedias are quite expensive.

7. Either the boys or their mother know where he is.

8. The Japanese is an industrious and economical people.

9. My brother as well as my parents have been to Europe.

10. The poet and novelist are going to attend the conference.

11. A number of plants and animals is in danger of extinction.

12. The educated is not necessarily wiser than the uneducated.

13. Not only the students but also their teacher seem to believe it.

14. Many an artist have attempted to capture the moods of nature.

[문법 연습 B] 각 문장의 주어를 찾아 밑줄을 치세요.

1. Very little is known about Aesop, the author of *Fables*.

2. How life began has been a topic of debate for many centuries.

3. Whosoever saves a single life is as if he saved the whole world.

4. So barren is much of the land that it is difficult even to raise sheep.

5. From a series of observed facts and phenomena a wider law uniting them all was formulated.

6. How we dispose of nuclear wastes and where we get rid of them have been serious social issues.

7. Whether or not the child eats what is put on his plate depends entirely upon what is put on his plate.

8. From the moment of our birth the customs into which we are born begin to shape our experience and behavior.

9. That secondhand smoke, like active smoking, can cause serious health problems has been shown by several studies.

10. Most helpful to the peaceful atmosphere that the children need but cannot produce for themselves is the presence of comforting music.

[실전 문법 A] 빈칸에 알맞은 낱말은?

1. _____ is done cannot be undone.

2. There was a small lake in the village, wasn't _____?

3. It is not what one has but what one is _____ matters.

4. Of all the states, _____ has so much open space as Montana.

5. _____ could be more ridiculous than to be angry with a baby.

6. _____ it is good for a man to realize that he is "the heir of all ages" is pretty commonly accepted.

7. _____ have been periods in history when remarkable progress was made within a relatively short span of time.

8. I think _____ must be very seldom that a writer looks upon any work of his on the whole with complete satisfaction.

9. _____ the soul survives death is a matter as to which opinions may differ, but _____ there is a soul seems unquestionable.

[실전 문법 B] 각 문항의 다섯 부분 중 어법에 맞지 않는 부분은?

1. [1]Five hundred dollars [2]are a big amount [3]for a person [4]to spend [5]in a day.

2. [1]Some fish, like salmon, [2]remember the precise taste [3]of the water [4]in which [5]it hatched a long time ago.

3. [1]There have been [2]much speculation about the effects [3]that a four-day or five-day workweek [4]would have [5]upon industry and economy.

4. [1]This should be noted [2]that our new products, [3] the tiny digital camera [4]and the brand-new copier, [5]represent modern electronic technology.

5. [1]The English may think [2]that all foreigners are frightfully funny. [3]In his eyes it is comical [4]that people talk foreign languages [5]and shake hands too often.

6. [1]Such mass media as radio, television and cinema, [2]helps mankind share the delights of the arts, [3]but none of them has [4]so lasting and profound an effect [5]as reading.

[필수 어휘 A] 다음 각 형용사의 명사형을 쓰세요.

1. poor: 2. high: 3. deep:

4. wise: 5. long: 6. wide:

7. cruel: 8. simple: 9. jealous:

10. strong: 11. fluent: 12. popular:

13. various: 14. modest: 15. accurate:

16. curious: 17. solitary: 18. miserable:

[필수 어휘 B] 다음 각 동사의 명사형을 쓰세요.

1. hate: 2. obey: 3. deny:

4. solve: 5. occur: 6. attend:

7. explain: 8. suspect: 9. describe:

10. pursue: 11. destroy: 12. consume:

13. neglect: 14. explode: 15. complain:

16. acquire: 17. conquer: 18. emphasize:

19. descend: 20. discover: 21. distinguish:

[필수 어휘 C] 밑줄 친 부분을 주어진 철자로 시작되는 낱말로 대체하세요.

1. Nothing will <u>stop</u> him from being an artist.   p _____

2. I believe they can <u>tell</u> the fox from the wolf.   d _____

3. She could not <u>account for</u> her foolish mistake.   e _____

4. How did the important discovery <u>come about</u>?   h _____

5. Science <u>brings about</u> many changes in our life.   c _____

6. He <u>got rid of</u> mud from his shoes and trousers.   r _____

7. I couldn't <u>make out</u> what she was trying to say.   u _____

8. Eva <u>makes believe</u> she knows nothing about it.   p _____

9. He waited for an hour but she did not <u>show up</u>.   a _____

10. A great earthquake <u>took place</u> in Kobe, Japan.   o _____

[구문 연습] 다음 문장을 우리말로 옮기세요.

1. There are few subjects within the compass of my interests that I have not lightly or seriously touched upon.

2. The fact is that every problem can be studied as such with an open mind without knowing what has already been learned about it.

3. Whatever one does is not only a reward in itself, but will be further rewarded in the sequel; and it is this that so few can understand.

4. Freedom of speech is now taken as a matter of course, but it has taken centuries to persuade people that liberty to express one's opinions is indispensable for the social life of human beings.

5. Just as it is vital for parents to live their own lives as fully as possible and to deepen their understanding of themselves to the utmost, so is it important for teachers and educators to do the same.

[작문 연습] 다음 문장을 영어로 옮기세요.

1. 내 컴퓨터에 무언가 문제가 있음에 틀림이 없다.

_____

2. 실례지만, 지하철역까지 걸어서 얼마나 걸릴까요?

_____

3. 그가 요전 날 서점에서 만난 것은 바로 내 누이였다.

_____

4. 내가 내일 아침 일찍 일어나는 것은 거의 불가능하다.

_____

5. 중요한 것은 네가 하는 모든 일에 최선을 다하는 것이다.

_____

[실전 독해 A] 각 문항의 물음에 답하세요.

1. _____ is one of the most universal and deep-seated of human passions. It is very noticeable in children before they are a year old, and has to be treated with the most tender respect by every educator. The very slight appearance of favoring one child at the expense of another is instantly ^{a)}observed and resented. Distributive justice, absolute and rigid, must be ^{b)}observed by anyone who has children to deal with.

> Q 1. 빈칸에 알맞은 낱말은?
>   1) Hate   2) Envy   3) Pride
>   4) Greed   5) Prejudice
>
>   2. 밑줄 친 a), b)의 각각의 명사형은?

2.   Pessimism is often portrayed as the sign of the intellectual, and optimism as the philosophy of the fool. Novelist James Cabell says, "The optimist proclaims that we live in the best of all possible worlds. The pessimist fears this is true." If you are an optimist, you probably look at life a little differently from many other people. Partly cloudy to you means mostly ^{a)}_____. If you lose your map and don't know where you are, you think of it as a chance to enjoy some sightseeing. When you lose your job, you think of it as a chance to ^{b)}_____ careers. Pessimists probably call you "unrealistic." They say you see the world "through rose-colored glasses" instead of "the way it really is"; they say you are a dreamer. But scientific research suggests that optimists may know something we can all learn from. The research links optimism to health and well-being; optimists tend to be healthier and happier.

> Q 1. 빈칸 a), b)에 들어갈 각 낱말은?
>
>   2. 이 글의 논지는?
>   1) Think positive.
>   2) Take your chance.
>   3) The optimist is not a dreamer.
>   4) The optimist enjoys life as it is.
>   5) Optimism is the sign of a happy man.

3. It is a ^{a)}_____ of a gentleman to say that he is one who never inflicts pain. He is mainly occupied in removing the obstacles which hinder the free action of those around him. The benefits he provides may be considered to be parallel to what is called comforts or conveniences in the affairs of ordinary life; that is, he is like an easy chair or a warm bath, which does its part in easing fatigue or providing warmth. The true gentleman carefully avoids whatever may cause a jolt in the minds of ^{b)}_____ with whom he is associated; his great concern is to make everyone feel at ease and at home. He is tender toward the bashful, gentle toward the distant, and merciful toward the absurd.

Q 1. 빈칸 a)에 들어갈 적절한 낱말은?

2. 빈칸 b)에 들어갈 낱말을 본문에서 찾으면?

4. So much sentimentality is attached to the rose in popular feeling that it is difficult to separate the original mythological and folkloric beliefs from the sentimental dross that surrounds the flower. Yet if we look into the beliefs, we find that the rose is much more than the mere symbol of romantic love invoked by every minor poet and painter. One of its most common associations in folklore, for example, is with death. The Romans often decked the tombs of the dead with roses; in fact, Roman ^{a)}_____ frequently specified that roses were to be planted on the grave. To this day, in Switzerland, cemeteries are known as rose gardens. The rose also has a long association with feminine beauty. Shakespeare mentions the rose more frequently than any other flower, often using it as a token of all that is lovely and good. For the Arabs, on the other hand, the rose was a symbol not of feminine but of ^{b)}_____ beauty. Later it became a sign of secrecy and silence. The expression *sub rosa*, "under the rose," is traced to a Roman belief. During the sixteenth and seventeenth centuries, it was common practice to carve or paint roses on the ceilings of council chambers to emphasize the intention of secrecy.

Q 1. 빈칸 a)에 들어갈 낱말은?
    1) arts   2) wills   3) myths
    4) customs   5) religions

2. 빈칸 b)에 들어갈 낱말은?

[실전 독해 B] 각 문항의 물음에 답하세요.

1   Most of the problems youngsters are seeking to solve were created for them by adults. It is, thus, little amusing to hear adults complaining and criticizing teen-agers, whom, they say, they cannot understand. It is understandable for them to fail to understand youngsters, but what I cannot understand is that they quickly forget <u>to, it, be, was, like, what, young</u>, especially to be a teen-ager.

　　　Q. 밑줄 친 7개의 낱말을 문맥에 맞게 배열하면?

2.　　Can you simply stay away from microbes and remain healthy? No. Microbes are found throughout your house and school, and on your body. Some helpful microbes even live *inside* your body. Your immune system doesn't work to get rid of these microbes, because they are essential for normal body functions, such as digestion. There are many harmful microbes, however, that the human immune system must recognize and fight. They include certain types of bacteria, fungi, protozoa, flatworms, hookworms, and roundworms. [a)]_____, the immune system must deal with viruses. These harmful microbes enter the human body through a cut in the skin, or through body openings such as nose or mouth. Other microbes, such as the fungus that causes athlete's foot, simply attach to the skin and cause disease there. Even before the immune system begins to do its job, the body tries to combat certain microbes and viruses with other defenses. You may have noticed that when you begin to get a cold, you sneeze and cough a lot, and you need to blow your nose frequently. Sneezing and coughing are reflexes that try [b)]_____.

　　　Q 1. 빈칸 a)에 들어갈 적절한 말은?
　　　　　1) Thus　　2) Similarly　　3) Otherwise
　　　　　4) In addition　　5) For example

　　　2. 빈칸 b)에 들어갈 적절한 말은?
　　　　　1) to fortify your immune system
　　　　　2) to protect your body from fever
　　　　　3) to keep you from catching a cold
　　　　　4) to warn you of the infectious disease
　　　　　5) to expel certain germs from your body

3.   A man can learn to use a hammer without any instruction whatever, even if instruction may speed up his progress toward skill. Human superiority depends upon observing as well as doing; few animals are capable of true observation prior to performing a trick, but a human being readily profits by _____.

   Q. 빈칸에 알맞은 낱말은?
      1) tools   2) instincts   3) example
      4) education   5) information

4.   [1]Because there are so many superstitions, it is not surprising that some of them are contradictory. [2]In Germany, it is good luck when the left eye twitches and bad luck when the right eye twitches. [3]Accidentally putting on clothes inside out brings good luck in Pakistan but bad luck in Costa Rica. [4]In Chile, young people won't take the last piece of food on the plate because it means they will never marry. [5]In Thailand, unmarried people take the last piece because it means they will marry someone good-looking.

   Q. 1)~5)의 문장 중 글의 흐름에 맞지 않은 것은?

5.   Humans have been fascinated by the concept of time for centuries. In Europe, in the fourteenth century, the hourglass was used. Time was measured by having a quantity of sand, water, or mercury [1]to run from the upper to the lower part over a set period of time. The first spring-powered clock was invented around 1510 by a German [2]named Peter Henlein. The power for this clock came from a metal coil inside called a mainspring. This was a more accurate timepiece than any previously used, but there was a problem; as the mainspring [3]unwound, the hands of the clock moved slower, and the clock lost time. Battery-powered clocks were first used in the 1840s, with electric and quartz-powered clocks [4]coming into use in the early 1900s. With the invention of battery and electric-powered clocks, there was no longer the need [5]to wind a mainspring.

   Q. 밑줄 친 1)~5)중 어법에 맞지 않는 것은?

[명작 감상]　　　Ernest Hemingway (1899 ~ 1961)

The Old Man and the Sea 『노인과 바다』

He was an old man who fished alone in a skiff in the Gulf Stream and he had gone eighty-four days now without taking a fish. In the first forty days a boy had been with him. But after forty days without a fish the boy's parents had told him that the old man was now definitely and finally *salao*, which is the worst form of unlucky, and the boy had gone at their orders in another boat which caught three good fish the first week. It made the boy sad to see the old man come in each day with his skiff empty and he always went down to help him carry either the coiled lines or the gaff and harpoon and the sail that was furled around the mast. The sail was patched with flour sacks and, furled, it looked like the flag of permanent defeat.

The old man was thin and gaunt with deep wrinkles in the back of his neck. The brown blotches of the benevolent skin cancer the sun brings from its reflection on the tropic sea were on his cheeks. The blotches ran well down the sides of his face and his hands had the deep-creased scars from handling heavy fish on the cords. But none of these scars were fresh. They were as old as erosions in a fishless desert.

Everything about him was old except his eyes and they were the same colour as the sea and were cheerful and undefeated.

"Santiago," the boy said to him as they climbed the bank from where the skiff was hauled up. "I could go with you again. We've made some money."

The old man had taught the boy to fish and the boy loved him.

"No," the old man said. "You're with a lucky boat. Stay with them."

"But remember how you went eight-seven days without fish and then we caught big ones everyday for three weeks."

"I remember," the old man said. "I know you did not leave me because you doubted."

"It was papa made me leave. I am a boy and I must obey him."

"I know," the old man said. "It is quite normal."

---

* Still waters run deep.　　깊은 물은 조용히 흐른다.
* Good words cost nothing.　　칭찬은 돈이 들지 않는다.

[확인 학습] 다음 문장을 우리말로 옮기세요.

1. The very slight appearance of favoring one child at the expense of another is instantly observed and resented.

2. The benefits he provides may be considered to be parallel to what is called comforts or conveniences in the affairs of ordinary life; that is, he is like an easy chair or a warm bath, which does its part in easing fatigue or providing warmth.

3. Human superiority depends upon observing as well as doing; few animals are capable of true observation prior to performing a trick, but a human being readily profits by example.

4. It made the boy sad to see the old man come in each day with his skiff empty and he always went down to help him carry either the coiled lines or the gaff and harpoon and the sail that was furled around the mast.

[words & phrases]

A1: favor 총애하다, at the cost of ~을 희생시키고, resent 분개하다, distribute 분배하다, justice 정의

A2: pessimism 비관주의, portray 묘사하다, intellectual 지성인, optimism 낙관주의, philosophy 철학, proclaim 선언하다/공포하다, well-being 복지/행복, tend to (do) ~하는 경향이 있다

A3: inflict 가하다, be occupied in ~에 종사하다, obstacle 장애물, hinder 방해하다, benefit 이익/혜택, parallel 평행하는/대응하는/유사한, what is called 소위/이른바, fatigue 피로, cause 초래하다, jolt 충격/동요, be associated with ~와 관련되다/교제하다, bashful 수줍어하는, absurd 불합리한

A4: folklore 민속, dross 찌꺼기/불순물, association 관련/연상, invoke 불러 일으키다, deck 장식하다, specify 명시하다, grave 무덤, cemetery (공동)묘지, secrecy 비밀/은밀, practice 관행, carve 파다/새기다, ceiling 천장, council 회의/의회, chamber 방/회의소, emphasize 강조하다, intention 의도

B1: seek 찾다/추구하다, adult 어른/성인, complain 불평하다, criticize 비난하다/비판하다

B2: microbe 미생물, immune system 면역체계, digestion 소화, fungus 버섯/균류, protozoa 원생동물, athlete's foot 무좀, combat 전투(하다), sneeze 재채기(하다), reflex 반사작용/반사운동,

B3: instruction 교육/지시, superiority 우월성, prior to ~보다 앞서, trick 재주/장난, profit 이익

B4: superstition 미신, contradictory 모순적인, twitch 경련/씰룩거리다, accidentally 우연히, plate 접시

B5: mercury 수은, invent 발명하다, accurate 정확한, timepiece 시계, quartz 석영, wind 감다/휘감다

C1: skiff 소형 범선, gaff 갈고리, harpoon 작살, furl 접다/감다, sail 돛, flour 밀가루, permanent 영원한, defeat 패배/패배시키다, gaunt 여윈, wrinkle 주름살, blotch 반점, benevolent 자비로운, blotch 종기/얼룩, reflection 반사, tropic 열대의, scar 흉터, erosion 침식, haul 끌어당기다, obey 복종하다

[실력 점검 A] 다음 각 동사의 우리말 뜻을 쓰세요.

1. resent: 2. reveal: 3. conceal:

4. punish: 5. furnish: 6. improve:

7. portray: 8. explore: 9. diminish:

10. invent: 11. replace: 12. condemn:

13. inspire: 14. capture: 15. distribute:

16. imitate: 17. classify: 18. formulate:

19. dispose of: 20. get rid of:

[실력 점검 B] 각 항목에 대응하는 영어 단어를 찾아 쓰세요.

보기   end, origin, species, dialect, content, disguise, moisture, consequence, miracle, evidence, statement, instrument, superiority, conception, phenomenon, expert, extinct, sufficient, aggressive, outstanding

1. 내용: 2. 증거: 3. 진술:

4. 개념: 5. 목적: 6. 기적:

7. 결과: 8. 도구: 9. 방언:

10. 현상: 11. 수분: 12. 기원:

13. 변장: 14. 종(種):   15. 우월성:

16. 전문가: 17. 충분한: 18. 뛰어난:

19. 멸종된: 20. 공격적인:

[실력 점검 C] 주어진 철자로 시작되는 알맞은 낱말을 쓰세요.

1. W_____ answered the phone was a very charming woman.

2. False friends are like our s_____, keeping close to us while we walk in the sunshine, but leaving us directly we cross into the s_____.

3. Socrates, the c_____, laid down his hammer and chisel and took up a spear and s_____ instead. He fought in several b_____, and Athens had no b_____ soldier.

명시 감상

The Red Wheelbarrow

W. C. Williams

so much depends
upon

a red wheel
barrow

glazed with rain
water

beside the white
chickens

* wheelbarrow 외바퀴 손수레, depend upon ~에 달려 있다/의존하다, glazed 반들반들한, 윤(광택)이 나는

Unit 3   동사

A. 동사의 종류

1) I *think*, therefore I *am*. Time *flies* like an arrow.

2) They *are* college students. The coffee *tastes* good.

3) She *likes* swimming. Her sister *wants* to live abroad.

4) He *gave* me the money. He *bought* me a book yesterday.

5) I *think* him to be honest. Why should we elect him Mayor?

B. 동사의 유형

1) I *hope* to see you soon. He *refused* to take the bribe.

   She *agreed* to pay for it. Would you *care* to go for a walk?

2) I *stopped* smoking. He *finished* writing his report.

   We *enjoyed* playing cards. Do you *mind* staying a little longer?

3) It may *cost* him his life. I *envy* you your fine garden.

   Forgive me my sins. It *saved* us much time and energy.

4) We *expected* you to come. What *caused* the plants to die?

   He *allowed* me to go. Money *enables* us to do a lot of things.

5) I *heard* him come in. We *saw* them enter the house.

   Let me know your address. Would you *have* me believe that?

6) I *had* my hair cut. Did you *have* your car fixed ?

   David *had* his bike stolen. She *had* her hat blown off.

7) The children *found* it exciting to throw stones at the dog.

   I *think* it very important that we should help our neighbors.

8) He is going to *sell* his house. I am not sure if his house will *sell*.

   Make hay while the sun shines. Hay *makes* better in small heaps.

9) *Put* it *on*. *Take* them *off*. *Put* your hat *on*. *Take off* your shoes.

   Get along well with your friends. I just can't *put up with* it.

   Thank you *for* coming. What *prevented* you *from* coming?

[필수 문법] 동사(verb)

* 문장의 술어 동사는 주어의 행위, 동작, 상태 등을 나타낸다.

* 동사는 완전 동사와 불완전 동사, 자동사와 타동사로 나뉠 수 있다.

* 불완전 동사는 보(충)어(complement)를, 타동사는 목적어(object)를 수반한다.

A. 동사의 종류

  1) S+**V**: 완전 자동사: Where *are* you?   The flower *blooms* in summer.

  2) S+**V**+C: 불완전 자동사: 명사/대명사/명사구/명사절이나 형용사/현재분사/
     과거분사 등이 보어가 될 수 있다: The cloth *feels* soft.   She *seems* (to be) happy.
     He *became* very excited.   We *kept* waiting.   She *went* blind.   The milk *turned* sour.

  3) S+**V**+O: 완전 타동사: 명사/대명사/명사구/명사절 등이 목적어가 될 수 있다:
     Do you *know* how to drive?   I *wonder* if he will come here tomorrow.

  4) S+**V**+O+O: 완전 타동사 (수여/여격 동사): 2개의 목적어, IO(간접목적어:"~에게")와
     DO(직접목적어:"~을/를") 취하는 동사: 이 형식은 "S+V+O"의 형식으로 전환될
     수도 있는데, 이 때는 동사에 따라 전치사 "to"나 "for"를 수반함:
        He *gave* the money *to* me.   (give/tell/show/lend/send/owe/bring 등의 경우)
        She *bought* a book *for* me.   (buy/make/get/do/order/leave/spare 등의 경우)

  5) S+**V**+O+C: 불완전 타동사: 목적어와 (목적격)보어의 관계는 주어와 술어동사의
     관계처럼 또 하나의 "서술적 관계(nexus)"이다: (=I think that *he is honest*.)

B. 동사의 유형

  1) hope/want/wish/care/agree/refuse/pretend 등의 동사는 to-부정사를 목적어로 취한다.

  2) stop/enjoy/finish/mind/avoid/consider/give up 등의 동사는 동명사를 목적어로 취한다.

  3) cost/envy/forgive/save/(ask) 동사는 "S+V+O+O"의 형식에서 "S+V+O"의 형식으로
     전환될 수 없다: "She *asked* many questions *of* me."의 문장은 널리 쓰이지는 않음.

  4) want/expect/cause/allow/enable 등의 동사는 to-부정사를 목적격 보어로 취한다.

  5) hear/see/watch/notice/feel 등의 지각동사와 let/make/have/(help) 등의 사역동사는,
     원형 부정사를 목적격 보어로 취한다: 동사 "help"는 to-부정사를 취하기도 함.

  6) have(=get)+목적어(사물)+과거분사: "~을 ~되게끔 시키다/당하다"의 뜻을 갖는다.

  7) find/make/think/believe 등의 동사는 흔히 "가목적어('it')+목적격보어(명사/형용사)
     +진목적어(명사구/명사절)" 구조를 취함: I made *it* a rule *to get up at six in the morning*.

  8) 자동사/타동사, 완전동사/불완전동사 양쪽으로 모두 쓰이는 동사도 적지 않다:
     He *made* toward the city hall. (=moved)   She will *make* a good wife. (=become)

  9) 동사는 흔히 부사/전치사와 결합하여 구동사(phrasal verb)나 동사구(verbal phrase)가
     된다.   * Put on *it*. (x) Take off *them*. (x): 목적어가 대명사인 경우, 반드시 동사와
     부사 사이에 위치해야 함: Put *them* on. (o) Put *your shoes* on. (o) Put on *your shoes*. (o)
     * Get along (with) ~(와) 잘 지내다/해나가다,   put up with ~을 참다/견디다
     * thank ~ for ~: ~에게 ~에 대해 감사하다,   prevent ~ from ~: ~을 ~못하게 하다/막다

[문법 연습 A] 틀린 곳을 고치세요.

1. I was stolen my bike yesterday.

2. Does this sentence sound rightly?

3. We provided them food and water.

4. Do you think what is he going to do?

5. That will save a lot of trouble for you.

6. Did you notice him to steal into the house?

7. They wanted her to marry with a man of wealth.

8. We hope you to win the first prize in the contest.

9. Do you want to discuss about the problem with me?

10. They succeeded to make contact with the kidnappers.

11. We did the mistake of leaving our window open last night.

12. Jane explained me why she had to be late for school this morning.

13. Don't approach to the problem from a purely economic perspective.

[문법 연습 B] 다음 문장에 쓰인 동사의 종류를 표시하세요.

1. We *called* him a taxi.   완전/불완전   자동사/타동사

2. We *called* him a fool.   완전/불완전   자동사/타동사

3. She *smiled* her brightest.   완전/불완전   자동사/타동사

4. They *painted* the door green.   완전/불완전   자동사/타동사

5. Please *make* yourself at home.   완전/불완전   자동사/타동사

6. Here *lies* William Shakespeare.   완전/불완전   자동사/타동사

7. It ill *becomes* you to be envious.   완전/불완전   자동사/타동사

8. All this will *come* right in the end.   완전/불완전   자동사/타동사

9. He *kept* me waiting at the bus stop.   완전/불완전   자동사/타동사

10. Her statement *turned out* to be false. 완전/불완전   자동사/타동사

11. His own efforts *made* him what he is. 완전/불완전   자동사/타동사

12. I *found* it impossible to convince him. 완전/불완전   자동사/타동사

[실전 문법 A] 빈칸에 알맞은 낱말을 쓰세요.

1. Most people seem to prefer dogs _____ cats.

2. The mist may _____ him from seeing very far.

3. The heavy rain has _____ the river to overflow.

4. The theory of evolution is _____ complex origin.

5. I _____ my picture taken at the shop the other day.

6. The gentleman made _____ difficult for us to refuse.

7. We are not trying to deprive you _____ daily necessaries.

8. Mr. Smith absented _____ from the meeting this morning.

9. She attributes her success _____ a friend's encouragement.

10. Such safety system will _____ the pilot to land without mishap.

11. Do you think that examinations _____ a large part in education?

[실전 문법 B] 각 문항의 다섯 부분 중 어법에 맞지 않는 부분은?

1. [1]Every effort [2]must be done [3]by modern men [4]to preserve [5]trees, plants, and wildlife.

2. [1]The automobile [2]has made possible [3]to work in the city [4]and yet live in the suburbs [5]many miles away.

3. [1]Recycling, [2]a process of conserving [3]mineral and timber wealth, [4]makes a great effect [5]on our society.

4. [1]Ultraviolet rays are [2]invisible to humans, [3]and the world would look very differently [4]if human eyes were [5]sensitive to them.

5. [1]Hundreds of wildlife refuges [2]have been established [3]throughout North America [4]to provide animals a safe place [5]in which to live.

6. [1]I do not like mystical language, [2]but I hardly know [3]how to express what I mean [4]without employing phrases [5]that sound poetically.

7. [1]When I entered into the room [2]with my daughter, [3]my husband was watching television [4]and my little boy was sleeping [5]beside him.

[필수 어휘 A] 다음 각 낱말의 동사형을 쓰세요.

1. rich: 2. large: 3. short:

4. long: 5. strong: 6. threat:

7. force: 8. simple: 9. poverty:

10. body: 11. prison: 12. danger:

[필수 어휘 B] 빈칸에 알맞은 동사를 택하세요.

1. If you don't have any butter, margarine will _____.

   1) do   2) fit   3) prefer   4) nourish   5) substitute

2. Some plants only _____ fruit once every twelve years.

   1) sow   2) bear   3) keep   4) grow   5) ripen

3. Who do you think will _____ the house when she dies?

   1) adopt   2) dwell   3) inherit   4) discard   5) appoint

4. I am glad John won the award; he thoroughly _____ it.

   1) makes   2) covers   3) prevails   4) confirms   5) deserves

5. Jane _____ to go back to work after she has had her baby.

   1) tends   2) tempts   3) attends   4) intends   5) contends

[필수 어휘 C] 밑줄 친 부분을 주어진 철자로 시작되는 낱말로 대체하세요.

1. Water consists of oxygen and hydrogen.   c_____

2. A fire broke out in a neighborhood school.   o_____

3. My mother brought up five children alone.   r_____

4. I came across a beautiful poem in the book.   e_____

5. Such a thing will never come to pass again.   h_____

6. We should do away with the death penalty.   a_____

7. He was completely taken in by the boy's story.   d_____

8. He made good and returned home a millionaire.   s_____

9. The book will turn out to be of some use to you.   p_____

10. I was invited to be foreman but I turned it down. r_____

[구문 연습] 다음 문장을 우리말로 옮기세요.

1. It is the artists who teach us to see new beauties in nature of whose existence we have never dreamed.

2. Let wealth be regarded by some society of the future as a mere means to the proper ends of human life.

3. I see to it that men are created equal, and I think it our duty and privilege that we make every effort to build an equal society.

4. The more important a thing is to us, the more difficult we find it to cut down our consumption and the less effect do changes in its prices have on the amount we buy.

5. I heartily wish that in my youth I had had someone of good sense to direct my reading. I sigh when I reflect on the amount of time I have wasted on books that were of no great profit to me. What little guidance I had I owe to a young man who came to live with the same family in Heidelberg as I was living with.

[작문 연습] 다음 문장을 영어로 옮기세요.

1. 오늘날의 내가 있게 된 것은 내 부모님 덕택이다.

   _____

2. 비가 몹시 와서 우리들은 어제 학교에 갈 수 없었다.

   _____

3. 그는 자기 딸이 시험에 합격한 것을 당연하게 여긴다.

   _____

4. 그녀는 좋은 친구를 사귀는 것이 어렵다는 것을 알았다.

   _____

5. 컴퓨터는 우리에게 많은 일을 신속하게 할 수 있게 해준다.

   _____

[실전 독해 A] 각 문항의 물음에 답하세요.

1.   In a world of competing states every nation seeks to protect itself. ① It wants other countries to become dependent on them but it does not want to become dependent on them. ② For whereas international trade makes nations more interdependent, they try to regulate their imports and exports in such a way that they will be more independent. ③ The basic wish of every nation is to be secure and prosperous but these selfish goals are unattainable. ④ In the world of the 21st century no country is secure from attack, and prosperous countries excite the envy of the impoverished majority. ⑤ This is one reason why the modern age has been called "the Age of Anxiety," but there are other reasons also for the strains and tensions that afflict modern society.

   Q. ① ~ ⑤ 중 다음 문장이 삽입되기에 적절한 곳은?
      This situation creates a paradox.

2.   For hundreds of years in Europe, religious art was almost the only type of art that existed. Churches and other religious buildings were filled with paintings that depicted people and stories from the Bible. Although most people couldn't read, they could still understand biblical stories in the pictures on church walls. By contrast, one of the main characteristics of art in the Middle East was its _____ of human and animal images. This reflects the Islamic belief that statues are unholy. By Islamic law, artists are not allowed to copy human or animal figures except on small items for daily use. Thus, on palaces, mosques, and other buildings, Islamic artists have created unique decoration of great beauty with images of flowers and geometric forms.

   Q 1. 빈칸에 들어갈 적절한 낱말은?
       1) variety   2) absence   3) worship
       4) mixture   5) harmony

    2. 이 글의 제목으로 적절한 것은?
       1) The Types of Religious Art
       2) The Religious Use of Images
       3) Characteristics of Religious Art
       4) The Function of Religious Buildings
       5) Art as a Reflection of Religious Faith

3.   Man must be the most aggressive and cruel of all living creatures. If we say a violent man is behaving "like a beast," we are slandering animals, as/no/so/for/man/beast/behaves/violently. When a territorial animal or bird encroaches upon the territory of another creature of the same species, the latter will only perform ritual gestures of hostility to warn off the intruder. _____, should a fight ensue, neither creature will be badly hurt, for the loser will save himself by making a gesture of submission. Normally one animal will only kill another for food, and rarely does an animal kill a member of its own species.

   Q 1. 밑줄 친 8개의 낱말을 문맥에 맞게 배열하면?

      2. 빈칸에 들어갈 적절한 말은?
        1) Instead   2) Besides   3) Similarly
        4) Furthermore   5) Nevertheless

4.   Everyone lies. Little lies, perhaps, which may not cause serious problems, but still they are lies. We fudge on how old we are, how much we weigh, what we are paid. Some people tell their children that Santa Claus will come on Christmas Eve.

   Consider the last time you got a phone call from someone you didn't want to talk to. Did you perhaps a)_____ falsely that you were just on your way out the door? Did you ever promise anyone, "we'll do lunch," when you know you'd never b)_____ together? Did you ever c)_____ for the phone to call in sick to work, then leap from bed to enjoy the day? Did you ever tell someone you d)_____ money to that the check was in the mail when it wasn't?

   Few excuses serve as many purposes as lying. We grow up to use lies, or at least little lies, to e)_____ things that should be done, to make people believe us, to get what we want, to buy time, to end conversation, and to f)_____ relationships going.

   The most understandable reason people lie is so they don't hurt others' feelings. But even though people lie for some good reasons, lying can be harmful. The most difficult thing for anyone to do is to tell others that he or she lied to them.

   Q. 빈칸 a) ~ f)에 들어갈 각 낱말의 번호는?
      1) get   2) have   3) reach   4) avoid   5) claim
      6) take   7) keep   8) made   9) owed   10) borrowed

41

[실전 독해 B] 각 문항의 물음에 답하세요.

1. Women are twice as likely as men to develop a headache. At least four thousand women in Phoenix have been reported to suffer from headaches, but as many as a third of all cases may never be revealed.

  Q. 이 도시의 두통 환자는 대략 몇 명?
    1) 6000명   2) 8000명   3) 9000명
    4) 10000명   5)12000명

2. The relationship between humans and animals dates back to the misty morning of history. The caves of southern France and northern Spain are full of wonderful depictions of animals. But long before art, we have evidence of the closeness of humans and animals. The bones of dogs lie next to those of humans in the excavated villages of northern Israel and elsewhere. This unity of death is terribly appropriate. It marks a relationship that is the most ancient of all, one that dates back at least to the Mesolithic Era. With the dog, the hunter acquired a companion and ally very early on, before agriculture, long before the horses and the cats. The companion animals were followed by food animals and then by those that provided enhanced _____. We may have domesticated those individual animals that were orphaned by our hunting ancestors. The steps from the home-raised wolfling to the domestic dog probably took countless generations. I bet it started with affection and curiosity. Only later did it become useful. The animal has a sense of smell and hearing several times more acute than our own, great advantages to a hunting companion and intrusion detector. The dog's defense behavior makes it an instinctive guard animal.

  Q 1. 빈칸에 들어갈 적절한 말은?
    1) power   2) friends   3) relation
    4) life and welfare   5) speed and range

   2. 이 글의 제목으로 적절한 것은?
    1) The Companion Animals
    2) The Dog as a Guard Animal
    3) The Origin of the Domestic dog
    4) The Domestication of Wild Animals
    5) The Relationship of Dogs and Humans

3. ①They sent us a _____ for the work they had done. ②The American Congress passed a special _____ forbidding the army to waste any more money. ③Can I have quarters for this one-dollar _____? ④There was a pretty _____ on the outside wall of the garden. ⑤The humming-bird has a long curving _____ for extracting nectar from blossoms.

   Q. ①～⑤의 문장의 빈칸에 공통으로 들어갈 낱말은?

4. Often people who hold higher positions in a given group overestimate their performance, ^{a)}while/though those who are in the lowest levels of the group underestimate theirs. Even if this may not be always true, it indicates that the actual position in a group has ^{b)}little/much to do with the feeling of personal confidence a person may have. Thus, members who hold higher positions in a group or feel that they have an important part to ^{c)}take/play in the group have more confidence in their own performance.

   Q. 밑줄 친 a)～c)에서 어법에 맞는 각 낱말은?

5. Employees often call their bosses by their first names, and they even sometimes joke freely with the president of the company.
   ⓐ Instead, they would rather think of the boss as an equal.
   ⓑ Obviously, however, the company president has more power than a lower-level employee.
   ⓒ This informal behavior and communication occur among people at all levels in the business and political worlds.
   ⓓ Despite this, many Americans choose not to be overly polite and formal with a person of a higher status.
In other words, the American tendency is to minimize status differences rather than to emphasize them.

   Q. ⓐ～ⓓ의 문장을 문맥에 맞게 배열하면?
   1) ⓐ-ⓒ-ⓑ-ⓓ   2) ⓑ-ⓒ-ⓐ-ⓓ   3) ⓑ-ⓒ-ⓓ-ⓐ
   4) ⓒ-ⓑ-ⓐ-ⓓ   5) ⓒ-ⓑ-ⓓ-ⓐ

[명작 감상]   Victor Hugo (1802 ~ 1885)
                 Les Misérables 『레 미제라블』

The door opened. It was flung widely open, as though in response to a vigorous and determined thrust. A man entered.

We know the man already. He stepped across the threshold and then stood motionless with the door still open behind him. His knapsack hung from his shoulder and his stick was in his hand. The firelight falling on his face disclosed an expression of exhaustion, desperation, and brutish defiance. He was an ugly and terrifying spectacle.

Mme Magloire was too startled even to exclaim. She stood trembling and open-mouthed. Mlle Baptistine half rose in alarm but then, as she turned towards her brother, her face recovered its customary tranquility.

The bishop was calmly regarding the stranger. He opened his mouth to speak, but before he could do so the man, leaning on his stick with both hands and gazing round at the three elderly people, said in a harsh voice:

"Look. My name is Jean Valjean. I'm a convict on parole. I've done nineteen years in prison. They let me out four days ago and I'm on my way to Pontarlier. I've walked from Toulon in four days and today I covered a dozen leagues. When I reached this place I went to an inn and they turned me out because of my yellow ticket-of-leave which I'd shown at the *Mairie* as I'm obliged to do. I tried another inn and they told me to clear out. Nobody wants me anywhere. I tried the prison and the doorkeeper wouldn't open. I crawled into a dog-kennel and the dog bit me and drove me out just as if he were a man and knew who I was. I thought I'd sleep in a field under the stars, but there weren't any stars and it looked as though it was going to rain, and no God to stop it raining, so I came back here hoping to find a doorway to sleep in. I lay down on a bench in the square outside and a good woman pointed to your door and told me to knock on it. So I've knocked. What is this place? Is it an inn? I've got money. I've got one hundred and nine francs and fifteen sous, the money I earned by nineteen years' work in prison. I'm ready to pay, I don't care how much, I've got the money. I'm very tired, twelve leagues on foot, and I'm hungry. Will you let me stay?"

[확인 학습] 다음 문장을 우리말로 옮기세요.

1. For whereas international trade makes nations more interdependent, they try to regulate their imports and exports in such a way that they will be more independent.

2. Nevertheless, should a fight ensue, neither creature will be badly hurt, for the loser will save himself by making a gesture of submission.

3. Thus, members who hold higher positions in a group or feel that they have an important part to play in the group have more confidence in their own performance.

4. I went to an inn and they turned me out because of my yellow ticket-of-leave I'd shown at the *Mairie* as I'm obliged to do. I crawled into a dog-kennel and the dog bit me and drove me out just as if he were a man and knew who I was.

[words & phrases]

A1: secure 안전한, prosper 번창하다, attain 달성하다, impoverish 가난하게 하다, afflict 괴롭히다

A2: religion 종교, depict 묘사하다, characteristic 특징, reflect 반영하다/반사하다, geometry 기하학

A3: aggressive 공격적인, slander 비방(하다), territory 영역, encroach 침범하다, ritual 의식/의례(의), hostile 적대적인, intrude 침입하다, ensue 결과로서 일어나다, submit to ~에 굴복하다/복종하다,

A4: fudge 속이다/날조하다, leap 뛰다/도약하다, check 수표, owe 빚지다, excuse 변명, purpose 목적

B1: be likely to (do) ~할 가능성이 있다, suffer from ~을 겪다, at least 적어도, reveal 드러내다

B2: depict 그리다/묘사하다, excavate 파다/발굴하다, Mesolithic 중석기 시대(의), acquire 획득하다, companion 친구/반려, ally 동맹국/협력자, enhance 높이다/고양하다, domesticate 길들이다, orphan 고아(로 만들다), ancestor 조상/선조, raised 키우다, wolfling 늑대 새끼, affection 애정, acute 예리한/날카로운, curiosity 호기심, intrude 침입하다, detect 탐지하다, instinct 본능

B3: Congress 미국 의회, forbid 금하다, quarter 25센트 동전, extract 추출하다/발췌하다, blossom 꽃

B4: overestimate 과대평가하다, have to do with ~와 관계가 있다, confidence 자신/확신, part 역할(role)

B5: employee 고용인, despite ~에도 불구하고, polite 공손한/정중한, status 지위/신분, tendency 경향

C1: as though ~ 마치 ~인 것처럼, determine 결심하다, threshold 문간/문지방, exhaust 지치게 하다, desperate 필사적인/절망적인, brute 짐승, defy 대항하다/반항하다, be startled 놀라다, customary 습관적/통상적, tranquil 고요한, bishop 주교, lean 기대다, convict 죄수, parole 가석방, inn 여관, ticket-of-leave 가석방 허가서, be obliged to (do) ~하지 않을 수 없다, kennel 개집, square 광장

[실력 점검 A] 다음 각 동사의 우리말 뜻을 쓰세요.

1. affect: 2. shrink: 3. enhance:

4. afflict: 5. utilize: 6. abandon:

7. define: 8. subdue: 9. preserve:

10. ignore: 11. extract: 12. cultivate:

13. invade: 14. console: 15. contribute:

16. collide: 17. exclude: 18. demonstrate:

19. encroach: 20. domesticate:

[실력 점검 B] 각 항목에 대응하는 영어 단어를 찾아 쓰세요.

보기 tame, flour, tribe, client, defeat, latitude, sacrifice, architect, insurance, dispute, obstacle, dignity, principal, evolution, molecule, tendency, employee, experiment, indifference, extraordinary

1. 경향: 2. 실험: 3. 분자:

4. 패배: 5. 희생: 6. 고객:

7. 존엄: 8. 종족: 9. 교장:

10. 보험: 11. 분쟁: 12. 진화:

13. 위도: 14. 무관심: 15. 건축가:

16. 장애물: 17. 밀가루: 18. 종업원:

19. 길들인: 20. 비범한:

[실력 점검 C] 다음 각 문장의 빈칸에 알맞은 낱말을 쓰세요.

1. My mother scolded me this morning _____ being rude to you.

2. Don't be persuaded _____ buying things you don't really want.

3. We tried to dissuade him _____ the feeling that he was a failure.

4. Little attention was _____ to their leaders' calls for independence.

5. There is this difference between happiness and _____: he who thinks himself the _____ man really is so, but he who thinks himself the wisest is generally the greatest _____.

명시 감상

Heaven

Langston Hughes

Heaven is
The place where
Happiness is
Everywhere.

Animals
And birds sing -
As does
Everything.

To each stone,
"How-do-you-do?"
Stone answers back,
"Well! And you?"

---

* heaven 천국, as does everything 모두가 (그렇게) 하듯이, How do you do? 안녕하세요? 처음 뵙겠습니다

Unit 4   조동사 I

A. May, Might

1) *May* I help you? Gather roses while you *may*.

2) It *may be* true. He *may have said* so.

3) Long *may* he live! May God forgive us!

4) You *might* ask him. *Might* I ask your name?

5) He is studying hard *so that* he *may* pass the examination.

6) She *may well* think so. *Well may* you ask why.

7) You *may as well* stay here. You *might as well* talk to the wall.

B. Can, Could

1) She *can* play the piano. What *can* I do for you?

2) It *cannot be* true. He *cannot have said* so.

3) *Could* you help me? *Could* I see Mr. Smith, please?

4) I *cannot* thank you *too* much. You *cannot* study *too* hard.

C. Must, Have to

1) You *must* do your best. You will *have to* see him.

2) You *must not* do it. You *don't have to* do it.

3) Everyone *must* die. What must be, *must* be.

4) It *must be* true. He *must have said* so.

D. Need, Dare

1) He *needs* to know it. She *dared* to doubt my sincerity.

2) You *need* not go there. How *dare* you talk to me like that?

3) We *didn't need* to hurry. We *needn't have hurried*.

E. Do, Did

1) I think as you *do*. He speaks English as well as she *does*.

2) I *do* hope to see you again. Only yesterday *did* I see him.

[필수 문법] 조동사(auxiliary)

* 좁은 의미의 조동사는 will, shall, can, may, must 등의 양태 조동사.
* 일반 동사의 의문문/부정문이나 강조/도치 문장에 도입되는 조동사 "do."
* 진행형/수동태에 도입되는 "be"동사, 완료형에 도입되는 "have"동사 등도 조동사.

A. May, Might

  1) 허락/가능: ~해도 좋다/~할 수 있다. May I come in? Yes, you may. No, you must not.

  2) 추측/추정: may be ~: ~일지도 모른다. may have p.p.: ~였을지도 모른다

  3) 소망/기원: =He may live long! =God may forgive us!

  4) 완곡한 표현: You might help us. You might pass me the paper, please.

  5) (so) that ~ may/can ~: ~하기 위해서, ~할 수 있도록 (= in order that ~ may/can ~)

  6) may (very) well ~: ~은 (너무나) 당연하다: =It is (quite) natural that she should think so.

  7) may as well ~: ~하는 게 (더) 낫다: =You *had better* stay here.

    might as well ~: 개연성이 없는 일을 가상해서 표현할 때 쓰는 가정법 시제임.

    may/might as well A as B: B하느니 A하는 게 낫다: You *may as well* stay here *as* go there.

B. Can, Could

  1) 가능/능력: =She *is able to* play the piano. =What *am* I *able to* do for you?

  2) 추측/추정: cannot be ~: ~일 리가 없다, cannot have p.p.: ~였을 리가 없다.

  3) 정중한 요청: Could you follow me? Could you give me a few examples?

  4) cannot ~ too ~ : 아무리 ~해도 지나치지 않다: Children *cannot* be taught English *too* early.

    We *cannot over*emphasize the importance of education. (아무리 강조해도 지나치지 않다)

C. Must, Have to

  1) must ~: ~해야만 한다 (=have to ~) * "have to"는 조동사로 분류되지는 않음.

    Must I do it? Yes, you must. No, you need not. (= No, you don't have to.)

  2) must not ~: ~해서는 안 된다, don't have to ~: ~할 필요가 없다 (=need not).

  3) 필연: (모든 사람은 반드시 죽는다.) (일어날 일은, 반드시 일어난다.)

  4) 추측/추정: must be ~: ~임에 틀림 없다, must have p.p.: ~였음에 틀림 없다.

D. Need, Dare

  1) 대체로 긍정문에서는 본동사로, 의문문/부정문에서는 조동사로 쓰인다.

  2) (=You do not need to go there.) (=How do you dare to talk to me like that?)

  3) did not need: ~할 필요가 없었다, need not have p.p.: ~할 필요가 없었는데.....

E. Do, Did

  1) 대동사: 예문에서 "do"와 "does"는 각각 "think"와 "speaks"를 대신한다.

  2) 강조/도치: *Do* be quiet. She *did* come. Never *did* he realize that.

[문법 연습 A] 틀린 곳을 고치세요.

1. God grants us peace and health!

2. He can't speak English, does he?

3. Must I go there? No, you must not.

4. All creatures are mortal; they may die.

5. They said that the rumor had to be true.

6. You had better not to smoke in the room.

7. Whatever can happen, I will do it without fail.

8. Telephone was invented by Graham Bell, did it?

9. No matter where you must go, I will follow you.

10. He has lived in New York, and so does his sister.

11. Little did I dreamed that she would get married to him.

12. We did not need to worry about them; they are all safe.

13. He may not have heard the news; he knows nothing about it.

14. You may as well try to move the mountain as try to persuade him.

[문법 연습 B] 조동사를 사용하여 고쳐 쓰세요.

1. It is possible they have arrived in Seoul.

_____

2. It is impossible that she has gone so far.

_____

3. It is certain that he has taken advantage of his friends.

_____

4. It is quite natural that she should be proud of her children.

_____

5. There was no need for him to meet them, but he met them.

_____

[실전 문법 A] 빈칸에 알맞은 낱말을 쓰세요.

1. A man _____ be rich and yet not be happy.

2. You cannot be _____ careful of your health.

3. She _____ have been ill; she looks very well.

4. We usually praise only that we _____ be praised.

5. It _____ have rained all day; the road is so muddy.

6. I _____ have a map somewhere, but I must have lost it.

7. You may as well go right away _____ stay here like this.

8. Never _____ I think that she would make such a mistake.

9. Not only _____ the sun give us light, but it also gives us heat.

10. I could not enter the room _____ thinking of my grandmother.

11. She has changed so much that you may _____ not recognize her.

12. Whatever faults he _____ have, she will never cease to love him.

[실전 문법 B] 각 문항의 다섯 부분 중 어법에 맞지 않는 부분은?

1. [1]As cannot be stressed [2]so strongly, [3]a university is [4]for forming broad outlooks, [5]for making whole persons.

2. [1]In a market system, [2]individual economical units [3]are free to interact [4]with one another [5]in the marketplace.

3. [1]I had some difficulty [2]to decide [3]between the Republican and the Democrat, [4]but I finally voted [5]for the latter.

4. [1]Those who have never [2]experienced and undergone [3]a rainy season [4]may not be able to imagine [5]what it is like.

5. [1]People have a curious habit [2]of thinking [3]that nature must always look [4]like the pictures [5]they are accustomed.

6. [1]We had better try to persuade her, [2]but it seems almost impossible; [3]we may as well expect [4]the sun to rise in the west [5]as try to change her mind.

[필수 어휘 A] 밑줄 친 각 낱말의 뜻은?

1. He spent the afternoon getting his car <u>mended</u>.

   1) fixed   2) rented   3) stolen   4) washed   5) crashed

2. Insects are greatly <u>affected</u> by body temperature.

   1) grown   2) harmed   3) spoiled   4) adapted   5) influenced

3. You can <u>alter</u> the appearance of a room by moving the furniture.

   1) make   2) change   3) arrange   4) decorate   5) consider

4. I think I <u>grasped</u> quite soon what was going on in my class.

   1) held   2) noticed   3) inferred   4) impaired   5) understood

5. The man put his hand to a weapon <u>concealed</u> under his coat.

   1) kept   2) hidden   3) covered   4) disguised   5) discovered

6. The business <u>thrives</u> under the guidance of a new manager.

   1) adjusts   2) succeeds   3) prospers   4) improves   5) increases

7. Large-scale industry <u>emerged</u> gradually as technology advanced.

   1) failed   2) vanished   3) improved   4) appeared   5) constructed

[필수 어휘 B] 밑줄 친 부분을 주어진 철자로 시작되는 낱말로 대체하세요.

1. I can't <u>figure</u> him <u>out</u>; he is a mystery.   u_____

2. It was very hard to <u>come by</u> these films.   o_____

3. He didn't know the meeting was <u>called off</u>.   c_____

4. She <u>takes after</u> her mother in many respects.   r_____

5. When can you <u>get through</u> (with) your work?   f_____

6. The country has <u>gone through</u> too many wars.   u_____

7. You have to <u>make allowances for</u> his position.   c_____

8. He <u>made up his mind</u> to apply for a scholarship.   d_____

9. We will have to <u>take</u> their feelings <u>into account</u>.   c_____

10. I think you <u>gave an account of</u> what happened.   e_____

11. How can I <u>get in touch with</u> you on weekend?   c_____

[구문 연습] 다음 문장을 우리말로 옮기세요.

1. In developing knowledge we must collaborate with our ancestors; otherwise we must begin, not where they arrived, but where they began.

2. As cannot be stressed too strongly, a university is for forming broad outlooks, for making whole persons; nobody wants the proverbial Jack, the dull boy, who has no time for play.

3. However arduous the task of a commander may be, he cannot face the men who shall live or die by his orders without sensing how much easier is his task than the one he has set them to perform.

4. A literary work must reach the minds and touch the feelings of its author's contemporaries. If a writer cannot do that, he may as well put his manuscript away in the safe, in the hope that there may be a generation for whom his work will come alive.

[작문 연습] 다음 문장을 영어로 옮기세요.

1. 우리가 사형을 폐지하는 것은 너무나 당연하다.

　　_____

2. 이 사진을 볼 때마다 나는 학창시절이 떠오른다.

　　_____

3. 그들은 그렇게 아침 일찍 출발할 필요가 없었는데.....

　　_____

4. 그는 지난 주말 국제 회의에 참석하지 못했을지도 모른다.

　　_____

5. 우리는 자연 환경과 생태계의 중요성을 아무리 강조해도 부족하다.

　　_____

[실전 독해 A] 각 문항의 물음에 답하세요.

1.   Our species is the only creative species, and it has only one creative instrument, the individual mind and spirit of a man. Nothing was ever created by two men. There are no good collaborations, whether in art, in music, in poetry, in mathematics, or in philosophy. Once the miracle of creation has taken place, the group can build and extend it, but the group can never ^{a)}_____ anything. The preciousness lies in the ^{b)}_____ mind of a man.

> Q. 빈칸 a), b)에 들어갈 각 낱말은?
>   1) add, creative   2) invent, lonely
>   3) attain, reasonable   4) prove, imaginative
>   5) achieve, cooperative

2.   From the earliest days the conviction has been growing among the people and their leaders that the government must be responsible for seeing that its citizens have a certain amount of education. That the government has this responsibility is shown by its constitution, law courts, and many school and local government decisions. _____, education has come to be universally regarded as a function of the government. The control of education by the government is not always desirable, but this control has come because of the early and ever growing belief that education is the foundation of a democratic government and cannot, therefore, be left too much to the desires of any individual or community. In a democracy the people cannot be permitted to remain ignorant even if some of them might desire to stay so.

> Q 1. 빈칸에 들어갈 적절한 말은?
>   1) In brief   2) Of course   3) Above all
>   4) In addition   5) For example

> 2. 이 글의 내용과 일치하지 않는 것은?
>   1) Education is indispensable to a democratic government.
>   2) Education is looked upon as a function of the government.
>   3) A certain amount of education is compulsory in a democracy.
>   4) The control of education by the government is always undesirable.
>   5) Education should not be distorted by any individual or community.

3. We find that Michael has broken a window in your basement. Maybe all little boys have to find out that balls can break glass, but I am sorry it was your window and not ours that he used for his a)_____. Max Schliemann, phone RI 5-8282, does repairing for us. If you will let him know when it would be convenient for you to b)_____ a new pane put in, he will replace the glass and charge the amount to us.

> Q 1. 빈칸 a), b)에 들어갈 각 낱말은?
> 1) work, make   2) game, order
> 3) mistake, change   4) experiment, have
> 5) excitement, prepare

4. A growing taste for shark and its fin has for the first time in 400 million years put the scourge of the sea at the wrong end of food chain. Commercial catches of this toothsome fish have doubled each year since 1980s, and shark populations are plunging. Sharks do for gentler fish what lions do for the wild beast; they check populations by feeding on the weak. Also, sharks apparently do not get cancer and may therefore harbor clues to the _____ of the disease.

> Q. 빈칸에 알맞은 낱말은?
> 1) future   2) nature   3) danger
> 4) patient   5) discovery

5. Some researchers distinguish primary emotions, which are thought to be universal, a)_____ secondary emotions, which include variations that are specific to cultures. The primary emotions are usually identified with fear, anger, joy, sadness, surprise, and disgust. Other psychologists doubt that surprise and disgust are true emotions; they also think that this list b)_____ universal emotions, such as love, hate, hope, pride, and empathy, which are difficult to measure physiologically.

> Q 1. 빈칸 a)에 들어갈 낱말은?

> 2. 빈칸 b)에 들어갈 적절한 말은?
> 1) draws up   2) leaves out   3) consists of
> 4) differs from   5) accounts for

[실전 독해 B] 각 문항의 물음에 답하세요.

1. Almost all nations in the 19th and 20th centuries became increasingly dependent on foreign markets, on selling goods to and buying goods from countries in other parts of the world. As the value of the international trade increased the ^{a)}people/peoples of the world became more dependent on one another. Countries that possessed a surplus of some ^{b)}community/commodity sought to exchange that surplus for goods they wanted but lacked the means to produce ^{c)}by/for themselves. International trade brought the nations of the world into closer contact. It made the countries more dependent on one another, and made ^{d)}it/them more important that they cooperate in supplying one another's needs for the benefit of all. The American economist, Henry George, summed up this situation very simply in three words: civilization is cooperation.

Q. 밑줄 친 a)~d)에서 문맥에 맞는 각 낱말은?

2. It is normally necessary for a creative scientist not only to have a new idea, but also to develop this idea, perform experiments and demonstrate that the concept is true often in the face of hostility and scorn. It can sometimes take a number of years before the majority of scientists accept a new development. ^{a)}_____, persistence is necessary if creativity in science is to be recognized by others. For example, Newton did not just tell the world that he believed the laws of mechanics were the same everywhere in the universe. He went on to calculate the orbits of the planets as inferred from the effects of gravity observed on earth, and then he compared his calculated orbits with experimentally observed orbits. It was the excellent ^{b)}_____ of this new theory with his experiments that persuaded scientists that Newton was right.

Q 1. 빈칸 a)에 들어갈 낱말은?
    1) Besides   2) However   3) Moreover
    4) Consequently   5) Nevertheless

  2. 빈칸 b)에 들어갈 낱말은?
    1) proof   2) notion   3) agreement
    4) foundation   5) application

3. [1]In many countries, nowadays, people are cutting down rain forests to make room for farms and lumberyards. [2]Many an organization is trying to save the forests. [3]They advise the countries not to cut down rain forests, explaining what consequences could be brought about by the destruction of the forests. [4]In spite of these advices and efforts, such areas as the Amazon Basin are quickly becoming deforested. [5]In fact, however, there has always been deforestation somewhere on the earth, and it is by no means a new phenomenon.

Q. 1)~5)의 문장 중 글의 흐름에 맞지 않는 것은?

4. The witch doctors of primitive tribes used a variety of methods to cure sick persons. Their methods seem ridiculous to us today, but some of them [1]<u>did help</u>. The cures that were used by the witch doctors are known [2]<u>to have real value</u> in those days. The plants that these early doctors [3]<u>used were</u> often drugs now understood [4]<u>to be medicinal</u> or pain-relieving. The respect and confidence the primitives [5]<u>had in their healer</u> gave some hope to the patients and helped them feel better.

Q. 밑줄 친 1)~5)중 어법에 맞지 않는 것은?

5. Like increasing millions of Americans who regularly follow a vigorous exercise program, I know that working out makes me feel good. ① Moreover, I am convinced that it contributes to both my physical and psychological well-being. ② But there is an added enticement you may not be aware of: keeping healthy may save you insurance dollars as well. ③ Life insurance companies reserve their best rate for those who meet certain health criteria. Of course smokers are not qualified. ④ Because of the medical links between smoking and such major killers as heart disease and lung cancer, insurance companies have been rewarding nonsmokers with lower rates for twenty years. ⑤ Today four out five life insurance companies offer them discounts averaging from 10 to 15 percent.

Q. ①~⑤중 다음 문장이 삽입되기에 적절한 곳은?
How can you trade a pound of flesh for an ounce of cash?

[명작 감상]   Henry David Thoreau (1817 ~ 1862)
         Walden, or Life in the Woods 『월든, 숲속에서의 생활』

Near the end of March, 1845, I borrowed an axe and went down to the woods by Walden Pond, nearest to where I intended to build my house, and began to cut down some tall arrowy white pines, still in their youth, for timber. It is difficult to begin without borrowing, but perhaps it is the most generous course thus to permit your fellow-men to have an interest in your enterprise. The owner of the axe, as he released his hold on it, said that it was the apple of his eye; but I returned it sharper than I received it. It was a pleasant hillside where I worked, covered with pine woods, through which I looked out on the pond, and a small open field in the woods where pines and hickories were springing up.

The ice in the pond was not yet dissolved, though there were some open spaces, and it was all dark colored and saturated with water. There were some slight flurries of snow during the days that I worked there; but for the most part when I came out on to the railroad, on my way home, its yellow sand heap stretched away gleaming in the hazy atmosphere, and the rails shone in the spring sun, and I heard the lark and pewee and other birds already come to commence another year with us. They were pleasant spring days, in which the winter of man's discontent was thawing as well as the earth, and the life that had lain torpid began to stretch itself.

One day, when my axe had come off and I had cut a green hickory for a wedge, driving it with a stone, and had placed the whole to soak in a pond hole in order to swell the wood, I saw a striped snake run into the water, and he lay on the bottom, apparently without inconvenience, as long as I stayed there, or more than a quarter of an hour; perhaps because he had not yet fairly come out of the torpid state. It appeared to me that for a like reason men remain in their present low and primitive condition; but if they should feel the influence of the spring of springs arousing them, they would of necessity rise to a higher and more ethereal life.

* Beauty is but skin deep.   미모는 한낱 거죽일 뿐.
* All is fair in love and war.   사랑과 전쟁에서는 모든 것이 정당하다.

[확인 학습] 다음 문장을 우리말로 옮기세요.

1. From the earliest days the conviction has been growing among the people and their leaders that the government must be responsible for seeing that its citizens have a certain amount of education.

2. I suppose that most adults take their language for granted and feel very little of the awe and excitement that must pass through a child when he or she is first learning to master language.

3. Because of the medical links between smoking and such major killers as heart disease and lung cancer, insurance companies have been rewarding nonsmokers with lower rates for twenty years.

4. It appeared to me that for a like reason men remain in their present low and primitive condition; but if they should feel the influence of the spring of springs arousing them, they would of necessity rise to a higher and more ethereal life.

[words & phrases]

A1: instrument 도구, collaborate 합작하다, once 일단 ~하면, miracle 기적, take place 생기다/일어나다
A2: conviction 확신, constitution 헌법, regard ~ as ~을 ~로 여기다, foundation 기초, ignorant 무지한
A3: basement 지하실, convenient 편리한, repair 수리하다, pane 창유리, replace 대신하다/대체하다
A4: shark 상어, scourge 천벌, toothsome 맛있는, plunge 뛰어들다/격감하다, harbor 제공하다/감추다
A5: universal 보편적인, identify ~ with ~을 ~와 동일시하다, empathy 감정이입, physiology 생리학
B1: goods 상품, means 수단, surplus 잉여, lack 부족(하다), benefit 이익/혜택, sum up ~을 요약하다
B2: hostile 적대적인, scorn 경멸, persist 고집하다/지속하다, orbit 궤도, infer 추론하다, gravity 중력
B3: rain forest 열대 우림, room 여지/공간, lumber 목재, consequence 결과, bring about ~을 초래하다
B4: primitive 원시인/원시적인, tribe 종족/부족, ridiculous 우스운/어리석은, relieve 덜다/경감하다
B5: vigorous 격렬한, work out 운동하다/훈련하다, be convinced 확신하다, contribute to ~에 기여하다,
    entice 유혹하다, insurance 보험, criterion 기준, qualify 자격을 주다, reward 보상/보답(하다)
C1: axe 도끼, intend 의도하다, pine 소나무, timber 목재, generous 관대한, enterprise 기획/기업/사업,
    hickory 호두 나무, dissolve 용해시키다, saturate 흠뻑 적시다, haze 안개/아지랑이, pewee 딱새,
    commence 시작하다, discontent 불만, thaw 해동/해빙(하다), torpid 마비된/무감각한/둔한, swell
    부풀다/부풀리다, stripe 줄무늬, state 상태, of necessity 반드시, ethereal 가뿐한/정신적인

[실력 점검 A] 다음 각 동사의 우리말 뜻을 쓰세요.

1. starve: 2. offend: 3. endeavor:

4. secure: 5. reform: 6. outweigh:

7. absorb: 8. abolish: 9. commence:

10. invest: 11. impose: 12. accumulate:

13. behold: 14. analyze: 15. compromise:

16. convey: 17. identify: 18. contemplate:

19. neglect: 20. convince:

[실력 점검 B] 각 항목에 대응하는 영어 단어를 찾아 쓰세요.

보기   awe, vanity, legend, protest, humility, maturity, territory, characteristic, suspicion, confidence, institution, instruction, constitution, indignant, significant, rusty, rational, ignorant, deficient, simultaneous.

1. 겸손: 2. 성숙: 3. 전설:

4. 항의: 5. 영토: 6. 헌법:

7. 신뢰: 8. 특징: 9. 의심:

10. 제도: 11. 경외: 12. 녹슨:

13. 가르침: 14. 허영심: 15. 합리적:

16. 부족한: 17. 무지한: 18. 동시적:

19. 분개한: 20. 중대한:

[실력 점검 C] 주어진 철자로 시작되는 알맞은 낱말을 쓰세요.

1. It is what u_____ we make of what we know that matters.

2. My mother's death brought h_____ to me the sorrow of life.

3. A r_____ person is one who does not talk very much to strangers.

4. It t_____ thirteen facial muscles to smile and forty-five to frown.

5. You should b_____ it in mind that a minor mistake in decision-making

   can r_____ in fatal failure in life.

명시 감상

The Example

W. H. Davies

Here's an example from
    A Butterfly;
That on a rough, hard rock
    Happy can lie;
Friendless and all alone
On this unsweetened stone.

Now let my bed be hard,
    No care take I;
I'll make my joy like this
    Small Butterfly,
Whose happy heart has power
To make a stone a flower.

* example 모범/본보기, butterfly 나비, lie 눕다/놓여있다, friendless 벗이 없는, take care 조심하다, 걱정/근심하다

Unit 5   조동사 II

A. Will, Would

1) It *will* rain tomorrow. I *will* tell you the truth.

2) *Will* you come with me? *Will* you have another cup of coffee?

3) Boys *will* be boys. Accidents *will* happen.

4) He *will* have his own way. He *would*n't take the bribe.

5) She *will* sit up late at night. We *would* dance together for hours.

6) *Will* you help me? *Would* you show me the way to the station?

7) Those who *would* succeed in life have to be honest and diligent.

B. Shall, Should

1) She *shall* not die. You *shall* have my answer tomorrow.

2) Shall I open the window? Shall he carry the box upstairs?

3) We *should* obey our parents. You *should* not speak so loud.

4) I *should have seen* him. You *should have been* more careful.

5) How *should* I know? Who *should* be there but Tom?

6) I wrote down her phone number *lest* I *should* forget it.

7) He suggests that they also *should* join the research team.

   She insisted that her son *should* go to Paris to study art.

8) It is strange that you *should* know so little about it.

   It is necessary that you *should* attend the meeting today.

   It is a pity that the children *should* do such a miserable thing.

C. Ought to, Used to

1) You *ought to* keep quiet here. You *ought* not *to* make a noise.

   I *ought to have worked* harder. I *ought* not *to have come* here.

2) He *used to* come every day. There *used to* be owls in the woods.

   What *used* she *to* say? She *used* not *to* answer.

[필수 문법] 조동사(auxiliary)

* 좁은 의미의 조동사는 will, shall, can, may, must 등의 양태 조동사.

* 일반 동사의 의문문/부정문이나 강조/도치 문장에 도입되는 조동사 "do."

* 진행형/수동태에 도입되는 "be"동사, 완료형에 도입되는 "have"동사 등도 조동사.

A. Will, Would

　1) 미래시제: 단순미래/의지미래의 조동사: "Unit 6: 필수 문법" 참조.

　2) 의지미래 의문문: 상대방(listener)의 의지/의향: "Unit 6: 필수 문법" 참조.

　3) 습성/경향: (머슴애는 머슴애인 법이다.) (사고는 일어나게 마련이다.)

　4) 고집: The door *won't* open. (현재)　He *would* go despite my warning. (과거)

　5) 습관: Why *will* you be late for every class? (현재)　He *would* sit still for hours. (과거)

　6) 정중한 요청: *Will/would* you do me a favor? (부탁 하나 들어주시겠습니까?)

　7) 소망/의도: (=wish to, intend to): One who *would* be a writer must read many books.

B. Shall, Should

　1) 의지미래: 평서문에서의 의지미래는 화자(speaker)의 의지: (=I *will* not let her die.)

　　(=I *will* give you my answer tomorrow.)　*You *shall* die. (=I *will* kill you.)

　2) 의지미래: 의문문에서의 의지미래는 상대방/청자(listener)의 의지/의향:

　　(=Do you want him to carry the box upstairs?)　*What *shall* she do? Let her wash dishes.

　3) 도덕적, 윤리적 당위/의무: Children *should* be taught to speak the truth.

　4) should have p.p.: "~했어야 했는데…(유감/후회)": She *should* not *have come* here.

　5) 고조된 감정 표출: (내가 어떻게 알겠니?) (Tom외에 누가 거기 있었겠니?)

　6) lest ~ should ~ = for fear (that) ~ should ~: "~할까 봐 (두려워서), ~하지 않도록"

　7) 요구(demand/require), 제안(suggest/propose/move/recommend), 명령(order/command),

　　주장(insist/urge)의 동사/명사에 수반되는 that-절에 사용되며, 흔히 생략되기도 함.

　8) "주관적 판단"의 형용사나 "놀람/뜻밖/유감/후회" 등의 감정을 나타내는 형용사나

　　명사에 수반되는 that-절에 사용됨: I am sorry (that) you *should* think I spoke ill of you.

C. Ought to, Used to

　1) ought to (=should): 당위/의무: They *ought to* be free, oughtn't they?

　　ought to have p.p. (=should have p.p.): "~했어야 했는데… (~하지 못해서 유감/후회)"

　2) used to (do): 과거의 습관/관행: 의문문이나 부정문에서는 두 가지의 형태가 가능:

　　= What *did* she *use* to say?　　= She *did* not *use* to answer.

　　* used to (do): ~하곤 했다(=would), ~했었다　* be used to (~ing): ~하는데 익숙하다:

　　She *is used to* caring for the children. (=She *is accustomed to* care[=caring] for the children.)

[문법 연습 A] 잘못된 부분을 고치세요.

1. I would rather die than living in dishonor.

2. It is impossible that we all must think alike.

3. Please remember that it ought to be not allowed.

4. We should come earlier; the train has already left.

5. She is not used to be spoken to in such a rude way.

6. We hid behind the trees lest they should not see us.

7. The doctor suggests that she takes a walk every day.

8. The court ordered that the plan would be carried out.

9. I told him what would happen, but he shouldn't listen.

10. "What will they do next?" "Let them clean the house."

11. She insisted that the accident should happen last night.

[문법 연습 B] 빈칸에 알맞은 조동사는?

1. Let's take a coffee break, _____ we?

2. Please keep an eye on him, _____ you?

3. I regret that my child _____ be so weak.

4. A drowning man _____ catch at a straw.

5. Don't you know oil _____ float on water?

6. Last year he _____ go fishing on weekends

7. None is so deaf as those who _____ not hear.

8. You _____ to have consulted with me beforehand.

9. We ran down the hill for fear rain _____ begin to fall.

10. You _____ have seen the sunrise; it was magnificent.

11. The proposal that he _____ join us was very reasonable.

12. He lives in town now, but he _____ to live in the country.

13. It is important that you _____ set your targets realistically.

14. If you _____ be a scientist, you have to study mathematics.

15. She turned her face away from me lest I _____ see her tears.

[실전 문법 A] 빈칸에 알맞은 낱말을 쓰세요.

1. Tom can speak Korean, and _____ can Jane.

2. Some people don't like coffee, and _____ do I.

3. The wealthy merchant could help us, if only he _____.

4. He moved that the case _____ be adjourned for a week.

5. I had to grab the iron rail at my side _____ I should slip off.

6. She could not help _____ around with a good deal of curiosity.

7. The Johnsons have lived in China for over ten years, _____ they?

8. "I was so worried about you." "I'm sorry. I _____ have called you."

9. They had to work hard so that they _____ earn a living in hard times.

[실전 문법 B] 각 문항의 다섯 부분 중 어법에 맞지 않는 부분은?

1. [1]The trading firm requires [2]that all workers and managers [3]are evaluated [4]for promotion [5]every six months.

2. [1]Well, it's too late [2]to do anything now. [3]If we had written down it [4]on the calendar, [5]we wouldn't have made this mistake.

3. [1]The judge told him [2]that he ought [3]to have not entered [4]his wife's room and bathroom [5]without her permission.

4. [1]The counselor used to say [2]that the feelings [3]of young children [4]were quite different [5]from their parents or teachers.

5. [1]It is essential [2]that each hiker carries [3]a flashlight, matches, [4]and extra food and clothes, [5]even if only a day hike is planned

6. [1]My aunt should not accompany us [2]to the lodging house [3]where Susan was staying alone, [4]but insisted on my going, [5]so I was obliged to go there.

7. [1]Rosa was afraid to see [2]Jimmy coming into her house, [3]so she insisted [4]that he left her house right away [5]or she would call the police immediately.

8. [1]Everyone's path is different, [2]so start your search now, [3]or if you know your passion, [4]make sure you make time for it [5]no matter how you may be busy.

[필수 어휘 A] 밑줄 친 낱말과 그 뜻이 비슷한 것은?

1. He acquired a knowledge of the language by careful study.

  1) strived 2) learned 3) revised 4) obtained 5) modified

2. They prohibited the use of wood as a construction material.

  1) banned 2) abused 3) avoided 4) favored 5) restricted

3. The minister declined to make a statement to the newspapers.

  1) agreed 2) disliked 3) refused 4) accepted 5) promised

4. An Englishman, unlike an American, is very reserved and discreet.

  1) polite 2) careful 3) logical 4) rational 5) economical

5. The sisters had a terrible quarrel, but later they became reconciled.

  1) got over 2) gave up 3) made up 4) left off 5) dropped by

6. From that time on his poetry has been read by succeeding generations.

  1) later 2) young 3) primary 4) prosperous 5) unprecedented

[필수 어휘 B] 빈칸에 알맞은 낱말을 고르세요.

1. He would _____ to violence to control his sons.

  1) tend 2) apply 3) resort 4) attempt 5) conform

2. Dinosaurs became _____ millions of years ago.

  1) rare 2) plenty 3) secure 4) extinct 5) obscure

3. The valleys are so _____ that three crops a year can grow.

  1) moist 2) fertile 3) sterile 4) barren 5) tropical

4. We have to save some money to _____ against a rainy day.

  1) lean 2) endure 3) provide 4) consume 5) preserve

5. She has been a valued _____ of our bank for many years.

  1) client 2) spouse 3) sibling 4) relative 5) colleague

6. How can you be so _____ to the sufferings of the children?

  1) trivial 2) hostile 3) generous 4) hospitable 5) indifferent

7. _____, one of the natural sciences, deals with energy and matter.

  1) Physics 2) Ecology 3) Genetics 4) Geometry 5) Astronomy

[구문 연습] 다음 문장을 우리말로 옮기세요.

1. It is strange that the devout should think God can be pleased when they slavishly pay him flowery compliments.

2. I have heard a story that really shows how what you are used to doing at home can be misunderstood in another country.

3. We should behave toward our country as women behave toward the men they love. A loving wife will do anything for her husband except to stop criticizing and trying to improve him. We should cast the same affectionate but sharp glance at our country.

4. My uncle had always hoped that I would go into the church, though he should have known that, stammering as I did, no profession could have been more unsuitable. When I told him that I wouldn't, he accepted my refusal with his usual indifference; a suggestion was made that I should become a civil servant.

[작문 연습] 다음 문장을 영어로 옮기세요.

1. 우리는 영화 보러 가자는 그의 제안에 동의했다.

2. 그녀는 그 시험에서 실수할까 봐 대단히 조심스러웠다.

3. 너는 그에게 그런 어리석은 질문은 하지 말았어야 했는데.....

4. 시인이 되고자 하는 사람은 모국어에 특별한 관심을 가져야 한다.

5. 그는 너무나 옹고집이어서 누구에게도 귀를 기울이려고 하지 않는다.

[실전 독해 A] 각 문항의 물음에 답하세요.

1. Many of us have observed in our travels that the best guides are often those who assert themselves least. They take us to the point where the view is best, step aside and let us look at it, assuming with a right sense of propriety that their forms are not essential to the landscape. They point out fine works in the galleries, and fine features of those works, but do not tell us _____. I am no huntsman, but I presume that huntsmen prefer guides who know where the game is but refrain from shooting it for them.

> Q. 빈칸에 들어갈 적절한 말은?
> 1) what to enjoy   2) how to respond
> 3) what to do with them   4) how to find the game
> 5) whom to keep company with

2. Reading poetry is not like reading prose. The virtue of prose is to say what it has to say directly and explicitly, using words in a single sense.

ⓐ The meaning is easily grasped since it lies upon the surface. Some readers can take in a whole sentence at a glance, and a legendary few can take in a whole paragraph.

ⓑ The greater rapidity with which we turn the pages of prose creates the illusion that we are covering more ground, but the ground covered should be measured by the amount of meaning absorbed, not by the number of words seen.

ⓒ Poetry cannot be read in this way. The virtue of poetry is to say what it has to say beautifully and by the power of suggestion, so that it is able to initiate an emotional response in the reader and to convey more meaning more powerfully than prose. The words expand in the reader's mind.

A page of poetry may be equal to many pages of prose in what it conveys; we absorb it more slowly because there is more to absorb.

> Q. ⓐ ~ ⓒ의 글을 문맥에 맞게 배열하면?
> 1) ⓐ-ⓒ-ⓑ   2) ⓑ-ⓒ-ⓐ   3) ⓑ-ⓐ-ⓒ
> 4) ⓒ-ⓐ-ⓑ   5) ⓒ-ⓑ-ⓐ

3. Most of our dreams have one characteristic in common: they do not follow the laws of logic that govern our waking thought. ① The categories of space and time are neglected. ② People who are dead, we see alive; events which we watch in the present, occurred many years ago. ③ We dream of two events occurring simultaneously when in reality they could not possibly occur at the same time. ④ It is simple for us to move to a distant place, to be in two places at once, to fuse two persons into one, or to have one person suddenly be changed into another. ⑤ Indeed, in our dream we are the creators of a world where time and space, which limit all the activities of our body, have no power.

Q. ①~⑤중 다음 문장이 삽입되기에 적절한 곳은?
We pay just as little attention to the laws of space.

4. Do you want a short love story? This one is long but small. I go to the Pike Place Market in Seattle almost every Saturday morning to shop and carry on a love affair.

For several years a)I've bought flowers from a youngish woman who is a refugee from one of the hill tribes of Indochina. For one thing, she has the freshest and most beautiful flowers. For another, she is a fresh and beautiful flower herself. I don't know her name, b)nor she mine. We don't speak the same language. To her, I must be just another customer.

She is spring to me. She's there with pussywillows, daffodils, and then irises. She's summer, with roses and sunflowers. She's fall, with mums and dahlias. As the growing season comes to an end, she brings stems of fall leaves to sell, and then it's over. In winter, I miss her.

When we exchange flowers and money, I always try to briefly and slyly touch her hand. I always insist c)she keeps the change and she always insists on giving me an extra flower.

Once I tried to buy all her flowers at once, but she just shook her head. "No." I don't know why. Maybe she, too, is in love with someone and wants to be there to sell him flowers d)when he will come.

Q. 밑줄 친 a)~d)중 어법에 맞지 않는 것은?
1) a, c   2) a, d   3) b, c   4) b, d   5) c, d

[실전 독해 B] 각 문항의 물음에 답하세요.

1. I would like to get some information about my legal rights and the rights of the police. Last week I had an experience with the police in my community. They took me to the police station and asked me a lot of questions. I didn't even know why I was there. I didn't have a lawyer with me and I felt angry and scared. I don't think that the police were right. But I am not sure about the things they can do. Please send me your pamphlet, *Know Your Rights*, so I can learn more about my legal rights. I want to know these things in case this ever happens to me again.

> Q 1. 이 글은 어떤 취지의 글인가?
>   1) inquiry   2) request   3) protest
>   4) gratitude   5) complaint
>
> 2. 이 글의 필자의 현재 심경은?
>   1) angry   2) serious   3) nervous
>   4) desperate   5) disappointed

2. There have been at different times and among different people many varying conceptions of the good life. To some extent the differences were subject to argument; this was when men differed as to the ^{a)}_____ to achieve a given end. Some think that prison is a good way of preventing crime; others hold that education would be better. A difference of this sort can be decided by sufficient evidence. But some differences cannot be tested in this way. Tolstoy condemned all war; others have held the life of a soldier doing battle for the right to be very noble. Here there was probably involved a real difference as to ends. Those who praise the soldier usually consider the punishment of sinners a good thing in itself; Tolstoy did not think so. On such a matter no ^{b)}_____ is possible. I cannot prove, thus, that my view of the good life is right. I just hope many people will agree to my view: the good life is one inspired by love and guided by knowledge.

> Q 1. 빈칸 a)에 들어갈 적절한 낱말은?
>   1) means   2) purpose   3) questions
>   4) beginning   5) consequence
>
> 2. 빈칸 b)에 들어갈 낱말을 본문에서 찾으면?

3. ①Women _____ two-fifths of the British labor force. ②What I didn't know I had to find out or _____. ③She seemed to take forever to _____ for the evening performance. ④I'm trying to _____ the time I lost while I was sick. ⑤Why don't you two forget your differences and _____?

   Q. 빈칸에 공통으로 들어갈 구동사(phrasal verb)는?

4. A crow, ready to die with hunger, flew with joy to a pitcher, which he saw at a distance. But when he came up to it, he found the water so low that with all his stooping and straining he was unable to reach it. Thereupon he tried to break the pitcher, then to overturn it, but his strength was not sufficient to do either. At last, seeing some small pebbles at hand, he dropped a great many of them, one by one, into the pitcher, and so raised the brim, and quench his thirst.

   Q. 이 글에 어울리는 속담은?
      1) No sweet without sweat.
      2) Many a little makes a mickle.
      3) Every cloud has a silver lining.
      4) While there is life, there is hope.
      5) Necessity is the mother of invention.

5. Studies have revealed that people react in different ways to different colors. [a] _____, humans tend to become more excited when exposed to red light and more passive with blue light. [b] _____, pink, which is closer to red than to blue, seems to be the most soothing color of all. This finding has implications for interior decorators, particularly those charged with deciding which colors to paint the walls of hospitals and prisons.

   Q 1. 빈칸 a)에 들어갈 적절한 말은?
      1) However   2) Therefore   3) Moreover
      4) In addition   5) For example

   2. 빈칸 b)에 들어갈 적절한 말은?
      1) Similarly   2) Naturally   3) Conversely
      4) Interestingly   5) Consequently

[명작 감상]　　　Jonathan Swift (1667 ~ 1745)

Gulliver's Travels 『걸리버 여행기』

My wife and family received me with great surprise and joy, because they concluded me certainly dead; but I must freely confess the sight of them filled me only with hatred, disgust and contempt, and the more by reflecting on the near alliance I had to them. For, although since my unfortunate exile from the Houyhnhnm country, I had compelled myself to tolerate the sight of Yahoos, and to converse with Don Pedro de Mendez, yet my memory and imaginations were perpetually filled with the virtues and ideas of those exalted Houyhnhnms. And when I began to consider that by copulating with one of the Yahoo species I had become a parent of more, it struck me with the utmost shame, confusion and horror.

As soon as I enter the room, my wife took me in her arms, and kissed me, at which, not having been used to the touch of that odious animal for so many years, I fell in a swoon for almost an hour. At the time I am writing it is five years since my last return to England: during the first year I could not endure my wife or children in my presence, the very smell of them was intolerable, much less could I suffer them to eat in the same room. To this hour they dare not presume to touch my bread, or drink out of the same cup, neither was I ever able to let one of them take me by the hand. The first money I laid out was to buy two young stone-horses, which I keep in a good stable, and next to them the groom is my greatest favourite; for I feel my spirits revived by the smell he contracts in the stable. My horses understand me tolerably well; I converse with them at least four hours every day. They are strangers to bridle or saddle, they live in great amity with me, and friendship to each other.

* 풍자 소설 *Gulliver's Travels*에 나오는 "Houyhnhnm"은 "인간의 건전한 이성을 갖춘 말(horse)." 그리고 "Yahoo"는 "인간의 모습을 한 짐승"을 가리키지만, 사실은 "짐승 같은 인간"을 뜻한다.

* Good medicine tastes bitter.　　좋은 약은 입에 쓰다.
* A wonder lasts but nine days.　　굉장한 일도 며칠이면 잊혀진다.
* As you sow, so shall you reap.　　심은 대로 거두리라.
* The pen is mightier than the sword.　　글(文)이 칼(武)보다 강하다.

[확인 학습] 다음 문장을 우리말로 옮기세요.

1. The virtue of poetry is to say what it has to say beautifully and by the power of suggestion, so that it is able to initiate an emotional response in the reader and to convey more meaning more powerfully than prose.

2. To some extent the differences were subject to argument; this was when men differed as to the means to achieve a given end.

3. But when he came up to it, he found the water so low that with all his stooping and straining he was unable to reach it.

4. When I began to consider that by copulating with one of the Yahoo species I had become a parent of more, it struck me with the utmost shame, confusion and horror.

5. During the first year I could not endure my wife or children in my presence, the very smell of them was intolerable, much less could I suffer them to eat in the same room.

[words & phrases]

A1: assert 주장하다, assume 가정하다, propriety 예의, presume 추정하다, refrain from ~을 삼가다

A2: prose 산문, virtue 덕/미덕, suggestion 암시, initiate 시작하다, convey 전달하다, expand 퍼지다, grasp 잡다/이해하다, legend 전설, illusion 환상/착각, measure 측정하다, absorb 흡수하다

A3: have ~ in common ~을 공유하다, logic 논리, neglect 무시하다/간과하다, simultaneously 동시에

A4: carry on ~을 계속하다, refugee 난민, tribe 부족, daffodil 수선화, mum 국화(=chrysanthemum)

B1: legal right 법적 권리, community 공동체/지역사회, be scared 겁먹다, in case (that) ~하는 경우에

B2: be subject to ~에 종속되다, ~을 조건으로 하다, argument 논쟁, as to ~에 관하여, end 목적, sufficient 충분한, condemn 비난하다, punish 벌주다/징벌하다, sin 죄/과오, state 진술하다

B3: two-fifths 5분의 2, labor force 노동력, performance 공연, take forever (시간이) 영원히 걸리다

B4: with all ~에도 불구하고, stoop 굽히다, pebble 자갈, brim 가장자리, quench 끄다, thirst 갈증

B5: reveal 드러내다, expose 노출시키다, soothe 진정시키다, imply 의미하다, decorate 장식하다

C1: disgust 혐오, contempt 경멸, reflect on ~을 숙고하다, alliance 결연, exile 추방, compel 강요하다, tolerate 참다, converse 대화하다, exalted 숭고한, copulate 교접하다, odious 역겨운, swoon 기절, lay out 투자하다, stable 마구간, groom 마부, contract 물들다, bridle 고삐, saddle 안장, amity 친교

[실력 점검 A] 다음 각 동사의 우리말 뜻을 쓰세요.

1. suit: 2. imply: 3. tolerate:

4. alter: 5. infect: 6. traverse:

7. grasp: 8. attract: 9. confront:

10. swear: 11. devote: 12. condemn:

13. desert: 14. assume: 15. penetrate:

16. expose: 17. prosper: 18. emphasize:

19. oppose: 20. reflect on:

[실력 점검 B] 각 항목에 대응하는 영어 단어를 찾아 쓰세요.

보기   gene, myth, theft, notion, luxury, therapy, principle, anecdote, contempt, factor, heredity, authority, prejudice, gravitation, acquaintance, hostile, inevitable, tropical, complicated, conventional

1. 경멸: 2. 권위: 3. 요인:

4. 치료: 5. 신화: 6. 면식:

7. 절도: 8. 편견: 9. 중력:

10. 일화: 11. 원리: 12. 개념:

13. 사치: 14. 유전: 15. 유전자:

16. 인습적: 17. 열대의: 18. 복잡한:

19. 적대적인: 20. 피할 수 없는:

[실력 점검 C] 빈칸에 알맞은 낱말은?

1. Two of _____ trade seldom agree.

   Birds of _____ feather flock together.

2. From the earliest time _____ had been observed that some relation

   existed _____ the tides and the moon. They were seen to be high when

   the moon is _____ or new, but why this should be so was not clearly

   understood _____ the law of gravitation gave the key to the riddle.

명시 감상

To-night

Edward Thomas

Harry, you know at night

The larks in Castle Alley

Sing from the attic's height

As if the electric light

Were the true sun above a summer valley:

Whistle, don't knock, to-night.

I shall come early, Kate:

And we in Castle Alley

Will sit close out of sight

Alone, and ask no light

Of lamp or sun above a summer valley:

To-night I can stay late.

---

* lark 종달새, attic 고미다락(방), as if~ 마치 ~인 것처럼, electric light 전등불, out of sight 아무도 안보는 곳에

Unit 6   시제

A.   현재 시제(present)

1) I *live* in Seoul. He *gets* up at six every morning.

2) Knowledge *is* power. The earth *moves* around the sun.

B.   과거 시제(past)

1) She *knew* his phone number. I *would* go fishing on weekends.

2) King Sejong and his scholars *invented* the Korean alphabet in 1443.

C.   미래 시제(future)

1) I *shall* be seventeen next month. *Will* it rain tomorrow?

2) I *will* never meet him again. *Shall* the boy wash your car?

D.   완료 시제(perfect)

1) He *has done* his homework. I *have lost* my watch.

   Have you ever *seen* a tiger? How long *have* you *lived* here in Korea?

   * She *has gone to* London. She *has been to* London.

2) The man claimed that he *had seen* a ghost.

   When we *got* to the station, the train *had* already *left*.

   * They *had hoped* to help the poor and the sick.

   * No sooner *had* we *left* home than it *began* to rain.

3) She *will have recovered* when you return from Europe.

   By this time next year he *will have taken* his doctor's degree.

   * I will return the book as soon as I *have* read *it*.

E.   진행 시제(progressive)

1) They *are playing* soccer. He *was playing* the guitar.

   I *will be waiting* for you. It *has been raining* for a week.

2) We *are having* lunch. They *were seeing* the sights of Rome.

3) She *is coming* later. What time *are* you *leaving*?

   It *is going to* rain. He *was going to* study earth science.

[필수 문법] 시제(tense)

* 동사의 어형 변화가 나타내는 어떤 행위/동작/상태의 시간적 관계.
* 일반적으로, 본동사에 의한 현재 시제와 과거 시제만을 시제로 인정한다.
* 조동사를 도입하는 미래/완료/진행형은 대개 별도의 "시제"로 보지 않는다.

A. 현재 시제: 1) 현재의 사실/습관   2) 불변의 "진리/속담"은 늘 현재시제로 표현.
   일반동사가 3인칭/단수/현재/직설법에 쓰이면 그 말미에 "~(e)s"를 덧붙인다.

B. 과거 시제: 1) 과거의 사실/습관   2) "역사적 사실"은 항상 과거시제로 표현.
   규칙 동사의 과거/과거분사의 어미는 "~ed": died, omitted, stopped, occurred 등.

C. 미래 시제: will/shall + 동사원형
   1) 단순 미래: 화자/청자의 의지와는 무관한 미래 사실: 미국 영어는 늘 "will"을 씀.
   2) 의지 미래: 평서문은 화자의 의지 표현, 의문문은 청자의 의지/의향에 대한 물음.
      평서문: I/We *will* ~.   You *shall* ~.   He/She/It/They *shall* ~.
      의문문: *Shall* I/we ~?   *Will* you ~?   *Shall* he/she/it/they ~?
      You *shall* hear from me. (=I *will* write to you.)   She *shall* have it. (=I *will* give it to her.)

D. 완료 시제: "have"동사 + 과거분사
   1) 현재 완료: 현재 시점에서의 행위/상태의 완료/결과/경험/계속(진행) 등을 나타냄:
      명백히 과거를 나타내는 낱말이나 어귀는 현재완료에 쓰일 수 없음: ago, when,
      yesterday, last night, just now 등 (단, "just"는 자주 쓰임: We *have just arrived* in Seoul.)
      * "런던에 가버렸다, 가고 없다"(결과), "런던에 갔다 왔다, 가본 적이 있다."(경험)
   2) 과거 완료: 과거의 어떤 일 보다 먼저 일어난 일을 나타냄: 과거의 특정 시점을
      기준하여, 그때까지의 어떤 행위의 완료/결과/경험/계속(진행) 등을 나타낸다:
      * "소망/의도"의 동사(hope/want/expect/intend)가 과거 완료형으로 쓰이면 이루지 못한
      일에 대한 유감/후회를 표현: =They hoped to have helped ~. (돕기를 희망했었는데.....)
      * no sooner ~ than ~; hardly(=scarcely) ~ when(=before) ~: ~하자마자 ~하다:
      = Hardly *had* we *left* home when it *began* to rain. (=As soon as we *left* home, it *began* to rain.)
   3) 미래 완료: 미래의 특정 시점을 기준하여, 그때까지의 행위의 완료/결과/경험/계속.
      * "시간/조건의 부사절"에서는 미래 시제 대신에 현재 시제를, 미래 완료 대신에 현재
      완료 시제를 사용함: I will go *if he comes*. (부사절) I don't know *if he will come*. (명사절)

E. 진행 시제: "be"동사 + 현재분사
   1) 현재/과거/미래/완료 진행형   2) 동작 동사: have(먹다/경험하다), see (관광하다):
      상태 동사 have, see, hear, know, like, resemble 등은 진행형으로 쓸 수 없다.
   3) 현재 진행형이 가까운 미래를 나타낼 수도 있다: "be going to (do)" (~하려 하고 있다)

[문법 연습 A] 틀린 곳을 고치세요.

1. When have you arrived in Seoul?

2. We have arrived in Seoul just now.

3. I have gone to Germany with my wife.

4. Three years passed since my father died.

5. She waited for a bus when I saw her this morning.

6. Danny had to sell the camera he bought the day before.

7. No sooner we sat down than we found it was time to go.

8. It will not be long before she will come to know the truth.

9. He lost his mother when his father was dead for three years.

10. I will help you with the work when I will have done with my job.

11. Sandy will read the book three times if she will read it once again.

[문법 연습 B] 다음 동사의 과거/과거분사와 우리말 뜻을 쓰세요.

1. lie   _____   _____   (거짓말하다   )

   lie   _____   _____   (   )

   lay   _____   _____   (   )

2. fall   _____   _____   (   )

   fell   _____   _____   (   )

3. find   _____   _____   (   )

   found   _____   _____   (   )

4. rise   _____   _____   (   )

   raise   _____   _____   (   )

5. saw   _____   _____   (   )

   sew   _____   _____   (   )

   sow   _____   _____   (   )

6. wind   _____   _____   (   )

   wound   _____   _____   (   )

[실전 문법 A] 빈칸에 알맞은 낱말을 쓰세요.

1. "_____ have you been?" "Pretty well."

2. "_____ have you been?" "I've been to my uncle's."

3. They have known each other since three years _____.

4. Didn't you know that blood _____ thicker than water?

5. I _____ expected to see her; she would never see me again.

6. She was one of the greatest novelists that _____ ever lived.

7. "Can you put the kettle on?" "No sooner said _____ done."

8. Scarcely had the boys seen me _____ they took to their heels.

9. It will not be long _____ he distinguishes himself in his class.

10. "How long have you lived here?" "Ever _____ I was married."

11. We had hardly returned home _____ we heard of his sudden death.

[실전 문법 B] 각 문항의 다섯 부분 중 어법에 맞지 않는 부분은?

1. [1]By the time [2]you will be graduated [3]from college, [4]you will have studied English [5]for more than ten years.

2. [1]The world will not be [2]a pleasant place to live in [3]unless the problem of global warming [4]will be solved [5]in the near future.

3. [1]Harvard, found in 1636, [2]is well known to the world [3]for its history and tradition [4]as the oldest university [5]in the United States.

4. [1]She was living [2]in the apartment house [3]for almost a year [4]before she came to know [5]her next-door neighbor.

5. [1]No sooner he closed his eyes [2]than he fell asleep; [3]he spent [4]the whole night [5]preparing for his final exams.

6. [1]Acute hearing [2]seems to help [3]most animals sense [4]the approach of tornados [5]long before people will do.

7. [1]As I approached my car [2]with my girlfriend, [3]I suddenly remembered [4]that I left my keys [5]on the cabinet in my office.

[필수 어휘 A] 밑줄 친 낱말과 그 뜻이 비슷한 것은?

1. They are going to <u>purchase</u> a new house in the country.

   1) buy   2) sell   3) rent   4) move   5) build

2. It is wrong to <u>ascribe</u> all that has happened simply to the war.

   1) owe   2) devote   3) attach   4) attribute   5) acknowledge

3. Both parties must agree to <u>abide by</u> the court's decision.

   1) prove   2) observe   3) inspect   4) consider   5) postpone

4. She did not <u>get over</u> her homesickness for some time.

   1) suffer   3) endure   3) undergo   4) overcome   5) experience

5. Being a bodyguard is obviously a <u>hazardous</u> occupation.

   1) busy   2) difficult   3) unusual   4) important   5) dangerous

6. He was <u>brooding</u> over the plan, trying to find some mistake in it.

   1) taking   2) talking   3) thinking   4) checking   5) examining

[필수 어휘 B] 빈칸에 들어갈 가장 적절한 낱말은?

1. The area is _____ to drought and floods and earthquakes.

   1) due   2) likely   3) subject   4) possible   5) supposed

2. She was older than I was, and not only in the _____ sense.

   1) strict   2) literal   3) natural   4) common   5) ordinary

3. Industrialization caused many people to move to _____ areas.

   1) rural   2) urban   3) central   4) crowded   5) secluded

4. This book is about change and how we can _____ to it.

   1) adapt   2) adopt   3) reply   4) apply   5) comply

5. He began to _____ upon memories of how she had lived her life.

   1) call   2) look   3) dwell   4) depend   6) recollect

6. We will restore the house wherever possible to its original _____.

   1) state   2) stage   3) statue   4) status   5) strategy

7. _____ is the scientific study of people, society, and culture.

   1) Ethics   2) Statistics   3) Theology   4) Archeology   5) Anthropology

[구문 연습] 다음 문장을 우리말로 옮기세요.

1. When he had gone, after an unusually pleasant little chat, she smiled to herself, but not without a slight fluttering of the heart.

2. If you bring curiosity to your work, it will cease to be merely a job and become a door through which you enter the best that life can give you.

3. I have never been much of a sightseer. So much enthusiasm has been expended over the great sights of the world that I can summon up very little when I am confronted with them.

4. No sooner had I got to school than I learned the problems of owning property. I used to dread the lost property lists which were read out twice a day. I would blush with humiliation as I had to get up in front of the school to collect the things I had lost.

[작문 연습] 다음 문장을 영어로 옮기세요.

1. 내 할아버님이 돌아 가신지 벌써 3년이 되었다.

   _____

2. 시골에서 전원 생활을 하신지 얼마나 되셨어요?

   _____

3. 그녀는 나를 만나자마자 내 친구 험담을 하기 시작했다.

   _____

4. 그는 그녀가 일주일 째 병원에 입원해 있다는 얘기를 들었다.

   _____

5. 내가 또다시 한번 그 산을 등정한다면 세 번 등정하는 셈이 된다.

   _____

[실전독해 A] 각 문항의 물음에 답하세요.

1. There was a Scotchman who married the tattooed woman from a sideshow so that his children could see moving picture [a)]_____. The Scotchman, in order to teach his small son thrifty habits, gave him a penny each day and saw to it that he deposited them in a white pig-bank. As soon as the boy had five pennies thus saved, the father removed coins and gave the lad a nickel in exchange and had him place it in a larger blue china bank. And when five nickels had been accumulated again the father took the smaller coins and gave him a [b)]_____ for them which the boy was taught to place in a large rusty iron box hidden beneath the floor.

> Q 1. 빈칸 a)에 알맞은 낱말은?
>   1) free   2) cheap   3) priceless
>   4) impressive   5) imaginative
>
> 2. 빈칸 b)에 알맞은 낱말은?

2. When a Japanese woman who lived in the United States arrived at work one morning, her boss asked her, "Did you get a plate?" "No...," she answered, wondering what in the world he meant. Why did the boss ask her about a plate? All day she wondered about her boss's strange question, but she was too embarrassed to ask him about it. At five o'clock, when she was getting ready to go home, her boss said, "Please be on time tomorrow. You were 15 minutes late this morning." "Sorry," she said. "My car wouldn't start, and....." Suddenly she stopped talking and began to smile. Now she understood. Her boss hadn't asked her, "Did you get a plate?" He had asked her, _____.

> Q. 빈칸에 알맞은 말은?
>   1) "Did you rent a car?"
>   2) "Did you get a start?"
>   3) "Did you have a car?"
>   4) "Did you get up late?"
>   5) "Did you get a license?"

3. I consider ignorance the primary enemy of mankind. ① The worst fool in the world is the man who will not admit anything that he cannot see or hear or feel, who has no place for imagination or vision. ② Man is capable of various kinds of education. He is possessed of physical, social, religious, intellectual and moral capabilities. ③ The education of all makes him complete; the education of part leaves him deficient. ④ The educated man is the man who can do something, and the quality of his work marks the degree of his education. ⑤ The best investment a young man can make is in good books, the study of which broadens the mind.

Q. ①~⑤중 다음 문장이 삽입되기에 적절한 곳은?
Each requires education.

4. The world we live in has changed a great deal in the last hundred years, and it is likely to change even more in the next hundred. Some people would like to stop these changes and go back to what they see as a purer and simpler age. But as history shows, the past was not that wonderful. It was not so bad for a privileged minority, though even they had to do without modern medicine, and childbirth was highly risky for women. But for the vast majority of the population, a)_____ . Anyway, even if one wanted to, one couldn't put the clock back to an earlier age. Knowledge and techniques can't just be forgotten. Nor can one prevent further advances in the future. Even if all government money for research were cut off, the force of competition would still bring about advances in technology. b)_____ , one cannot stop inquiring minds from thinking about basic science, whether or not they were paid for it.

Q 1. 빈칸 a)에 알맞은 문장은?
1) life was nasty and short
2) doctors were not available
3) happiness lay in ignorance
4) science meant something new
5) knowledge was not power at all

2. 빈칸 b)에 알맞은 낱말은?
1) However   2) Therefore   3) Moreover
4) Nevertheless   5) Consequently

[실전 독해 B] 각 문항의 물음에 답하세요.

1. The _____ of the United States established a political system comprising a national and federal government. It greatly enhanced the power of central government but carefully divided its function into three distinct branches—executive, legislative, and judicial. The principle of separation of powers was applied throughout the document. Carefully measured checks and balances were inserted to prevent the acquisition or concentration of power in any one branch and also for the purpose of protecting minority rights from the potential rule of the majority. In their powers to amend the supreme law and to elect the president and members of the Senate, the states gained a role in applying checks and balances.

Q 1. 빈칸에 들어갈 적절한 낱말은?

   2. 밑줄 친 "their"가 가리키는 것은?
      1) majority   2) the states   3) three branches
      4) minority rights   5) checks and balances

2. Facts can be discovered through observation, calculation, or reliable report. You can observe that your tropical fish 1)swim, the snow outside is cold, and your infant niece cries. One or more of your five senses—sight, hearing, touch, taste, smell—can tell you such things. A piece of steak weighs twelve ounces and a gasoline engine has 250 horsepower. You cannot observe 2)those things, but they can be determined by reliable calculation. The South Pole is much colder than Florida, and Marilyn Monroe was once married to Joe DiMaggio. You probably know 3)none of those things from observation, but you probably do know them through reliable report. Any fact can be observed or calculated, if not by the average person, at least by someone with special training or special instruments. Thus, presently 4)existing facts can be proved even if they are not readily accessible, and past facts also can be proved. But proof that rests on someone else's observation or calculation, and thus on report, is 5)less certain than your own observation or your own carefully checked calculation.

   Q. 밑줄 친 1) ~ 5)중 어법에 맞지 않는 것은?

3.   Suppose an unkempt and tattered man passes three women on the street. One woman might remark, "His clothes are dirty and ragged." Another might say, "He must not work for a living." The third might add, "He's disgusting." All three women would be making a statement about the same person, but they would be making three different kinds of statement: the statement of report, the statement of _____, and the statement of value judgment.

> Q. 빈칸에 들어갈 적절한 낱말은?
>   1) attitude   2) emotion   3) inference
>   4) experience   5) assumption

4.   With regard to the question of reading, our difficulties arise not from the lack of quantity, but from the true discrimination of quality. In the very multiplicity and variety of the volumes placed at our disposal we find our _____. The question is not one of finding books in sufficient numbers, but in selecting those which inform, enrich, elevate and gladden the mind.

> Q. 빈칸에 들어갈 적절한 낱말은?
>   1) tragedy   2) limitation   3) satisfaction
>   4) contradiction   5) embarrassment

5.   Whatever the novelist writes is the expression of his personality and it is the manifestation of his innate instincts, his feelings and his experiences. The subjects he chooses, the characters he invents and his attitude toward them, are conditioned by his bias. However hard he tries to be objective, he remains the slave of his idiosyncrasies. However hard he tries to be impartial, he cannot help taking sides. He arranges his facts in such a manner as to capture and hold readers' attention.

> Q. 이 글의 요지로서 적절한 것은?
>   1) The novelist is at the mercy of his prejudice.
>   2) The novelist wants to express his personality.
>   3) The novelist must try to be objective and impartial.
>   4) The novelist makes efforts to capture readers' attention.
>   5) The novelist is a man of strong views and powerful feelings.

[명작 감상] Charles Dickens (1812 ~ 1870)

Great Expectations 『위대한 유산』

The early dinner-hour at Joe's, left me abundance of time, without hurrying my talk with Biddy, to walk over to the old spot before dark. But, what with loitering on the way, to look at old objects and to think of old times, the day had quite declined when I came to the place.

There was no house now, no brewery, no building whatever left, but the wall of the old garden. The cleared space had been enclosed with a rough fence, and, looking over it, I saw that some the old ivy had struck root anew, and was growing green on low quiet mounds of ruin. A gate in the fence standing ajar, I pushed it open, and went in.

A cold silvery mist had veiled the afternoon, and the moon was not yet up to scatter it. But, the stars were shining beyond the mist, and the moon was coming, and the evening was not dark. I could trace out where every part of the old house had been, and where the brewery had been, and where the gates, and where the casks. I had done so, and was looking along the desolate garden-walk, when I beheld a solitary figure in it.

The figure showed itself aware of me, as I advanced. It had been moving towards me, but it stood still. As I drew nearer, I saw it to be the figure of a woman. As I drew nearer yet, it was about to turn away, when it stopped, and let me come up with it. Then, it faltered as if much surprised, and uttered my name, and I cried out:

"Estella!"

"I am greatly changed. I wonder you know me."

The freshness of her beauty was indeed gone, but its indescribable majesty and its indescribable charm remained. Those attractions in it, I had seen before; what I had never seen before, was the saddened softened light of the once proud eyes; what I had never felt before, was the friendly touch of the once insensible hand.

We sat down on a bench that was near, and I said, "After so many years, it is strange that we should thus meet again, Estella, here where our first meeting was! Do you often come back?"

"I have never been here since."

"Nor I."

[확인 학습] 다음 문장을 우리말로 옮기세요.

1. Carefully measured checks and balances were inserted to prevent the acquisition or concentration of power in any one branch and also for the purpose of protecting minority rights from the potential rule of the majority.

2. With regard to the question of reading, our difficulties arise not from the lack of quantity, but from the true discrimination of quality. In the very multiplicity and variety of the volumes placed at our disposal we find our embarrassment.

3. However hard he tries to be objective, he remains the slave of his idiosyncrasies. However hard he tries to be impartial, he cannot help taking sides. He arranges his facts in such a manner as to capture and hold readers' attention.

4. Those attractions in it, I had seen before; what I had never seen before, was the saddened softened light of the once proud eyes; what I had never felt before, was the friendly touch of the once insensible hand.

[words & phrases]

A1: tattoo 문신, thrifty 검소한, remove 제거하다, china 도자기, accumulate 축적하다, rusty 녹슨

A2: plate 접시/금속판, wonder 궁금하게 여기다, in the world 도대체, be embarrassed 당황하다,

A3: ignorance 무지, religion 종교, capability 능력, deficient 부족한, invest 투자하다, broaden 넓히다

A4: privilege 특권, minority 소수, majority 다수, medicine 의약/의학, inquire 문의하다/탐구하다

B1: comprise 구성하다, enhance 높이다, executive 행정부/집행부, legislative 입법부, judicial 사법부, principle 원리/원칙, apply 적용하다/응용하다, check and balance 견제와 균형, insert 삽입하다, acquire 획득하다, concentrate 집중하다, rule 통치(하다), amend 고치다/수정하다, Senate 상원

B2: reliable 믿을 만한, tropical 열대의, infant 유아, niece 조카딸, calculate 계산하다, the South Pole 남극, instrument 도구/기구, readily 쉽사리, accessible 접근할 수 있는, rest on ~에 의존하다

B3: kempt 말쑥한, tatter 넝마/누더기, ragged 누더기를 걸친, disgusting 혐오스러운, statement 진술

B4: with regard to ~에 관하여, discriminate 구별하다, multiple 다수의, disposal 처분, sufficient 충분한

B5: manifest 명시하다, innate 타고난/내재적, instinct 본능, objective 객관적인, bias 편견/선입견, idiosyncrasy 특이성, impartial 공평한, cannot help (~ing) ~하지 않을 수 없다, taker sides 편들다

C1: abundance 풍부, loiter 빈둥거리다, decline 기울다, brewery 양조장, enclose 둘러싸다, ivy 담쟁이, ajar 조금 열려져, mist 안개/운무, scatter 흩트리다, trace 흔적을 밟다, cask 통, desolate 쓸쓸한, solitary 고독한, aware of ~을 인식하는, still 고요한/정지된, be about to (do) 막 ~하려고 하다, falter 머뭇거리다, utter 말하다/내뱉다, majesty 위엄, attraction 매력, insensible 둔감한/무감각한

[실력 점검 A] 다음 각 동사의 우리말 뜻을 쓰세요.

1. exalt: 2. falter: 3. compete:

4. dwell: 5. persist: 6. generate:

7. distort: 8. accuse: 9. maintain:

10. reduce: 11. surpass: 12. fascinate:

13. sustain: 14. disdain: 15. anticipate:

16. decline: 17. deserve: 18. participate:

19. enclose: 20. precede:

[실력 점검 B] 각 항목에 대응하는 영어 단어를 찾아 쓰세요.

보기   torch, logic, barrier, fallacy, prestige, intuition, obstinacy, autobiography, cause, sermon, sculpture, revolution, controversy, relative, opponent, theoretical, ethical, perilous, deliberate, simultaneous.

1. 친척: 2. 대의: 3. 조각:

4. 혁명: 5. 오류: 6. 논쟁:

7. 논리: 8. 명성: 9. 장벽:

10. 햇불: 11. 설교: 12. 완고함:

13. 직관: 14. 자서전: 15. 반대자:

16. 위험한: 17. 윤리적: 18. 동시적:

19. 이론적: 20. 고의적:

[실력 점검 C] 주어진 철자로 시작되는 알맞은 낱말은?

1. A computer is powerful in t_____ of speed and capacity.

2. To comprehend a man's life it is necessary to know not m_____ what he does, but also what he purposely leaves u_____.

3. If art were merely a record of the appearances of n_____, the closest imitation would be the most satisfactory w_____ of art, and the time would be fast approaching w_____ photography should replace painting.

명시 감상

The Master

Lao-tzu

Without opening your door,
You can open your heart to the world.
Without looking out your window,
You can see the essence of Tao.

The more you know,
The less you understand.

The Master arrives without leaving,
sees the light without looking,
achieves without doing a thing.

* Lao-tzu 老子 (중국 춘추 전국 시대의 "無爲 自然" 사상가), Tao 도(道), master 선생/대가, achieve 성취하다

Unit 7   부정사

A. 부정사의 용법

1) *To teach* is *to be taught*. I expected him *to come*.

He likes *to go* to the movies. I don't know *what to say*.

* You may come if you want *to*.   *She told me *not to be* late.

2) There are many sights *to see* in Rome and Athens.

Give me something cold *to drink*. I need a pencil *to write with*.

3) He went out *to see* his friends. She grew up *to be* a novelist.

I am glad *to see* you again. He must be crazy *to talk* like that.

B. 부정사의 주어/시제

1) The book is difficult *for children to understand*.

It is impossible (*for us/you*) *to master* English in a few years.

* I wanted *you to go* there.   * It is very *kind of you* to help me.

* It is *too* difficult for me *to* read. He is tall *enough to* touch the ceiling.

2) He seems *to be* rich. She seems *to have been* ill.

C. 원형 부정사

1) I saw someone *move* in the dark. Let me *tell* you something.

2) You had better not *smoke*. I would rather *die* than *surrender*.

3) We cannot but *admire* him. She did nothing but *complain*.

D. 독립 부정사

1) He is, *so to speak*, a walking dictionary.

2) *To do her justice*, she is not a respectable woman.

3) *To make matters worse*, they were almost always unreliable.

4) There is no time to do all the work, *to say nothing of* the cost.

E. "be"동사 + to-부정사

1) We *are to meet* at six.   2) Not a soul *was to be seen* in the street.

3) You *are* not *to smoke* here.   4) The poet *was to die* very young.

5) If you *are to enter* the college, you have to be diligent in your studies.

[필수 문법] 부정사(infinitive)

* 어형 변화를 하지 않은 기본 형태의 동사를 말한다.

* 조동사 다음이나 명령문에 사용됨은 물론, 문장에서 여러 가지 기능을 한다.

* to-부정사와 ("to"없는) 원형 부정사가 있으며, 단순형과 완료형이 있다.

A. 부정사의 용법

  1) 명사적 용법: 문장의 주어, (주격/목적격) 보어, 목적어의 기능을 한다.

    *부정사의 반복을 피하는 대부정사(=want *to come*). * "not/never"는 부정사의 앞에 둔다.

  2) 형용사적 용법: 앞에 있는 명사/명사구를 수식하는 기능: "볼 거리," "마실 것"

  3) 부사적 용법: 동사/형용사/부사를 수식하는 기능을 한다: 문장의 내용에 따라서 어떤 행위/행동의 "목적/결과/원인/이유(판단의 근거)" 등의 의미를 갖는다.

B. 부정사의 주어/시제

  1) 부정사의 주어: "for+목적격"의 형태로 나타나며, 일반 주어 "for us/you/them"이나 주절의 주어와 동일한 (부정사의) 주어는 생략된다: I wanted (*for me*) to go there. 생략된다. * S+V+O+C의 문형에서는 부정사의 주어를 나타내는 전치사 "for"는 생략된다. * 사람의 성격/성품을 나타내는 형용사 (kind, nice, wise, smart, silly, foolish, cruel, careful, careless, considerate, presumptuous) 다음에는 "of+목적격"을 사용한다.

    * (=It is *so* difficult *that* I *cannot* read it.) (=He is *so* tall *that* he *can* touch the ceiling.)

  2) 부정사의 시제: 단순형의 시제는 술어동사의 시제와 일치하며, 완료형의 시제는 술어동사의 시제보다 앞섬: (=It *seems* that he *is* rich.) (=It *seems* that she *was/has been* ill.)

C. 원형 부정사

  1) 지각동사(hear/listen/see/watch/feel)나 사역동사(let/have/make/help)의 목적격 보어.

  2) had better ~: ~하는 것이 더 낫다.　would rather ~ than ~: ~하느니 차라리~하겠다.

  3) cannot (help) but ~: ~하지 않을 수 없다(cannot help ~ing). do nothing but ~: ~하기만 한다.

    * I couldn't but *obey* them. =I couldn't help *obeying* them. =I had no choice but *to obey* them.

D. 독립[절대] 부정사

  1) 말하자면/이를테면(=as it were)　　2) ~을 공평하게 평하자면　　3) 설상가상으로

  4) ~은 말할 것도 없고(=not to speak of ~)　* not to say ~: ~라고 말할 수는 없지만

E. "be"동사 + to-부정사

  1) 예정(=be going to)　2) 가능(=can)　3) 당위(=must/should)　4) 운명(=be destined to)

  5) 소망/의도(=wish/want/expect/intend to)　* You are *to blame*. (=You should *be blamed*.)

[문법 연습 A] 잘못된 곳을 고치세요.

1. I had my sister to find me a house.

2. The table is too heavy for me to lift it.

3. They had no house to live at that time.

4. The baby does nothing but to cry all day.

5. She wishes for a friend to open her mind.

6. I am sorry to have not answered your e-mail.

7. He is said to be wounded in the Vietnam War.

8. We have no choice but wait until he will come back.

9. She noticed an old man to be seated in the front row.

10. You had better get your children clean their own rooms.

11. The webtoon is enough interesting to attract young readers.

12. I would go out for a walk rather than staying at home like this.

13. Young people have a tendency of listening only to popular music.

[문법 연습 B] 같은 뜻의 다른 문장으로 고치세요.

1. The sisters are so proud that boys cannot speak to them.

_____

2. The question was so easy that everybody could answer it.

_____

3. It seemed that she was on good terms with her neighbors.

_____

4. It seems that the old man has been living alone in the house.

_____

5. I think that it is almost impossible to finish the work in a week.

_____

6. You would be very wise to consult with him about the problem.

_____

[실전 문법 A] 빈칸에 알맞은 낱말은?

1. When will it suit you _____ us to call?

2. He was so tall _____ to touch the ceiling.

3. To do him _____, he is honest but obstinate.

4. How stupid _____ you to make such a mistake!

5. _____ girls to marry young is not altogether bad.

6. You should know whom to keep company _____.

7. "Would you prefer to go?" "No, I prefer not _____."

8. They are learning _____ to operate the new machine.

9. Are your children old _____ to take care of themselves?

10. To be frank _____ you, they don't care much for your plan.

11. We felt _____ our duty to make it public as soon as possible.

12. I finally found my watch, _____ to discover that it had stopped.

[실전 문법 B] 각 문항의 다섯 부분 중 어법에 맞지 않는 부분은?

1. [1]As we grow older, [2]we come to understand [3]that both our fears and hopes [4]are mostly illusions [5]and are to be not taken too seriously.

2. [1]Though the Romans became [2]masters of the world, [3]they were not so proud [4]to learn useful lessons [5]from the people they conquered.

3. [1]The sign of intelligence in reading [2]is the ability of reading [3]different things differently [4]according to [5]their worth or importance.

4. [1]Her face was cold and pale, [2]and when she put her hand on my cheek [3]and laid my head on her chest, [4]I felt a cold shuddering [5]to pass all through me.

5. [1]The world is a pleasant place to live [2]as soon as we accept the fact [3]that other people, as well as ourselves, [4]have a right [5]to live a happy life.

6. [1]Why are some people easily hooked on cigarettes [2]while others drop the habit after a few puffs? [3]According to a study, [4]heredity plays a role in [5]why people start, stop or continue to smoke.

[필수 어휘 A]   접두사를 사용하여 반의어를 쓰세요.

1. legal: 2. mortal: 3. regular:

4. finite: 5. honest: 6. famous:

7. noble: 8. normal: 9. ordinary:

10. ability: 11. fortune: 12. nutrition:

[필수 어휘 B]   빈칸에 들어갈 적절한 낱말은?

1. A story intended to teach a moral truth is a _____ .

   1) myth   2) fable   3) novel   4) legend   5) biography

2. A _____ line runs straight up from the bottom to the top.

   1) front   2) coast   3) border   4) vertical   5) horizontal

3. Teachers should not _____ the students who are not bright.

   1) forbid   2) suspect   3) protect   4) humiliate   5) encourage

4. He is a terrible boss; he _____ people for the slightest mistake.

   1) fires   2) evades   3) removes   4) evaluates   5) interrupts

5. It took great self-control not to _____ her feeling of shock.

   1) depict   2) betray   3) reduce   4) indicates   5) exaggerate

6. My brother is so _____ that he is often deceived by his friends.

   1) timid   2) jealous   3) prudent   4) arrogant   5) credulous

7. This was thought to be a _____ Van Gogh, but in fact it's a fake.

   1) general   2) generous   3) genuine   4) ingenious   5) ingenuous

[필수 어휘 C]   밑줄 친 부분의 우리말 뜻은?

1. She is pretty, not to say beautiful or attractive.   _____

2. She can speak French, not to speak of English.   _____

3. He finished the job at the expense of his health.   _____

4. The ship was at the mercy of the stormy weather.   _____

5. They are at their wits' end about computer crimes.   _____

6. These paintings as often as not end up in London.   _____

94

[구문 연습] 다음 문장을 우리말로 옮기세요.

1. If your name is to live at all, it is so much more to have it live in people's hearts rather than only in their brains.

2. Once people have learned to learn in a given way, it is extremely difficult for them to learn in any other way.

3. I find it wholesome to be alone the greater part of the time. To be in company, even with the best, is soon wearisome and dissipating.

4. It would be as presumptuous of me to overhaul the human soul as for an astronomer to remake the solar system. All I want to do is to help the patients understand who God made them to be.

5. The most important thing in an argument, next to being right, is to leave an escape door for your opponent, so that he can gracefully swing over to your side without too much apparent loss of face.

[작문 연습] 다음 문장을 영어로 옮기세요.

1. 신라 왕조의 수도였던 경주에는 볼거리가 많다.

2. 너희들은 늦어도 밤 열 시까지는 집에 들어와야 한다.

3. 그는 한국 전통 음악과 악기에 관심이 있었던 것 같다.

4. 그녀는 자라서 저명한 시인이 되었으며, 여든까지 살았다.

5. 나는 그들에게 누구에게도 결코 거짓말하지 말라고 충고했다.

[실전 독해 A] 각 문항의 물음에 답하세요.

1. It is always easy to pick faults in other people. None of us is perfect at all. The sad thing is that many people seem to find ^{a)}_____ so difficult to overlook faults in others. They ignore the good things in a person's character and concentrate on the bad. A Persian writer once said: "If you know a man who has ten faults and one good quality, try to think as little of the faults as you can, and to make the most of his one good quality. And if you know a man who has ten virtues and one fault, praise him for the former and do all you can do to ^{b)}_____ the latter."

> Q 1. 빈칸 a)에 알맞은 낱말은?
>
> 2. 빈칸 b)에 알맞은 낱말은?
>   1) forget   2) prefer   3) forgive
>   4) conceal   5) criticize

2. Satire is the type of writing which most closely resembles sarcasm, and it is usually used to expose foolishness or injustice. As a result, writing satires has, in many countries, often been a dangerous occupation, and satirists have spent more years in prison than perhaps any other kind of writers. A satirist may simply present the speech and habits—exaggerated for humorous effect—of a group of people whom he or she wants to ridicule. A satirist may also express an opinion about a social or political issue. To do this, the writer pretends to adopt a viewpoint that is opposed to his or her own and then makes such outrageous proposals that the reader will be convinced that such a viewpoint is foolish. The success of satire depends on the reader being skilled enough to determine _____.

> Q. 빈칸에 알맞은 말은?
>   1) how to read efficiently
>   2) what to do for public good
>   3) how to solve a social problem
>   4) what the writer's true opinion is
>   5) whom he or she wants to ridicule

3. It is not always when things are going from bad to worse that revolutions break out. _____, it oftener happens that when a people that has put up with an oppressive rule over a long period without protest suddenly finds the government relaxing its pressure, it takes up arms against it. Thus the social order overthrown by a revolution is almost always better than the ^{a)}one immediately preceding it, and experience teaches us that, generally speaking, the most perilous moment for a bad government is ^{b)}one when it seeks to mend its ways.

Q 1. 빈칸에 알맞은 말은?
　　1) However　　2) Therefore　　3) Moreover
　　4) In addition　　5) On the contrary

　2. 밑줄 친 a), b)의 "one"이 각각 가리키는 것은?

4. More than two-thirds of all astronauts suffer from motion sickness while traveling in space. In the gravity-free environment, the body cannot distinguish up from down. The body's internal balance system sends confusing signals to the brain, which can result in nausea lasting as long as a few days.

ⓐ One of the most common is the loss of muscle mass and bone density. Another effect of the weightless surroundings is that astronauts tend not to use their legs as much, so the muscles gradually atrophy.

ⓑ This, combined with the shift of fluid to the upper body and the resulting loss of essential minerals such as calcium, causes bones to weaken. Bone density can decrease at a rate of 1 to 2 percent a month, and many astronauts are unable to walk properly upon their return to earth.

ⓒ A body that is deprived of gravity also experiences changes in the distribution of bodily fluids. More fluid than normal ends up in the face, neck, and chest, resulting in a puffy face, bulging neck veins, and a slightly enlarged heart. Throughout the duration of a mission, astronauts' bodies experience some potentially dangerous disorders.

Q. ⓐ~ⓒ의 글을 문맥에 맞게 배열하면?
　　1) ⓐ-ⓒ-ⓑ　　2) ⓑ-ⓐ-ⓒ　　3) ⓑ-ⓒ-ⓐ
　　4) ⓒ-ⓐ-ⓑ　　5) ⓒ-ⓑ-ⓐ

[실전 독해 B] 각 문항의 물음에 답하세요.

1.   The Japanese, though superficially resembling their Chinese neighbors, are a very distinctive people. Comparisons which represent the Chinese as the Greeks of the Far East and the Japanese as its Romans are apt to be misleading, but it is certainly true that the Chinese resemble the Greeks in their passion for art and philosophy, and the Japanese the Romans in their power of assimilation, their lack of originality and their readiness for discipline. Just as the Greeks civilized the Romans, _____ the Chinese have civilized the Japanese, and Buddhism has done for both much of what Christianity did for the Greek and Roman world.

    Q 1. 빈칸에 알맞은 낱말은?

       2. 이 글의 내용과 일치하지 않는 것은?
          1) The Japanese are accustomed to absorbing foreign cultures.
          2) The lack of originality is characteristic of the Japanese culture.
          3) Buddhism is to the Chinese what Christianity is to the Romans.
          4) The Chinese culture has something to do with the Greek culture.
          5) The Chinese are to the Japanese as the Greeks are to the Romans.

2.   A schoolboy stole his classmate's writing tablet and took it to his mother, who instead of reproving him praised him. Another time he brought her a stolen cloak, [a)]of/for which she praised him still more highly. When he grew up to be a young man he ventured on more serious thefts. But one day he was caught in the act, whereupon his hands were tied behind his back and he was led off to execution. His mother went with him, [b)]beat/beating her breast, and he said that he wanted to whisper something in her ear. The moment she went up to him, he took the lobe of her ear in his teeth and bit it. She reproached him for his unfilial conduct: not content with the other crimes he had committed, he had now done grievous bodily harm to his mother. "The time when you [c)]could/should have reproved me," he said, "was when I committed my first theft and brought you the tablet I had stolen. Then I should not have ended up in the hands of the executioner."

    Q. 밑줄 친 a) ~ c)에서 어법에 맞는 각 낱말은?

3. ①We'll certainly take your feelings into _____. ②She gave a full _____ of what had happened the night before. ③It is of little _____ to me whether you go or stay. ④On no _____ must strangers be let in. ⑤I would like to open a checking _____ with you.

    Q. ①~⑤의 문장의 빈칸에 공통으로 들어갈 낱말은?

4. It is important to remember that many life-saving medicines are created from certain plants or animals. The purple foxglove is, for example, the main source of the drug digitalis. Without this drug, over 3 million people in the U.S. alone would die every year within seventy-two hours of suffering a heart attack. To ensure that we have a long-term supply of digitalis well into the future, we must make sure that the purple foxglove and its habitat do not become endangered or extinct. To preserve the quality of our lives, and the lives of future generations, we must protect plants and animals now, and in the future.

    Q. 이 글의 주제는?
      1) The purple foxglove
      2) The endangered wildlife
      3) The life-saving medicines
      4) The preservation of species
      5) The importance of environment

5. From my fifteenth year I have lived as solitary a life as a modern can have. ① I mean by this that the number of hours, days, months, and years that I have spent alone has been immense and extraordinary. ② I propose, therefore, to describe the experience of human loneliness exactly as I have known it. ③ The reason that impels me to do this is not that I think my knowledge of loneliness is different in kind from that of other men. ④ The whole conviction of my life now rests upon the belief that loneliness, far from being a rare and curious phenomenon to myself and to a few other solitary men, is the central and inevitable fact of human existence. ⑤

    Q. ①~⑤중 다음 문장이 삽입되기에 적절한 곳은?
    Quite the contrary.

[명작 감상]　　　James Joyce (1882 ~ 1941)
　　　　　　　　Dubliners 『더블린 사람들』

She was fast asleep. Gabriel, leaning on his elbow, looked for a few moments unresentfully on her tangled hair and half-open mouth, listening to her deep-drawn breath. So she had had that romance in her life: a man had died for her sake. It hardly pained him now to think how poor a part he, her husband, had played in her life. He watched her while she slept as though he and she had never lived together as man and wife. His curious eyes rested long upon her face and on her hair: and, as he thought of what she must have been then, in that time of her first girlish beauty, a strange friendly pity for her entered his soul. He did not like to say even to himself that her face was no longer beautiful, but he knew that it was no longer the face for which Michael Furey had braved death....

The air of the room chilled his shoulders. He stretched himself cautiously along under the sheets and lay down beside his wife. One by one, they were all becoming shades. Better pass boldly into that other world, in the full glory of some passion, than fade and wither with age. He thought of how she who lay beside him had locked in her heart for so many years that image of her lover's eyes when he had told her that he did not wish to live. Generous tears filled Gabriel's eyes. He had never felt like that himself towards any woman, but he knew that such a feeling must be love....

A few light taps upon the pane made him turn to the window. It had begun to snow again. He watched sleepily the flakes, silver and dark, falling obliquely against the lamplight. The time had come for him to set out on his journey westward. Yes, the newspapers were right: snow was general all over Ireland. It was falling on every part of the dark central plain, on the treeless hills, falling softly upon the Bog of Allen and, farther westward, softly falling into the dark mutinous Shannon waves. It was falling, too, upon every part of the lonely churchyard on the hill where Michael Furey lay buried. It lay thickly drifted on the crooked crosses and headstones, on the spears of the little gate, on the barren thorns. His soul swooned slowly as he heard the snow falling faintly through the universe and faintly falling, like the descent of their last end, upon all the living and the dead.

[학인 학습] 다음 문장을 우리말로 옮기세요.

1. On the contrary, it oftener happens that when a people that has put up with an oppressive rule over a long period without protest suddenly finds the government relaxing its pressure, it takes up arms against it.

2. The whole conviction of my life now rests upon the belief that loneliness, far from being a rare and curious phenomenon to myself and to a few other solitary men, is the central and inevitable fact of human existence.

3. He thought of how she who lay beside him had locked in her heart for so many years that image of her lover's eyes when he had told her that he did not wish to live.

[words & phrases]

A1: overlook 너그럽게 봐주다, make the most of ~을 가장 중시하다, the former 전자, the latter 후자

A2: satire 풍자, resemble 닮다, sarcasm 비꼼/빈정거림, occupation 직업, exaggerate 과장하다, ridicule 비웃다/조롱하다, pretend ~인 체하다, adopt 채택하다, outrageous 포학한, be convinced 확신하다

A3: revolution 혁명, put up with ~을 참다/견디다, oppressive 억압적인, protest 항의/항변, arms 무기, overthrow 타도하다/전복하다, precede 선행하다, perilous 위험한, mend 고치다/수선(개선)하다

A4: astronaut 우주 비행사, suffer from ~을 겪다, motion sickness 멀미/현기증, gravity 중력, nausea 메스꺼움, last 지속되다, mass 질량, density 밀도, atrophy 쇠퇴하다, fluid 액체/체액, deprive ~ of ~ ~에게서 ~을 빼앗다, gravity 중력, vein 혈관, distribution 분배/분포, duration 지속, disorder 장애

B1: superficial 피상적인, compare 비교하다, represent 묘사하다, be apt to (do) ~하기 쉽다, assimilate 흡수하다/동화하다, lack 부족(하다), originality 독창성, discipline 훈육/교육, Buddhism 불교

B2: tablet 서판/명판, reprove 꾸짖다, cloak 외투/망토, theft 절도, execute 집행하다/처형하다, lobe 귓불, reproach 꾸짖다, filial 효성스러운, grieve 슬퍼하다, should have p.p. ~했어야 했는데.....

B3: take ~ into account ~을 고려하다, of little account 중요하지 않은, on no account 결코 ~이 아닌

B4: purple 자주색, heart attack 심장마비, term 기간, habitat 서식지, extinct 멸종된, preserve 보존하다

B5: immense 엄청난, extraordinary 비범한, impel 재촉하다, conviction 확신, rest on ~에 의지하다/의존하다, far from ~이기는커녕, rare 드문/진귀한, phenomenon 현상, inevitable 피하지 못할

C1: fast 굳게/단단히, resent 분개하다, tangled 헝클어진, for one's sake ~을 위해서, play a part in ~에 역할을 하다, as though ~ 마치 ~인 것처럼, brave (위험을) 무릅쓰다, cautious 조심스러운, shades 저승/죽음/영혼, wither 시들다, generous 관대한/풍부한, tap 가볍게 두드림, pane 창유리, oblique 비스듬한, set out 출발하다/시작하다, plain 평원, mutinous 반항적, bury 파묻다/매장하다, swoon 기절하다/쇠약해지다, crooked 구부러진, headstone 묘석, thorn 가시(나무), descend 하강하다

[실력 점검 A] 다음 각 동사의 우리말 뜻을 쓰세요.

1. carve:	2. grieve:	3. deplore:
4. digest:	5. obtain:	6. flourish:
7. stagger:	8. wander:	9. conceive:
10. deliver:	11. irrigate:	12. astonish:
13. deplete:	14. appoint:	15. condense:
16. deprive:	17. pretend:	18. cooperate:
19. tolerate:	20. overlook:	

[실력 점검 B] 각 항목에 대응하는 영어 단어를 찾아 쓰세요.

보기 conflict, meadow, fragment, contract, affection, organism, abundant, novelty, ancestor, privilege, gratitude, ingredient, respective, contemporary, comet, identical, substantial, superficial, transparent, inexhaustible

1. 감사:	2. 초원:	3. 애정:
4. 갈등:	5. 특권:	6. 성분:
7. 조상:	8. 계약:	9. 풍부한:
10. 혜성:	11. 파편:	12. 새로움:
13. 유기체:	14. 투명한:	15. 동일한:
16. 상당한:	17. 당대의:	18. 각각의:
19. 무진장한:	20. 피상적인:	

[실력 점검 C] 주어진 철자로 시작되는 알맞은 낱말은?

1. Through my father-in-law I was able to get into easy c_____
   with a number of persons whom o_____ I should have known
   only from a distance.

2. It is true that we don't know what we've got until we l_____ it,
   as the old saying g_____. But it is also true that we often don't know
   what we have been m_____ until it arrives.

명시 감상

Lucy

William Wordsworth

She dwelt among the untrodden ways
   Beside the springs of Dove,
A maid whom there were none to praise
   And very few to love:

A violet by a mossy stone
   Half hidden from the eye.
—Fair as a star, when only one
   Is shining in the sky.

She lived unknown, and few could know
   When Lucy ceased to be;
But she is in her grave, and, oh,
   The difference to me!

* dwell 거주하다, tread 밟다, spring 샘, praise 칭찬하다, violet 제비꽃, moss 이끼, cease 멈추다, grave 무덤

Unit 8 동명사

A. 동명사의 용법

1) *Learning* Korean is not easy. My job is *teaching* English.

2) It stopped *raining*. She enjoys *telling* them fairy tales.

3) Thank you for *coming*. He is proud of *being* an artist.

4) *smoking* room, *swimming* suit, *sleeping* car, *magnifying* glass

B. 동명사의 주어/시제

1) *George's returning* so soon surprised all of us.

   Pardon *me saying* it. I really hate *my sister('s) meeting* him.

2) I am sure of his *being* a schoolteacher.

   I am sure of his *having been* a schoolteacher.

3) He forgot *posting* the letter. He forgot *to post* the letter.

   She remembers *meeting* him. She remembers *to meet* him.

C. 동명사의 관용적 구문

1) We *couldn't help* laugh*ing* at the funny sight.

2) *It is no use* cry*ing* over spilt milk. *It is no good* argu*ing* with them.

3) *There is no* account*ing* for tastes. *There is* no liv*ing* without love.

4) She *makes a point of* tak*ing* a walk every morning.

5) When we *were on the point of* go*ing* out, it began to rain.

6) The young boy *came near to* be*ing* run over by the car.

7) *On* arriv*ing* in New York, I called him up on the phone.

8) *Far from* tak*ing* my advice, he did just what I warned him against.

9) *How about* play*ing* tennis? *What do you say to* play*ing* tennis?

10) *When it comes to* play*ing* golf, Tom is one of the best players.

11) *It goes without saying* that honesty is the best policy.

12) The books are *worth* read*ing*. They are *busy* do*ing* their homework.

13) My shoes *want* mend*ing*. His house *needed* paint*ing*.

[필수 문법] 동명사(gerund)

* 동사 기본형의 말미에 "~ing"을 붙인다는 점에서, 현재 분사와 그 형태가 같으나,
* 현재 분사가 형용사적 성격을 갖는다면, 동명사는 명사적 성격을 갖는다.
* 부정사의 경우처럼, 단순형("~ing)"과 완료형("having + 과거분사")이 있다.

A. 동명사의 용법

　1) 문장의 주어나 보어로 쓰인다: *Seeing* is *believing*. (백문이 불여일견)

　2) 동사 "stop/enjoy/finish/mind/avoid/escape/deny/consider" 등의 목적어로 쓰인다.

　3) 전치사의 목적어로 쓰인다:　He insisted on *paying* for the meal.

　4) "용도/기능"의 복합어: (흡연실/수영복/침대차/확대경): *living* room, *sleeping* bag,

B. 동명사의 주어/시제

　1) 동명사의 주어: 원칙적으로 명사/대명사의 소유격을 사용하지만, 동사/전치사의
　　목적어로 쓰인 동명사의 주어로서는 흔히 (명사/대명사의) 목적격이 사용된다.

　2) 동명사의 시제: 단순형의 시제는 술어동사의 시제와 일치하며, 완료형의 시제는
　　술어동사의 시제보다 앞섬: (=I *am* sure that he *is* ~.) (=I *am* sure that he *was/has been* ~.)

　3) 동사 "forget, remember"의 목적어로 동명사가 오면 과거 사실을, to-부정사가 오면
　　미래 사실을 나타냄: (그 편지를 부친 것을 잊었다.) (그 편지를 부칠 것을 잊었다.)

C. 동명사의 관용적 구문

　1) cannot help ~ing (~하지 않을 수 없다):　=We *couldn't but laugh* at the funny sight.

　2) it is no use(=good) ~ing (~해도 소용없다):　=It is *of no use to cry* over spilt milk.

　3) there is no ~ing (~하는 것은 불가능하다):　=*It is impossible to account* for tastes.

　4) make a point of ~ing (~하는 것을 규칙으로 삼다):　=She *makes it a rule to take* a walk ~.

　5) be on the point of ~ing" (막 ~하려고 하다):　=When we *were about to go* out, it began ~.

　6) come/go near to ~ing (거의 ~할 뻔하다):　=The young boy *narrowly escaped being* run ~.

　7) on/upon ~ing (~하자마자):　=*As soon as I arrived* in New York, I called him up ~.

　8) far from ~ing (~이기는커녕, 결코 ~이 아닌):　She is *far from being* content with the result.

　9) what do you say to ~ing (~하는 것이 어때?):　=*What do you think about playing* tennis?

　10) when it comes to ~ing (~으로 말하자면):　=*As for playing* golf, Tom is one of the best ~.

　11) it goes without saying that ~ (~은 말할 필요도 없다):　=*It is needless to say* that ~.

　12) 형용사 "worth"와 "busy"는 흔히 "~ing"를 수반함: =*It is worthwhile to read* the books.
　　=It is worth (your) while to read the books.　　=They *are busy with* their homework.

　13) 동사 "want/need"가 수반하는 (능동형의) 동명사는 흔히 "수동"의 의미를 갖는다:
　　=My shoes need *to be mended*.　　=His house needed *to be painted*.

[문법 연습 A]　잘못된 부분을 고치세요.

1. I have spent the entire morning to wash the floor

2. He narrowly escaped to be injured in the accident.

3. She is looking forward to see her son this summer.

4. Half way up the mountain we stopped taking a rest.

5. Why don't you consider to move to a larger house?

6. Don't forget to receive a lot of applications last year.

7. What do you say to go fishing with me this weekend?

8. My brother is very busy to prepare for mid-term exams.

9. They were strongly opposed to develop nuclear weapons.

10. He went to America with a view to study computer science.

11. Please excuse me for having not answered your letter earlier.

12. The plants need to water; the leaves are starting to go brown.

13. The professor devoted his whole life to study Korean history.

14. He is proud of his father being educated in Oxford and Harvard.

[문법 연습 B]　동명사 구문으로 고치세요.

1. He regretted that he was not able to help his sister.

_____

2. We insisted that they should be invited to the party.

_____

3. It is impossible to know what will happen tomorrow.

_____

4. It was very difficult for me to find his new office in town.

_____

5. She was convinced that her son had been innocent of the crime.

_____

6. I have no doubt that there will be many youngsters at the concert.

_____

[실전 문법 A] 빈칸에 알맞은 낱말을 쓰세요.

1. I believe he is honest; he is above _____ lies.

2. When I heard of his death, I felt _____ crying.

3. He is trying to find something worth _____ to do.

4. They always tried their best to avoid _____ mistakes.

5. It is _____ no use to sit and wait for success to come.

6. The students were punished _____ being late for school.

7. You will have to speak up, for she is hard _____ hearing.

8. She complains of _____ being too warm here in summer.

9. _____ the clock striking nine, he turned on the television.

10. Animals can do all they have to do without _____ taught.

11. Is there any chance _____ you having a holiday this year?

12. _____ being smart, she is kind, generous, and considerate.

[실전 문법 B] 각 문항의 다섯 부분 중 어법에 맞지 않는 부분은?

1. ¹⁾As you may know, ²⁾losing leaves help ³⁾some trees and plants ⁴⁾conserve water ⁵⁾in the wintertime.

2. ¹⁾For some people, ²⁾Memorial Day went by ³⁾unnoticed. ⁴⁾They didn't even stop thinking ⁵⁾what the day was all about.

3. ¹⁾All of us have had the experience ²⁾of being misunderstood, ³⁾of being not able ⁴⁾to find right words ⁵⁾to get across our meaning.

4. ¹⁾When it comes to modify the landscape ²⁾in a major way, ³⁾the beaver ranks second ⁴⁾only to humans ⁵⁾among all living creatures.

5. ¹⁾I thought I would buy ²⁾something for her birthday, ³⁾and I entered the shop on the corner, ⁴⁾as I remembered ⁵⁾to see a pretty hat there.

6. ¹⁾If the project is successful ²⁾then it should not need extra funds, ³⁾and if it is not successful ⁴⁾then it is scarcely worth ⁵⁾to support and encourage.

7. ¹⁾Those who are being treated ²⁾for high blood pressure ³⁾should self-monitor at home ⁴⁾in addition to have their blood pressure ⁵⁾checked at the doctor's clinic.

[필수 어휘 A] 빈칸에 들어갈 가장 적절한 낱말은?

1. David had to drive his friends to their _____ homes.

   1) tidy   2) native   3) decent   4) suitable   5) respective

2. Smokers _____ a great risk of dying from lung cancer.

   1) run   2) keep   3) make   4) outlive   5) undergo

3. They were on good _____ with the people in the village.

   1) arms   2) ideas   3) terms   4) customs   5) manners

4. Long summer and plentiful rainfall are _____ to the crops.

   1) fertile   2) thirsty   3) ultimate   4) favorable   5) moderate

5. "No Vacancy" means that no room is _____ at the moment.

   1) asked   2) reserved   3) possible   4) available   5) accessible

6. The police searched all the house but failed to find any _____.

   1) trap   2) clue   3) criminal   4) incidents   5) circumstances

[필수 어휘 B] 밑줄 친 부분과 그 뜻이 가장 가까운 것은?

1. My father has been working for a law firm for twenty years.

   1) clerk   2) court   3) client   4) company   5) profession

2. With some selfish end in view, she has been very nice to her friends.

   1) close   2) result   3) purpose   4) attitude   5) conclusion

3. The professor seems to have a profound understanding of Shakespeare.

   1) deep   2) clear   3) definite   4) thorough   5) superficial

4. The soil on the factory site was contaminated with lead and mercury.

   1) mixed   2) filled   3) replaced   4) polluted   5) investigated

5. You will have to read the story several times to make sense of it.

   1) enjoy   2) explain   3) criticize   4) summarize   5) understand

6. During the long career as a dentist, he laid by a large amount of money.

   1) earned   2) saved   3) raised   4) donated   5) accumulated

7. The office building was designed to take advantage of the sun's warmth.

   1) use   2) receive   3) improve   4) conserve   5) compensate

[구문 연습] 다음 문장을 우리말로 옮기세요.

1. Recycling mean finding ways to use products a second time. The motto of the recycling movement is "Reduce, Reuse, Recycle."

2. Plagiarism is one of the most common ways of infringing on the copyright. Plagiarizing the work of another person means passing it off as one's own.

3. There is nothing new about people cutting down trees. While there are some reasons for cutting trees, there are also fatal consequences for life on earth.

4. The human mind has no more power of inventing a new value than of imagining a new primary color, or, indeed, of creating a new sun and a new sky for it to move in.

5. An open mind is all very well in its way, but it ought not to be so open that there is no keeping anything in or out of it. It should be capable of shutting its doors sometimes, or it may be found a little drafty.

[작문 연습] 다음 문장을 영어로 옮기세요.

1. 할 가치가 있는 일은 잘 할 가치가 있다.

　_____

2. 그 어린애는 하마터면 개한테 물릴 뻔했다.

　_____

3. 건강이 재산 보다 우선임은 말할 필요도 없다.

　_____

4. 그는 그녀가 빌려준 소설책을 읽느라고 온밤을 지샜다.

　_____

5. 그녀는 자신의 생각을 영어로 전달하는 데 어려움이 없었다.

　_____

[실전 독해 A] 각 문항의 물음에 답하세요.

1.   A primitive man, on meeting other men, will first have experienced fright. His fear will make him see these men as larger and stronger than himself; he will give them the name "the giants." After many experiences, he will discover that the supposed giants are neither larger nor stronger than himself, and that their stature did not correspond to the idea he had originally linked to the word "giant." He will then invent another name that he has in common with them, such as, for example, the word "man," and will retain the word "giant" for the false object that impressed him while he was being deluded.

　　Q. 이 글의 주제는?
　　　1) 언어의 기원　 2) 언어의 변천
　　　3) 언어의 한계　 4) 언어의 허상과 진실
　　　5) 언어 의식의 발달 과정

2.   Besides society's changing view of the role men play in relation to childcare, social scientists are also re-examining the contribution a father makes to his child's welfare and development. Researchers have found evidence to suggest that a father plays a part in child development that is quite different from ^{a)}_____ of the mother. According to the research, fathers tend to be more playful, thus encouraging children to develop in a different way emotionally and physically than a child might under a mother's ^{b)}_____ care. Studies have also found that the presence of the father in the home can contribute to lower juvenile crime rates, a decrease in child poverty, and lower rates of teenage pregnancy. Differences in parenting styles between men and women are also believed to contribute to children's ability to understand and communicate emotions in different ways. The research supports claims by some groups that the ^{c)}_____ of a father in the family is the single biggest social problem of modern society.

　　Q 1. 빈칸 a)에 들어갈 적절한 낱말은?

　　　2. 빈칸 b)에 들어갈 적절한 낱말은?
　　　　1) excessive　 2) unselfish　 3) exclusive
　　　　4) subjective　 5) unbalanced

　　　3. 빈칸 c)에 들어갈 적절한 낱말은?

3.　Unfortunately, humans have gained the ability to change the environment very quickly, and many times organisms cannot adapt quickly enough to survive these changes in the environment. ① When a whole species dies out, we say the organism has become extinct. A great many animals and plants are threatened with extinction. ② Whales and dolphins, gorillas and wild elephants are now classified as endangered species. These animals face extinction unless we control the fishing, hunting, and land development that threaten the species and their habitats. ③ Extinction can result from entirely natural causes. Dinosaurs, for example, became extinct millions of years ago, before humans appeared on the earth. ④ Scientists today are worried by the rate at which extinctions are occurring. Our planet is currently losing about three species per day, a rate that is expected to accelerate to three per hour in less than ten years. ⑤ If so, sooner or later, 20 percent of all the earth's species could be gone forever.

　　Q. ①~⑤중 다음 문장이 삽입되기에 적절한 곳은?
　　　But most extinctions are now caused by human intervention.

4.　It is possible to distinguish levels of word usage such as formal and informal. Although such a distinctions is probably less prominent or important than it was thirty years ago, some language is still recognizably more formal or informal than other language.

　　ⓐ Most people know the various levels and instinctively use them
　　　at the right times.
　　ⓑ In fact, some situations seem to call for language more or less formal
　　　than other situations do.
　　ⓒ We expect a debate in the legislature, a sermon in church, or an article
　　　in a scholarly journal to be more formal than the language of the lounge,
　　　the fraternity house, or popular magazines.

While we should focus more on accuracy and precision than on levels of usage, it is helpful to be aware of the different usages which affect our level of speaking and writing.

　　Q. ⓐ ~ ⓒ의 문장을 문맥에 맞게 배열하면?
　　　1) ⓐ-ⓒ-ⓑ　　　2) ⓑ-ⓐ-ⓒ　　　3) ⓑ-ⓒ-ⓐ
　　　4) ⓒ-ⓐ-ⓑ　　　5) ⓒ-ⓑ-ⓐ

[실전 독해 B] 각 문항의 물음에 답하세요.

1. The process we call seeing, which we all take for granted, is unbelievably complicated. We see not "what is there" but what we have been taught to see there. The human eye is a lens that only receives images; these images are referred to the brain, ^{a)}_____ they must be patterned and given meaning. And meaning is a convention that stems from our education and our expectations. We see things as we are, not ^{b)}_____.

    Q 1. 빈칸 a)에 들어갈 적절한 낱말은?

       2. 빈칸 b)에 들어갈 적절한 어구나 어절은?

2. One of the most urgent problems in teaching handwriting is presented by the left-handed child. The traditional policy has been to attempt to induce all children to write with their right hands. Parents and teachers alike have an antipathy to the child's using his left hand. ^{a)}_____, psychologists have shown beyond a doubt that some persons are naturally left-handed and that it is much more difficult for them to do any skilled act with the right hand than with the left hand. Some believe, ^{b)}_____, that to compel a left-handed child to write with his right hand may make him nervous and may cause stammering. There seems to be some cases in which this is true, although in the vast majority of children who change over, no ill effects are noticed. ^{c)}_____ these difficulties, left-handedness sometimes seems to cause mirror writing—writing from right to left—and reversals in reading, as reading "was" for "saw."

    Q 1. 빈칸 a)에 들어갈 적절한 낱말은?
        1) Besides   2) Likewise   3) Nonetheless
        4) On the one hand   5) On the other hand

      2. 빈칸 b)에 들어갈 적절한 말은?
        1) however   2) therefore   3) of course
        4) furthermore   5) for example

      3. 빈칸 c)에 들어갈 적절한 말은?
        1) Due to   2) With all   3) Instead of
        4) Regardless of   5) In addition to

3. What is art? [1]According to one definition, it is the creation of something that appeals to our sense of beauty. [2]This definition may include painting, drawing, sculpture, and architecture, or performing arts such as music and drama. [3]Cultural and historical influences, as well as one's own perception of what is aesthetically pleasing, play a part in what one believes to be art. [4]To some people, art is the depiction of an object—a painting or sculpture, for example. [5]For others, art may be a blank canvas, or a piece of chalk.

Q. 1)~5)의 문장 중 이 글의 요지에 해당되는 것은?

4. No study of the United States [1]would be complete without a discussion of immigrants because America is a nation of immigrants. For 400 years, a nation of over 200 million people [2]was built by persons who came from all parts of the world and [3]all walks of life. Every aspect of American life, from business to athletics, has been influenced [4]in one way or another by immigrants. No one could ever completely understand this "teeming nation of nations," as the poet Walt Whitman called it, [5]without first knowing something about the history of America's leading import.

Q. 밑줄 친 1)~5)중 어법에 맞지 않는 것은?

5. In the public mind, challenges to Darwin's theory of evolution are associated with the biblical creationists who periodically remove their children from schoolrooms where they are being taught that _____. What most people do not know is that for much of the twentieth century, and especially in recent years, scientists have been fighting among themselves about Darwin and his ideas.

Q. 빈칸에 들어갈 적절한 문장은?
   1) man evolved from monkeys
   2) man was really created by God
   3) man is essentially similar to other animals
   4) the creation of man can be explained scientifically
   5) the notion of evolution differs from that of creation

[명작 감상]   Thomas Bulfinch (1796 ~ 1867)
             Mythology 『신화』

"The inhabitants of this valley say that your husband is a terrible and monstrous serpent, who nourishes you for a while with dainties that he may by and by devour you. Take our advice. Provide yourself with a lamp and a sharp knife; put them in concealment that your husband may not discover them, and when he is sound asleep, slip out of bed, bring forth your lamp, and see for yourself whether what they say is true or not. If it is, hesitate not to cut off the monster's head, and thereby recover your liberty."

Psyche resisted these persuasions as well as she could, but they did not fail to have their effect on her mind, and when her sisters were gone, their words and her own curiosity were too strong for her to resist. So she prepared her lamp and a sharp knife, and hid them out of sight of her husband. When he had fallen into his first sleep, she silently rose and uncovering her lamp beheld not a hideous monster, but the most beautiful and charming of the gods, with his golden ringlets wandering over his snowy neck and crimson cheek, with two dewy wings on his shoulders, whiter than snow, and with shining feathers like the tender blossoms of spring. As she leaned the lamp over to have a nearer view of his face, a drop of burning oil fell on the shoulder of the god, startled with which he opened his eyes and fixed them full upon her; then, without saying one word, he spread his white wings and flew out of the window. Psyche in vain endeavouring to follow him, fell from the window to the ground. Cupid, beholding her as she lay in the dust, stopped his flight for an instant and said, "O foolish Psyche, is it thus you repay my love? After having disobeyed my mother's commands and made you my wife, will you think me a monster and cut off my head? But go; return to your sisters, whose advice you seem to think preferable to mine. I inflict no other punishment on you than to leave you forever. Love cannot dwell with suspicion." So saying, he fled away, leaving poor Psyche prostrate on the ground, filling the place with mournful lamentations.

* Psyche is the Greek name for a *butterfly*, and the same word means the *soul*. The fable of Cupid and Psyche suggests that the human soul is purified by sufferings and misfortunes and is thus prepared for the enjoyment of true and pure happiness. In works of art, Psyche is represented as a maiden with the wings of a butterfly.

[확인 학습] 다음 문장을 우리말로 옮기세요.

1. Besides society's changing view of the role men play in relation to childcare, social scientists are also re-examining the contribution a father makes to his child's welfare and development.

2. Cultural and historical influences, as well as one's own perception of what is aesthetically pleasing, play a part in what one believes to be art.

3. Challenges to Darwin's theory of evolution are associated with the biblical creationists who periodically remove their children from schoolrooms where they are being taught that man evolved from monkeys.

4. Psyche resisted these persuasions as well as she could, but they did not fail to have their effect on her mind, and when her sisters were gone, their words and her own curiosity were too strong for her to resist.

[words & phrases]

A1: primitive 원시적/원시인, fright 놀라움, stature 키/신장, correspond to ~에 대응하다/일치하다, invent 발명하다, have ~ in common ~을 공유하다, retain 보유하다, object 물체, delude 속이다

A2: besides ~외에도, examine 검토하다, contribution 기여/공헌, evidence 증거, encourage 격려하다, presence 현존/존재, juvenile 아동/소년소녀(의), poverty 가난, pregnancy 임신, claim 주장(하다)

A3: organism 유기체, adapt 적응하다, threat 위협, extinct 멸종된, classify 분류하다, habitat 서식지,

A4: prominent 현저한, instinct 본능, more or less 다소, debate 토론(하다), legislature 입법부, sermon 설교, article 글/기사, scholar 학자, fraternity 남학생 사교클럽, accurate 정확한, precise 적확한,

B1: take ~ for granted ~을 당연시 하다, complicated 복잡한, refer to ~에 보내다, convention 인습/관습, stem from ~로부터 생기다/유래하다, as we are 우리의 모습대로, as they are 그들의 모습대로

B2: urgent 긴급한, policy 정책, attempt 시도하다, induce 권유하다, antipathy 반감, compel 강요하다, cause 초래하다, stammer 말을 더듬다, majority 다수, ill 아픈/나쁜, reverse 뒤집다/거꾸로하다

B3: define 정의하다, include 포함하다, sculpture 조각, architecture 건축, perceive 인식하다, aesthetic 미학적, play a part in ~에 역할을 하다, depict 그리다/묘사하다, blank 빈/백지(의), chalk 분필

B4: immigrant 이민자, athletics 운동경기, influence 영향을 미치다, teem 충만하다, import 수입(하다)

B5: evolution 진화, biblical 성경의/성서적, creationist 창조론자, periodical 정기적, remove 제거하다,

C1: inhabitant 주민, serpent 뱀, nourish 육성하다, dainty 진미, devour 먹어 치우다, conceal 숨기다, recover 회복하다, persuade 설득하다, curiosity 호기심, behold 보다, hideous 끔직한, ringlet(=curl), crimson 진홍색, wander 배회하다, feather 깃털, blossom 꽃, endeavor 애쓰다, inflict 입히다/가하다, dwell 거주하다, suspicion 의심, flee 달아나다, prostrate 엎드린/mourn 통곡하다/lament 한탄하다

[실력 점검 A] 다음 각 동사의 우리말 뜻을 쓰세요.

1. trace: 2. depict: 3. compel:

4. cease: 5. endow: 6. conceal:

7. foster: 8. devour: 9. reinforce:

10. linger: 11. justify: 12. embarrass:

13. fasten: 14. involve: 15. impoverish:

16. vanish: 17. indicate: 18. accompany:

19. confine: 20. stammer:

[실력 점검 B] 각 항목에 대응하는 영어 단어를 찾아 쓰세요.

보기   lead, adult, infant, benefit, formula, affliction, commodity, inhabitant, gift, vague, decent, absurd, colony, eminent, ingenuity, continent, regulation, crucial, anonymous, involuntary

1. 납: 2. 재능: 3. 공식:

4. 성인: 5. 상품: 6. 주민:

7. 혜택: 8. 고통: 9. 유아:

10. 규정: 11. 대륙: 12. 창의성:

13. 식민지: 14. 익명의: 15. 저명한:

16. 모호한: 17. 결정적인: 18. 무심결의:

19. 불합리한: 20: 품위 있는:

[실력 점검 C] 주어진 철자로 시작되는 알맞은 낱말은?

1. Those who have not d_____ themselves at school need not

   on that account be d_____.

2. Most people are mirrors, r_____ the moods and emotions of

   the times; f_____ are windows, bringing light to bear on the dark

   corners w_____ troubles fester. The whole p_____ of education

   is to turn mirrors into windows.

명시 감상

The Flower

Robert Creeley

I think I grow tensions
like flowers
in a wood where
nobody goes.

Each wound is perfect,
encloses itself in a tiny
imperceptible blossom,
making pain.

Pain is a flower like that one
like this one,
like that one,
like this one.

---

* tension 긴장, wound 상처, enclose (봉해)넣다, tiny 아주 작은, imperceptible 미세한/감지할 수 없는, blossom 꽃

Unit 9 분사

A. 분사의 용법

1) He is *working*. I have *done* it. The window was *broken*.

2) *Barking* dogs seldom bite. They were *wounded* soldiers.

3) She stood *gazing* at the pond. She seems very *tired*.

4) He kept me *waiting*. I heard my name *called*.

5) I saw a farmer *working* in the field.

   Look at the mountain *covered* with snow.

B. 분사 구문

1) *Coming* home late at night, I found him waiting for me.

   Very *surprised* at the news, she didn't know what to do.

   Turning to the left, you will find the post office on your right.

   Admitting what they say, I still think they are in the wrong.

   Starting in the morning, we arrived in Seoul in the evening.

   While crossing the street, the boy was run over by the car.

2) *Having finished* the work, they went out to have a drink.

   Mr. Kim, *born* in America, wants to be a Korean citizen.

3) *Winter coming on*, it's time to buy warm clothes.

   She was reading a book, *her baby sleeping* in bed.

C. 분사의 기타 용법

1) She walked to the bus stop, with a man *following* her.

   They are sitting on the floor, with their eyes *closed*.

2) *Considering* her age, your mother looks very young.

   Judging from his accent, he must be an Englishman

   Generally speaking, women live longer than men.

   Taking all things into account, Mr. Smith is a reliable man.

   Granted/Granting that he's in hospital, he can't do us much harm.

[필수 문법] 분사(participle)

* 동사 변화형의 하나로서, 동사적 성격을 갖는 한편 형용사적 성격도 갖는다.
* 동사가 나타내는 행위/동작/상태의 "능동적 진행"의 의미를 갖는 현재 분사와
* 동사가 나타내는 행위/동작/상태의 "수동적 완료"의 의미를 갖는 과거 분사가 있다.

A. 분사의 용법
  1) 현재 분사는 진행형에 쓰이며, 과거 분사는 완료형이나 수동태에 쓰인다.
  2) 명사를 수식하는 형용사적 역할을 한다: an *exciting* game, the *broken* window
  3) 주격 보어로 쓰임: Tom was sitting *watching* television. I became *acquainted* with him.
  4) 목적격 보어로 쓰임: I saw her *coming* here. She always leaves things *undone*.
  5) 분사가 앞에 있는 명사를 수식하는 경우에는, 명사와 분사 사이에 "관계대명사＋
     be동사"가 생략되어 있다: ＝I saw a farmer (who was) *working* in the field. ＝Look at
     the mountain (which is) *covered* with snow. I know the girl (who is) *talking* with Jane.

B. 분사 구문: (접속사) ＋ (주어) ＋ 현재분사/과거분사
  * 분사 구문에서는 접속사는 대개 생략되며, 주절의 주어와 동일한 주어도 생략됨.
  * 수동태 분사 구문에서는, "being"이나 (완료 분사 구문의) "having been"은 생략된다.
  * 대체로 종속절을 줄인 것이 분사 구문이지만, 등위절을 줄인 경우도 흔히 있다.
  * 보다 명확한 의미 전달을 위해서라면, 종속 접속사를 생략하지 않을 수도 있다.
  1) ＝*When I came* home late at night, I found him waiting for me.
     ＝*As she was very surprised* at the news, she didn't know what to do.
     ＝*If you turn* to the left, you will find the post office on your right.
     ＝*(Al)though I admit* what they say, I still think they are in the wrong.
     ＝*We started* in the morning, *and* (we) arrived in Seoul in the evening.
     ＝*While he was crossing* the street, the boy was run over by the car.
  2) 완료 분사 구문: 시제가 주절의 시제보다 앞선다: (＝*After they had finished* the work,
     they went out to have a drink.) (＝Mr. Kim, *though he was born* in America, wants to be ~.)
  3) 독립 분사 구문: 주절의 주어와는 상이한 주어를 가진 분사 구문을 말한다:
     (＝*As winter comes on*, it's time ~.) (＝She was reading ~, *and her baby* was sleeping ~.)

C. 분사의 기타 용법
  1) "with＋명사/대명사＋분사": 부가적인 상황을 묘사할 때 흔히 쓰이는 문어체 구문:
     (＝She walked ~, *and a man followed her*.) (＝They are sitting ~, *and their eyes are closed*.)
  2) 비인칭 독립 분사 구문: 일반주어 "one, we, you" 등이 생략된 관용적 분사 구문:
     (~을 고려하면, ~에 비해서) (~으로 판단하건대) (일반적으로 말하면)
     (모든 것을 고려하면) (~라고 치더라도, ~사실을 인정한다 하더라도)

[문법 연습 A] 다음 각 동사의 현재 분사형을 쓰세요.

1. lie: 2. die: 3. dye:

4. stop: 5. admit: 6. prefer:

7. picnic: 8. mimic: 9. escape:

[문법 연습 B] 각 문장의 잘못된 부분을 고치세요.

1. He is very smart, comparing with other students.

2. The dying and the died were carried on stretchers.

3. While waiting for the bus, a thunderstorm came up.

4. Dressing in pink, she was like a flower in full bloom.

5. I was so amusing that I talked with him almost an hour.

6. She stood leaning against the tree, with her arms folding.

7. We speaking strictly, he is not a scientist but an inventor.

8. Being cold and windy, we gave up climbing the mountain.

9. The new hotel, locating on the hill, commands a fine view.

10. He felt very pleasant whenever he completed a piece of work.

11. Having not read the book, he could not make any comment on it.

[문법 연습 C] 분사 구문을 어절(clause)로 고치세요.

1. Walking along the street, I met an old friend of mine.

_____

2. Picking up a stone, the boy threw it at the barking dog.

_____

3. The rock, seen from a distance, looks like a human face.

_____

4. Born in America, she could have succeeded as a physicist.

_____

5. Having lived in China for a year, he still couldn't speak Chinese.

_____

[실전 문법 A] 빈칸에 알맞은 낱말은?

1. Do to others as you would be _____ by.

2. I wish I could make myself _____ in English.

3. He stood there _____ his hands in his pockets.

4. _____ by surprise, they did not know what to do.

5. _____ being no bus available, we had to take a cab.

6. There is a saying that a _____ stone gathers no moss.

7. _____ up in a good family, he is really nice and gentle.

8. All things _____ into account, you had better quit the job.

9. They went to the photographer's to have their pictures _____.

10. Eight planets move around the sun, the earth _____ one of them.

[실전 문법 B] 각 문항의 다섯 부분 중 어법에 맞지 않는 부분은?

1. [1]Lobsters have [2]compound eyes [3]which consist of [4]hundreds of lenses [5]joining together.

2. [1]The first vaccine [2]ever developed [3]was used to fight [4]a smallpox, a disease resulted [5]from infection by a virus.

3. [1]The dam is used [2]to control flooding, [3]provide water for irrigation, [4]generating electricity [5]for the urban and industrial area.

4. [1]When a child, [2]my father sometimes took me for a walk [3]in the late afternoon. [4]We would wander through the pasture, [5]not hurrying.

5. [1]Now considering a major poet [2]of the 19th century, [3]Emily Dickinson was unknown [4]to the literary world [5]during her lifetime.

6. [1]His music was hardly popular [2]with the public, [3]and he found it [4]all but impossible [5]to have his music performing.

7. [1]I recall how good it was to be a child, [2]exploring the hills and fields, [3]watching the miracles of the changing seasons, [4]and exciting about the mysteries [5]that even my father could not answer.

[필수 어휘 A] 밑줄 친 부분과 그 뜻이 가장 가까운 것은?

1. It is <u>vital</u> to keep an accurate record of every symptom of the disease.

   1) useful   2) absurd   3) crucial   4) intricate   5) effective

2. I've always been very <u>cautious</u> about giving people my phone number.

   1) hasty   2) careful   3) worried   4) courteous   5) ridiculous

3. He is still <u>awkward</u> with a knife and fork and drops food at each meal.

   1) slow   2) clumsy   3) incapable   4) concerned   5) unfamiliar

4. Her husband was a lawyer, and when he died he left her very <u>well off</u>.

   1) rich   2) famous   3) grateful   4) desirable   5) comfortable

5. I asked her exactly why she wanted to leave, but she was <u>at a loss</u>.

   1) tired   2) scared   3) excited   4) astonished   5) embárrassed

6. All of you must know that a holiday this year is <u>out of the question</u>.

   1) strict   2) missing   3) doubtful   4) impossible   5) favorable

7. Elizabeth had to <u>give up</u> her job to look after her invalid mother.

   1) lose   2) replace   3) abandon   4) disclose   5) persevere

8. We couldn't <u>rule out</u> the possibility that they would come after all.

   1) prove   2) predict   3) exclude   4) overcome   5) determine

[필수 어휘 B] 밑줄 친 부분을 주어진 철자로 시작되는 낱말로 대체하세요.

1. His theory was <u>anything but</u> new or original.   n_____

2. The building will be <u>all but</u> completed in a week.   a_____

3. He explained it to her but <u>left out</u> some details.   o_____

4. They carried on from where they had <u>left off</u>.   s_____

5. He needs a father, someone he can <u>look up to</u>.   r_____

6. We should not <u>look down upon</u> the handicapped.   d_____

7. She wants to <u>take part</u> in the anti-drugs campaign.   p_____

8. The new system will <u>take the place of</u> the old one.   r_____

9. If there's anything you want to see, just <u>drop by</u>.   v_____

10. I am <u>looking forward to</u> seeing you next month.   a_____

[구문 연습] 다음 문장을 우리말로 옮기세요.

1. The man sat in front of the girls, his dusty face masking his age, dressed in a plain brown suit that did not fit him.

2. Convinced that pockets are natural places to put things into, I have always kept them filled with a variety of things.

3. The division between "popular" and "classical" music has been fairly clearly defined, with those active on one sphere rarely trespassing in the other, and never more so than today.

4. An ass, having put on a lion's skin, wandered about to frighten all the animals he met with. Seeing a fox, he tried to alarm him also. But the fox, having heard his voice, said, "I should have been frightened too, if I had not heard you bray."

[작문 연습] 다음 문장을 영어로 옮기세요.

1. 그 피고인은 살인죄로 밝혀져서 종신형을 선고 받았다.

_____

2. 꽃밭에서는 작은 나비들이 날아다니는 어느 화창한 봄날이었다.

_____

3. 모든 것을 고려해보면 그는 그렇게 나쁜 사람인 것 같지는 않다.

_____

4. 그 책은 평이한 영어로 씌어져 있어서 읽기가 그렇게 어렵지 않다.

_____

5. 고인은 많은 학생들과 동료들에게서 존경을 받는 위대한 학자였다.

_____

[실전 독해 A] 각 문항의 물음에 답하세요.

1. Man's _____ is a wonderful thing: it is so full of anguish and of magic and he never comes to know it as it is, until it has gone from him forever. It is the thing he cannot bear to lose, it is the thing whose passing he watches with infinite sorrow and regret, it is the thing whose loss he must lament forever, and it is the thing whose loss he really welcomes with a sad and secret joy, the thing he would never willingly re-live again, could it be restored to him by any magic.

Q. 빈칸에 알맞은 낱말은?
   1) life   2) love   3) dream
   4) youth   5) friendship

2. Edison defined genius as "1 percent inspiration and 99 percent perspiration." He demonstrated this belief by working for days at a time, stopping only for short naps. He experimented in the field of medicine, came close to the invention of the radio, and predicted the use of atomic energy. Edison always tried to develop devices that would work under ordinary conditions, could not easily get out of order, and were easy to repair. He also improved the inventions of other persons, such as the telephone, the typewriter, and the motion picture. Edison once admitted that he "tried everything" while working on his inventions. He generally ignored scientific theory and mathematical study that might have saved him time. When about 10,000 experiments with a storage battery failed to produce results, a friend tried to console him. "Why, I have not failed," Edison said. "I've just found 10,000 ways that won't _____."

Q 1. 빈칸에 알맞은 낱말은?
   1) work   2) exist   3) prove
   4) develop   5) improve

   2. 이 글의 내용과 일치하지 않는 것은?
      1) 에디슨은 매우 낙관적인 사람이었다.
      2) 에디슨은 원자력의 사용을 예측하였다.
      3) 에디슨은 발명의 실용성을 매우 중시하였다.
      4) 에디슨은 과학적 이론을 다양하게 응용하였다.
      5) 에디슨은 남들의 발명품을 개량하기도 하였다.

3. The value of will training in preparing a boy for life ^{a)}_____ be overemphasized. A well-balanced personality is not a gift; it is not something we are born with; it is an achievement. Some persons are richly endowed at birth; but ^{b)}_____ their advantages they fail to achieve a successful adjustment. Others less gifted, but who have a strong will to succeed, rise to great heights because they have made the most of their endowments. There are ^{c)}_____ people who could not do better if they would.

> Q 1. 빈칸 a)에 들어갈 적절한 낱말은?
>
> 　2. 빈칸 b)에 들어갈 적절한 말은?
> 　　1) with　　2) without　　3) besides
> 　　4) for all　　5) on account of
>
> 　3. 빈칸 c)에 들어갈 적절한 낱말은?

4. After driving his flock to pasture one day a goatherd noticed that it was joined by some wild goats. In the evening he drove them all to his cave. The next day he was prevented by foul weather from taking them to the usual pasture and had to attend to them indoors.

　ⓐ When the weather cleared he took them all out to pasture, and as soon as they set foot on the mountains the wild goats took to their heels. The herdsman charged them with ingratitude for deserting him after the special attention he had shown them.

　ⓑ He gave his own animals a ration that was just enough to save them from being famished, but he heaped the fodder generously before the newcomers in the hope of increasing his flock by domesticating them.

　ⓒ They turned around and told him that this was precisely what had put them on their guard against him. "We came to you only yesterday," they said, "and yet you treated us better than your old charges. Obviously, therefore, if others join your flock later on, you will make much of them at our expense."

> Q. ⓐ~ⓒ의 글을 문맥에 맞게 배열하면?
> 　1) ⓐ-ⓒ-ⓑ　　2) ⓑ-ⓐ-ⓒ　　3) ⓑ-ⓒ-ⓐ
> 　4) ⓒ-ⓐ-ⓑ　　5) ⓒ-ⓑ-ⓐ

[실전 독해 B] 각 문항의 물음에 답하세요.

1.   When we say "She has a nice car!" we say it with some tone of envy, admiration, or possibly blame of excessive wealth. Among people whose general income level is such that a car is taken more or less for granted, the statement is not emotional; it is just a statement of fact, a confirmation of what was supposed. And we can imagine that there may be people, though we have never known any, among whom "She has a nice car!" means that she is not rich enough to afford a nice house or yacht, or helicopter.

    Q. 이 글의 주제는?
      1) fact and emotion
      2) the relativity of wealth
      3) two kinds of statement
      4) objects of envy and blame
      5) symbols of general income

2.   While both art and science are ultimately concerned with the pursuit of truth, the process and methods employed by the artist on the one hand, and by the scientist on the other, [a)]_____. The scientist, whether physical or social, is concerned principally with the problem of analyzing materials or events, while the method of the artist is primarily synthesizing. The scientist isolates, breaks things down and separates matter into its constituent parts for purposes of analysis; the artist selects his materials, assembles, composes and builds. The scientist has to concern himself with the objective world of facts and phenomena; the artist deals more with the [b)]_____ world of human life and action.

    Q 1. 빈칸 a)에 들어갈 말은
      1) make little difference
      2) are quite familiar to us
      3) vary to considerable degree
      4) are very simple and humble
      5) have nothing to do with truth

    2. 빈칸 b)에 들어갈 적절한 낱말은?

3. ①She never quite overcame the sense of being out of _____, of being an outsider. ②I would _____ him among the ten most brilliant scientists of his age. ③The children didn't think anyone could take the _____ of their mother or father. ④The talks will take _____ in Vienna next week. ⑤The old system has died and a new one has sprung up to take its _____.

　　Q. ①~⑤의 문장의 빈칸에 공통으로 들어갈 낱말은?

4.　It is ironic that bureaucracy [1)]is primarily a term of scorn. In reality, bureaus are [2)]among the most important institutions in every part of the world. [3)]Not only they provide employment for a significant fraction of the world's population, but they also make [4)]critical decisions that shape the economic, political, educational, social, moral and [5)]even religious lives of nearly everyone on earth.

　　Q. 밑줄 친 1)~5)중 어법에 맞지 않는 것은?

5.　The Bible, while mainly a religious document, is secondarily a book of history and geography. ① Selected historical materials were included in the text for the purpose of illustrating and underlining the teaching of the Christian God. ② Historians and archeologists have learned to rely on the amazing accuracy of historical memory in the Bible. ③ The smallest references to persons and places and events contained in the accounts of the Exodus, _____, or the biographies of such Biblical heroes as Abraham and Moses and David, can lead to extremely important historical discoveries. ④ The archeologists' efforts are not directed at "proving" the correctness of the Bible, which is neither necessary nor possible, any more than belief in God can be scientifically demonstrated. ⑤ The historical clues in the Bible can lead the experts to a knowledge of lost cities and civilizations.

　　Q 1. 빈칸에 들어갈 적절한 말은?
　　　　1) moreover　　2) therefore　　3) as a result
　　　　4) for instance　　5) in other words

　　2. ①~⑤중 다음 문장이 삽입되기에 적절한 곳은?
　　　　It is quite the opposite, in fact.

[명작 감상]　　Mark Twain (1835 ~ 1910)

The Adventures of Huckleberry Finn 『헉클베리 핀의 모험』

Sometimes we'd have that whole river all to ourselves for the longest time. Yonder was the banks and the islands, across the water; and maybe a spark— which was a candle in a cabin window—and sometimes on the water you could see a spark or two—on a raft or a scow, you know; and maybe you could hear a fiddle or a song coming over from one of them crafts. It's lovely to live on a raft. We had the sky, up there, all speckled with stars, and we used to lay on our backs and look up at them, and discuss about whether they was made, or only just happened—Jim he allowed they was made, but I allowed they happened; I judged it would have took too long to *make* so many. Jim said the moon could a *laid* them; well, that looked kind of reasonable, so I didn't say nothing against it, because I've seen a frog lay most as many, so of course it could be done. We used to watch the stars that fell, too, and see them streak down. Jim allowed they'd got spoiled and was hove out of the nest.

Once or twice of a night we would see a steamboat slipping along in the dark, and now and then she would belch a whole world of sparks up out of her chimbleys, and they would rain down in the river and look awful pretty; then she would turn a corner and her lights would wink out and her pow-wow shut off and leave the river still again; and by-and-by her waves would get to us, a long time after she was gone, and joggle the raft a bit, and after that you wouldn't hear nothing for you couldn't tell how long, except maybe frogs or something.

After midnight the people on shore went to bed, and then for two or three hours the shores was black—no more sparks in the cabin windows. These sparks was our clock—the first one that showed again meant morning was coming, so we hunted a place to hide and tied up, right away

---

* "Mark Twain"은 작가 Samuel L. Clemens의 필명. 이 글은 문법이나 단어에 있어 잘못 된 곳이 흔히 있다. 이것은 주인공 Huck이 어린이이고, 또 다른 주인공 Jim은 정규 교육을 받지 못한 흑인 노예이기 때문이다. "lay"는 "lie(눕다)"의 잘못, "allow"는 "think"의 뜻, "took"은 "taken"의 잘못, "a laid"는 "lay(낳다)"의 잘못, 그리고 "chimbley"는 "chimney(굴뚝)"의 잘못된 발음.

[확인 학습]   다음 문장을 우리말로 옮기세요.

1. It is the thing whose loss he really welcomes with a sad and secret joy, the thing he would never willingly re-live again, could it be restored to him by any magic.

2. While both art and science are ultimately concerned with the pursuit of truth, the process and methods employed by the artist on the one hand, and by the scientist on the other, vary to considerable degree.

3. The archeologists' efforts are not directed at "proving" the correctness of the Bible, which is neither necessary nor possible, any more than belief in God can be scientifically demonstrated.

4. Some persons are richly endowed at birth; but for all their advantages they fail to achieve a successful adjustment. Others less gifted, but who have a strong will to succeed, rise to great heights because they have made the most of their endowments.

[words & phrases]

A1: anguish 고뇌, bear 참다/견디다, infinite 무한한, sorrow 슬픔, lament 한탄하다, restore 회복하다
A2: inspiration 영감, perspire 땀을 흘리다, nap 낮잠/선잠, experiment 실험(하다), console 위로하다
A3: will 의지/의지력, emphasize 강조하다, gift (타고난) 재능, endow 부여하다, adjust 적응하다
A4: pasture 풀밭/초원, goatherd 염소지기, take to one's heels 달아나다, charge 비난하다/위탁(관리), gratitude 감사, desert 버리다, ration 배급/식량, famish 굶주리게 하다, fodder 사료, domesticate 길들이다, guard 경계/조심, make much of 중시하다, at one's expense ~을 희생시키고,
B1: admire 칭송하다, excessive 과도한, state 진술하다, confirm 확인하다, afford ~을 살 여유가 있다
B2: be concerned with ~에 관계되다, pursue 추구하다, employ 고용하다, principle 원리/원칙, analyze 분석하다, synthesize 통합하다, isolate 격리하다/고립시키다, constituent 요소/성분, assemble 모으다/조립하다, compose 구성하다, objective 객관적, phenomenon 현상, deal with ~을 다루다
B3: overcome 이기다/극복하다, out of place 부적절한, take the place of ~을 대신하다, spring 샘(솟다)
B4: bureaucracy 관료주의, scorn 경멸, institution 제도/기관, fraction 파편/분수, critical 비판적/중대한
B5: geography 지리, illustrate 예증하다, archeology 고고학, accurate 정확한, reference 언급/참고/참조 account 설명, Exodus 출애굽기, biography 전기, A is not B any more than C is D (=A is no more B than C is D) A가 B 아닌 것은 C가 D 아닌 것과 같다. demonstrate 입증하다, expert 전문가
C1: yonder 저쪽에, bank 강둑, spark 불빛, raft 뗏목, scow 짐배, fiddle 깽깽이(바이올린), craft 배/선박, speckle 작은 반점, streak 줄무늬(지다), spoil 망치다, heave 내던지다, still 고요한, joggle 흔들다

[실력 점검 A] 다음 각 동사의 우리말 뜻을 쓰세요.

1. rear: 2. lessen: 3. advertise:

4. inflict: 5. derive: 6. illustrate:

7. detect: 8. endow: 9. constitute:

10. reside: 11. betray: 12. determine:

13. certify: 14. emerge: 15. investigate:

16. restore: 17. consume: 18. supplement:

19. contain: 20. interfere with:

[실력 점검 B] 각 항목에 대응하는 영어 단어를 찾아 쓰세요.

보기   comb, throne, forgery, compass, spectator, manuscript, contradiction, trait, frugal, summit, disgust, perfume, appearance, catastrophe, compliment, status, elaborate, prospective, perspiration, indispensable

1. 땀: 2. 빗: 3. 지위:

4. 혐오: 5. 향수: 6. 재앙:

7. 정상: 8. 원고: 9. 특성:

10. 위조: 11. 찬사: 12. 모순:

13. 왕위: 14. 외모: 15. 구경꾼:

16. 나침반: 17. 검소한: 18. 정교한:

19. 예상되는: 20. 필수불가결한:

[실력 점검 C] 빈칸에 들어갈 적절한 낱말을 쓰세요.

1. She was as _____ as her word, and arrived at the appointed time.

2. _____ we travel in space or in time, to make it worth _____
   we must travel in imagination also.

3. There is no one of our natural passions so hard to subdue _____
   pride. Even if I could conceive that I had completely overcome it,
   I should probably be _____ of my humility.

명시 감상

After Work

Gary Snyder

The shack and a few trees
float in the blowing fog

I pull out your blouse,
warm my cold hands
        on your breasts.
you laugh and shudder
peeling garlic by the
            hot iron stove.
bring in the axe, the rake,
the wood

we'll lean on the wall
against each other
stew simmering on the fire
as it grows dark
            drinking wine.

* shack 오두막, float 떠다니다, peel 껍질을 벗기다, garlic 마늘, ax(e) 도끼, rake 갈퀴, simmer 끓다, lean 기대다

Unit 10 관계사

A. 관계 대명사

1) I have two sisters *who* are younger than you.

I have two sisters, *who* are younger than you.

2) The boy *who* is playing the violin is my brother.

I have a friend *whose* mother is a famous actress.

This is the girl (*whom*) I want to introduce to you.

3) She likes the flower *which* is in full bloom.

I have a book *whose* author is still unknown.

This is the book (*which*) I am going to read tonight.

4) *What* I know about you is that you know nothing about me.

Reading is to the mind *what* exercise is to the body.

We often judge a man not by *what he is* but by *what he has*.

5) I want you to marry such a man *as* will make you happy.

There is no rule *but* has some exceptions.

Don't use more words *than* are necessary.

B. 관계 형용사

1) I gave her *what* money I had with me.

2) He may come here, in *which* case I will ask him.

C. 관계 부사

1) I still remember the day *when* you were born.

2) This is the house *where* I lived ten years ago.

3) This is (*the way*) how we solved the problem.

4) Tell me (*the reason*) why you are late for school.

D. 복합 관계사

1) I will lend the book to *whoever* wants to read it.

2) *Whatever* orders he gives are obeyed.

3) Come and see me *whenever* you feel you have to talk.

[필수 문법] 관계사(relative)

* 뒤쪽 어절의 첫머리에 놓여서, 앞쪽 어절의 어떤 말(선행사)을 가리킴과 동시에
* 앞쪽 어절과 뒤쪽 어절을 서로 연결시키는 접속사의 기능을 담당하는 낱말.
* 관계사에는 관계 대명사, 관계 형용사, 관계 부사, 그리고 복합 관계사가 있다.

A. 관계 대명사: "접속사 + 대명사"의 기능을 하는 낱말.

  1) 제한적 용법: "너보다 어린 누이가 둘 있다." (누이는 둘 이상 수도 있음)
     계속적 용법: "누이가 둘 있는데, 그 누이들은 너보다 어리다." (누이는 둘 뿐임)

  2) 선행사가 사람일 경우: 주격/who(=that), 소유격/whose, 목적격/whom(=that)

  3) 선행사가 사물: 주격/which(=that), 소유격/whose(=of which), 목적격/which(=that)
    *소유격의 경우에는 다음 문장도 가능: =I have a book *of which the author*(=*the author of which*) is still unknown. *선행사가 사람이든 사물이든, 관계 대명사 목적격은 생략될 수 있다. *관계 대명사 "which"는 흔히 앞쪽 어절 전체의 내용이나 그 내용의 일부분을 가리키기도 한다: *She changed her mind, which* made him very angry.
    He resolved *to stop smoking, which* would not be so easy. He was *rich, which* I was not.

  4) what ~ (= that which ~, the thing that ~): 대부분의 관계대명사절은 선행사를 수식/한정하는 형용사절이지만, "what ~"어절은 명사절이다: what I know (내가 아는 것)
    * A is to B what (=as) C is to D: "A가 B에 대한 관계는 C가 D에 대한 관계와 같다."
    * what he is (그의 모습/인품), what he has (그의 재산), what I am/was (현재/과거의 나)

  5) (유사)관계대명사: "as, but, than" 등은 거의 주격으로 쓰이지만, "such ~ *as* ~, as ~ *as* ~, the same ~ *as* ~" 등의 구문에 사용되는 "as"는 목적격으로 사용되는 경우도 있다. "than"은 비교급 구문에 사용되며, "but"은 부정("not")의 뜻을 담고 있다: =There is no rule *that*(=which) has *not* some exceptions.

B. 관계 형용사: "접속사 + 형용사"의 기능을 하는 낱말.

  1) "what"은 명사 "money"를 수식함: =I gave her all the money (that) I had with me.

  2) "which"는 명사 "case"를 수식함: "~, 그가 여기 오는 경우에 그에게 물어 보겠다."

C. 관계 부사: "접속사 + 부사"의 기능을 하는 낱말.

  1) when (=in/at/on which): = I still remember the day *on which* you were born.

  2) where (=in/at/on which): = This is the house *in which* I lived ten years ago.

  3) how (=in which): = This is the way *in which* we solved the problem.

  4) why (=for which): = Tell me the reason *for which* you are late for school.

D. 복합 관계사: 철자가 "~ever"로 끝나는 낱말로서, 선행사를 내포하고 있음.

  1) 관계 대명사: = I will lend the book to *anyone who* wants to read it.

  2) 관계 형용사: = Any orders that he gives are obeyed.)

  3) 관계 부사: = Come and see me *anytime when* you feel you have to talk.

[문법 연습 A] 잘못된 부분을 고치세요.

1. This is the girl whom I spoke the other day.

2. I know the house in which coal miners inhabit.

3. He wants to buy the same watch that he has lost.

4. There are several ways by which this can be done.

5. She really believed that he told her about his father.

6. Whoever that violates traffic regulations will be fined.

7. The teacher said that he would punish whomever told a lie.

8. Ireland is the country which I want you to stay for over a week.

9. My mother had two sisters, that were destined to die very young.

10. She met a young man whom she believed came of a good family.

11. John is the only one of the students who are able to speak German.

12. They have three children, but none of whom wants to live with them.

[문법 연습 B] 관계사를 사용하여 두 문장을 결합하세요.

1. The newcomer is from Korea. He is smart and handsome.

_____

2. She was married to a man. I thought he was very wealthy.

_____

3. He was absent from school. I didn't know that he was absent.

_____

4. She is reciting a poem. I cannot remember the title of the poem.

_____

5. The day will come. You will really understand your parents then.

_____

6. They went to their uncle's in Seoul. They stayed there for a month.

_____

7. He spoke English very fluently. I was surprised at the great fluency.

_____

[실전 문법 A]   빈칸에 알맞은 낱말을 쓰세요.

1. Three is to twelve _____ five is to twenty.

2. He is just such a teacher _____ we all admire.

3. There are no parents _____ love their children.

4. Sam is English by birth _____ anyone may say.

5. He was a foreigner, _____ I knew from his accent.

6. We have to raise as much money _____ is necessary.

7. An object _____ shape is like a ball is called a globe.

8. This is _____ I don't want to keep company with them.

9. Tony is determined to make friends with _____ likes him.

10. She has changed very much; she is not _____ she used to be.

11. He believes in public ownership, _____ idea I am opposed to.

12. The book is interesting, and _____ is better still, very instructive.

[실전 문법 B]   각 문항의 다섯 부분 중 어법에 맞지 않는 부분은?

1. [1]Every tyrant or dictator [2]has a specially keen [3]and hostile instinct [4]for whomever keeps up [5]human dignity and independence.

2. [1]The teacher mentioned [2]the names of five students [3]whom he thought deserved [4]to represent his class [5]for a year.

3. [1]Most of us spend 59 minutes an hour [2]living in the past [3]with regret for lost joys, [4]or in a future [5]when we dread or long for.

4. [1]Most scientists agree [2]that the amount of carbon dioxide [3]has reached the point [4]which an increase in temperature [5]is imminent.

5. [1]The part of the ocean floor [2]where slopes gently away [3]from the continent [4]is called [5]the continental shelf.

6. [1]Learning is defined [2]in psychology [3]as the process [4]which behavior changes [5]as a result of experience.

7. [1]The students carefully listened [2]to the old professor, [3]but still they couldn't understand [4]that he was trying to mean [5]in his lecture on foreign affairs.

[필수 어휘 A] 각 항목의 반대성의 낱말을 쓰세요.

1. hen: 2. god: 3. hero:

4. duke: 5. bride: 6. widow:

7. witch: 8. waiter: 9. nephew:

[필수 어휘 B] 다음 각 낱말의 복수형을 쓰세요.

1. ox: 2. die: 3. mouse:

4. thief: 5. crisis: 6. stimulus:

7. sheep: 8. formula: 9. manservant:

10. have-not: 11. passer-by: 12. phenomenon:

[필수 어휘 C] 각 문장의 밑줄 친 부분의 뜻은?

1. The doctor has a <u>reputation</u> of being good with children.

   1) cure   2) fame   3) game   4) method   5) character

2. They are very <u>reserved</u> people, the English.

   1) quiet   2) polite   3) thrifty   4) humble   5) rational

3. I know that you have always been quite <u>candid</u> with me.

   1) kind   2) frank   3) modest   4) patient   5) tolerant

4. She seems <u>content</u> just to sit in front of the television all day.

   1) tired   2) bored   3) excited   4) pleased   5) satisfied

5. His <u>principal</u> interest in life was to be the richest man in Asia.

   1) main   2) whole   3) general   4) intense   5) immense

6. Local residents want to <u>retain</u> the existing character of the area.

   1) enjoy   2) change   3) improve   4) preserve   5) advocate

7. Both parties must agree to <u>abide by</u> the court's decision.

   1) accept   2) ignore   3) observe   4) embrace   5) reconcile

8. As soon as the children saw my brother, they <u>took to their heels</u>.

   1) fled   2) cried   3) followed   4) vanished   5) scattered

[구문 연습] 다음 문장을 우리말로 옮기세요.

1. There are those who are so scrupulously afraid of doing wrong that they
   seldom venture to do anything.

2. What is called a high standard of living consists, in considerable measure, in
   arrangements for avoiding muscular energy, for increasing sensual pleasure.

3. The long unmeasured pulse of time moves everything. There is nothing hidden
   that it cannot bring to light, nothing once known that may not become unknown.

4. Cyberspace, the media space in which people interact with computer
   technology, has some risk of harming healthy human life, generating new
   crimes and widening the gap between the haves and the have-nots.

5. The best part of my youth, the critical four years when I should have had the
   opportunity of studying, reflecting and sometimes loafing, I spent in mastering
   hard, practical little tricks for getting ahead in a tough environment.

[작문 연습] 다음 문장을 영어로 옮기세요.

1. 부지런하지 않은 사람은 어떤 일에도 성공할 수 없다.

   _____

2. 우리들 모두가 자유와 정의를 옹호하고 실천할 때가 왔다.

   _____

3. 개인이 국가에 대한 관계는 세포가 신체에 대한 관계와 같다.

   _____

4. 내가 정말 하고 싶은 것은 너와 함께 유럽 여행을 가는 것이다.

   _____

5. 네가 어디를 간다 하더라도 집처럼 편안한 곳은 찾지 못할 것이다.

   _____

[실전 독해 A] 각 문항의 물음에 답하세요.

1. ¹⁾<u>Most</u> complete and healthy sleep that can be taken in the day is in summer-time, out in a field. There is, perhaps, no solitary sensation so exquisite as ²⁾<u>that</u> of slumbering on the grass or hay, ³⁾<u>shaded</u> from the hot sun by a tree, with the consciousness of a fresh but light air ⁴⁾<u>running</u> through the wide atmosphere, and the sky ⁵⁾<u>stretching</u> far overhead upon all sides.

Q. 밑줄 친 1)~5)중 어법에 맞지 않는 것은?

2. There are two kinds of twins, and each is produced in a different way. Identical twins look so much alike that it is hard to tell them apart. This is because such twins are really one person who became two. About once in every 300 times, when a fertilized egg is just beginning to grow into a baby, something causes it to split in half. Each half grows into a separate baby. Since the babies came from the same egg and the same sperm, they carry exactly the same genes. So identical twins are always of the same sex and are exactly alike in their hereditary traits. Any differences are caused by their not having had the same _____.

Fraternal twins are born two or three times as often as identical twins. They may be as completely different as any two children born separately in a family. The reason is that fraternal twins result when the mother, instead of producing one egg, as is the usual case, produces two eggs. Each egg is fertilized by a different sperm. Thus fraternal twins are different in their heredity. One may be a boy, the other a girl. Or if they are of the same sex, one may look and be quite different from the other.

Q 1. 빈칸에 들어갈 적절한 어구는?
    1) cells and genes   2) eggs and sperms
    3) nature and nurture   4) organs and intestines
    5) environment and experiences

2. "이란성 쌍둥이"가 태어날 확률은?
    1) 1/60 ~ 1/90   2) 1/100 ~ 1/150
    3) 1/200 ~ 1/300   4) 1/300 ~ 1/450
    5) 1/600 ~ 1/900

3. It is a strong belief among certain groups of people that the medical community should take every possible step to keep a person alive, without regard for the quality of that person's life. But other people argue just as strongly that patients who are confronting a life of pain and encumbrance on others have the _____ to decide for themselves whether or not to continue with life-prolonging therapies and medications. When the quality of life has disintegrated, when there is no hope of reprieve, when there is intense and ever present pain, does the patient have the _____ to be put to death?

   Q. 빈칸에 공통으로 들어갈 적절한 낱말은?

4. People feel safer behind some kind of physical barrier. If a social situation is in any way threatening, then there is an immediate urge to set up such a barricade. For a tiny child faced with a stranger, the problem is usually solved by hiding behind its mother's body and peeping out at the intruder to see what he or she will do next. If the mother's body is not available, then a chair or some other piece of solid furniture will ^{a)}_____. If the stranger insists on coming closer, then the peeping face must be hidden too. If the insensitive intruder continues to approach despite these obvious signals of fear, then there is nothing for it ^{b)}_____ to scream or flee. This pattern is gradually reduced as the child matures. In teenage girls it may still be detected in the giggling cover-up of the face, with hands or papers, when acutely or jokingly embarrassed. But by the time we are adults, the childhood hiding which dwindled to ^{c)}_____, is expected to disappear altogether, as we bravely stride out to meet our guests, friends, relatives, colleagues, clients or customers.

   Q 1. 빈칸 a)에 들어갈 적절한 낱말은?
       1) be   2) do   3) keep   4) make   5) apply

    2. 빈칸 b)에 들어갈 적절한 낱말은?
       1) as   2) nor   3) but   4) even   5) only

    3. 빈칸 c)에 들어갈 적절한 어구는?
       1) a way of life   2) a kind of habit
       3) normal behavior   4) adolescent shyness
       5) juvenile delinquency

[실전 독해 B] 각 문항의 물음에 답하세요.

1.   Fundamental to the existence of science is a body of established facts which come from observation and experiment. Without facts we have no science. Facts are to the scientist ^{a)}_____ words are to the poet. The scientist has a love of facts, even of isolated facts, similar to the poet's love of words. But a collection of facts is not science any more than a collection of words, or a dictionary, is poetry. Around his facts the scientist weaves a logical pattern or theory which gives the facts order and meaning. ^{b)}_____, no one can look at the brilliant night sky without emotion, but the realization that the earth and planets move in great orbits according to simple laws gives proportion and significance to this experience. A scientific theory goes far beyond the facts because it has unforeseen consequences which can be applied to new facts or be tested by experiment.

　　Q 1. 빈칸 a)에 들어갈 적절한 낱말은?

　　　2. 빈칸 b)에 들어갈 적절한 말은?
　　　　1) Thus　　2) Besides　　3) However
　　　　4) Of course　　5) For example

2.   A Japanese-style conversation is like a game of bowling, not like tennis or volleyball. You wait for your turn. ① It depends on such things as whether you are older or younger, a close friend or a relative stranger to the previous speaker, in a senior or junior position, and so on. ② When your turn comes, you step up to the starting line with your bowling ball and carefully bowl it. Everyone else stands back and watches politely, murmuring encouragement. ③ Everyone waits until the ball has reached the end of the alley and watches to see if it knocks down all the pins, or only some of them, or none of them. There is a pause, while everyone registers your score. ④ Then, after everyone is sure that you have completely finished your turn, the next person in line steps up to the same starting line, with a different ball. ⑤ He doesn't return your ball, and he does not begin from where your ball stopped. There is no rush, no scramble for the ball.

　　Q. ①～⑤중 다음 문장이 삽입되기에 적절한 곳은?
　　　And you always know your place in line.

3. ¹⁾Coal has been substituted for oil, ²⁾and oil is being used up so fast. ³⁾What is true of oil is equally true of other natural resources. ⁴⁾Everyday, many square miles of forest are turned into newspaper, ⁵⁾but there is no known process by which newspaper can be turned into forest.

> Q. 1) ~ 5)중 문맥(context)에 맞지 않는 것은?

4. The European traveler in America—at least I may judge by myself—is struck by two peculiarities: first the extreme similarity of outlook in all part of the United States, and secondly the passionate desire of each locality to prove that it is peculiar and different from every other. The second of these is, of course, caused by the first. Every place wishes to have a reason for local pride, and therefore cherishes whatever is distinctive in the way of geography or history or tradition. The greater is the uniformity that in fact exists, the more eager becomes the search for _____ that may mitigate it.

> Q. 빈칸에 들어갈 적절한 낱말은?
> 1) virtues   2) reasons   3) traditions
> 4) differences   5) communities

5. ⓐ Who knows what the chimpanzees will be like forty million years hence? It should be of concern to us all that we permit them to live, that we at least give them the chance to evolve.

ⓑ They have the ability to solve quite complex problems, they can use and make tools for a variety of purposes, their social structure and methods of communication with each other are elaborate, and they show the beginnings of self-awareness.

ⓒ Yes, we humans definitely overshadow the chimpanzee. The chimpanzee is, nevertheless, a creature of immense significance to the understanding of humans. Just as they are overshadowed by us, so the chimpanzees overshadow all other animals.

> Q. ⓐ~ⓒ의 글을 문맥에 맞게 배열하면?
> 1) ⓐ-ⓒ-ⓑ   2) ⓑ-ⓐ-ⓒ   3) ⓑ-ⓒ-ⓐ
> 4) ⓒ-ⓐ-ⓑ   5) ⓒ-ⓑ-ⓐ

[명작 감상]　　　D. H. Lawrence (1885 ~ 1930)

Sons and Lovers 『아들과 연인』

When the light was fading, and Mrs. Morel could see no more to sew, she rose and went to the door. Everywhere was the sound of excitement, the restlessness of the holiday, that at last infected her. She went out into the side garden. Women were coming home from the wakes, the children hugging a white lamb with green legs, or a wooden horse. Occasionally a man lurched past, almost as full as he could carry. Sometimes a good husband came along with his family, peacefully. But usually the women and children were alone. The stay-at-home mothers stood gossiping at the corners of the alley, as the twilight sank, folding their arms under their white aprons.

Mrs. Morel was alone, but she was used to it. Her son and her little girl slept upstairs; so, it seemed, her home was there behind her, fixed and stable. But she felt wretched with the coming child. The world seemed a dreary place, where nothing else would happen for her—at least until William grew up. But for herself, nothing but this dreary endurance—till the children grew up. And the children! She could not afford to have this third. She did not want it. The father was serving beer in a public house, swilling himself drunk. She despised him, and was tied to him. This coming child was too much for her. If it were not for William and Annie, she was sick of it, the struggle with poverty and ugliness and meanness.

She went into the front garden, feeling too heavy to take herself out, yet unable to stay indoors. The heat suffocated her. And looking ahead, the prospect of her life made her feel as if she were buried alive.

The front garden was a small square with a privet hedge. There she stood, trying to soothe herself with the scent of flowers and the fading, beautiful evening. Opposite her small gate was the stile that led uphill, under the tall hedge between the burning glow of the cut pastures. The sky overhead throbbed and pulsed with light. The glow sank quickly off the field; the earth and the hedges smoked dusk. As it grew dark, a ruddy glare came out on the hilltop, and out of the glare the diminished commotion of the fair.

* Honesty is the best policy.　　정직함이 최선의 정책.
* Time and tide wait for no man.　　세월은 사람을 기다리지 않는다.

[확인 학습] 다음 문장을 우리말로 옮기세요.

1. There is, perhaps, no solitary sensation so exquisite as that of slumbering on the grass or hay, shaded from the hot sun by a tree,

2. A collection of facts is not science any more than a collection of words, or a dictionary, is poetry. Around his facts the scientist weaves a logical pattern or theory which gives the facts order and meaning.

3. Other people argue just as strongly that patients who are confronting a life of pain and encumbrance on others have the right to decide for themselves whether or not to continue with life-prolonging therapies and medications

[words & phrases]

A1: solitary 고독한, exquisite 멋진/절묘한, slumber 잠/잠자다, hay 건초, conscious of ~을 의식하는

A2: identical 동일한, fertilize 수정(수태)시키다, split 쪼개(지)다, sperm 정자, gene 유전자, heredity 유전, trait 특성, cause 초래하다, fraternal 형제의, result 결과로서 일어나다, instead of ~대신에

A3: confront 직면하다, encumber 방해하다, disintegrate 분해하다/붕괴하다, reprieve (집행)유예/구제

A4: barrier 장벽, threaten 위협하다, urge 충동, peep 엿보다, intrude 침입하다, available 이용 가능한, insist on ~을 주장하다, insensitive 둔감한, despite ~에도 불구하고, flee 달아나다/도망치다, reduce 줄이다/감소하다, mature 성숙한/성숙하다, detect 탐지하다, acute 예리한, embarrassed 당황한, adult 성인/어른, dwindle 줄다, stride 활보하다, relative 친척, colleague 동료, client 고객/단골손님

B1: fundamental 근본적, existence 존재, establish 설립하다/확립하다, observation 관찰, experiment 실험(하다), A is to B what[=as] C is to D (A가 B에 대한 관계는 C가 D에 대한 관계와 같다), similar 유사한, isolate 고립시키다, A is not B any more than C is D (A가 B아닌 것은 C가 D아닌 것과 같다), logical 논리적, theory 이론, order 질서, planet 행성, orbit 궤도, proportion 조화/균형 significance 의미/중요성, foresee 예견하다, consequence 결과, apply to ~에 적용하다/응용하다

B2: volleyball 배구, relative 비교적, previous 이전의, murmur 속삭이다, alley 길/골목, scramble 쟁탈

B3: substitute 대신하다/대체하다, natural resource 천연 자원, square 정사각형/제곱, process 과정/공정

B4: peculiar 독특한, extreme 극단적인, similarity 유사성, passion 열정/정열, locality 지방(성), cherish 소중히 하다, distinctive 뚜렷한/구별되는, geography 지리, uniform 획일적인, mitigate 완화하다

B5: concern 관심/걱정, evolve 진화하다, tool 연장, purpose 목적, elaborate 정교한, awareness 인식, overshadow ~보다 낫다/우월하다, nevertheless 그럼에도 불구하고, immense 엄청난

C1: fade 사라지다, infect 전염시키다, wakes 휴일축제, lurch 비틀거리다, twilight 황혼, stable 안정된, wretched 비참한, dreary 황량한/처량한, public house 선술집, swill 폭음하다, despise 멸시하다, if it were not for ~이 없다면, poverty 가난, mean 미천한/비열한, suffocate 질식시키다, prospect 전망/예상, hedge 울타리, soothe 진정시키다, scent 향기, throb 두근거리다, pulse 맥박(치다), dusk 황혼/땅거미, ruddy 붉은, glare 섬광, diminish 줄다, commotion 소동/동요, fair 장/시장

[실력 점검 A] 다음 각 동사의 우리말 뜻을 쓰세요.

1. split: 2. fade: 3. despise:

4. breed: 5. banish: 6. recognize:

7. infect: 8. beware: 9. encourage:

10. adjust: 11. preach: 12. humiliate:

13. soothe: 14. cherish: 15. suffocate:

16. prevail: 17. destroy: 18. substitute:

19. intrude: 20. integrate:

[실력 점검 B] 각 항목에 대응하는 영어 단어를 찾아 쓰세요.

보기   folly, intact, neutral, reptile, mutual, puberty, laboratory, descendant, orbit, asset, virtue, epoch, ladder, twilight, stimulus, installment, conference, dormitory, unprecedented, comprehensive

1. 황혼: 2. 후손: 3. 자극:

4. 시대: 5. 미덕: 6. 할부:

7. 궤도: 8. 우둔: 9. 자산:

10. 회담: 11. 기숙사: 12. 사춘기:

13. 사다리: 14. 파충류: 15. 실험실:

16. 중립적인: 17. 포괄적인: 18. 상호간의:

19. 본래대로의: 20. 전례가 없는:

[실력 점검 C] 다음의 빈칸에 들어갈 적절한 낱말은?

1. All men are equal before the law _____ of their social status.

2. A man is defined not so much by himself _____ by his friends.

3. The jury and the judge had to _____ the crime home to the accused.

4. It is curious how we humans learned to make things _____ of metal.

5. Music has a great advantage _____ poetry in that it is a _____
   language common to all nations.

명시 감상

Arrival

W. C. Williams

And yet one arrives somehow

finds himself loosening the hooks of

her dress

in a strange bedroom—

feels the autumn

dropping its silk and linen leaves

about her ankles.

The tawdry veined body emerges

like a winter wind . . . !

* somehow 여하튼/어쨌든, loosen 풀다/끄르다, ankle 발목, tawdry 야한/비속한, emerge 나타나다, vein 정맥/혈관

Unit 11   연결사

A. 전치사(preposition)

1) He will be back *in* an hour. He will be back *within* an hour.

2) I have lived here *for* ten years. I was born *during* the war.

3) We will finish the work *by* six. We will stay here *till* tomorrow.

4) I was sitting *between* the twins. I was sitting *among* the crowd.

5) They swam *across* the river. The river flows *through* the city.

6) She followed him *into* the shop. She was coming *out of* the shop.

7) There is a fly *on* the ceiling. It is hidden *beneath* the blanket.

8) The lamp hung *over* the table. She was waiting *under* the tree.

9) The sun rises *above* the horizon. The sun sets *below* the mountain.

10) He is really a man *of* culture. Young soldiers fought *with* courage.

B. 접속사(conjunction)

1) We were wet *and* tired. They are poor *but* cheerful.

   He is cautious, *or* rather timid. I was lost, *so* I bought a street map.

   They were surprised, *for* it was almost ten o'clock.

2) *Once* you have signed, you won't be able to cancel the contract.

   Even if they take a cab, they will still miss the train.

   She felt *as if* she had been lying in the sun for hours.

   The instant I saw him I knew he was an old friend of mine.

   Every time he takes an exam, Charles makes a couple of mistakes.

   Now that I've got a car, I don't get as much exercise as I used to.

   As far as I know, it's true. *As long as* I live, I will never forget it.

3) Just *as* food nourishes our body, *so* books nourish our mind.

   He is *not only* kind *but also* smart. I don't know *whether* he is glad *or* sorry.

   You must *either* sing *or* dance. *Neither* you *nor* I am to blame for it.

   She loves him *not because* he is handsome *but because* he is kind and honest.

4) Tony was fairly stable, *while* Bonny was severely disturbed.

   Young *as* he is, Jack is wise. Woman as she was, Jane was brave.

   You should *not* despise a man *because* he is poorly dressed.

   It never rains *but* it pours. No man is so old *but* he may learn.

[필수 문법] 연결사(connective)

* 낱말/어구/어절을 서로 연결시켜 주는 기능을 하는 낱말.
* 관계사를 제외한다면, 연결사에는 전치사와 접속사가 있다.
* 접속사에는 등위 접속사, 종속 접속사, 상관 접속사가 있다.

A. 전치사: 명사/대명사/명사구/명사절의 앞에 놓여, 앞뒤의 낱말/어구를 연결시킴.
　1) in: ~지나면/경과하면, within: ~이내에.　*in/within* a month (한 달 있으면/이내에)
　2) for: 경과된 기간, during: 지속된 기간.　*during* the night/summer (밤/여름 동안)
　3) by: 특정 시점까지의 행위의 완료, till: 특정 시점까지의 행위의 계속
　4) between: 둘 사이에, among: 셋 이상의 사이에.　*between* A and B, *among* the people
　5) across: 가로질러/횡단하여, through: 통과/관통하여.　*across* the street, *through* the gate
　6) into: (밖에서) 안으로, out of: (안에서) 밖으로.　in: ~안에, out: ~밖(끝)에.
　7) on (표면/접촉면) 위에, beneath (표면/접촉면) 밑에:　*on/beneath* the wall/floor
　8) over (수직선상의) 바로 위에, under (수직선상의) 바로 밑에.　*over/under* the bridge
　9) above ~보다 위에(=higher than ~), below ~보다 밑에(lower than ~).　*above/below* the knee
　10) of+추상명사=형용사 ("교양 있는 사람"), with+추상명사=부사 ("용감하게 싸웠다")
　　The cow is an animal *of* (*great*) *use*. = The cow is a (*very*) *useful* animal.
　　Treat it *with great care*. = Treat it (*very*) *carefully*.　*with courage (=courageously)
　* instead of ~대신에, in front of ~의 앞에/정면에(↔behind), in spite of (=despite) ~에도
　　불구하고, with all ~에도 불구하고, in addition to (=besides) ~외에도, as for ~로 말하자면,
　　as to (=about) ~에 관하여, as of ~현재로, regarding(=concerning) ~에 관해서(=about)

B. 접속사: 낱말과 낱말, 어구와 어구, 어절과 어절을 서로 연결하는 기능.
　1) 등위 접속사: and (순접/첨가), but (역접/대조), or (보완/환언), so (결과), for (이유)
　2) 종속 접속사: as, when, while, because, since, after, before, until, if, unless, (al)though;
　　once 일단 ~하면; even if (=even though, although) 비록 ~이지만/일지라도; as if ~
　　(=as though) 마치 ~인 것처럼; the instant (=the moment, as soon as) ~하자 마자;
　　every time (=whenever) ~할 때마다; now that (=since) ~이므로; as far as (=so far as,
　　insofar as) ~하는 한 (거리/정도의 개념); as/so long as ~하는 한 (시간적 개념)
　3) 상관 접속사: (just) as ~, so ~ (꼭) ~이듯이, ~하다; not only ~ but (also) ~; whether ~ or ~;
　　either ~ or ~; neither ~ nor ~; not because ~ but because ~; both ~ and ~(=at once ~ and ~)
　4) 접속사 구문: while(=whereas) ~인 한편/반면에(=*While* Tony was fairly stable, Bonny ~.);
　　(=*Though* he is young, Jack is wise.) (=*Though* she was *a woman*, Jane was very brave.);
　　not ~ because ~이기 때문에 ~이지는/하지는 않다; 관계 대명사 "but"의 경우처럼,
　　종속 접속사 "but" 또한 "not"의 의미를 담고 있다: (=It never rains *without* pouring.)
　　(=No man is so old *that* he may *not* learn. 배울 수 없을 만큼 나이 든 사람은 없다.)
　* 명사 (the) fact/idea/doubt/belief/proof/possibility/reason 등에 수반되는 접속사 "that"은
　　그 명사와 that-절이 동격임을 나타낸다: There is no *proof that* he killed the woman.

[문법 연습 A] 다음 각 쌍의 우리말 뜻을 쓰세요.

1. ask for ~:

  ask after ~:

2. consist in ~:

  consist of ~:

3. apply to ~:

  apply for ~:

4. succeed in ~:

  succeed to ~:

5. attend to ~:

  attend on ~:

6. compare ~ to ~:

  compare ~ with ~:

7. look after ~:

  take after ~:

8. be anxious for ~:

  be anxious about ~:

9. by oneself:

  for oneself:

10. beside oneself:

  in spite of oneself:

11. be due to ~:

  be due to (do):

12. be obliged to ~:

  be obliged to (do):

13. of no account:

  on no account:

14. come to one's feet:

  take to one's heels:

15. out of question:

  out of the question:

16. be concerned with ~:

  be concerned about ~:

[문법 연습 B] 각 문장의 빈칸에 알맞은 전치사를 쓰세요.

1. They are still _____ table.

2. We have fossils _____ great value.

3. The boys are _____ an age.

4. Will you cut it _____ the scissors?

5. She took me _____ the hand.

6. She was dancing _____ the music.

7. He patted me _____ the back.

8. _____ my surprise, they were all gone.

9. Her father died _____ cancer.

10. We mistook her _____ her sister.

11. Christine lay _____ her face.

12. Final exams are near _____ hand.

13. I bought it _____ ten dollars.

14. You have to read _____ the lines.

15. He is leaning _____ the wall.

16. Are you _____ the plan or for it?

17. The copier is _____ of order.

18. Something's wrong _____ my car.

19. They did it _____ confidence.

20. Jessie looks young _____ her age.

[실전 문법 A] 빈칸에 알맞은 낱말은?

1. None _____ the brave deserves a fair.

2. _____ David away, we've got more room.

3. As _____ snowboarding, he is second to none.

4. _____ all his learning, he is the simplest of men.

5. The social situation has changed _____ recognition.

6. Just _____ a man is rich, you can't say that he is happy.

7. He decided to major in botany, _____ the study of plants.

8. Laugh _____ they would, he maintained the story was true.

9. Now _____ it is October, the leaves are beginning to turn red.

10. There was a heated argument _____ to who should be appointed.

11. As Frenchmen enjoy their wine, _____ Germans enjoy their beer.

12. Of course I agreed, _____ who would reject such a wonderful offer?

13. She had no intention _____ spending her whole life working in a bank.

[실전 문법 B] 각 문항의 다섯 부분 중 어법에 맞지 않는 부분은?

1. [1]A dark suit is preferable [2]than a light one [3]for evening wear, [4]particularly [5]on a rainy day.

2. [1]We do hope [2]that he won't be involved [3]in any corruption cases [4]like many politician [5]have been.

3. [1]As everybody knows, [2]democracy is based [3]on the idea [4]which all men have equal rights [5]before the law.

4. [1]If someone maintains [2]that two and two are five, [3]or Canada is on the equator, [4]you feel pity [5]rather than anger.

5. [1]A friend of mine lived [2]in a little shabby house, [3]of which the ceiling was so low [4]that we had to move in and out [5]with our hands and knees.

6. [1]A scholar cannot rest with learning something; [2]he has to tell about it feely and fully. [3]The world may sometimes not care to listen, [4]but the scholar must keep telling [5]until he will succeed in communicating.

[필수 어휘 A] 각 문장의 빈칸에 가장 알맞은 낱말은?

1. No visitors are allowed _____ in the most exceptional cases.

   1) as   2) save   3) despite   4) without   5) concerning

2. _____ its wide acceptance, Darwinism is today in trouble.

   1) Like   2) Except   3) Due to   4) With all   5) Regardless of

3. The girl _____ blind when she was just nineteen months old.

   1) went   2) left   3) came   4) found   5) recognized

4. The pain nearly _____ him mad, but I couldn't help him at all.

   1) took   2) drove   3) turned   4) proved   5) caused

5. This glass dish is very _____; you must handle it with care.

   1) valid   2) subtle   3) fragile   4) trifling   5) transparent

6. She allowed them to share her house and its superb _____.

   1) heir   2) contents   3) souvenirs   4) residence   5) reputation

7. Most infections are contagious before any _____ are noticed.

   1) clues   2) traits   3) methods   4) symptoms   5) conditions

8. The _____ to being taken prisoner was to die fighting bravely.

   1) way   2) obstacle   3) decision   4) hardship   5) alternative

[필수 어휘 B] 밑줄 친 부분의 우리말 뜻은?

1. He opened the book at random.

2. Ten to one the train will be late.

3. She is in charge of the kindergarten.

4. Can you share a room for the time being?

5. You're just arguing for the sake of arguing.

6. Without her glasses she is as good as blind.

7. Basic issues of health and safety are at stake.

8. He insulted me in the presence of my friends.

9. This is all nonsense as far as I am concerned.

10. We're quite rich, but not in terms of happiness.

[구문 연습] 다음 문장을 우리말로 옮기세요.

1. There is no act, however trivial, but has its train of consequences,
   as there is no hair so small but it casts its shadow.

2. Just as we appreciate warmth because we have experienced cold,
   so we appreciate what love means all the more because we know what it is
   to have feeling of hate.

3. As more and more women take on jobs, either to increase the family's
   income or to build a career for themselves, the more the traditional pattern
   of families changes.

4. We should not pay attention to a man delivering a lecture or a sermon on
   his "philosophy of life" until we know exactly how he treats his wife, his
   children, his neighbors, his friends, and his enemies.

[작문 연습] 다음 문장을 영어로 옮기세요.

1. 달이 지구의 주위를 돌듯이 지구는 태양의 주위를 돈다.

2. 그 학생은 나에게 조용히 다가와 아무 말없이 무릎을 꿇었다.

3. 풍경이 너무나 아름다워서 나는 그 곳에 영원히 머물고 싶었다.

4. 그녀를 만나고서야 비로소 그는 사랑이 무엇인지를 알게 되었다.

5. 그를 좋아해서가 아니라 싫어하지 않기 때문에 나는 그를 만난다.

[실전 독해 A] 각 문항의 물음에 답하세요.

1.   There is little need to speak of the pleasures and advantages of travel. New lands, new peoples, new experiences, all ¹⁾alike offer to the traveler the opportunity of a wider knowledge. And greater than any knowledge ²⁾gained is the influence ³⁾which travel exerts on habits of thought, and on one's attitude to one's fellow man. A juster appreciation of the real values in life, and a deeper realization of the oneness of mankind—these are some of the results which travel, rightly ⁴⁾pursuing, cannot fail to produce. Quite apart, _____, from all of these things, desirable as they are, is the pleasure of travel in itself. This is for some the main, and for ⁵⁾others at least an important motive. To the real traveler no joy is so keen, no pleasure so lasting, as that of travel itself.

   Q 1. 빈칸에 들어갈 적절한 말은?
       1) in fact   2) however   3) therefore
       4) furthermore   5) in other words

   2. 밑줄 친 1)~5)중 어법에 맞지 않는 것은?

2.   ⓐ One wheel in a watch would not be able to understand that without the other wheel turning in the opposite direction there would be no watch. What is true of the watch is equally true of all social organizations.

   ⓑ All that is lacking is the proper sympathy for the other fellow's contentions, and the understanding that society is a system of interdependencies where each of us needs the others and none stands altogether by himself.

   ⓒ The doctor entertains no very high opinion of most human activity, for he knows that sick people can do nothing and that he is the one who can help to restore them to health. The fireman realizes that a successful career in any field is impossible to pursue from a house that has been burned down and that his own enterprise, and his alone, is the core of the social universe. Of course each is partly correct in his assumptions.

   Q. ⓐ~ⓒ의 글을 문맥에 맞게 배열하면?
      1) ⓐ-ⓒ-ⓑ   2) ⓑ-ⓐ-ⓒ   3) ⓑ-ⓒ-ⓐ
      4) ⓒ-ⓐ-ⓑ   5) ⓒ-ⓑ-ⓐ

3. The human body is a complex machine. From the day you are born your body grows and changes in response to your environment, diet, and habits. [1]The body has many different organ systems that work together to allow you to breathe, move, see, talk, and digest food all at the same time. [2]There are about sixty muscles in your face, for example; you use twenty of them to smile but forty to frown. [3]Most of time you are unaware of what is happening in your body; usually it is only when you get sick or feel pain that you notice. [4]Bad habits like smoking, drinking too much alcohol, and eating junk food damage your body; as with any machine, the better you take care of it, the longer it will last. [5]Of course, the best way to take care of your amazing machine is to eat the right foods, do regular exercise, get enough sleep, and try to smile.

Q. 1)~5)의 문장 중 글의 흐름에 맞지 않는 것은?

4. Before beginning to decorate a room it is essential to consider for what purpose the room is to be used. Each room in a house has its individual uses: some are made to sleep a)_____, and b)_____ are for dressing, eating, study, or conversation. Whatever the uses of a room, they are seriously interfered with if it is not preserved as a small world by itself. Privacy is one of the first requisites of civilized life. If the drawing-room is a part of the hall and the library a part of the drawing-room, all three will be equally unfitted to serve their special purpose. The indifference to privacy, which has sprung up in modern times, is of complex origin. It is probably due in part to the fact that many houses are built and decorated by people unfamiliar with the habits of those for whom they are building. The individual <u>who are, the room, to occupy, of the people, tastes and habits</u> must be taken into account. It must not be "a library" or "a drawing-room," but the library or the drawing-room best suited to the master or mistress of the house which is being built and decorated. The individuality in the decoration of the house consists not in an attempt to be different from other people at the cost of comfort, c)_____ d)_____ the desire to be comfortable in one's own way.

Q 1. 빈칸 a)~d)에 들어갈 각각의 낱말은?

2. 밑줄 친 5개의 어군을 문맥에 맞게 배열하면?

[실전 독해 B] 각 문항의 물음에 답하세요.

1. Middle children usually look outside of the family for approval and acceptance and are therefore more social and less conservative than other children. They try to obtain from their peers the attention their older brothers and sisters received from their parents. By finding their strength outside the family, they learn valuable skills that prepare them for adult life. These might include diplomatic skills, the ability to listen and relate to others, and knowing how to _____. It is no coincidence that many middle children end up in managerial and leadership positions.

> Q. 빈칸에 들어갈 적절한 말은?
> 1) work and play   2) run a business
> 3) make a fortune   4) love and be loved
> 5) negotiate and compromise

2. Elements are fundamental substances that cannot be reduced by chemical reactions to anything else. John Dalton figured out that each element is composed of tiny [1]articles/particles called atoms, and that each atom of each element is the same as every other atom for that element—but different from the atoms of any other element. Whenever matter changes, the atoms themselves do not change; according to Dalton, they just [2]rearrange/reproduce themselves. Dalton's basic ideas turned out to be correct, although scientists did not become sure that atoms existed until the twentieth century. It is not really surprising that it took so long to prove the existence of atoms. After all, they were far too small to be seen, even with the best microscopes. So all kinds of [3]experiences/experiments and analyses had to be brought together over a long period time before scientists knew the "atomic theory" was correct.

> Q. 밑줄 친 1 ~ 3)에서 문맥에 맞는 각 낱말은?
> 1) articles   rearrange   experiences
> 2) articles   reproduce   experiments
> 3) particles   reproduce   experiences
> 4) particles   rearrange   experiments
> 5) particles   reproduce   experiments

3. ①Kim used to _____ a wig when he went out in the evening. ②Shall I _____ the microwave? ③We're planning to _____ a concert to raise money for famine victims. ④I don't see why you have to _____ a phony English accent. ⑤She _____ a lot of weight after the children were born.

    Q. 빈칸에 공통으로 들어갈 구동사(phrasal verb)는?

4. There are many factors that can cause a plant or animal species to become endangered. The main cause of species endangerment is humanity's destruction of both aquatic and terrestrial habitats. Soil, air and water pollution, as well as deforestation, can all destroy a habitat. This can then cause a large number of plants or animals to die. Another cause of endangerment is exploitation of animals. Uncontrolled hunting of whales in the last century, for example, caused many whale species to become endangered. A third cause of endangerment is the _____ for animal parts for use in certain foods or medicines.

    Q. 빈칸에 들어갈 적절한 낱말은?
      1) threat   2) demand   3) purpose
      4) extinction   5) consumption

5. For hundreds of years scientists [1)]have debated the nature of light. After performing many experiments, Sir Isaac Newton decided that light must be made up of tiny particles. But a Dutch physicist, named Christian Huygens, thought that light behaves like waves on water [2)]and that it must consist of waves. Today we believe that Newton and Huygens were both right: light behaves like particles *and* like waves. When it travels, light acts like the wave you make when you toss a pebble into a pond. When it is being absorbed or [3)]given off by matter it acts like particles. We call particles of light "photons." But they shouldn't be thought of as little specks. Photons are packets of pure energy with no mass. You shouldn't think of light [4)]as changing from photon to wave and back again. Light always has the properties of both. If the double nature of light is hard to visualize, don't worry. It's so peculiar that everybody has trouble [5)]to picture it.

    Q. 밑줄 친 1)~5)중 어법에 맞지 않는 것은?

[명작 감상]　　　Hermann Hesse (1877 ~ 1962)

Demian 『데미안』

At times I was dissatisfied with myself and tortured with desire: I believed I could no longer bear to have her near me without taking her in my arms. She sensed this, too, at once. Once when I had stayed away for several days and returned bewildered she took me aside and said: "You must not give way to desires which you don't believe in. I know what you desire. You should, however, either be capable of renouncing these desires or feel wholly justified in having them. Once you are able to make your request in such a way that you will be quite certain of its fulfillment, then the fulfillment will come. But at present you alternate between desire and renunciation and are afraid all the time. All that must be overcome. Let me tell you a story."

And she told me about a youth who had fallen in love with a planet. He stood by the sea, stretched out his arms and prayed to the planet, dreamed of it, and directed all his thoughts to it. But he knew, or felt he knew, that a star cannot be embraced by a human being. He considered it to be his fate to love a heavenly body without any hope of fulfillment and out of this insight he constructed an entire philosophy of renunciation and silent, faithful suffering that would improve and purify him. Yet all his dreams reached the planet. Once he stood again on the high cliff at night and gazed at the planet and burned with love for it. And at the height of his longing he leaped into the emptiness toward the planet, but at the instant of leaping "it's impossible" flashed once more through his mind. There he lay on the shore, shattered. He had not understood how to love. If at the instant of leaping he had had the strength of faith in the fulfillment of his love he would have soared into the heights and been united with the star.

"Love must not entreat," she added, "or demand. Love must have the strength to become certain within itself. Then it ceases merely to be attracted and begins to attract. Sinclair, your love is attracted to me. Once it begins to attract me, I will come. I will not make a gift of myself, I must be won."

---

* Good medicine tastes bitter.　　좋은 약은 입에 쓰다.
* It is never too late to mend.　　허물을 고침에는 때가 따로 없다.

[확인 학습] 다음 문장을 우리말로 옮기세요.

1. Most of time you are unaware of what is happening in your body; usually it is only when you get sick or feel pain that you notice.

2. Quite apart, however, from all of these things, desirable as they are, is the pleasure of travel in itself. This is for some the main, and for others at least an important motive.

3. It is probably due in part to the fact that many houses are built and decorated by people unfamiliar with the habits of those for whom they are building.

4. He considered it to be his fate to love a heavenly body without any hope of fulfillment and out of this insight he constructed an entire philosophy of renunciation and silent, faithful suffering that would improve and purify him.

[words & phrases]

A1: opportunity 기회, exert 발휘하다, appreciate 인식하다, pursue 추구하다, keen 예리한/강렬한
A2: organize 조직하다, lack 부족(하다), contend 주장하다, interdependency 상호의존(성), by oneself 혼자서/외로이, entertain 마음에 품다, enterprise 사업/기업/진취성, core 핵심, assume 가정하다
A3: response 반응, diet 식품/음식, organ 장기/기관, digest 소화하다, frown 찡그리다, last 지속되다
A4: interfere with ~을 방해하다/간섭하다, preserve 보존하다, requisite 필요조건, indifference 무관심, origin 기원/근원, due to ~때문에, occupy 점령하다/차지하다, take ~ into account ~을 고려하다, suit 적합(하게)하다, consist in ~에 (놓여)있다, attempt 시도(하다), at the cost of ~을 희생시키고
B1: approval 찬성/승인, conservative 보수적인, peer 동료, diplomat 외교관, coincidence 우연의 일치
B2: element 요소/원소, substance 물질, figure out ~을 이해하다, be composed of ~로 구성되어 있다, particle 입자, arrange 배열하다, turn out ~임이 판명되다, microscope 현미경, analyze 분석하다
B3: wig 가발, kettle 솥, raise 모금하다, famine 기아/기근, victim 희생자, phony 가짜의/엉터리의
B4: factor 요인, aquatic 물의/수중의, terrestrial 지상의, habitat 서식지, exploit 착취하다/남획하다
B5: debate 토론(하다), experiment 실험(하다), behave 행동하다, consist of ~로 구성되어 있다, pebble 자갈/조약돌, absorb 흡수하다, speck 조각/파편, mass 질량, property 성질/특성, peculiar 독특한
C1: torture 고문(하다), bear 참다, bewilder 당혹케하다, give way to ~에 굴복하다, renounce 체념하다, justify 정당화하다, fulfill 성취하다, alternate 번갈아하다, overcome 이기다/극복하다, embrace 포옹하다/포용하다, fate 운명, heavenly body 천체, insight 통찰력, suffering 고통, cliff 절벽, long 갈망하다, leap 뛰다, shatter 부수다, soar 비상하다, entreat 간청하다, attract 끌다/매혹하다

[실력 점검 A] 다음 각 동사의 우리말 뜻을 쓰세요.

1. soar:

2. exert:

3. approve:

4. defer:

5. tempt:

6. embrace:

7. rebuke:

8. occupy:

9. negotiate:

10. shatter:

11. exploit:

12. encounter:

13. entreat:

14. modify:

15. contaminate:

16. declare:

17. contend:

18. accommodate:

19. restrain:

20. compromise:

[실력 점검 B] 각 항목에 대응하는 영어 단어를 찾아 쓰세요.

보기   insult, ceiling, torture, divorce, analysis, inherent, banquet, fertilizer, pursuit, famine, digestion, spectator, diplomat, obligation, modest, terrestrial, obscure, courteous, prestigious, disinterested

1. 이혼:

2. 기근:

3. 모욕:

4. 분석:

5. 소화:

6. 고문:

7. 천장:

8. 추구:

9. 연회:

10. 의무:

11. 비료:

12. 구경꾼:

13. 외교관:

14. 유명한:

15. 지상의:

16. 겸손한:

17. 희미한:

18. 본래의:

19. 사심 없는:

20. 예의 바른:

[실력 점검 C] 주어진 철자로 시작되는 적절한 낱말은?

1. I would like to get in t_____ with him as soon as possible.

2. At present, in the most c_____ countries, freedom of speech is taken as a matter of c_____ and seems a perfectly simple thing. We are so a_____ to it that we look upon it a_____ natural right. But this right has been acquired only in quite r_____ times, and the way to its attainment has l_____ through lakes of blood.

명시 감상

Tomorrow, and Tomorrow, and Tomorrow

William Shakespeare

Tomorrow, and tomorrow, and tomorrow,

Creeps in this petty pace from day to day,

To the last syllable of recorded time;

And all our yesterdays have lighted fools

The way to dusty death. Out, out, brief candle!

Life's but a walking shadow, a poor player

That struts and frets his hour upon the stage

And then is heard no more: it is a tale

Told by an idiot, full of sound and fury,

Signifying nothing.

— from *Macbeth*

* creep 기다, petty 사소한, syllable 음절, strut 활보하다, fret 안달하다, idiot 바보, fury 분노, signify 의미하다

Unit 12   지시사

A. 지시사의 품사

1) *This* is Mr. Smith. I know *that*. *Such* were the results.

2) I like *these* children. There were no computers *those* days.

3) Did he go to bed *this* early? It won't take *that* much time.

B. 지시사의 용법

1) Who is *this*, please? *This* is Lydia (speaking).

My sister makes a mistake, *and that* very often.

2) The weather of Seoul is milder than *that* of New York.

The girls in your class are prettier than *those* in my class.

3) *One who* is not diligent will never prosper.

Those who live in glass houses should not throw stones.

   * *Those present* were all surprised at the news.

4) She was *so* beautiful *that* he found it difficult to win her.

They have the eyes *so* located *as to* give panoramic vision.

I really enjoyed the movie, and *so* did my wife.

   * He is not interested in politics, and *neither* is his wife.

5) She was *such* a beautiful woman *that* he found it difficult to win her.

We have to sell the products in *such* a way *as to* make a profit.

She is really a good woman and is known *as such* to everyone.

I will plant flowers, *such as* roses, geraniums and sunflowers.

6) He has two sons; *one* is a doctor and *the othe*r is a schoolteacher.

Some students like football, and *others* like baseball.

   * Five of the books are mine; *the others* are my brother's.

   * To know is *one thing*, and to teach is *another*.

7) Of cows and pigs, *the former* seems more valuable than *the latter*.

   * Ability and industry are both necessary, but *this* often does more than *that*.

   * Vice and virtue are before you; *the one* leads you to peace and happiness,

   the other to misery and suffering.

[필수 문법] 지시사(demonstrative)

* 특정한 사람이나 사물 또는 특정 내용을 가리키는 기능을 하는 낱말.
* 그 담당하는 품사에 따라 지시 대명사, 지시 형용사, 지시 부사로 나뉜다.

A. 지시사의 품사

  1) 대명사: 주어, 목적어, 보어의 기능: Who's *this*? *This* is Tom (speaking).

  2) 형용사: 명사를 수식: I met him *this* morning. Who's *that* boy over there?

  3) 부사: 형용사/부사를 수식: It was about *this* high. He hasn't gone *that* far.

B. 지시사의 용법

  1) 전화/무선상의 주어 "this": 누구세요?(=Who's calling, please?), *This* is Radio K.

    ~, and that ~: "그것도/더구나": (내 누이는 실수를 한다, 그것도 아주 흔히.)

  2) 동일한 명사의 반복 사용을 피하기 위한 "that" (=the weather), "those" (=the girls).

  3) one who (=he who) ~하는 사람; those who ~하는 사람들 (스스로 흠이 있는 자들은 남을 평해서는 안된다.) * =*Those* (*who were*) *present* were all surprised at the news.

  4) "so ~ that ~"이나 "such ~ that ~"구문: 흔히 "너무나 ~해서 ~하다"로 번역되지만, 사실 지시부사 "so(그렇게)"나 지시형용사 "such(그러한)"는 that-절의 내용을 가리킴.

    "so ~ as to ~"나 "such ~ as to ~"구문: "so"나 "such"는 "as to ~"의 내용을 가리킴.

    "so+(조)동사+주어": (~역시/또한 그렇다): He has come and *so has his wife*.

    * 부정문에서는 "neither"를 사용함: I don't like him, and *neither does my friend*.

    A: He is looking forward to seeing them. B: *So is she*. (그녀 역시/또한 그렇다.)

    A: She is very kind and considerate. B: *So she is*. (그녀는 과연/정말 그렇다.)

  5) 지시사 "so"나 "such": that-절이나 "as to ~"의 내용을 가리킴: (=She was *so beautiful a woman* that he found ~.) (우리는 그 제품을 이익을 낼 그런 방식으로 팔아야 한다.)

    "as such": "그것으로서, 그 자체로서": (그러한 여인으로서 알려져 있다.)

    "such as ~": "가령 ~과 같은" : (=I will plant *such* flowers *as* roses, geraniums ~.)

    * You can use my car, *such as* it is. (제 차를 사용하세요, 변변치 않지만.)

  6) one ~, the other ~: (하나는 ~, 다른 하나는 ~): 둘 사이를 구분할 때 사용함.

    some ~, others ~: (몇몇은 ~, 나머지는 ~): 여럿을 둘로 구분할 때 사용함.

    * 한 쪽의 수가 확정되면, 다른 한 쪽의 수도 확정되므로 "*the* others"가 된다.

    * "아는 것과 가르치는 것은 별개의 문제." (=To know and to teach are *one thing another*.)

    It is *one thing* to play a computer game; quite *another* to understand how it works.

  7) the former (전자), the latter (후자): 소가 돼지보다 더 가치 있는 것 같다.

    * this (후자), that (전자): 후자(근면)가 흔히 전자(능력)보다 더 많은 것을 한다.

    * the one (전자/후자), the other (후자/전자): 글의 내용에 의해 전자/후자가 결정됨: 예문에서는 "the one"은 후자(virtue:미덕), "the other"은 전자(vice:악덕)를 가리킴.

[문법 연습 A]　잘못된 부분을 고치세요.

1. The boy raised his hands one after another.

2. I haven't seen him for a week, and so did she.

3. If you are allowed to go out, and so I should be.

4. Some were killed, and the others were captured.

5. One who my sister hates, my brother tends to like.

6. We were very nervous that we couldn't sleep at all.

7. The climate of Korea is a little different from Japan.

8. Three of the girls agreed with me, but others did not.

9. None of the two sisters was invited to the birthday party.

10. The book is such written as to give a wrong idea of the facts.

11. The population of South Korea is twice as large as North Korea.

12. The twins are so much alike that I can't tell the one from the other.

[문법 연습 B]　빈칸에 알맞은 낱말은?

1. Some say it is true, _____ not.

2. I don't like this tie; show me _____.

3. She is not _____ a fool as to believe it.

4. To say is one thing, and to do is quite _____.

5. It _____ happens that we have the same birthday.

6. The door was shut, and _____ were the windows.

7. He can't speak French, and _____ can his brother.

8. She was so fortunate _____ to pass the examination.

9. Children are easily influenced by _____ around them.

10. It is not an agreement as _____, but it will serve as one.

11. The temperature here is higher than _____ of San Francisco.

12. The ears of the rabbit are much longer than _____ of the dog.

13. Tom is _____ honest a student that his teacher is proud of him.

[실전 문법 A] 빈칸에 알맞은 낱말은?

1. Dinner's on the table, _____ as it is.

2. It is one thing to hear, and it is quite _____ to see.

3. _____ scientists as Newton are rare in human history.

4. Man is _____ made that he can't remember long without a symbol.

5. Their diet was _____ that they weren't getting the necessary vitamins.

6. It is said that his dress is _____ of a gentleman but his manners are _____ of a clown.

7. Both the mind and the body are important to human beings; _____ is concerned with their activity, and _____ is with their creativity.

8. Labor and temperance are the two best physicians; the _____ sharpens the appetite, and the _____ prevents indulgence to excess.

[실전 문법 B] 각 문항의 다섯 부분 중 어법에 맞지 않는 부분은?

1. [1]Most eagles have [2]so long, broad wings and tails [3]that they look clumsy [4]while they are [5]on the ground.

2. [1]The sun is too much hotter [2]than the earth [3]that matter can exist [4]only as a gas, [5]except at the solid core.

3. [1]Despite these similarities [2]with other creatures, [3]however, [4]the evolution of mankind [5]differs from other species.

4. [1]I have subscriptions [2]to two newspapers. [3]One is put out in the morning [4]and another is published [5]in the afternoon.

5. [1]She was very surprised [2]to find her brother in the club [3]that she had to hide [4]behind the curtain [5]lest he should see her.

6. [1]In any matter [2]which the public has imperfect knowledge, [3]public opinion is as likely to be erroneous [4]as is that of an individual [5]equally uninformed.

7. [1]The story of the city mouse [2]and the country mouse [3]is one version of the debate [4]between the people who prefer city life [5]and who prefer county life.

[필수 어휘 A] 밑줄 친 낱말의 뜻은?

1. We should underline{initiate} a direct talk with the trade union.

   1) try   2) start   3) reject   4) demand   5) postpone

2. She couldn't understand his refusal to underline{confront} reality.

   1) face   2) evade   3) accept   4) reform   5) overcome

3. I still remember in underline{minute} detail everything that happened.

   1) tiny   2) exact   3) trivial   4) specific   5) important

4. The police underline{maintained} that she acted alone in the shooting.

   1) found   2) proved   3) claimed   4) indicted   5) suspected

5. They wanted the foreign troops to underline{withdraw} from their country.

   1) retreat   2) outlive   3) protect   4) descend   5) separate

6. According to scientists, migratory birds can underline{withstand} the winter.

   1) avoid   2) resist   3) prepare   4) hibernate   5) undertake

7. He gave an underline{impartial} view of the state of affairs in the Middle East.

   1) absurd   2) hostile   3) neutral   4) friendly   5) coherent

8. He joined his hands together in Indian underline{fashion} and gave a little bow.

   1) spirit   2) vogue   3) manner   4) imitation   5) discipline

[필수 어휘 B] 밑줄 친 부분의 우리말 뜻은?

1. Fame or money counts for little.   _____

2. The maternal love came home to me.   _____

3. I suppose you two have a lot in common.   _____

4. She may get in the way of your ambitions.   _____

5. People tend to fall back on easier solutions.   _____

6. Don't have anything to do with those people.   _____

7. Please help yourself to the cake and the fruit.   _____

8. We think it difficult to make both ends meet.   _____

9. You must try to make the most of your ability.   _____

10. They'll have to make do with what they have.   _____

[구문 연습] 다음 문장을 우리말로 옮기세요.

1. Progress is the gradual result of the unending battle between human reason and human instinct, in which the former slowly but surely wins.

2. We have a firm belief that a natural diet, close to that eaten by primitive man, is likely to be most suitable for the human digestion.

3. Language is so much a part of our daily activities that we may come to look upon it as an automatic and natural act like winking and breathing.

4. No man, however well-informed, can come to such fullness of understanding as to safely judge and dismiss the customs or institutions of his society.

5. Actions speak more honestly than words; the inferences we draw from people's non-verbal behavior are more secure than those that we base upon what they say about themselves.

[작문 연습] 다음 문장을 영어로 옮기세요.

1. 좋아하는 것과 사랑하는 것은 아주 별개의 문제다.

_____

2. 한국의 문화적 전통은 일본이나 중국하고는 매우 다르다.

_____

3. 어떤 이들은 삶을 축복으로 여기고, 다른 이들은 저주로 여긴다.

_____

4. 그녀에 대한 그의 사랑은 거의 매일 그녀에게 편지를 쓸 정도였다.

_____

5. 전자를 숨기고 후자를 드러내어 과장하려는 널리 퍼진 음모가 있다.

_____

[실전 독해 A] 각 문항의 물음에 답하세요.

1. The efforts to make our environment free from pollution sometimes clash head on with other urgent problems. For instance, if a factory closes down because it cannot meet pollution standards of the government, a large number of workers suddenly find themselves without jobs. Questioning the quality of the air they breathe becomes less important than worrying about the next _____. Can you think of any ways to resolve this? I hope you will suggest some practical and applicable methods to get out of this hard situation.

> Q. 빈칸에 들어갈 적절한 낱말은?
> 1) priority   2) solution   3) paycheck
> 4) generation   5) opportunity

2. You need stress in your life! Without stress, life would be dull and unexciting. Stress adds flavor, challenge, and opportunity to life. Too much stress, of course, can have a serious effect on your mental and physical well-being. A major challenge in this complex world of today is to learn how to [a]_____ stress so that it does not become too much. You may think of major crises such as natural disasters, war and death as main sources of stress. On a day-to-day basis, however, it is the small things that cause stress: waiting in line, having car trouble, getting stuck in a traffic jam, or having too many things to do in a limited time. In fact, stress is so personal to each of us that what may be relaxing to one person may be stressful to another. For example, if you are an executive who likes to keep busy all the time, "taking it easy" at the beach on a beautiful day may feel extremely frustrating, non-productive, and upsetting. That is to say, you may be emotionally distressed from [b]_____.

> Q 1. 빈칸 a)에 들어갈 적절한 말은?
> 1) cope with   2) think over   3) come about
> 4) take advantage of   5) make the best of

> 2. 빈칸 b)에 들어갈 적절한 말은?
> 1) working hard   2) spending money
> 3) doing nothing   4) wasting time on trifles
> 5) getting together for a party

3. Botany, the study of plants, occupies a peculiar position in the history of human knowledge. ① It is almost impossible to know today just what our Stone Age ancestors knew about plants, but judging from what we can observe of preindustrial societies that still exist, a detailed learning of plants and their properties must be extremely ancient. ② Plants are the basis of the food pyramid for all living things, even for other plants. ③ They have always enormously important to the welfare of people, not only for food, but also for shelter, clothing, dyes, tools, weapons, medicines, and many other purposes. ④ Tribes living today in the jungles of the Amazon recognize literally hundreds of plants and know many properties of each. ⑤ Unfortunately, the more industrialized we become the farther we move from direct contact with plants, and the _____ distinct our knowledge of botany grows.

Q 1. 빈칸에 들어갈 적절한 낱말은?

2. ①~⑤중 다음 문장이 삽입되기에 적절한 곳은?
This is logical.

4. Architecture is an art and any art must give us pleasure, or else is bad art, or we are abnormally blind. We are in general too hardened and insensitive to architecture as an art and to the joy it may bring to us.

ⓐ This false doctrine has strengthened in us until our eyes are dulled and our minds are deadened to all the fine deep pleasure that we might otherwise experience from our ordinary surroundings.

ⓑ Therefore we think architecture as some vague, learned thing dealing with French cathedrals or Italian palaces or Greek temples, not with New York or Chicago streets or Los Angeles suburbs.

ⓒ It is the constant nearness of architecture that has blinded us in this way. We forget that it is an art of here and now, because it is with us every day, and because we must have houses to live in we are apt to think of them solely as abiding places.

Q. ⓐ~ⓒ의 글을 문맥에 맞게 배열하면?
  1) ⓐ-ⓒ-ⓑ   2) ⓑ-ⓐ-ⓒ   3) ⓑ-ⓒ-ⓐ
  4) ⓒ-ⓐ-ⓑ   5) ⓒ-ⓑ-ⓐ

[실전 독해 B] 각 문항의 물음에 답하세요.

1.   No doubt some men are much more gifted than others. But let two men start in life; the one with brilliant abilities, but idle, careless, and self-indulgent; the other comparatively slow, but careful, diligent, and high-principled, and he will in time distance his brilliant competitor. Labor without genius will do more in the long run than genius without labor. No cleverness, no advantage in life, no rich friend or powerful relations will make up for the want of _____ and character.

   Q 1. 빈칸에 들어갈 낱말은?
       1) talent   2) industry   3) aptitude
       4) ambition   5) personality

2.   Demades, the Athenian, condemned a man of his city whose trade was to sell what is needed for funerals, on the ground that he asked too high a profit, and that he could only make this profit by the death of a great many people. This seems ill-reasoned judgment, since no profit can be made except at another's expense, and so by this rule we should have to condemn every sort of gain.

   The merchant thrives on the ^{a)}_____ of youth; the farmer on the high price of ^{b)}_____; the architect on the ^{c)}_____ of houses; the offices of the law on men's ^{d)}_____ and contentions; even the honor ant practice of ministers of religion depend on our ^{e)}_____ and our deaths. No physician takes pleasure in the ^{f)}_____ even of his friends, says an ancient Greek comedy-writer, no soldier in the ^{g)}_____ of his city, and so on. And what is worse, let anyone search his heart and he will find that our inward ^{h)}_____ are for the most part born and nourished at the ⁱ⁾_____ of others. One man's profit is another's loss.

   As I was reflecting on this, the fancy came to me that here nature is merely following her habitual policy. Natural scientists hold that the birth, nourishment and growth of each thing mean the change and decay of something else.

   Q. 빈칸 a)~i)에 들어갈 각 낱말의 번호는?
       1) cost   2) grain   3) health   4) collapse
       5) suits   6) vices   7) peace   8) diseases
       9) wishes   10) extravagance

3.   Man is an animal, and his happiness depends on his [1]physiology more than he likes to think. This is a humble conclusion, but I cannot make myself [2]believe it. Unhappy businessmen, I am convinced, [3]would increase their happiness more by walking six miles every day than by any conceivable change of philosophy. This, [4]incidentally, was the opinion of Thomas Jefferson, who on this ground deplored the horse. Language would have [5]failed him if he could have foreseen the motor-car.

　　Q. 밑줄 친 1)～5)중 그 쓰임이 잘못된 것은?

4.   When we speak of values or value orientations, our focus should always be on cultures, not on nations. A nation is a political entity which may contain within it many quite different cultures; ＿＿＿＿＿＿, national borders may politically distinguish areas which are culturally identical. The lines drawn in Europe during the 19th century slicing up Africa into European colonies produced some nations which contain many different cultures, and cruelly divided unified cultures into separate nations. Within the United States, we may say there are different cultures or, as is more commonly said, different subcultures.

　　Q. 빈칸에 들어갈 적절한 낱말은?
　　　1) however　　2) therefore　　3) similarly
　　　4) consequently　　5) nevertheless

5.   After I was married and had lived in Japan for a while, my Japanese gradually improved to the point [1]where I could take part in simple conversations with my husband and his friends and family. And I began to notice that often, when I joined in, [2]the others would look startled, and the conversational topic would come to a halt. After this happened several times, [3]it became clear to me that I was doing something wrong. But for a long time, I didn't know what it was. Finally, [4]after listening carefully to many conversations, I discovered [5]what was my problem. Even if I was speaking Japanese, I was handling the conversation in a Western way.

　　Q. 밑줄 친 1)～5)중 어법에 맞지 않는 것은?

[명작 감상]   Ralph Waldo Emerson (1803 ~ 1882)
Farming

The glory of the farmer is that, in the division of labors, it is his part to create. All trade rests at last on his primitive activity. He stands close to Nature; he obtains from the earth the bread and the meat. The food which was not, he causes to be. The first farmer was the first man, and all historic nobility rests on possession and use of land. Men do not like hard work, but every man has an exceptional respect for tillage, and a feeling that this is the original calling of his race, that he himself is only excused from it by some circumstance which made him delegate it for a time to other hands. If he has not some skill which recommends him to the farmer, some product for which the farmer will give him corn, he must himself return into his due place among the planters. The profession has in all eyes its ancient charm, as standing nearest to God, the first cause.

Then the beauty of Nature, the tranquility and innocence of the countryman, his independence and his pleasing arts,—the care of bees, of poultry, of sheep, of cow, the dairy, the care of hay, of fruits, of orchards and forests, and the reaction of these on the workman, in giving him a strength and plain dignity like the face and manners of Nature,—all men acknowledge. All men keep the farm in reserve as an asylum where, in case of mischance, to hide their poverty,—or a solitude, if they do not succeed in society. And who knows how many glances of remorse are turned this way from the bankrupts of trade, from mortified pleaders in courts and senates, or from the victims of idleness and pleasure? Poisoned by town life and town vices, the sufferer resolves: "Well, my children, whom I have injured, shall go back to the land, to be recruited and cured by that which should have been my nursery, and now shall be their hospital."

The farmer's office is precise and important, but you must not try to paint him in rose-color; you cannot make pretty compliments to fate and gravitation, whose minister he is. He represents the necessities. It is the beauty of the great economy of the world that makes his comeliness. He bends to the order of the seasons, the weather, the soils and crops, as the sails of a ship bend to the wind. He represents continuous hard labor, year in, year out, and small gains. He is a slow person, timed to Nature, and not to city watches.

[확인 학습] 다음 문장을 우리말로 옮기세요.

1. Unfortunately, the more industrialized we become the farther we move from direct contact with plants, and the less distinct our knowledge of botany grows.

2. This false doctrine has strengthened in us until our eyes are dulled and our minds are deadened to all the fine deep pleasure that we might otherwise experience from our ordinary surroundings.

3. Every man has an exceptional respect for tillage, and a feeling that this is the original calling of his race, that he himself is only excused from it by some circumstance which made him delegate it for a time to other hands.

4. If he has not some skill which recommends him to the farmer, some product for which the farmer will give him corn, he must himself return into his due place among the planters.

[words & phrases]

A1: effort 노력, urgent 긴급한/위급한, meet 충족시키다, resolve 해결하다, applicable 적용할 수 있는

A2: flavor 맛/풍미, crisis 위기, disaster 재해, executive 임원, frustrate 좌절시키다, distress 괴롭히다

A3: botany 식물학, ancestor 조상/선조, property 특성, dye 염료/염색, tribe 부족/종족, logical 논리적

A4: architecture 건축, be apt to (do) ~ 경향이 있다, abide 체류하다, vague 모호한, learned 학문적인, cathedral 성당, temple 절/사원, suburbs 교외/근교, doctrine 주의/원칙, otherwise 그렇지 않더라면

B1: gift (타고난) 재능, indulgent 방종한, distance 앞지르다, relation 친족/친척, make up for 보충하다

B2: condemn 비난하다, funeral 장례식, profit 이익, reason 사유하다, at one's expense ~을 희생시키고, thrive 번창하다, architect 건축가, contend 다투다/주장하다, physician 내과의사, nourish 기르다, reflect on ~을 반성하다/숙고하다, habitual 습관적인, hold 생각하다/주장하다, decay 부패(하다)

B3: physiology 생리학/생리현상, conceive 품다/생각하다, incidentally 첨언하면, deplore 개탄하다

B4: orientation 방침/지향, entity 실체, border 경계, identical 동일한, colony 식민지, unify 통합하다

B5: improve 개선하다/향상되다, startle 놀라게 하다, halt 멈춤/멈추다, even if~ 비록 ~일지라도

C1: rest on ~에 의존하다, primitive 원시적, nobility 귀족, obtain 얻다, till 경작하다, calling 직업, excuse 용서하다/면제하다, delegate 대의원/위임하다, recommend 추천하다, due 마땅한, cause 원인/대의, tranquil 고요한, poultry 가금, dairy 낙농업, orchard 과수원, dignity 존엄성, acknowledge 인정하다, reserve 예비/준비, asylum 은신처/피난처, mischance 불운, remorse 후회, bankrupt 파산한/파산자, mortify 굴욕감을 느끼게 하다, plead 탄원하다/간청하다, senate 의회, vice 악덕, resolve 결심하다, recruit 보충하다/보양하다, nursery 육아실/양성소, office 일/직분, compliment 찬사, gravitation 중력, minister 성직자/대행자, necessities 생필품, comely 어여쁜/아름다운, soil 토양, crop 농작물

[실력 점검 A] 다음 각 동사의 우리말 뜻을 쓰세요.

1. deter: 2. hover: 3. vomit:

4. retain: 5. thrive: 6. discard:

7. startle: 8. recruit: 9. execute:

10. assert: 11. irritate: 12. frustrate:

13. nourish: 14. explode: 15. overwhelm:

16. conceive: 17. overcome: 18. manufacture:

19. recommend: 20. acknowledge:

[실력 점검 B] 각 항목에 대응하는 영어 단어를 찾아 쓰세요.

보기   spouse, violence, mammal, heritage, pressure, incident, precaution, tension, capacity, prosperity, candidate, offspring, preference, destination, alert, innate, fortune, rational, desperate, exclusive

1. 압력: 2. 폭력: 3. 능력:

4. 자손: 5. 번영: 6. 선호:

7. 유산: 8. 긴장: 9. 예방책:

10. 재산: 11. 사건: 12. 후보자:

13. 목적지: 14. 배우자: 15. 포유류:

16. 내재적인: 17. 합리적인: 18. 독점적인:

19. 절망적인: 20. 방심 않는:

[실력 점검 C] 빈칸에 들어갈 적절한 낱말은?

1. Every problem can be studied as _____ with an open and empty mind, without prejudice, without knowing _____ has been learned about it.

2. Here is a story about four people named Everybody, Somebody, Anybody and Nobody: There was an important job to be done and Everybody was sure that _____ would do it. _____ could have done it, but _____ did it. _____ got angry about that, because it was _____'s job. He or she didn't know that "Everybody's business is _____'s business."

명시 감상

Leisure

W. H. Davies

What is this life if, full of care,
We have no time to stand and stare.

No time to stand beneath the boughs
And stare as long as sheep or cows.

No time to see, when woods we pass,
Where squirrels hide their nuts in grass.

No time to turn at Beauty's glance,
And watch her feet, how they dance.

No time to wait till her mouth can
Enrich that smile her eyes began.

A poor life this if, full of care,
We have no time to stand and stare.

* leisure 여유/여가, stare 응시하다, bough 큰 나무 가지, squirrel 다람쥐, glance 일견/눈짓, enrich 풍요롭게 하다

Unit 13 태

A. 태의 전환

1) He *reads* the book.   The book *is read* by him.

   He *read* the book.   The book *was read* by him.

   He *will read* the book.   The book *will be read* by him.

2) She *has read* the book.   The book *has been read* by her.

   She *is reading* the book.   The book *is being read* by her.

   She *has been reading* the book. The book *has been being read* by her.

B. 수동태의 유형

1) He told *me a story*.   *I* was told a story by him.

   She gave *me the money*.   *The money* was given (to) me by her.

2) *We* called him Johnny.   He was called Johnny (*by us*).

   They speak English in India.   English is spoken in India (*by them*).

3) We saw her *meet* the man.   She was seen *to meet* the man (by us).

   He made me *do* the work.   I was made *to do* the work by him.

4) She must *take care of* him.   He must *be taken care of* by her.

   They *speak well of* the boy.   The boy *is well spoken of* (by them).

5) *Open* the window.   *Let* the window *be opened*.

   Don't open the window.   Don't *let* the window *be opened*.

6) *Who* invented the machine?   *By whom* was the machine invented?

   Have *you* paid for the book?   Has *the book* been paid for (by you)?

7) *They say* that he is honest.   *It is said* that he is honest.

   They said that he was honest.   *He was said* to be honest.

C. 기타 수동태

1) The fence *is made of* wood.   Wine *is made from* grapes.

2) He *is known to* the people.   A man *is known by* his friends.

3) I *am tired from* walking.   I *am tired of* quarreling with you.

[필수 문법] 태(voice)

* 동사의 형태가 나타내는 주어와 동사 사이의 행위 관계의 방향성.
* 능동태(active)와 수동태(passive)로 구분되며, 수동태는 (술어)동사가
  "be동사+과거분사"의 형태로 나타나는 것이 그 특징이다.

A. 태의 전환
  1) 능동태의 목적어가 수동태의 주어가 되며, 능동태의 주어는 "by+목적격"으로
     변환되어 수동태의 "be동사+과거분사" 다음에 놓인다. * 목적어를 수반하는
     (술어) 동사라 하더라도 have/lack/resemble 등의 동사는 수동태로 전환될 수 없음.
  2) 완료형의 수동태: 능동태의 (술어)동사가 "have been +과거분사"로 변환된다.
     진행형의 수동태: 능동태의 (술어)동사가 "be being +과거분사"로 변환된다.
     완료 진행형의 수동태: 능동태의 (술어)동사가 "have been being +과거분사"로 변환됨.

B. 수동태의 유형
  1) 2개의 목적어(간접목적어+직접목적어)를 가지는 동사는 원칙적으로 2개의 수동태:
     (=A story was told (to) me by him.) (=I was given the money by her.) *그러나 유의할 점은,
     buy/make/write/sell/send/sing 등의 동사의 경우에는 직접목적어만이 수동태의 주어가
     될 수 있음: "He bought her a doll."의 경우, "A doll was bought (for) her by him."만 성립
     가능하며, "She was bought a doll by him."의 문장은 성립되지 않음에 유의할 것.
  2) 능동태의 일반주어(we/you/they)에서 변환된 수동태의 "by us/you/them"은 생략됨.
  3) 지각동사/사역동사에 수반된 원형 부정사는 수동태에서는 to-부정사로 변환된다.
  4) 동사구/구동사는 한 묶음으로 취급되지만, "She took good care of him."의 경우에는,
     "He was *taken good care of* by her."와 "*Good care* was taken of him by her." 둘 다 가능.
  5) 명령문의 수동태는 "let"동사를 이용한다: "*Let* the window *not* be opened."도 가능함.
  6) 의문문이 수동태가 되면, 문장의 주어는 (첫)조동사와 과거분사 사이에 놓인다.
  7) "They say/said that ~"의 구문은, 2개의 수동태가 가능하며, "by them"은 생략된다:
     * They *say* that he *was* rich. → It *is* said that he *was* rich. He *is* said *to have been* rich.

C. 기타 수동태
  1) be made of ~: 물리적(형태) 변화의 경우,   be made from ~: 화학적(성질) 변화의 경우
  2) be known to ~: ~에게 알려지다(정보/면식),   be known by ~: ~으로 식별되다(판단)
  3) be tired from ~: ~에 지치다 (육체적 피로),   be tired of ~: ~에 싫증나다 (정신적 피로)
     be interested in ~에 관심을 갖다, 흥미를 느끼다,   be covered with ~으로 덮여 있다
     be satisfied(=contented) with ~에 만족하다,   be pleased with ~에 기뻐하다/즐거워하다
     be surprised/amazed/astonished/astounded/frightened/startled at ~에 놀라다 (= marvel at ~)

[문법 연습 A] 수동태 문장으로 고치세요.

1. We heard the woman call her daughter.

_____

2. What do you call this flower in English?

_____

3. No one has ever answered such a serious question.

_____

4. The government paid no attention to pre-school education.

1) _____

2) _____

5. They said that he would arrive in Seoul at ten in the morning.

1) _____

2) _____

6. Nobody believes that she was accused of assault and battery.

1) _____

2) _____

[문법 연습 B] 각 문장의 빈칸에 알맞은 전치사를 쓰세요.

1. Bread is made _____ flour.

2. The wall is built _____ stones.

3. He is known _____ his novels.

4. A tree is known _____ its fruit.

5. Amy was engaged _____ Tim.

6. John is engaged _____ business.

7. She is possessed _____ jewels.

8. He is possessed _____ prejudice.

9. Coal was replaced _____ oil.

10. Oil was substituted _____ coal.

11. Water is frozen _____ ice.

12. I am contented _____ the result.

13. It is divided _____ two parts.

14. He was sentenced _____ death.

15. Paul was deprived _____ sight.

16. She was robbed _____ her purse.

17. He is absorbed _____ the book.

18. I was informed _____ his arrival.

19. She is faced _____ bankruptcy.

20. The hall is crowded _____ guests.

[실전 문법 A] 각 문항의 바른 문장은?

1. 1) He is much resembled by his son.

   2) No notice was taken of what he said.

   3) The singer is well known by teenagers.

   4) They are said to stay at the hotel yesterday.

   5) It was resulted from some misunderstanding.

2. 1) Let it be not regarded as a matter of course.

   2) His warnings were not listened by anybody.

   3) The woman is spoken ill of by her neighbors.

   4) The general is reported to be killed in the war.

   5) She was often made a fool of by her classmates.

[실전 문법 B] 각 문항의 다섯 부분 중 어법에 맞지 않는 부분은?

1. [1]To rank as a masterpiece, [2]a work of art must transcend [3]the ideals of the period [4]in which [5]it was created.

2. [1]Acupuncture therapy is becoming [2]widely accepted [3]in many countries, [4]though it once considered [5]a primitive kind of treatment.

3. [1]Opportunity is the only thing [2]we may give [3]to the young, [4]and it has to be sought diligently [5]and even to create.

4. [1]Thanks to [2]the newly invented vaccine, [3]the liver disease [4]has now been disappeared [5]in almost all continents of the world.

5. [1]When we got to the restaurant, [2]we told that there would be [3]thirty-minute wait, [4]and so we headed [5]for another place.

6. [1]The students offered [2]a small box of chocolates [3]instead of cash [4]as payment for their participation [5]in a marketing survey.

7. [1]A man asking to define [2]the essential characteristics of a gentleman [3]would presumably reply: [4]the horror of forcing others into positions [5]from which he himself would draw back.

[필수 어휘 A] 밑줄 친 부분과 그 뜻이 비슷한 것은?

1. They <u>deal</u> in rice, fish, meat, fruits and vegetables.

 1) reap   2) trade   3) produce   4) exchange   5) cultivate

2. He kept on nagging until I couldn't <u>stand</u> it any longer.

 1) bear   2) deny   3) accept   4) deserve   5) stimulate

3. The explosion in the mine could have a terrible <u>consequence</u>.

 1) fate   2) result   3) purpose   4) disaster   5) obstacle

4. Their contribution to the project was relatively <u>insignificant</u>.

 1) rare   2) stable   3) infinite   4) enormous   5) negligible

5. All the children <u>made off</u> at the sight of the old, weird man.

 1) fled   2) stared   3) laughed   4) vanished   5) marveled

6. Exhausted, she checked her watch and decided to <u>call it a day</u>.

 1) stop   2) leave   3) repair   4) cancel   5) postpone

7. She <u>made up her mind</u> to leave Seoul and live in the countryside.

 1) cared   2) strove   3) longed   4) resolved   5) intended

8. The pasture <u>runs out of</u> the most nutritious plants for cows and goats.

 1) grows   2) contains   3) exhausts   4) reduces   5) devastates

[필수 어휘 B] 밑줄 친 부분을 주어진 철자로 시작되는 낱말로 대체하세요.

1. We will have to <u>make up</u> for their loss.   c _____

2. All substances are <u>made up</u> of molecules.   c _____

3. I can't <u>put up with</u> your rudeness any more.   t _____

4. When in Seoul, we <u>put up</u> at a youth hostel.   s _____

5. She <u>set about</u> cleaning and sweeping the house.   s _____

6. They may have broken the window <u>on purpose</u>.   i _____

7. The theater was closed down <u>for good (and all)</u>.   f _____

8. The girls visited the orphanage <u>from time to time</u>.   o _____

9. Don't you know it's raining <u>cats and dogs</u> outside?   h _____

[구문 연습] 다음 문장을 우리말로 옮기세요.

1. Life and books must be shaken and taken in right proportions. A boy brought up alone in a library turns into a bookworm; brought up alone in the fields, he turns into an earthworm.

2. The microscope has been rapidly perfected since the introduction of better kinds of lenses early in the nineteenth century, so that it is now possible to magnify minute objects to more than two thousand times their diameters.

3. The meaning of life in the West has ceased to be seen as anything more lofty than the "pursuit of happiness," a goal that has been solemnly guaranteed by constitutions.

4. If you are interested in the things you are doing, it is not because you were born with a natural interest for that particular kinds of things, but because you have learned to be interested in doing them.

[작문 연습] 다음 문장을 영어로 옮기세요.

1. 그 은행은 간밤에 수십만 달러를 강탈 당했다.

2. 집에 오는 길에 나는 소나기를 만나 흠뻑 젖었다.

3. 저질러진 일은 결코 되돌릴 수 없다는 것을 모르니?

4. 그의 삼촌은 한국 동란 중에 행방불명이 되었다고 한다.

5. 그 강아지는 바로 옆집 이웃에 의해 잘 보살펴지고 있었다.

[실전독해 A] 각 문항의 물음에 답하세요.

1. In many Middle Eastern countries, cleanliness has religious overtones that link spiritual and physical purification. The Jewish people have many religious laws relating to hygiene, both personal and in preparation of food. Muslims, too, live by some very strict rules related to cleanliness. ^{a)}_____, they are required to wash certain parts of their bodies, such as their feet and hands, before they pray. For them, baths are a sort of ritual, a major affair that takes longer than an hour. Bathing begins with a steam, followed by rubbing the body with a hard towel, then soaping and rinsing. People usually want to lie down after a bath. Since it takes so long and is so exhausting, they indulge in baths once a week. And they believe daily washing dries out the skin and hair, ^{b)}_____ is actually true.

Q 1. 빈칸 a)에 들어갈 적절한 말은?
1) Moreover   2) Therefore   3) Of course
4) In addition   5) For example

2. 빈칸 b)에 들어갈 적절한 낱말은?

2. Teaching is supposed to be a professional activity requiring long and complicated training as well as official certification. However, teaching need not be the province of a special group of people nor need it be looked upon as a technical skill. Teaching can be more like guiding and assisting than forcing information into a supposedly empty head. If you have a certain skill you should be able to share it with someone. You do not have to get certified to convey what you know to someone else or to help them in their attempt to teach themselves. All of us, from the very youngest children to the oldest members of our cultures, should come to realize our own potential as teachers. We can share what we know, however little it might be, with someone who needs that knowledge or skill.

Q. 이 글의 요지는?
1) Teaching is like guiding and assisting.
2) It is not difficult to be a good teacher.
3) Teaching is not a professional activity.
4) Every person has the potential to be a teacher.
5) We need some skill or knowledge to teach others.

3.   Science seeks to explain the endlessly diverse phenomena of nature by ignoring the uniqueness of particular events, concentrating on what they have in common and finally abstracting some kind of "law," in terms of which they make sense and can be effectively dealt with. Science may thus be defined as the reduction of multiplicity to _____ :

Q. 빈칸에 들어갈 적절한 낱말은?
   1) unity   2) theory   3) analysis
   4) creativity   5) classification

4.   The first thing that a teacher should endeavor to produce in his students is, if democracy is to survive, the kind of tolerance which springs from an effort to understand those who are different from ourselves. It is perhaps a natural human impulse to view with _____ all manners and customs different from those which we are accustomed to.

Q. 빈칸에 들어갈 적절한 말은?
   1) envy and pride   2) horror and disgust
   3) interest and concern   4) sense and sensibility
   5) hostility and hospitality

5.   [1]The hurricane that hits the coast starts as an innocent circling disturbance hundreds—even thousands—of miles out to sea, traveling aimlessly over water warmed by the summer sun and carried westward by the trade winds. [2]The average life of a hurricane is only about nine days, but it contains almost more power than we can imagine. [3]The energy in the heat released by a hurricane's rainfall in a single day would satisfy the entire electrical needs of the United States for more than six months. [4]Water, not wind, is the main source of death and destruction in a hurricane; a typical hurricane brings 6- to 12-inch downpours resulting in sudden floods. [5]Worst of all is the powerful movement of the sea—the mountains of water moving toward the low-pressure center of the hurricane; the water level rises as much as 15 feet above normal as it moves toward shore.

Q. 1)~5)의 문장 중 글의 전체적인 흐름에 맞지 않는 것은?

[실전 독해 B] 각 문항의 물음에 답하세요.

1. (A) Pockets are what women need more of. It is always dangerous to generalize, but it seems quite safe to say that, on the whole, the men of the world, at any given time, are carrying about a much greater number of pockets than ^{a)} _____ the women of the world, and that the "pockety" men enjoy more power and wealth than the "pocketless" women ^{b)}_____.

(B) No one has investigated the role that pockets have played in preventing women from attaining the social status and rights that could and should be theirs. ① Consider your average woman dressed for office work; if she is wearing a dress or skirt and blouse, she is probably wearing zero pockets, or one or two at most. ② And consider your average successful executive; how many pockets does he wear to work? ③ His pockets are for carrying money, credit cards, identification, important messages, pens, keys, and an impressive-looking handkerchief. ④ And held close to the body. Easily available. Neatly classified. Pen in the inside coat pocket. Keys in the back left trouser pocket. ⑤ Efficiency. Order. Confidence.

(C) What does a woman have to match this organization? A purse? Even a large purse is no match for a suitful of pockets. If the woman carrying a purse is so lucky as to get an important phone number or market tip from the executive with whom she is lunching, can she write it down? Can she find her pen? Perhaps she can, but it will probably be buried under three old grocery lists, two combs, cosmetics, a checkbook, and a wad of Kleenex. The executive could have whipped his pen in and out of his pocket and written ten important messages on the table napkin in the time she is still digging and searching, like a busy little prairie dog, for her pen. What can a pocketless woman do?

Q 1. (A)글의 빈칸 a), b)에 들어갈 각각의 낱말은?

2. (B)글의 ①~⑤중 다음 문장이 삽입되기에 적절한 곳은?
All the equipment essential to running the world.

3. (A)~(C)의 글을 문맥에 맞게 배열하면?
1) (A)-(C)-(B)   2) (B)-(A)-(C)   3) (B)-(C)-(A)
4) (C)-(A)-(B)   5) (C)-(B)-(A)

2. ①The journey will _____ us about a week. ②It may _____ a lot of courage to admit your mistake. ③You will have to _____ the boxes to the office this weekend. ④They wanted him to _____ her advice and see a doctor. ⑤If we _____ wage-earning as a whole, then women come a long way below average.

    Q. ①~⑤의 문장의 빈칸에 공통으로 들어갈 낱말은?

3. "Consider the lilies of the field; they toil not, neither do they spin: yet Solomon in all his glory was not arrayed like one of these." But I think that if anybody thinks a lily achieves full lilyhood without the most extraordinary application of effort and ingenuity, he had better take a first-year course in botany. The lily is a natural *Oxonian*: it presents a fragile and exquisite appearance on the surface, and underground it is working furiously.

    Q. 이 글에서 "Oxonian"이 의미하는 것은?
      1) 지혜로운 식물   2) 흔하지만 특이한 식물
      3) 독창적인 예술가   4) 부단히 노력하는 존재
      5) 연약하지만 강인한 존재

4. One of the biggest differences among many Western, Asian, and African cultures 1)is the use of eye contact. In the United States, people make eye contact when they talk to others. If a person avoids eye contact, others might think they are being dishonest or that they lack confidence. If two people 2)are having a conversation and the listener is not making eye contact, the speaker may think that the listener 3)is not interesting. In many Asian cultures, however, making direct eye contact with someone is considered bold or aggressive. In many African cultures, making direct eye contact 4)with an older person or a person of higher social rank or status is often considered rude and disrespectful. In many Asian and African cultures, children are taught to lower their eyes 5)when talking to their elders, or those of higher rank, as a way to show respect.

    Q. 밑줄 친 1)~5)중 어법에 맞지 않는 것은?

[명작 감상]   Nathaniel Hawthorne (1804 ~ 1864)
              The Scarlet Letter   주홍 글자

When the young woman—the mother of this child—stood fully revealed before the crowd, it seemed to be her first impulse to clasp the infant closely to her bosom; not so much by an impulse of motherly affection, as that she might thereby conceal a certain token, which was wrought or fastened into her dress. In a moment, however, wisely judging that one token of her shame would but poorly serve to hide another, she took the baby on her arm, and, with a burning blush, and yet a haughty smile, and a glance that would not be abashed, looked around at her townspeople and neighbors. On the breast of her gown, in fine cloth surrounded with an elaborate embroidery and fantastic flourishes of gold thread, appeared the letter "A." It was so artistically done, and with so much fertility and gorgeous luxuriance of fancy, that it had all the effect of a last and fitting decoration to the apparel which she wore; and which was of a splendor in accordance with the taste of the age, but greatly beyond what was allowed by the sumptuary regulations of the colony.

The young woman was tall, with a figure of perfect elegance on a large scale. She had dark and abundant hair, so glossy that it threw off the sunshine with a gleam, and a face which, besides being beautiful from regularity of feature and richness of complexion, had the impressiveness belonging to a marked brow and deep black eyes. She was ladylike, too, after the manner of the feminine gentility of those days; characterized by a certain state and dignity, rather than by the delicate, evanescent, and indescribable grace, which is now recognized as its indication. And never had Hester Prynne appeared more ladylike, in the antique interpretation of the term, than as she issued from the prison. Those who had before known her and had expected to behold her dimmed and obscured by a disastrous cloud, were astonished, and even startled, to perceive how her beauty shone out and made a halo of the misfortune and ignominy in which she was enveloped. It may be true that, to a sensitive observer, there was something exquisitely painful in it.

---

* 이 소설의 제목은 "주홍 글씨"로 널리 알려져 있지만, 여기에서는 "주홍 글자"로 옮겨본다. 여주인공 Hester Prynne이 정성스럽게 예쁜 수를 놓아 자신의 앞가슴에 달고 있는 문자 "A"는 "adultery(간통)" 또는 "adulteress(간통한 여인)"의 첫머리 글자를 의미하기 때문이다.

[확인 학습] 다음 문장을 우리말로 옮기세요.

1. No one has investigated the role that pockets have played in preventing women from attaining the social status and rights that could and should be theirs.

2. Science seeks to explain the endlessly diverse phenomena of nature by ignoring the uniqueness of particular events, concentrating on what they have in common and finally abstracting some kind of "law."

3. Never had Hester Prynne appeared more ladylike, in the antique interpretation of the term, than as she issued from the prison.

4. It seemed to be her first impulse to clasp the infant closely to her bosom; not so much by an impulse of motherly affection, as that she might thereby conceal a certain token, which was wrought or fastened into her dress.

[words & phrases]

A1: overtone 함축/의미, purify 정화하다, hygiene 위생(학), ritual 의식/의례, indulge in ~에 탐닉하다

A2: suppose 추측하다, complicated 복잡한, certify 증명하다, province 영역, look upon ~ as ~을 ~로 여기다, force 강요하다, convey 전달하다, attempt 시도(하다), potential 잠재력/잠재적인

A3: phenomenon 현상, ignore 무시하다, have ~ in common ~을 공유하다, abstract 추상하다/요약하다, in term of ~의 견지에서, make sense 이해되다, deal with ~을 다루다, reduce 줄이다/바꾸다/옮기다

A4: endeavor 애쓰다/노력하다, tolerance 관용, spring 샘/샘솟다, impulse 충동, accustomed 익숙한

A5: disturb 교란하다, aim 목적/목표, the trade wind 무역풍, contain 담다, flood 홍수, pressure 압력

B1: generalize 일반화하다, match 상대/적수, grocery 식료품, comb 빗, cosmetic 화장품, whip 채찍/휘두르다, investigate 조사하다, role 역할, at most 기껏해야, identification 신분증, available 이용 가능한, classify 분류하다, trouser(s) 바지, efficiency 효율성, confidence 자신/확신

B2: had better ~하는 것이 더 낫다, courage 용기, wage 임금/급료, as a whole 전체로서, average 평균

B3: toil 수고(하다), spin (실을) 잣다, array 치장하다, extraordinary 비범한, application 적용/응용, ingenuity 독창성, botany 식물학, fragile 연약한, exquisite 절묘한/섬세한, furious 격노한/맹렬한

B4: lack 부족(하다), bold 대담한, aggressive 공격적인, status 지위/신분, rude 무례한, lower 낮추다

C1: reveal 드러내다, impulse 충동, bosom 가슴, not so much A ~ as B (A라기 보다는 B), affection 애정, token 표/표식, wrought 만들어진, fasten 부착하다, haughty 오만한/당당한, abash 무안하게 하다, elaborate 정교한, embroider 수놓다, flourish 장식체, fertility 비옥함, gorgeous 화려한/찬란한 luxuriance 풍성함, apparel 의복, splendor 광채, sumptuary 사치를 금하는, regulation 규정, colony 식민지, abundant 풍부한, glossy 윤이 나는, complexion 안색, brow 이마, state 위풍, dignity 위엄, evanescent 덧없는/섬세한, antique 고래의/구식의, interpret 해석하다, term 말/용어, issue 나오다, obscure 흐리게 하다, disaster 재난/재해, halo 후광/영광, ignominy 치욕, envelop 둘러싸다

[실력 점검 A] 다음 각 동사의 우리말 뜻을 쓰세요.

1. adorn: 2. instill: 3. hinder:

4. wither: 5. impair: 6. threaten:

7. rejoice: 8. disturb: 9. attribute:

10. inhabit: 11. revolve: 12. embroider:

13. remove: 14. regulate: 15. complicate:

16. indulge: 17. smuggle: 18. discriminate:

19. descend: 20. generate:

[실력 점검 B] 각 항목에 대응하는 영어 단어를 찾아 쓰세요.

보기   prey, drawer, obesity, symptom, allowance, amphibian, inconvenience, garment, proverb, drought, chimney, equation, prophecy, substance, detergent, distinct, tranquil, competent, instructive, confidential

1. 물질: 2. 속담: 3. 용돈:

4. 서랍: 5. 증상: 6. 불편:

7. 먹이: 8. 가뭄: 9. 세제:

10. 의복: 11. 굴뚝: 12. 비만:

13. 예언: 14. 방정식: 15. 양서류:

16. 유능한: 17. 고요한: 18. 은밀한:

19. 뚜렷한: 20. 교훈적인:

[실력 점검 C] 주어진 철자로 시작되는 적절한 낱말은?

1. The monarch carried out the plan at the c_____ of many lives.

2. The president was wondering whom to promote in John's p_____.

3. No man, however brilliant or well-informed, can come to s_____ fullness of understanding as to safely judge and dismiss the c_____ and institutions of his society, for these are the wisdom of g_____ after centuries of experiment in the laboratory of h_____.

명시 감상

Music, When Soft Voices Die

P. B. Shelley

Music, when soft voices die,

Vibrates in the memory —

Odours, when sweet violets sicken,

Live within the sense they quicken.

Rose leaves, when the rose is dead,

Are heaped for the beloved's bed;

And so thy thoughts, when thou art gone,

Love itself shall slumber on.

* vibrate 진동하다, odour 냄새/향기, heap 쌓다, thy (=your), thou art (=you are), slumber on ~을 베고/깔고 잠자다

Unit 14 법

A. 직설법(indicative)

1) He *has* done with the work. She *will* come here tomorrow.

2) They *are* watching television. We *had* a good time at the party.

B. 명령법(imperative)

1) *Do* in Rome as the Romans do. *Be* quiet here in the library.

2) *Work* hard, *and* you will succeed in your study or business.

　Work hard, *or* you will not succeed in your study or business.

C. 가정법(subjunctive)

1) If this rumor *be* true, anything may happen.

2) If it *should* rain tomorrow, the meeting might be canceled.

3) If I *were* in America, I *could learn* English better.

4) If he *had* not *been* there, she *would have been* drowned.

5) If you *had listened* to me, you *wouldn't be* in such trouble now.

D. 가정법 구문

1) If I *were to* die tomorrow, I should never forget your name.

2) I wish I *were* a schoolteacher. I wish I *had been* a schoolteacher.

3) She talks as if it *were* true. She talks as though it *had been* true.

4) It's time we *were* going. It is high time you *learned* to behave yourself.

5) He studied hard; *otherwise* he could not have entered the college.

6) *Without* his help, she could not succeed in business.

　But for her advice, he might not have succeeded in business.

7) A true artist *would* be interested in the ugly as well as in the beautiful.

　Your attendance at the meeting *would have encouraged* the students.

8) *Were* I to ask you to scrub my back, what would you say?

　Had I *known* that you hadn't heard, I wouldn't have told you.

9) *Suppose* something should go wrong, what would you do then?

　She was prepared to come, *provided* that she might bring her daughter.

[필수 문법] 법(mood)

* 문장 진술에 있어, 그 진술에 대한 특정한 태도를 술어 동사의 형태로써 나타내는 것.
* 객관적 사실을 진술하는 직설법(: fact-mood), 상대방에게 어떤 행위를 명하는
  명령법, 조건/요망/가능성 등을 가상해서 진술하는 가정법(: thought-mood) 등.

A. 직설법(indicative)

  1) 대부분의 진술은 객관적인 기정 사실에 관한 직설법의 진술이라고 할 수 있음.

  2) 현재/과거 시제가 각각 현재/과거 사실을 나타냄: 시제(tense)와 시간(time)의 일치.

B. 명령법(imperative)

  1) 주어 "you"는 대개 생략되고, 문장의 첫 머리에 부정사(동사의 기본형)가 사용됨.

  2) 명령문, and ~ : "~하라, 그러면 ~할 것이다."

     명령문, or ~ : "~하라, 그렇지 않으면 ~할 것이다."

C. 가정법(subjunctive)

  1) 가정법 현재: 오늘날에는 거의 직설법으로 대치됨: =If this rumor *is* true, ~.

  2) 가정법 미래: 조건절에서 "should"를 사용: 실현될 가능성이 희박함을 나타냄.

  3) 가정법 과거: 현재의 사실/상황에 대한 가정: =As I *am not* in America, I *cannot* learn~.

  4) 가정법 과거 완료: 과거의 사실에 대한 가정: =As he *was* there, she *was* not drowned.

  5) 혼합 가정법: 종속절의 시제와 주절의 시제가 상이함: =As you *did not listen* to me,
     you *are* in such trouble now. If he *had studied* hard then, he *would* now *be* a college student.

D. 가정법 구문

  1) were to ~: 실현될 가능성이 거의 없는 미래 사실에 대한 가정의 경우에 사용.

  2) I wish (that) ~: "학교 교사라면 좋으련만" (=I *would rather* I *were* a schoolteacher.)
     "학교 교사였다면 (지금) 좋으련만" (=I *would rather* I *had been* a schoolteacher.)

  3) as if (=as though) ~: "(마치) 사실인 것처럼 얘기한다" "사실이었던 것처럼 얘기한다"

  4) It is (high) time (that) ~: ~해야 할 때이다: =It's (high) time (that) we *should* be going.

  5) otherwise: (만약) 그렇지 않(았)다면: =*if he had not studied hard*, he could not have ~.

  6) without (=but for) ~: ~이 없(었)다면: =*If it were not for* his help, she could not succeed ~.
     =*If it had not been for* her advice, he might not have succeeded in business.

  7) 문장의 주어가 조건절을 함축하고 있는 경우: =*If he were a true artist*, he would be ~.
     =*If you had attended* the meeting, *it would have encouraged* the students.

  8) 조건절의 접속사 "if"가 생략되면, 주어와 (조)동사가 도치됨: =*If I were to ask* ~.
     =If I had known that you hadn't heard, ~.   * *Could* I afford it, I would buy a boat.

  9) "if"의 대용: suppose/supposing (that) ~ = if ~; provided/providing (that) ~ = if ~, if only ~
     Supposing (that) we are late, what will he say? I'll come *providing* (that) it is fine tomorrow.

[문법 연습 A]　잘못된 부분을 고치세요.

1. It is high time all of you stop smoking.

2. I would rather you go home right away.

3. At times my mother wished she was a man.

4. I really wish I worked harder in my school days.

5. She talked as though she read the book when in college.

6. If you can write lucidly and simply, you would write perfectly.

7. To hear him speak English, you will take him for an American.

8. If they are to be taken by surprise, they would never be surprised.

9. It would be pleasant living providing she is living in a nice house.

10. She was singing as nicely as if she once was a professional singer.

11. If you would have been careful, you could have prevented the fire.

12. Had it not been for your advice, I may have made a serious mistake.

13. If he were not killed in the accident, he would be thirty years old now.

[문법 연습 B]　빈칸에 알맞은 낱말은?

1. What _____ we should fail again?

2. I wish you _____ have come with me.

3. Oh, _____ I listened to my parents then!

4. Be careful, _____ you will bump your head.

5. What would you do if war _____ to break out?

6. One more day, _____ the vacation will be over.

7. It is time that all the children _____ going home.

8. She felt as though she _____ stumbling up a mountain.

9. If I _____ in your place, I would never do such a thing.

10. Usually, _____ not always, we write "cannot" as one word.

11. Thousands of families would have died _____ his leadership.

12. It's perfectly harmless, Sandy; _____ I wouldn't have done it.

13. _____ it not for water, no living things could exist on the earth.

[실전 문법 A] 빈칸에 알맞은 낱말은?

1. Some are wise, some are _____ .

2. _____ for you, I would be dead now.

3. The camel is, as it _____ , a ship in the desert.

4. _____ it ever so humble, there is no place like home.

5. _____ I met you before, I could have recognized you at once.

6. He would have been frozen to death _____ we had found him.

7. It may be quite natural that they _____ have refused our request.

8. The suspect demanded that he _____ be allowed to call his lawyer.

9. She suggested that her secretary _____ responsible for the schedule.

[실전 문법 B] 각 문항의 다섯 부분 중 어법에 맞지 않는 부분은?

1. [1]I heartily wish [2]that in my youth [3]I had someone [4]of good sense
   [5]to direct my reading.

2. [1]I could be justly blamed [2]if I saw [3]only people's faults [4]and was blind
   [5]to their virtues.

3. [1]It is very important [2]that you will realize [3]that human labor is [4]not merely
   a physical activity [5]but it is also a mental activity.

4. [1]Scarcely had the words [2]left her lips [3]before she secretly wished [4]she did
   not speak [5]in that way.

5. [1]If Kevin would have been [2]more careful, [3]he could have avoided [4]the crash
   [5]that wrecked his car.

6. [1]We must reduce the amount [2]of violence on television. [3]Otherwise we will
   feel [4]as if the world is [5]a bad place to live in.

7. [1]It is required [2]of all students [3]that they will attend [4]at least three quarters of
   the lectures [5]every semester.

8. [1]If all the land in Mexico [2]is not high but low, [3]it would be a very hot country,
   [4]because it is not far from the equator; [5]temperature also depends on altitude.

[필수 어휘 A] 다음 각 낱말의 반의어(대칭어)를 쓰세요.

1. vice: 2. quality: 3. success:

4. verse: 5. comedy: 6. ancestor:

7. export: 8. optimist: 9. employer:

10. urban: 11. natural: 12. concrete:

13. guilty: 14. foreign: 15. negative:

16. fertile: 17. inferior: 18. maternal:

19. mental: 20. material: 21. objective:

22. vertical: 23. absolute: 24. increase:

25. add: 26. divide: 27. produce:

28. ascend: 29. include: 30. construct:

[필수 어휘 B] 다음 각 문장의 빈칸에 알맞은 낱말은?

1. Let's meet here tomorrow. What time shall we _____ it?

   1) get 2) have 3) make 4) take 5) arrange

2. A computer can _____ and remember a great deal of information.

   1) store 2) utilize 3) relieve 4) improve 5) comprehend

3. Nancy is very _____; she is often moved to tears in the theater.

   1) tidy 2) timid 3) cautious 4) sensitive 5) impressionable

4. _____ duties are concerned with the running of a home and family.

   1) Mutual 2) Ethical 3) Private 4) Domestic 5) Feminine

5. In the last game of the season they suffered a humiliating _____.

   1) defeat 2) obstacle 3) triumph 4) strategy 5) withdrawal

6. A _____ is an excellent work of art produced by a writer or artist.

   1) myth 2) fable 3) souvenir 4) monument 5) masterpiece

7. Ugly new buildings have taken the _____ of the medieval ones.

   1) order 2) place 3) miracle 4) tradition 5) landscape

8. At last it's come _____ to him how much he owes to his parents.

   1) true 2) home 3) much 4) realistic 5) conscience

[구문 연습] 다음 문장을 우리말로 옮기세요.

1. The current spirit of cooperation among various branches of the sciences has led to a number of discoveries which might not otherwise have been made.

2. Were they pressed hard enough, most men would probably confess that political freedom—that is to say, the right to speak freely and to act in opposition—is a noble ideal rather than a practical necessity.

3. Without various inventions industry might have continued its slow progress—firms becoming larger, trade more widespread, and division of labor more minute—but there would have been no industrial revolution

4. What would I have done differently in my 20s and 30s if I had known then what I know now? For one thing, I would have laughed more. And I would have grieved less. I would have understood earlier that not all losses are permanent and that some things lost were not worth keeping.

[작문 연습] 다음 문장을 영어로 옮기세요.

1. 내 아들이 그 병원에서 일하는 의사라면 좋으련만.

_____

2. 만일 해가 서쪽에서 뜬다면 우리들에게 무슨 일이 일어날까?

_____

3. 산소와 수소가 없다면 한 방울의 물도 형성될 수 없을 것이다.

_____

4. 젊은 시절에 열심히 일했더라면 그는 지금 편히 살 수 있을텐데.

_____

5. 나의 온 삶을 문학에 바쳤더라면 나는 더 나은 작가가 되었을까?

_____

[실전 독해 A] 각 문항의 물음에 답하세요.

1. The _____ is a guide on the journey of learning. As a guide, because of his experience, his knowledge of the road and of the travelers, and of his great interest in their learning, he assumes major responsibility for the trip. He establishes the aims and limits of the trip according to the travelers' needs and abilities. He determines the way to be followed, makes every aspect of the journey more meaningful, and evaluates progress. The journey has often been used in literature and history to represent the life of man or some part of that life.

Q. 빈칸에 들어갈 적절한 낱말은?
　　1) writer　　2) scholar　　3) teacher
　　4) historian　　5) philosopher

2. Friendship is a gift that we offer because we must. It cannot grow where there is any calculated choice. To give it as the reward of virtue would be to set a price upon it, and those who do that have no friendship to give. If you choose your friends on the ground that you are virtuous and want virtuous _____, you are not nearer to true friendship than if you choose them for commercial reasons. Though you may find virtues in a friend, he was your friend before you found them, and though you may choose the virtuous to be your friends they may not choose you. It is enough for any man that he has the divine power of making friends, and he must leave it to that power to, be, his, will, who, friends, determine.

Q 1. 빈칸에 들어갈 적절한 낱말은?
　　1) profit　　2) company　　3) behavior
　　4) achievement　　5) relationship

　2. 밑줄 친 7개의 낱말을 문맥에 맞게 배열하면?

　3. 이 글의 요지는?
　　1) Friendship is above reason.
　　2) Making friends is a great virtue.
　　3) We should not set a price on friendship.
　　4) Everyone has the divine power of making friends.
　　5) Friendship is an unconditional gift we give to the virtuous.

3.　The behavior of rats, according to recent studies, is greatly affected by space. If their living conditions become too crowded, their behavior patterns and even their health change perceptibly. They cannot eat and sleep well, and signs of fear become obvious. The more crowded they are, the more they tend to bite, and even kill, each other. Thus, for rats, population and _____ are directly related. Is this a natural law for human society as well?

Q. 빈칸에 들어갈 적절한 낱말은?
　　1) habitat　　2) instinct　　3) violence
　　4) cooperation　　5) environment

4.　We are all inclined to accept conventional forms of colors as the only correct ones. Children sometimes think that stars must be starshaped, though naturally they are not. The people who insist that in a picture [1)]the sky is blue, and the grass green, are not very different from these children. They get very indignant if they see other colors in a picture, but if we try to forget all we have heard about green grass and blue skies, and look at the world [2)]as if we had just arrived from another planet on a voyage of discovery and were seeing it for the first time, we may find that things are apt to have the most surprising colors.

　　New painters sometimes feel [3)]as if they were on such a voyage of discovery. They want to see the world afresh, and to discard all the accepted notions and prejudices [4)]about flesh being pink and apples yellow or red. It is not easy to get rid of these preconceived ideas, but the artists who succeed best in doing so produce the most exciting works. It is they who teach us to see new beauties in nature [5)]of whose existence we had never dreamed. If we follow them and learn from them, even a glance out of our window may become a thrilling adventure.

Q 1. 밑줄 친 1)~5)중 어법에 맞지 않는 것은?

　　2. 다음 중 이 글의 내용과 일치하는 것은?
　　　　1) Few children like to paint the sky blue in their pictures.
　　　　2) It is children and artists who find new beauties in nature.
　　　　3) People are different from each other in their choice of colors.
　　　　4) Good artists are willing to give up conventional ideas and notions.
　　　　5) Even a glance out of the window is necessary for drawing a picture.

[실전 독해 B] 각 문항의 물음에 답하세요.

1. Some unexpected changes at my home will make it impossible for me to take my part on the program for the Women's Club this winter. I am very sorry as I am decidedly interested in the topic assigned to me and should have enjoyed doing the necessary reading. I hesitate to ask someone to take my place before informing you as you may have someone in mind; but if you haven't, I think Ms. Wallace may be willing. She has a cousin who has been in Lima on business and has therefore close access to material on Peru.

Q. 이 글은 어떤 취지의 글인가?
1) 감사   2) 문의   3) 부탁
4) 초대   5) 추천

2. Here is a way of winning a Nobel Prize without trying. The first step is to obtain the names of a number of recent Nobel Prize winners in scientific subjects. Their recent papers should then be photocopied and divided into groups at random. The first group might contain a paper from a chemist, a physicist and a biologist, for example. Send the chemist copies of the papers from the physicist and biologist, with a covering letter saying that you are sure he will realize the importance and relevance of these papers to his own work. [a]_____, send the physicist copies of the papers from the chemist and biologist, and so on until you have many Nobel Prize winners studying the papers of other Nobel Prize winners in different fields. The chances are that one of these creative scientists will make connections with the work of the others and [b]_____ a brilliant idea. He will then contact you, congratulate you on your vision, and ask you to be a joint author of the paper. With some luck, you could win a Nobel Prize.

Q 1. 빈칸 a)에 들어갈 적절한 말은?
1) However   2) Therefore   3) Similarly
4) Additionally   5) Consequently

2. 빈칸 b)에 들어갈 적절한 말은?
1) use up   2) bring up   3) bring about
4) come up with   5) catch up with

3. ¹⁾The nervous system of insects is very different from ours; insects are not capable of thought. ²⁾When we smell good food, we think to ourselves, "I'm hungry! I'd like to eat that." ³⁾In the human body, such messages are carried by nerve cells called neurons. ⁴⁾But when an insect smell its food, its nervous system makes its muscles move its body toward the food. ⁵⁾The insect doesn't think about what it is doing; it just does it.

Q. 1) ~ 5)의 문장 중 글의 흐름에 맞지 않는 것은?

4. Meaning does not exist only on the page or in the mind of the reader. It is created by an interaction between reader and text. Based on their general knowledge and the information in a text, good readers develop predictions about what they will read next; then they read to see if their expectations will be confirmed. If they are not confirmed, they reread, stopping at several points and creating new predictions. In fact readers cannot always predict precisely what an author will talk about next, but they can use clues from the text and their general knowledge to predict content more efficiently.

Q. 이 글의 제목으로 가장 적절한 것은?
   1) Predictions in Reading   2) The Meaning of Reading
   3) Who is a Good Reader?   4) Reading as an Active Process
   5) The Interaction of the Reader and the Author

5. Simple things like doors sometimes have confusing designs. Have you ever had trouble opening a door? ① Have you ever pushed on a door that pulls open, or pulled on a door that pushes open? ② When you have trouble opening a door, it's probably because the door is poorly designed. ③ Well-designed doors tell people exactly what to do. ④ A door with a handle tells people to pull; a door with a bar tells people to push. If you're pulling at a door that pushes open, the door probably has a handle on it. ⑤ It has a bad design. You shouldn't blame yourself, thus, if you have trouble with a thing you use every day. You should blame its maker or designer.

Q. ① ~ ⑤중 다음 문장이 삽입되기에 적절한 곳은?
   The door is giving you the wrong signal.

[명작 감상]　　　Fyodor M. Dostoyevsky (1821 ~ 1881)

Crime and Punishment　죄와 벌

On a very hot evening at the beginning of July a young man left his little room at the top of a house in Carpenter Lane, went out into the street, and, as though unable to make up his mind, walked slowly in the direction of Kokushkin Bridge.

He was lucky to avoid a meeting with his landlady on the stairs. His little room under the very roof of a tall five-story building was more like a cupboard than a living-room. His landlady, who also provided him with meals and looked after him, lived in a flat on the floor below. Every time he went out, he had to walk past her kitchen, the door of which was practically always open; and every time he walked past that door, the young man experienced a sickening sensation of terror which made him feel ashamed and pull a wry face. He was up to the neck in debt to his landlady and was afraid of meeting her.

It was not as though he were a coward by nature or easily intimidated. Quite the contrary. But for some time past he had been in an irritable and overstrung state which was like hypochondria. He had been so absorbed in himself and had led so cloistered a life that he was afraid of meeting anybody, let alone his landlady. He was crushed by poverty, but even his straitened circumstances had ceased to worry him lately. He had lost all interest in matters that required his most immediate attention and he did not want to bother about them. As a matter of fact, he was not in the least afraid of his landlady, whatever plots she might be hatching against him. But rather than be forced to stop on the stairs and listen to all the dreary nonsense which did not concern him at all, to all those insistent demands for payment, to all those threats and complaints, and have to think up some plausible excuse and tell lie - no! A thousand times better to slip downstairs as quietly as a mouse and escape without being seen by anybody.

This time, however, as he reached the street, his fear of meeting his landlady surprised even himself.

"Good Lord!" he thought to himself, with a strange smile, "here I am thinking of doing such a thing and at the same time I am in a jitter over such a trivial matter. Well, of course, everything is in a man's own hands, and if he lets everything slip through his fingers, it is through sheer cowardice...."

[확인 학습] 다음 문장을 우리말로 옮기세요.

1. If you choose your friends on the ground that you are virtuous and want virtuous company, you are not nearer to true friendship than if you choose them for commercial reasons.

2. It is they who teach us to see new beauties in nature of whose existence we had never dreamed.

3. He had been so absorbed in himself and had led so cloistered a life that he was afraid of meeting anybody, let alone his landlady.

4. Rather than be forced to stop on the stairs and listen to all the dreary nonsense which did not concern him at all, to all those insistent demands for payment, to all those threats and complaints, and have to think up some plausible excuse and tell lie - no! A thousand times better to slip downstairs as quietly as a mouse and escape without being seen by anybody.

[words & phrases]

A1: assume 떠맡다, responsibility 책임, aim 목적/목표, evaluate 평가하다, represent 묘사[기술]하다

A2: calculate 계산하다, reward 보상/보답(하다), virtue 미덕, commercial 상업적인, divine /신성한,

A3: rat 쥐, affect 영향을 미치다, crowded 혼잡한, obvious 분명한, tend to ~경향이 있다, as well 또한

A4: be inclined to ~경향이 있다, indignant 성난, voyage 항해, be apt to ~경향이 있다, discard 버리다, notion 개념, prejudice 편견, flesh 살/육신, get rid of ~을 제거하다, conceive 품다/생각하다

B1: assign 할당하다, hesitate 망설이다/주저하다, take one's place ~을 대신하다, access 접근(하다)

B2: obtain 얻다/획득하다, at random 임의로, chemist 화학자, physicist 물리학자, biologist 생물학자, relevance 관련/적절, chances 가망/가능성, congratulate 축하하다, joint author 공동 저자

B3: nerve 신경, insect 곤충/벌레, differ from ~와 다르다, be capable of ~을 할 수 있다, muscle 근육

B4: predict 예측하다, confirm 확인하다, clue 단서 content 내용, precise 정밀한, efficient 효율적인

B5: confuse 혼란시키다, have trouble (~ing) ~에 어려움을 겪다, bar 빗장/가로대, blame 비난하다

C1: carpenter 목수, lane 골목길, as though ~ 마치 ~인 것처럼, make up one's mind 결심하다, stair(s) 계단 wry 뒤틀린, debt 빚, landlady 여주인, look after ~을 돌보다, flat 아파트, coward 비겁자, intimidate 겁주다, irritable 성마른, overstrung 너무 긴장한, hypochondria 우울증, cloister 수도원/은둔시키다, crush 으깨다/뭉개다, strait 해협/궁핍, bother 고민하다, plot 음모/계략, threat 위협, complaint 불평, plausible 그럴듯한, jitter 불안감/신경과민, trivial 사소한, sheer 순전한/완전한, cowardice 비겁

[실력 점검 A] 다음 각 동사의 우리말 뜻을 쓰세요.

1. rule: 2. leak: 3. install:

4. grab: 5. deem: 6. qualify:

7. plead: 8. inhibit: 9. beckon:

10. assign: 11. induce: 12. evaluate:

13. pursue: 14. outvote: 15. overtake:

16. enclose: 17. evaporate: 18. undermine:

19. summon: 20. intimidate:

[실력 점검 B] 각 항목에 대응하는 영어 단어를 찾아 쓰세요.

보기   dairy, victim, figure, refuge, funeral, altitude, agriculture, conviction, labor, harsh, routine, disaster, impulse, bankrupt, acquisition, consciousness, thirsty, abstract, tranquil, redundant

1. 재난: 2. 충동: 3. 농업:

4. 일과: 5. 노동: 6. 의식:

7. 고도: 8. 숫자: 9. 확신:

10. 피난: 11. 낙농: 12. 습득:

13. 희생자: 14. 장례식: 15. 거친:

16. 목마른: 17. 추상적: 18. 파산한:

19. 고요한: 20. 불필요한:

[실력 점검 C] 다음의 빈칸에 들어갈 적절한 낱말은?

1. My brother has much knowledge, and experience as _____.

2. _____ all the large fortune he inherited from his father, he was _____ a man of high character that he lived a simple life.

3. We cannot know _____ much about the language we speak every day of our life, but most of us can get along fairly well _____ knowing very much about our language.

명시 감상

The Supreme Good

Lao-tzu

The supreme good is like water,

which nourishes all things without trying to.

It is content with the low places that people disdain.

Thus it is like Tao.

In dwelling, live close to the ground.

In thinking, keep to the simple.

In conflict, be fair and generous.

In governing, don't try to control.

In work, do what you enjoy.

In family life, be completely present.

When you are content to be simply yourself

and don't compare or compete,

everybody will respect you.

* nourish 기르다/육성하다, be content with ~에 만족하다, disdain 경멸하다, dwell 거주하다, conflict 갈등/싸움

Unit 15 화법

A. 평서문의 화법 전환

1) He says, "I am busy today." He *says* that *he is busy today*.

   He said, "I am busy today." He *said* that *he was busy that day*.

2) She says to me, "I loved you." She *tells* me that *she loved me*.

   She said to me, "I loved you." She *told* me that *she had loved me*.

3) He said, "Eight planets move around the sun."

   He said that eight planets *move* around the sun.

   He said to me, "The Korean War *broke out* in 1950."

   He told me that the Korean War *broke out* in 1950.

   She said, "I *could* help all of them if I *were* really wealthy."

   She said that she *could* help all of them if she *were* really wealthy.

B. 의문문의 화법 전환

1) I said to him, "How long have you lived in this town?"

   I *asked* him *how long he had lived in that town*.

2) He said to me, "Can you find my new office in town?"

   He *asked* me *if I could find his new office in town*.

C. 명령문의 화법 전환

1) He said to me, "Do as you would be done by."

   He *told* me *to do* as I would be done by.

2) She said to him, "Please don't make a noise in the library."

   She *asked* him *not to make* a noise in the library.

D. 복합문의 화법 전환

1) He said, "How fine it is! Let's go hiking."

   He *remarked* how fine it was, and *suggested* that we (should) go hiking.

2) She said to me, "He is handsome, but he isn't my type."

   She *told* me (that) he was handsome, but *that* he wasn't her type.

[필수 문법] 화법(narration)

* 특정 시점에서 행하여진 어떤 이의 진술을 타인에게 전달하는 방식.
* 본래의 진술 그대로를 차용하여 전달하는 방식을 직접 화법이라 하며,
* 전달자의 입장에서 객관화하여 전달하는 방식을 간접 화법이라 한다.

A. 평서문의 화법 전환

1) 전달동사 "say, said"는 간접 화법에서도 대체로 그대로 사용한다. 간접 화법으로
   전환할 때는 특히 인칭/시제/부사의 변환에 유의하여야 한다. * 부사의 변환:
   this/that; here/there; now/then; ago/before; today/that day; tomorrow/the following
   (=next) day; yesterday/the day before(=the previous day); last night/the night before 등.
   * 감탄문의 경우, 전달동사가 "cry (out), shout, exclaim, remark" 등으로 변환되기도 함:
   They said, "We've won the game!" → They shouted(=exclaimed) that they had won the game.
2) 전달동사 "say to, said to"는 간접 화법에서는 대체로 각각 "tell, told"로 변환된다.
3) 시제 일치의 예외: 불변의 진리/습관은 항상 현재 시제로, 역사적 사실은 항상
   과거 시제로 표현되며, 가정법의 시제는 변환 없이 원래의 시제 그대로 사용함.
   * 불변의 습관: Mary *told* me (that) she always *gets up* at six in the morning.

B. 의문문의 화법 전환

   * 전달동사 "say to, said to"는 간접 화법에서는 각각 "ask, asked"로 변환된다.
1) 의문사가 있는 경우에는, 그 의문사가 간접 화법의 접속사 역할을 한다.
2) 의문사가 없는 경우에는, (연결하는) 접속사로서 "if"나 "whether"를 도입한다.

C. 명령문의 화법 전환

   * 전달동사 "say to, said to"는 간접 화법에서는 대체로 "tell, told"로 변환되지만,
1) 피전달문(전달하는 내용)에 따라서 흔히 "ask, advise, order/command" 등의 동사로
   변환되며, 피전달문은 "to-부정사"로 연결된다: (=He *advised* me to do as I would ~.)
2) 부드러운 명령이나 완곡한 요청/부탁의 경우에는 "ask"동사를 사용한다:
   He said to me, "Will you do me a favor?" → He *asked* me to do him a favor.

D. 복합문의 화법 전환

1) 피전달문의 종류와 내용에 따라서 간접 화법의 (술어)동사와 구문을 선택한다.
   He said to me, "How pretty she is! Do you know who she is?"
   → He *told* me that she was very pretty, *and asked if* I knew who she was."
2) 간접화법에서, 등위접속사 "and, but, or" 바로 다음의 접속사 "that"은 생략 불가.
   She said, "It was a fine day, and I went out for a walk."
   → She said (that) it had been a fine day, and *that* she had gone out for a walk.

* 묘출(묘사) 화법: 흔히 소설 문체에서 사용되는 화법으로서, 전달하는 내용을 좀
   더 생생하게 표현하기 위해 직접 화법의 요소를 부분적으로 채용한 간접 화법:
   He asked me *could I come with him.* (=He asked me *if I could come with him.*)

[문법 연습 A]　잘못된 부분을 고치세요.

1. I said to her that he was a real gentleman.

2. He asked them where were his wife and children.

3. She told me that she had been to Sandy's last night.

4. The boy told me that he saw the girl a few days ago.

5. Columbus believed that the earth was round like a ball.

6. He asked me that I could understand what he was saying.

7. We didn't know that there was no rule without an exception.

8. They said that the Korean alphabet had been invented in 1443.

9. The old man said that he would fly to his children if he was a bird.

10. I told her that my son had a bad cold, and he couldn't go to school.

[문법 연습 B]　간접 화법의 문장으로 고치세요.

1. He said, "It is three years since my father died."

_____

2. She said to me, "Did you see my brother yesterday?"

_____

3. The captain said to his men, "Keep an eye on the prisoners."

_____

4. She said to him, "Could you show me the way to the church?"

_____

5. He said to her, "Please don't forget to see me here tomorrow.

_____

6. She said to me, "Where have you been? Let's go out for lunch."

_____

7. He said, "What a lovely girl she is! I wish she were my girlfriend."

_____

8. She said to him, "I liked you very much, but I didn't love you at all."

_____

[실전 문법 A] 각 문항의 다섯 부분 중 어법에 맞지 않는 부분은?

1. [1]She asked me [2]why I didn't tell her right away [3]that she had the wrong number. [4]Before I could answer her, [5]she hanged up the phone.

2. [1]From its beginnings [2]in the 1890's, [3]newspaper comics appealed [4]not only to adults [5]but to youngsters.

3. [1]Once people have learned [2]to learn [3]in a given way, [4]they are very difficult to learn [5]in any other way.

4. [1]Only after he finishes [2]his military service [3]he would be able [4]to get married [5]to the woman he wants.

5. [1]Dried leaves [2]continue to hang [3]on the branches [4]of some deciduous trees [5]until new leaves will appear.

6. [1]I've never worked in a factory, [2]but some of my friends did. [3]Your factory employs [4]both male and female workers, [5]doesn't it?

[실전 문법 B] 각 문항의 다섯 부분 중 어법에 맞지 않는 부분은?

1. [1]"I took a shower [2]this morning," [3]said Betty, [4]"and that's why I couldn't [5]answer the phone."

2. [1]The complex relationship [2]between poet and poetry [3]has been [4]a primary concern of literate critics [5]in recent years.

3. [1]They had trouble [2]finding out [3]whether the resources of the country [4]laid in the coastal area [5]or in the mountains.

4. [1]The reason why I was late [2]is because the subway train [3]broke down in the tunnel [4]and we had to wait [5]for almost half an hour.

5. [1]Plankton, the collective name [2]for minute marine animals and plants, [3]are the basic foodstuff [4]for every creature [5]that lives in the ocean.

6. [1]The deceased insisted, in his will, [2]that his son spent half the inheritance [3]within the next three years. [4]If he didn't, [5]the money would be given to a mental hospital.

[필수 어휘 A] 각 문장의 빈칸에 알맞은 낱말은?

1. It makes _____ to adopt labor-saving methods.

   1) deal   2) role   3) sense   4) favor   5) effect

2. I'd like to pay by _____, please, rather than in cash.

   1) bill   2) check   3) credit   4) change   5) account

3. Scott's novels were written to get him out of _____.

   1) debt   2) fame   3) vanity   4) disorder   5) question

4. I have completely no _____ how he made such a mistake.

   1) way   2) idea   3) doubt   4) evidence   5) possibility

5. Mr. Kim, the Korean student, has a good _____ of English.

   1) point   2) grade   3) control   4) fluency   5) command

[필수 어휘 B] 밑줄 친 부분과 그 뜻이 가장 가까운 것은?

1. It wasn't your fault; you have nothing to <u>reproach</u> yourself with.

   1) imply   2) blame   3) regret   4) excuse   5) concern

2. The committee has 10 members, each <u>eminent</u> in his or her field.

   1) gifted   2) decent   3) famous   4) obscure   5) ingenious

3. Politicians are usually <u>expert</u> at turning a crisis to their advantage.

   1) skilled   2) excited   3) pleased   4) astonished   5) contented

4. The document's <u>ambiguous</u> wording makes it very difficult to follow.

   1) vague   2) logical   3) definite   4) abstract   5) complicated

5. Familiarity with routine did not <u>diminish</u> the horror of living in prison.

   1) affect   2) endure   3) reduce   4) conceal   5) eliminate

6. Jefferson's ideas are based on the <u>notion</u> that all men are created equal.

   1) belief   2) theory   3) attitude   4) principle   5) conception

7. I go jogging every morning and <u>work out</u> with weights twice a week.

   1) finish   2) continue   3) perform   4) exercise   5) endeavor

8. The researchers are trying to get the <u>up-to-date</u> information on genetics.

   1) new   2) latest   3) current   4) modern   5) important

[구문 연습] 다음 문장을 우리말로 옮기세요.

1. Someone, it is said, reproached Aristotle for having been too merciful to a wicked man. "I have indeed been merciful to the man," he answered, "but not to his wickedness."

2. A sheep was being shorn clumsily. "If it's my wool that you want," it said, "don't cut so close. If it's my flesh that you're after, kill me outright. Don't torture me to death by inches."

3. "Mr. Shaw," asked a reporter, "if you could live your life over and be anybody you've known, or any person from history, who would be you?" "I would choose," replied Shaw, "to be the man George Bernard Shaw could have been, but never was."

4. Once when I asked, on the phone, how Dad was, Mother said, casually, "I think something's wrong with him. He's sitting in the living room without anything on." "Nothing on?" I repeated, concerned. "Yes," Mother replied, "he's got the TV off, the radio off and the computer off."

[작문 연습] 다음 문장을 영어로 옮기세요.

1. 숲속에서 사슴을 본 적이 있느냐고 그녀는 나에게 물었다.

_____

2. "오늘 신문에 뭐 새로운 게 있니?"라고 그는 나에게 말했다.

_____

3. 그의 어머님은 몇 해 전에 돌아가셨다고 그는 나에게 말했다.

_____

4. "이번 주말에 골프 치는 게 어때?"라고 그는 그녀에게 말했다.

_____

5. 하늘은 스스로 돕는 자를 돕는다고 담임 선생님께서 말씀하셨다.

_____

[실전 독해 A] 각 문항의 물음에 답하세요.

1. It is no mere accident that people have twisted the Biblical saying into "Money is the root of all evil," when it reads "Love of money is the root of all evil"—thus transferring the blame from their own _____ to the coinage itself.

> Q. 빈칸에 들어갈 적절한 낱말은?
> 1) greed   2) wealth   3) vanity
> 4) selfishness   5) temptation

2. ⓐ Many parents don't want to face it, but the world today is a lot different than it was when they were kids. Our streets, and our schoolyards, are full of violent people. The best way to prepare young people to face the world is to show them what it's really like. TV does this.

ⓑ Your recent column on TV violence gave a very one-sided view of the subject. I agree that there is a lot of violence on TV, but you only have to open the newspaper, turn on the radio, or look out of your window to see that violence is a way of life. TV shows just reflect that reality.

ⓒ TV can also help young people to overcome the prejudices that can lead to violence. Television brings people of every culture, creed, religion, and race into others' living rooms. Someone once said that TV was "the great equalizer," because it allows us to see every kind of person in the world, and helps us feel a connection with them.

> Q 1. ⓐ ~ ⓒ의 단락을 문맥에 맞게 배열하면?
> 1) ⓐ-ⓒ-ⓑ   2) ⓑ-ⓐ-ⓒ   3) ⓑ-ⓒ-ⓐ
> 4) ⓒ-ⓐ-ⓑ   5) ⓒ-ⓑ-ⓐ
>
> 2. 이 글에서 필자가 주장하는 바는?
> 1) TV 폭력물은 긍정적인 효과도 있다.
> 2) TV 폭력물은 폭력적인 현실을 조장한다.
> 3) TV 폭력물은 문화적, 인종적 편견을 낳는다.
> 4) TV 폭력물에 대한 생각은 사람마다 다를 수 있다.
> 5) TV 폭력물이 젊은이들에게 미치는 영향은 심각하다.

3. ①You should have had the _____ to turn off the electricity before touching the wires. ②She was at last beginning to _____ what the trouble was. ③Living away from home had given him a _____ of freedom and independence. ④She may not be lying in the strict _____ of the word, but she is certainly hiding something from us. ⑤He was an unusually able detective with a sort of sixth _____ for tracking down burglary suspects.

Q. ①~⑤의 문장의 빈칸에 공통으로 들어갈 낱말은?

4. A good way to find out what another person is thinking or feeling is to ask him directly. ① He may not answer, or if he does answer he may not answer truly, but very often he will. ② The fact that the information people give about themselves can be deceptive does not entail that it is never to be trusted. ③ It may be that the inferences we draw from people's gestures and facial expressions are more secure than those which we base upon what they say about themselves. ④ But were it not that we can rely a great deal upon words, we should know still less about each other than we do now. ⑤

Q. ①~⑤중 다음 문장이 삽입되기에 적절한 곳은?
We do not depend upon it alone.

5. A smile costs nothing but creates much. It enriches those who receive without impoverishing those who give. It happens in a flash and the memory of it sometimes lasts forever. _____ are so rich that they can get along without it; they are richer for its benefits. It creates happiness in the home, fosters good will in a business and is the countersign of friends. It is rest to the weary, daylight to the discouraged, sunshine to the sad, and nature's best antidote for trouble. Yet it cannot be bought, begged, borrowed or stolen, for it is something that is no earthly good to anybody until it is given away. Nobody needs a smile so much <u>to, as, who, give, have, left, none, those</u>.

Q 1. 빈칸에 들어갈 적절한 낱말은?

2. 밑줄 친 8개의 낱말을 문맥에 맞게 배열하면?

[실전 독해 B] 각 문항의 물음에 답하세요.

1. One day an unlucky fox who was trying to get a drink of water fell into a deep well and could not get out. Along came a thirsty goat and asked the fox if the water was good. "Oh yes," said the fox, "the water is excellent." And the fox told the goat to jump in and have a drink. Without stopping to think, the goat jumped into the well and took a long drink. Then both animals began to wonder how they would get out of the well. "I have an idea," said the fox. "Put your feet against the wall, and I will climb on top of you to get out. After I am out, I'll pull you up too." So the fox climbed onto the goat's shoulders and out over the edge of the well. Then the fox started to leave. The goat cried out, "What about me? Aren't you going to help me out?" "You have more hairs on your chin than brains in your head," the fox answered and left.

    Q. 이 글이 주는 교훈이 아닌 것은?
       1) Plan ahead.   2) Second thoughts are best.
       3) Don't trust anybody.   4) Look before you leap.
       5) The biter is sometimes bit.

2. A woman in Ohio put her baby into the washing-tub, and its dirty frock and petticoat into the cradle, and set her little boy to rock it. She did not discover her mistake until the baby cried out when she pinned its left leg to the line, as she hung it out in the yard to dry.

    The *Nashville Observer* informs us of another case, which took place in the person of an old lady, who, after stirring the fire with her knitting needle, proceeded to knit with the poker, and did not discover her error till she commenced scratching her head with it.

    We learn from the *Nashville Banner*, that a land-agent down there, by name Hiram Botts, having to ride out in great haste one day last week, actually clapped the saddle upon his own back instead of his mare's, and never found out the mistake till he was quite fatigued with vainly trying to get upon himself.

    Q. 이 글의 제목으로 적절한 것은?
       1) People in Haste   2) The Absence of Mind
       3) Terror and Horror   4) How to Make a Mistake
       5) The Wise and the Foolish

3.   Isn't it nice that the new year starts [1]in the dead of winter, when the primitive in each of us believes [2]that we will never see spring again? Right in mid gloom, here comes the new year [3]with all its hopefulness untarnished. Isn't it wonderful? I mean, [4]who would care about the new year [5]if it is in mid July?

 Q. 밑줄 친 1)~5)중 어법에 맞지 않는 것은?

4.   People are always talking about originality or creativity; but what do they mean? The moment we are born, the world begins to work upon us, and this goes to the end till we cease to be. What can we call our own, after all, except energy, strength, and will? If I could give an account of all that I owe to others, there would be _____.

 Q. 빈칸에 들어갈 적절한 말은?
  1) much to share   2) little to give them
  3) nothing to say   4) but little of my own
  5) a great deal for them.

5.   The lawyer happened to be very busy at the moment a young man called on him. "Won't you please take a chair and wait?" he said, looking up politely from his desk. "I don't think you understand," interrupted the youth impatiently, "I am Reverend Jackson's son." "Oh," said the lawyer, looking up from his desk again, "in that case [a]_____. Most of us can't react constantly with that much wit. But we can react with tolerance. While we can't get a reputation for being [b]_____, we can get a reputation for being nice. And being nice is much more important when it comes to making friends. When you don't think you can take the other fellow's arrogance, it's good to be reminded of what Emerson once said: "Every man I meet is in some way my superior; and in that I can learn of him."

 Q 1. 빈칸 a)에 들어갈 적절한 말은?
   1) I'll help you   2) you don't have to wait
   3) please be patient   4) please take two chairs
   5) I'll be with you in a minute

  2. 빈칸 b)에 들어갈 적절한 말은?
   1) wise   2) polite   3) honest
   4) modest   5) brilliant

[명작 감상]   Leo N. Tolstoy (1828 ~ 1910)
            Anna Karenina 『안나 까레니나』

All happy families are alike but an unhappy family is unhappy after its own fashion.

Everything had gone wrong in the Oblonsky household. The wife had found out about her husband's relationship with their former French governess and had announced that she could not go on living in the same house with him. This state of affairs had already continued for three days and was having a distressing effect on the couple themselves, on all the members of the family, and on the domestics. They all felt that there was no sense in their living together under the same roof and that any group of people who chanced to meet at a wayside inn would have more in common than they, the members of the Oblonsky family, and their servants. The wife did not leave her own rooms and the husband stayed away from home all day. The children strayed all over the house, not knowing what to do with themselves. The English governess had quarreled with the housekeeper and had written a note asking a friend to find her a new place. The head-cook had gone out right at dinner-time the day before. The under-cook and the coachman had given notice....

Oblonsky was a straightforward man in his dealings with himself. He could not deceive himself into believing that he repented of his conduct. He could not now do penance for something he had reproached himself for half a dozen years ago when he had first been unfaithful to his wife. He could not beg forgiveness because he, a handsome, susceptible man of thirty-four, was not in love with his wife, who was the mother of five living and two dead children and only a year younger than himself. He only regretted that he had not managed to hide things from her better. Nevertheless, he felt the full gravity of his position and pitied his wife, his children, and himself. Perhaps he would have been more successful in hiding his wrongdoing from his wife had he suspected the effect that the discovery would have upon her. He had never clearly thought the matter out but had vaguely imagined that she had long since guessed his unfaithfulness and was turning a blind eye to it. She was a good mother but she was already faded and plain and no longer young, a simple, uninteresting woman; so it seemed to him that she really ought to be indulgent. But it proved to be quite the opposite.

[학인 학습] 다음 문장을 우리말로 옮기세요.

1. The fact that the information people give about themselves can be deceptive does not entail that it is never to be trusted.

2. None are so rich that they can get along without it; they are richer for its benefits. Nobody needs a smile so much as those who have none left to give.

3. She did not discover her mistake until the baby cried out when she pinned its left leg to the line, as she hung it out in the yard to dry.

4. Any group of people who chanced to meet at a wayside inn would have more in common than they, the members of the Oblonsky family, and their servants.

5. Perhaps he would have been more successful in hiding his wrongdoing from his wife had he suspected the effect that the discovery would have upon her.

[words & phrases]

A1: accident 사고/우연, transfer 옮기다/이동하다, coinage 주조화폐, arrogance 거만, selfish 이기적인
A2: violent 폭력적, reflect 반영하다, overcome 극복하다, prejudice 편견, creed 신조, race 인종/종족
A3: electricity 전기, independence 독립, detective 탐정/형사, burglary 강도질/도둑질, suspect 용의자
A4: deceptive 현혹시키는, entail 수반하다, infer 추론하다, secure 안전한, rely (up)on ~을 신뢰하다
A5: impoverish 가난하게 하다, benefit 이득/혜택, foster 육성하다, good will 호의, antidote 해독제
B1: fox 여우, goat 염소, well 샘/우물, thirsty 목마른, shoulder 어깨, edge 모서리/가장자리, chin 턱
B2: frock 아동복, petticoat 속치마/소아복, cradle 요람, take place 일어나다/발생하다, poker 부지깽이,
   commence 시작하다, agent 중개인, haste 서두름, saddle 안장, mare 암말, fatigue 피로(하게 하다)
B3: in the dead of winter 한겨울에, primitive 원시인/원시적, gloom 어둠/우울/침울, tarnish 더럽히다
B4: originality 독창성, cease 멈추다, will 의지, give an account of ~에 대한 설명을 하다, owe 빚지다
B5: Reverend 성직자에 대한 경칭, tolerate 참다/관용하다, reputation 명성/평판, superior 우월한 (사람)
C1: fashion 방식, governess 여자 가정교사, distress 고통/괴롭히다, , have an effect on ~에 영향을 미치다,
   domestic 하인, sense 뜻/의미, have ~ in common ~을 공유하다, stray 흩어지다, notice 통고/통지,
   deceive 속이다, repent 후회하다, conduct 행위/행동, penance 참회/속죄, reproach 꾸짖다/비난하다,
   unfaithful 부정한/불충한, forgive 용서하다, manage to (do) 그럭저럭 ~하다, susceptible 다감한,
   grave 중대한, suspect 의심하다, vague 모호한, fade 시들다, plain 평이한, indulgent 무른/관대한

[실력 점검 A] 다음 각 동사의 우리말 뜻을 쓰세요.

1. store: 2. infer: 3. suspect:

4. stifle: 5. tarnish: 6. infuriate:

7. impart: 8. expand: 9. stimulate:

10. reverse: 11. deceive: 12. embezzle:

13. exempt: 14. examine: 15. transcend:

16. convert: 17. withstand: 18. appreciate:

19. measure: 20. exaggerate:

[실력 점검 B] 각 항목에 대응하는 영어 단어를 찾아 쓰세요.

보기   oath, well, insect, device, insight, faculty, priority, despair, celebrity, defect, planet, odious, prophet, criminal, patience, opportunity, expenditure, velocity, perpetual, inconsistent

1. 행성: 2. 벌레: 3. 인내:

4. 능력: 5. 결점: 6. 실망:

7. 맹세: 8. 지출: 9. 장치:

10. 우물: 11. 기회: 12. 유명인:

13. 속도: 14. 우선권: 15. 통찰력:

16. 예언자: 17. 범죄자: 18. 영속적:

19. 불쾌한: 20. 일관성이 없는:

[실력 점검 C] 주어진 철자로 시작되는 적절한 낱말은?

1. Were it not for dust the sky would a_____ absolutely black, and
   stars would be v_____ even at noonday.

2. Everyone, however insignificant, has an e_____ on someone else,
   just as a stone sends out ripples when it is cast into s_____ water.
   There is no one who does not a_____ others in some way or another.

명시 감상

The Lake Isle of Innisfree

W. B. Yeats

I will arise and go now, and go to Innisfree,
And a small cabin build there, of clay and wattles made;
Nine bean rows will I have there, a hive for the honey bee,
And live alone in the bee-loud glade.

And I shall have some peace there, for peace comes dropping slow,
Dropping from the veils of the morning to where the cricket sings;
There midnight's all a glimmer, and noon a purple glow,
And evening full of the linnet's wings.

I will arise and go now, for always night and day
I hear lake water lapping with low sounds by the shore;
While I stand on the roadway, or on the pavement gray,
I hear it in the heart's core.

* isle 작은 섬, wattle 섞가래, hive 꿀벌통, glade 숲속의 빈터, glimmer 희미한 빛, linnet 홍방울새, lap 물결치다

Unit 16 비교

A. 원급/비교급/최상급

1) He is *young*. He is *younger* than my brother.

  She is *beautiful*. She is *more beautiful* than her sister.

2) He is *the tallest* (boy) of all. She is *the most beautiful* in my class.

  He runs *fastest* of all the boys. The days are *longest* in summer.

3) She likes you *better* than me. He is one of the *best* singers in Korea.

  The weather gets *worse*. Winter was the *worst* season for them.

B. 비교 구문의 유형

1) We *prefer* fish *to* meat. Their products are *inferior to* ours.

2) She is *prettier* than her sister. She is *more pretty* than beautiful.

3) Betty is *the nicer* of the two. I love him *all the more* for his faults.

4) *The higher* one goes, *the rarer* becomes the air. *The more, the better*.

5) *The brightest boy* couldn't answer all the questions in the oral test.

6) You are *the last* to blame. He was *the last* man I wanted to see.

7) It is *a most* important thing. It is one of *the most* important things.

8) He can speak German, *much more* English or French.

  He can't speak English, *much less* French or German.

9) She is *as* pretty *as* her sister. She was *not so* happy *as* her sister.

  Tim had almost three times *as much* money *as* Tom had.

  He made five mistakes in *as many* pages. I thought *as much*.

10) They did *not so much as* greet their neighbors.

  The representative is *not so much* a statesman *as* a politician.

  The whale is *no more* a fish *than* the penguin is.

11) Seoul is the largest city in Korea.

  = Seoul is the largest of all the cities in Korea.

  = Seoul is larger than any other city in Korea.

  = No (other) city in Korea is larger than Seoul.

  = No (other) city in Korea is so large as Seoul.

[필수 문법] 비교(comparison)

* 형용사나 부사의 어형 변화가 나타내는 둘 혹은 여럿 사이의 양태의 비교.
* 대부분의 형용사/부사는 규칙 변화를 하지만, 불규칙 변화를 하는 것도 있다.

A. 원급/비교급/최상급

  1) 비교급: 원급+"~er" : longer/easier/bigger/heavier/greater 등 (대개 1~2음절의 낱말)
      more+원급: more difficult, more important 등 (2~3음절 이상의 낱말).

  2) 최상급: 원급+"~est" : oldest, wisest, tallest, easiest, biggest, greatest, prettiest 등
      most+원급: most difficult, most important, most beautiful 등. * 명사를 수식
          하는 형용사의 최상급 앞에는 정관사 "the"를 붙여야 함.

  3) 불규칙 변화: good/well — better — best   bad/ill — worse — worst
      many/much — more — most   little — less — least
      in — inner — in(ner)most   out — outer — out(er)most
      old — older/elder — oldest, eldest (나이/순위): my elder brother
      far — farther/further — farthest/furthest (거리/정도): further information
      late — later/latter — latest/last (시간/순서): the latest news (최신 소식)

B. 비교 구문의 유형

  1) "than"을 쓰지 않고 "to"를 쓰는 비교급 낱말: prefer A to B (A를 B보다 더 좋아하다)
      be inferior/superior to ~보다 열등/우월하다,   be junior/senior to ~보다 연하/연상이다.

  2) 하나의 대상 내부에서의 비교: "~er"비교급이 아닌 "more"비교급을 사용한다.

  3) for, because, of the two 등에 의해 한정될 때는 비교급에서도 정관사 "the"를 붙인다.

  4) the+비교급~ , the+비교급~ : "~일수록/할수록, 더욱 ~하다": The sooner, the better.

  5) 최상급 앞에 "even(심지어 ~조차도)"이 생략된 경우: =*Even* the brightest boy ~.

  6) (너는 비난할 자격이 없다.) (그는 내가 가장 만나고 싶지 않은 사람이었다.)

  7) a most = very,   the most ~(최상급).   * *most* people, *most* of the people: "대부분(의)"

  8) much more (=still more) ~: "하물며 ~은 말할 것도 없고": 부정문은 much(=still) less ~.

  9) as ~ as ~: 동등(대등) 비교 구문: 미국 영어에서는 "She was *not as* happy *as* her sister."
      "as many," "so many"는 같은 수, "as much"는 같은 양: So many men, *so many* minds.

  10) not so much as ~조차도 않다: He's gone *without so much as* saying a word.
      not so much A as B (=not A so much as B): A라기 보다는 B이다: (=The representative is
      not a statesman *so much as* a politician. 그 의원은 정치가라기 보다는 정치꾼이다.)
      A is no more B than C is D (=A is not B any more than C is D): A가 B아닌 것은 C가
      D아닌 것과 같다: =The whale is *not* a fish *any more than* the penguin is (a fish).

  11) 비교 구문의 전환: 원급/비교급/최상급을 사용한 같은 뜻의 다양한 표현들.

[문법 연습 A] 잘못된 곳을 고치세요.

1. My father prefers tea than coffee.

2. Of the two girls, Minnie is prettier.

3. The young man was wiser than clever.

4. He's had a holiday and looks better for it.

5. I don't think I have anything farther to say.

6. She spent the later part of her life in Greece.

7. It is the most dangerous to play with explosives.

8. The woman looked very older than her husband.

9. Danny is brightest of all the students in the group.

10. The building is the last thing in modern architecture.

11. Their submarines were shown up as superior as ours.

12. She is kinder than any other girls in the neighborhood.

13. As you grow old, you will realize that life is really short.

[문법 연습 B] 빈칸에 알맞은 낱말은?

1. She is two years senior _____ my sister.

2. The more one has _____ more one wants.

3. Ten people gathered like so _____ ghosts.

4. They went as _____ as the subway station.

5. Three hours went by like as _____ minutes.

6. The baby can't even walk, much _____ run.

7. He knows _____ than to make such a mistake.

8. She just left _____ so much as saying goodbye.

9. He is not so much a scientist _____ an engineer.

10. She had almost twice as much money _____ I had.

11. Your mother looks much _____ old than my mother.

12. We have ten tickets, but we will need as _____ again.

13. He worked _____ harder, because his salary was raised.

218

[실전 문법 A] 같은 뜻의 다른 문장으로 고치세요.

Mt. Baekdu is the highest mountain in the Korean peninsula.

= Mt. Baekdu _____

= Mt. Baekdu _____

= No (other) mountain _____

= No (other) mountain _____

[실전 문법 B] 각 문항의 다섯 부분 중 어법에 맞지 않는 부분은?

1. [1]All this is part of modern commercial life [2]even if it is not [3]as an essential activity [4]as most participants [5]care to believe.

2. [1]I would prefer [2]a phrase or sentence [3]that was easy and unaffected [4]than a phrase or sentence [5]that was simply grammatical.

3. [1]The greatness of a people [2]is no more determined [3]by their number [4]than the greatness of a person [5]is not determined by his or her height.

4. [1]I was very embarrassed [2]to find my uncle there; [3]he was the last person [4]I had never expected [5]to see in such a place.

5. [1]The force of gravity is stronger [2]at the North or South Pole [3]than at the equator [4]because the poles are close [5]to the Earth's center.

6. [1]Nothing in the world gives us [2]so much real pleasure [3]as making things. [4]Have you ever tried to think [5]exactly what does making a thing mean?

7. [1]One who merely learns [2]pieces of information by heart [3]can hardly be said to know anything— [4]still more, [5]to understand what he knows.

8. [1]Radio has had as much influence on the world [2]like any other communication device. [3]And television is another major instrument of communication, [4]permitting us to see [5]as well as to hear the performer.

9. [1]The more area a map covers, [2]the more detail it can show; [3]a small map of the world will probably show [4]nothing but such major features [5]as countries, capital cities, and landforms.

[필수 어휘 A] 다음 형용사의 우리말 뜻은?

1. historic: 2. economic:
   historical: economical:
3. credible: 4. imaginary:
   credulous: imaginative:
5. industrial: 6. comparable:
   industrious: comparative:
7. respectful: 8. impressive:
   respectable: impressionable:
9. momentary: 10. desirable:
   momentous: desirous (of):
11. sensible: 12. considerable:
    sensitive (to):   considerate (of):

[필수 어휘 B] 각 문장의 밑줄 친 부분의 뜻은?

1. She felt sure she could <u>outshine</u> all the other competitors.

   1) stifle   2) admire   3) deceive   4) surpass   5) overtake

2. They didn't seem to <u>comprehend</u> how hard he had struggled.

   1) know   2) accept   3) imagine   4) realize   5) understand

3. His quiet manner was sometimes mistaken for being <u>indolent</u>.

   1) lazy   2) angry   3) modest   4) cautious   5) arrogant

4. As a birds is warm-blooded, its body temperature is <u>constant</u>.

   1) high   2) proper   3) natural   4) moderate   5) invariable

5. They are worried about the recent worldwide <u>surplus</u> of crude oil.

   1) crisis   2) excess   3) supply   4) demand   5) shortage

6. The photographs were <u>next to</u> useless, but they were all we had.

   1) even   2) really   3) almost   4) seldom   5) completely

7. <u>More often than not</u> the patient recovers in a few days or weeks.

   1) Rarely   2) Usually   3) Probably   4) Certainly   5) Sometimes

[구문 연습] 다음 문장을 우리말로 옮기세요.

1. The envious person deprives others of their advantages, which to him is as desirable as it would be to secure the same advantages himself.

2. The more we consider the question of primitiveness in language, the less reasonable does it seem to call any language inferior or primitive.

3. People are never so ready to believe you as when you say things in dispraise of yourself, and you are never so much annoyed as when they take you at your word.

4. Much remains to be discovered about what causes some people to be more intelligent, more able, or to have greater application than others.

5. It is philosophy, not science, that should be uppermost in any culture or civilization, simply because the questions it can answer are more important. It should be clear that the more science we possess the more we need philosophy, because the more power we have the more we need direction.

[작문 연습] 다음 문장을 영어로 옮기세요.

1. 너희들이 술과 담배를 즐기면 즐길수록 끊기가 더 어려워진다.

_____

2. 그 공공 도서관은 우리들이 가진 책의 열 배 이상을 갖고 있다.

_____

3. 솔직히 말하면 그는 진정한 예술가라기 보다는 단순한 모방꾼이다.

_____

4. 나이가 들수록 우리들은 삶은 살 가치가 있다는 것을 깨닫게 된다.

_____

5. 독도가 일본의 섬이 아닌 것은 대마도가 한국의 섬이 아닌 것과 같다.

_____

[실전 독해 A] 각 문항의 물음에 답하세요.

1. The majority of men are ^{a)}_____ uninterested in the workings of nature in general as they are in the processes taking place in their own bodies. For many there is something indecent and unnatural in trying to understand the world which they live in. For these the glories of a sunset fade before an explanation of how these gay colors are produced; a description of the wonderful growth of a baby from the fertilized egg is something horrible, to be thrust away and ^{b)}_____ from contemplation like thoughts of death.

> Q 1. 빈칸 a)에 들어갈 낱말은?
>
> 　 2. 빈칸 b)에 들어갈 낱말은?
> 　　 1) kept　　 2) derived　　 3) brought
> 　　 4) separated　　 5) distinguished

2. A brand name and its brand image are very important in advertising. In fact, advertisements without brand names can fail completely. If a furniture dealer ^{a)}<u>put</u> out an advertisement, "Buy some more furniture now," he would fail; people are not told to buy a particular brand of furniture.

Sometimes an advertising agency accidentally chooses a name that produces unhappy or unpleasant feelings. It is very easy to make a mistake, especially in a foreign country. A ^{b)}<u>brand-new</u> perfume called "No. 4" was advertised in Japan, but no one bought it. Why? In Japanese the number of four is also the word for "death."

At times a brand name loses any real meaning for consumers; it becomes ^{c)}<u>too</u> well known that people use it for other products of the same kind. *Hoover,* for instance, is the brand name—the trademark for a particular kind of vacuum cleaner. But we now use this name for any kind of vacuum cleaner. In the end, the word goes into the dictionary ^{d)}<u>with</u> a capital letter.

> Q. 밑줄 친 a) ~ d)중 잘못된 것은?
> 　 1) a, b　　 2) a, c　　 3) b, c
> 　 4) b, d　　 5) c, d

3. Things should be seen from a distance—never close, but always from a distance. Seen close, their charm disappears and only their innate ugliness remains. Nothing is so beautiful _____ it betrays some defects on close inspection.

> Q. 빈칸에 알맞은 낱말은?
> 1) as   2) nor   3) but
> 4) that   5) what

4. Like others who had a Puritan education, I had the habit of meditating on my sins, foolishness, and deficiencies. I seemed to myself—no doubt justly—a miserable being. Gradually I learned to be indifferent to myself and my deficiencies; I came to center my attention increasingly upon external objects: the state of the world, various branches of knowledge, individuals for whom I felt affection. External interests, it is true, bring each its own possibility of pain: the world may be plunged in war, knowledge in some direction may be hard to achieve, friends may die. But pains of these kinds do not destroy the essential quality of life, as do those that spring from _____.

> Q. 빈칸에 들어갈 적절한 어구는?
> 1) bad habits of life   2) a variety of feelings
> 3) the loss of interests   4) the disgust with self
> 5) ignorance and indifference

5. Aristotle could not have understood a page of modern physics or biology, but Socrates and his friends would have had little trouble in following most current discussions of human affairs. And as to technology, we have made immense strides in controlling the physical and biological worlds, but our practice in government, education, and much of economics has not greatly improved.

> Q. 이 글의 요지로서 적절한 것은?
> 1) No one can understand all the fields of modern science.
> 2) Aristotle was not so intelligent as Socrates and his friends.
> 3) Nothing is so difficult to understand as physics and biology.
> 4) Technology has greatly contributed to the improvement of our life.
> 5) Natural sciences have made far more progress than social sciences.

[실전 독해 B] 각 문항의 물음에 답하세요.

1. ⓐ Early in history, the women stayed at home to care for the children, to tend the fire, and to gather the food. They did individual work. Women had to be self-sufficient. They had to be able to find food for themselves and their children. Meanwhile, the men went out in a group to hunt for food. Therefore, the men developed a "<u>pack mentality</u>" like dogs. All dogs, whether wolves in the wild or tame dogs in cities, seem to enjoy the company of other members of their kind.

ⓑ In general, artists like cats. Painters, musicians, sculptors, and actors— these people are likely to prefer cats to dogs. Like cat's personality, the cat lover's personality is likely to be independent, individual and distinct. More women than men prefer cats, perhaps because women tend to be more independent than men, says Morris. On the other hand, soldiers prefer dogs. The idea of group loyalty is natural to dogs and dog-loving human beings. In general more men prefer dogs.

ⓒ Who likes cats, and who likes dogs? According to Desmond Morris, an anthropologist and watcher of both people and animals, there are serious differences between cat lovers and dog lovers. Cats don't need people, says Morris, though they like to be pampered by their people. A cat is not likely to please anyone but itself. On the other hand, dogs tend to be dependent on their owners. And dogs try to please their owners. These animal characteristics are reflected in the characteristics of the people who like them.

Q 1. ⓐ~ⓒ의 단락을 문맥에 맞게 배열하면?
   1) ⓐ-ⓒ-ⓑ   2) ⓑ-ⓐ-ⓒ   3) ⓑ-ⓒ-ⓐ
   4) ⓒ-ⓐ-ⓑ   5) ⓒ-ⓑ-ⓐ

2. 밑줄 친 "pack mentality"와 동일한 뜻의 낱말이나 어구를
   ⓑ~ⓒ의 단락에서 찾으면?

3. 이 글의 내용과 일치하지 않는 것은?
   1) Both men and dogs may be characterized by a "pack mentality."
   2) The dog's personality seems to be reflected in that of the dog lover.
   3) Women were self-sufficient and they didn't have to depend on men.
   4) Morris' theory is concerned with the people attracted to cats or dogs.
   5) Artists tend to be more independent and individual than other people.

2.   Your castles in the air are the best castles to possess, and keep a quiet mind. In them no taxes, no housemaids, no men-at-arms bother and no slavery of property exists. Their architecture is always perfect, the prospect of and from them is always delightful, and in fact, without them the greater part of humanity would have no house in which to shield their souls against the storm of life.

Q. 이 글은 무엇에 관한 것인가?
   1) 정신 수련   2) 공상의 효용성
   3) 가상 현실   4) 환상적 유토피아
   5) 현대 건축의 완벽성

3.   The mental world of the ordinary man comprises beliefs which he has accepted without questioning and to which he is firmly attached; he is instinctively hostile to anything that would upset the established order of this familiar world. A new idea or conception, inconsistent with some of the beliefs he holds, means the necessity to rearrange his mind; and this process is laborious, requiring a painful expenditure of brain energy.

Q. 이 글을 다음과 같이 요약하였다.
   빈칸에 들어갈 각각의 낱말은?
   People in general are not so much progressive
   _____ _____ in their way of thinking.

4.   Although computers can perform complex calculations with astonishing rapidity and index vast quantities of data, they have never been able to "understand" human language. At present, any task a computer _____ to do must be spelled out, step by step, in terms of a computer language. A misplaced comma or period will foul the computation. For anyone who has even a passing acquaintance with computer-programming, the possibility that a machine might learn to understand the ambiguities of plain English is little short of astounding.

Q. 빈칸에 들어갈 적절한 것은?
   1) asks   2) asked   3) asking
   4) is asked   5) to be asked

[명작 감상]   Jean-Jacques Rousseau (1712 ~ 1778)
            The Confessions 『고백록』

I was born at Geneva in 1712, the son of Issac Rousseau, a citizen of that town, and Susanne Bernard, his wife. My father's inheritance, being a fifteenth part only of a very small property which had been divided among as many children, was almost nothing, and he relied for his living entirely on his trade of watchmaker, at which he was very highly skilled. My mother was the daughter of a minister of religion and rather better-off. She had besides both intelligence and beauty, and my father had not found it easy to win her.

Their love had begun almost with their birth; at eight or nine they would walk together every evening along La Treille, and at ten they were inseparable. Sympathy and mental affinity strengthened in them a feeling first formed by habit. Both being affectionate and sensitive by nature, were only waiting for the moment when they find similar qualities in another; or rather the moment was waiting for them, and both threw their affections at the first heart that opened to receive them. Fate, by appearing to oppose their passion, only strengthened it. Unable to obtain his mistress, the young lover ate out his heart with grief, and she counseled him to travel and forget her. He travelled in vain, and returned more in love than ever, to find her he loved still faithful and fond. After such a proof, it was inevitable that they should love one another for all their lives. They swore to do so, and Heaven smiled on their vows....

My uncle Bernard, who was an engineer, went to serve in the Empire and Hungary under Prince Eugene, and distinguished himself at the siege and battle of Belgrade. My father, after the birth of my only brother, left for Constantinople, where he had been called to become watchmaker to the Sultan's Seraglio. While he was away my mother's beauty, wit, and talents brought her admirers, one of the most pressing of whom was M. de la Closure, the French Resident in the city. His feelings must have been very strong, for thirty years later I have seen him moved when merely speaking to me about her. But my mother had more than her virtue with which to defend herself; she deeply loved my father, and urged him to come back. He threw up everything to do so, and I was the unhappy fruit of his return. For ten months later I was born, a poor and sickly child, and cost my mother her life. So my birth was the first of my misfortunes.

[확인 학습] 다음 문장을 우리말로 옮기세요.

1. The majority of men are as uninterested in the workings of nature in general as they are in the processes taking place in their own bodies

2. Seen close, their charm disappears and only their innate ugliness remains. Nothing is so beautiful but it betrays some defects on close inspection.

3. For anyone who has even a passing acquaintance with computer-programming, the possibility that a machine might learn to understand the ambiguities of plain English is little short of astounding.

4. My father's inheritance, being a fifteenth part only of a very small property which had been divided among as many children, was almost nothing, and he relied for his living entirely on his trade of watchmaker, at which he was very highly skilled.

[words & phrases]

A1: majority 다수, decent 품위 있는, fertilize 수정시키다, contemplate 숙고하다, thrust 밀다/밀어내다

A2: advertise 광고하다, accidental 우연한, perfume 향기/향수, consume 소비하다, capital letter 대문자

A3: innate 타고난/내재적인, but ~하지 않을 만큼, betray 드러내다, defect 결함/결점, inspect 조사하다

A4: Puritan 청교도, meditation 명상, deficiency 부족/결여, affection 애정, plunge 뛰어들다/던져넣다

A5: as to ~에 관해서, immense 광대한, stride 활보(하다)/진보, practice 실행/관행, improve 향상되다

B1: tend 돌보다, sufficient 충분한, pack 떼/무리, tame 길들인/길들이다, company 동반/교제, sculptor 조각가, personality 개성, independent 독립적인, distinct 뚜렷한, loyalty 충성/충직, anthropology 인류학, pamper 응석받이로 키우다, characteristic 특징/특징적인, reflect 반사하다/반영하다

B2: man-at arms 병사/군인, property 재산, architecture 건축(물), prospect 전망/가망, shield 보호하다

B3: comprise ~으로 구성되어 있다, attached 붙이다/부착하다, instinct 본능, hostile 적대적인, upset 뒤엎다, establish 확립하다, consistent 일관된, laborious 힘든/고된, expenditure 지출/경비/비용

B4: index 색인(을 넣다), acquaintance 지식/면식, ambiguous 모호한/다의적, little short of 거의/가까운

C1: heritance 상속(재산), as many 같은 수(=fifteen), minister 목사, well-off 유복한, besides 게다가 sympathy 동정/공감, affinity 유사성/친화력, affection 애정, sensitive 민감한, similar 유사한, fate 운명, appear to (do) ~처럼 보이다, oppose 반대하다, obtain 얻다, mistress 애인/정부, grief 슬픔, in vain 헛되이, inevitable 피할 수 없는, swear 맹세하다, vow 맹세/서약, distinguish oneself 뛰어나다, siege 포위 공격, admire 칭송하다, virtue 미덕/정조, urge 재촉하다, misfortune 불행/불운

[실력 점검 A] 다음 각 동사의 우리말 뜻을 쓰세요.

1. tend:	2. exult:	3. aspire:
4. evolve:	5. admire:	6. respire:
7. exceed:	8. include:	9. perspire:
10. plunge:	11. inspect:	12. astound:
13. bestow:	14. menace:	15. comprise:
16. implore:	17. swallow:	18. withdraw:
19. recollect:	20. illuminate:	

[실력 점검 B] 각 항목에 대응하는 영어 단어를 찾아 쓰세요.

보기 fuel, germ, villain, illegal, prospect, stubborn, periodical, immigrant, anxiety, harvest, appetite, reaction, archive, statistics, emergency, colleague, urgent, editorial, temporary, supplementary

1. 수확:	2. 통계:	3. 식욕:
4. 세균:	5. 연료:	6. 전망:
7. 이민:	8. 악당:	9. 동료:
10. 걱정:	11. 위급:	12. 사설:
13. 반응:	14. 불법적:	15. 일시적:
16. 긴급한:	17. 완고한:	18. 보충적:
19. 문서 보관소:	20. 정기 간행물:	

[실력 점검 C] 주어진 철자로 시작되는 적절한 낱말은?

1. Do you really believe that the pen is m_____ than the sword?

2. Man had s_____ built the first cities before he began to try to get away from them. This paradox is as old as city i_____.

3. Bad weather and poor road condition bring a_____ some accidents, but, generally, such factors appear to be of minor s_____ compared with the mental and p_____ condition of the driver.

명시 감상

Stopping by Woods on a Snowy Evening

Robert Frost

Whose woods these are I think I know.
His house is in the village though;
He will not see me stopping here
To watch his woods fill up with snow.

My little horse must think it queer
To stop without a farmhouse near
Between the woods and frozen lake
The darkest evening of the year.

He gives his harness bells a shake
To ask if there is some mistake.
The only other sound's the sweep
Of easy wind and downy flake.

The woods are lovely, dark and deep,
But I have promises to keep,
And miles to go before I sleep,
And miles to go before I sleep.

* though 그러나, queer 이상한/야릇한, farmhouse 농가, harness 馬具, sweep 쓸기, downy flake 솜털같은 눈송이

Unit 17 문체

A. 간결(brevity)

1) Writers have their own styles (*that are used in their works*).

2) Iris wishes to be a teacher (*in the future*) when she grows up.

3) There are still many primitive tribes in the world (*we live in*).

4) You may have received a letter from a stranger (*you have never met*).

B. 도치(inversion)

1) Long may *you* live! How happy is *the boy who wins the race*!

2) *Blessed* are the poor in spirit, for *theirs* is the kingdom of heaven.

3) *What he said* I still remember. *Not a word* did she say to me.

4) *There* comes the bus! *Little* did I dream of ever seeing you here.

5) He is happy today, and *so is she*. He didn't come, and *neither did she*.

C. 강조(emphasis)

1) I *do* remember. He *does* know it. She *did* keep her words.

2) He did it *himself*. The President *herself* could not find the answer.

3) Have you *ever* seen a hippopotamus? I have *never* been to Europe.

4) It was *much* worse than I thought. We faced a *far* greater problem.

5) The hotel is *right* on the beach. Have you any interest *whatever*?

6) She used *this very* pen. This is *the very* book I have been looking for.

7) What *on earth* are you doing? Where *in the world* could they be?

8) It was *her* that he met yesterday. It was *yesterday* that he met her.

D. 병렬(parallelism)

1) Rachel is *kind*, *smart*, and very *beautiful*.

2) Mr. Lee speaks English *fluently* and *accurately*.

3) He is interested *not in* physics *but in* metaphysics.

4) May I have your *name*, *address*, and *phone number*?

5) Michael was *loved by* his wife and *respected by* his children.

6) The party was planned by the students *of art* and *of medicine*.

7) Charles likes *swimming*, *watching* videos, and *playing* the guitar.

8) They want *a glass of water*, *two cups of coffee*, and *three cans of beer*.

[필수 문법] 문체(style)

* 글이나 문장의 전반적인 모양이나 특징.
* 글과 문장은 무엇보다도 언어의 경제성에 맞게 간결해야 하며,
* 문장 특정 부분의 도치, 강조, 병렬의 경우에는 그 원리에 맞아야 함.

A. 간결: 제시된 각 예문의 일부분은 그 의미가 중첩되는 불필요한 부분임.
   1) 작가들은 (자신의 작품에서 사용되는) 자기 자신의 문체를 갖고 있다.
   2) 아이리스는 (미래에) 자신이 성장했을 때 선생님이 되기를 소망한다.
   3) (우리가 사는) 세상에는 아직도 많은 원시 부족들이 있다.
   4) 당신은 (만나본 적도 없는) 낯선 이로부터 편지 한 통을 받았을 지도 모른다.

B. 도치: 주어 아닌 다른 요소가 문두에 놓이면 흔히 "주어/(조)동사"가 도치된다.
   1) 주어의 도치: =You may live long!   =*The boy who wins the race* is very happy.
   2) 보어의 도치: =The poor in spirit are *blessed*, for the kingdom of heaven is *theirs*.
   3) 목적어의 도치: =I still remember *what he said*.   =She did *not* say *a word* to me.
   4) 부사(구)의 도치: =The bus comes *there*!   =I *little* dreamed of ever seeing you here.
   5) =He is happy today, and *she is happy, too*.   =He didn't come, and *she didn't, either*.

C. 강조: 문장의 특정 부분을 강조하여 표현하는 방법이나 방식.
   1) 동사의 강조: 강조를 위한 조동사 "do, does, did"를 도입함: Do be quiet. He *did* come.
   2) 재귀 대명사: 흔히 강조사(intensifier)로 쓰이며 "(자신이) 직접, (자기) 스스로"의 뜻.
   3) 강조사 "ever"는 흔히 (현재/과거) 완료형에 쓰이며, "never"는 "not"의 강조형.
   4) 비교급의 강조: much, far, still, even, a lot (훨씬)   5) right (바로), whatever (무엇이든).
   6) 강조 어구: on earth, in the world (도대체)   7) this very (바로 이), the very (바로 그).
   8) 강조 구문("it is ~ that ~"): 강조되는 부분이 "it is"와 "that"의 사이에 놓이게 된다:
      It was *he* that(=who) met her yesterday.   It is *not him but you* that(=whom) I love.

D. 병렬: 문장 내에서의 문법적 기능이 서로 같은 요소들은 그 모양이나 형태에 있어서도
   서로 같아야 함: 병렬/대구 구조에 적용되는 표현의 일관성을 위한 "평행원칙(parallelism)"
   1) Rachel was *kind, smart*, and *of great beauty*. (x)
   2) Mr. Lee speaks English *fluently* and *with accuracy*. (x)
   3) He is interested *not in* physics *but* metaphysics. (x)
   4) May I have your *name, address*, and *what's your phone number*? (x)
   5) Michael *was loved by* his wife, and his children *respected* him. (x)
   6) The party was planned by the *students of art* and *medical students*. (x)
   7) Charles likes *swimming, watching* videos, and *to play* the guitar. (x)
   8) They want *a glass of water, two cups of coffee*, and *three beers*. (x)
   * 운(rhyme)을 맞춘 경쾌한 표현들: *Nurture* passes *nature*. (양육이 태생보다 중요)
      Haste makes *waste*. A friend *in need* is a friend *indeed*. (어려울 때 친구가 진정한 친구)

[문법 연습 A] 잘못된 부분을 고치세요.

1. We didn't know whether to go or stay and help.

2. Will you tell me your name, age, and where you live?

3. They could neither be happy in the city nor in the country.

4. A wise man is defined not by what he knows but what he does.

5. He is the man who works hard and who is admired by all of us.

6. She told me about Alfred Nobel and that he invented dynamite.

7. Paul has a strong desire that he wishes to be a sculptor like Rodin.

8. They complained both of the climate and the people of the country.

9. Such a disaster as an earthquake can happen at any time or even now.

[문법 연습 B] 밑줄 친 부분을 강조하세요.

1. <u>Who</u> is going to take care of the children?

_____

2. They are fighting for <u>their freedom and independence</u>.

_____

3. Women did <u>not</u> gain the vote <u>until after the First World War</u>.

_____

[문법 연습 C] 밑줄 친 부분을 도치하세요.

1. The rain came <u>down</u> with a clap of thunder.

_____

2. My teacher was <u>so angry</u> that he didn't know what to do.

_____

3. He <u>never</u> thought that she was about to go on stage again.

_____

4. Women did <u>not</u> gain the vote <u>until after the First World War</u>.

_____

[실전 문법 A] 빈칸에 알맞은 강조사는?

1. I found it at the _____ bottom of the box.

2. You can ask me questions on any topic _____.

3. Jack has loved trains _____ since his boyhood.

4. How on _____ do we raise half a million dollars?

5. I have no time _____ now to discuss your problems.

6. She was afraid of the _____ idea of going home alone.

7. *Anna Karenina* is one of the best novels _____ written.

8. There is no scientific evidence _____ to support such a view.

9. Others might find odd what one finds perfectly normal _____.

[실전 문법 B] 각 문항의 다섯 부분 중 어법에 맞지 않는 부분은?

1. ¹⁾It is the joints ²⁾of the human body ³⁾that movements ⁴⁾of the bones ⁵⁾take place.

2. ¹⁾Not until he was awarded ²⁾the Pulitzer Prize in 1947 ³⁾Charles Ives received ⁴⁾any degree of recognition ⁵⁾for his work.

3. ¹⁾Excessive weight, ²⁾cigarette smoking, ³⁾and lack of exercise ⁴⁾are the three big causes ⁵⁾of ill health and early dying in our society.

4. ¹⁾Only in recent years ²⁾people have begun to realize ³⁾that wild animals, kept within limited territory, ⁴⁾do more good ⁵⁾than harm.

5. ¹⁾It is well known ²⁾that the elephant, like the dog, ³⁾relies more ⁴⁾on its sense of smell ⁵⁾than any other sense.

6. ¹⁾She has many a hobby, ²⁾such as swimming, ³⁾stamp collecting, ⁴⁾listening to music, ⁵⁾and reading detective stories.

7. ¹⁾He doesn't write ²⁾for money or fame; ³⁾he writes because he has a burning desire ⁴⁾to express what was seen, heard and felt ⁵⁾in his everyday life.

8. ¹⁾We have been surrounded by birds ²⁾all our lives, ³⁾yet very feeble is our observation ⁴⁾that many of us cannot tell the song of a thrush ⁵⁾from the song of a blackbird.

[필수 어휘 A] 각 문장의 밑줄 친 낱말의 뜻은?

1. Who wants to leave the children to <u>perish</u> from starvation?

   1) die   2) suffer   3) escape   4) protect   5) prevent

2. He was aware that his wife was a <u>prudent</u> manager of money.

   1) timid   2) stingy   3) selfish   4) careful   5) generous

3. If this policy is reversed, we will never achieve our <u>objective</u>.

   1) profit   2) status   3) purpose   4) business   5) reputation

4. In fact, his departure was <u>abrupt</u> and completely unexpected.

   1) urgent   2) sudden   3) delayed   4) unknown   5) surprising

5. The young man had the great virtues of <u>humility</u> and kindliness.

   1) faith   2) honesty   3) modesty   4) affection   5) friendliness

6. I thought that this would have a <u>negligible</u> effect on the temperature.

   1) vital   2) normal   3) negative   4) enormous   5) insignificant

[필수 어휘 B] 각 문장의 밑줄 친 부분의 뜻은?

1. If there is one thing I <u>loathe</u>, it is long car journeys.

   1) hate   2) avoid   3) consider   4) hesitate   5) condemn

2. The boys will probably <u>grumble</u> about having to do the work.

   1) learn   2) worry   3) discuss   4) tolerate   5) complain

3. She didn't want to <u>humiliate</u> the student in front of his friends.

   1) scold   2) shame   3) praise   4) punish   5) persuade

4. They could recoup these costs from the extra harvest <u>yielded</u>.

   1) saved   2) earned   3) planned   4) produced   5) remained

5. There were some <u>priceless</u> things in the attic of the old house.

   1) useful   2) useless   3) expensive   4) valuable   5) invaluable

6. In his letters to me he rarely <u>referred to</u> social and political events.

   1) liked   2) blamed   3) explained   4) mentioned   5) suggested

7. Ms. Lee <u>availed herself of</u> every opportunity to improve her English.

   1) used   2) sought   3) practiced   4) registered   5) encountered

[구문 연습] 다음 문장을 우리말로 옮기세요.

1. Fortunate is the man who at the right moment meets the right friend; fortunate also the man who at right moment meets the right enemy.

2. That the beauty of life is a thing of no moment, I suppose few people would venture to assert, and yet most civilized people act as if it were none.

3. It is the values which are attached to such words as "liberty" or "democracy" that are being called in question today.

4. So great is the disparity between human speech and any form of animal communication that it remains the most difficult human trait for which to provide an evolutionary account.

5. Not until severe energy shortage and heavy pollution began to interfere with everyday life did we start to question our irresponsible use of the earth's resources, and to see nature as a force to be protected as well as used.

[작문 연습] 다음 문장을 영어로 옮기세요.

1. 내가 그 젊은이를 길에서 우연히 만난 것은 바로 그저께였다.

_____

2. 그와 사랑에 빠지게 될 줄은 그녀는 거의 꿈에도 생각지 못했다.

_____

3. 상대성 이론과 그것의 우리 생활에의 적용에 대해서 생각해보자.

_____

4. 그 절과 계곡이 너무나 조화로워서 그 풍경은 하나의 예술품이었다.

_____

5. 우리 지능 저하의 원인들 가운데는 지난 반 세기의 TV 시청도 있다.

_____

[실전독해 A] 각 문항의 물음에 답하세요.

1. A young boy and his doting grandmother were walking long the shore in Daytona Beach when a huge wave appeared out of nowhere, sweeping the child out to sea. The horrific woman fell to her knees, raised her eyes to the heavens and begged the Lord to return her beloved grandson. And, lo, another wave reared up and deposited the stunned child on the sand before her. The grandmother looked the boy over carefully. He was fine. But still she stared up angrily toward the heavens. "When we came," she snapped indignantly, _____.

    Q. 빈칸에 들어갈 적절한 말은?
        1) "he had a hat!"　　2) "we were very happy!"
        3) "it was a fine day!"　　4) "the waves were friendly!"
        5) "we didn't have to see a doctor!"

2. I guess it is true that big and strong things are much less dangerous than small soft weak things. Nature makes the small and weak reproduce faster. And that is not true of course. The ones that did not reproduce faster than they died, disappeared. But how about little faults, little pains, little worries? The cosmic ulcer comes not from great concerns, but from little irritations. And great things can kill a man but if they do not he is stronger and better for them. A man is destroyed by the duck nibblings of nagging, ragweed, athlete's foot, small bills, telephones (wrong number), the common cold, and boredom. All of these are the negatives, the tiny frustrations, and _____.

    Q 1. 빈칸에 들어갈 적절한 말은?
        1) they are still worse　　2) we know little about them
        3) they come to no good　　4) no one is stronger for them
        5) it is you that can get over them

    2. 이 글의 제목으로 적절한 것은?
        1) The Negatives　　2) The Weak and the Strong
        3) The Survival of the Fittest　　4) The Danger of Small Things
        5) The Advantages of the Small and Weak

3. In the United States, Mother's Day is celebrated every year on the second Sunday in May. The origin of this holiday dates back to May 10, 1908. On that day, Anna May Jarvis held church services to honor her own mother, who [1]had died two years earlier. From this beginning, Anna started a national movement. She made the suggestion that one day [2]was set aside each year for people to honor their mothers, living or deceased. Anna's proposal caught on. In 1914, President Wilson [3]asked people to fly the national flag on Mother's Day to show love and respect for their mothers. Anna [4]had meant Mother's Day to be a religious holiday, but businesses were turning it into a commercial, or money-making, event. They began selling Mother's Day candy, flowers, greeting cards, and other merchandise. Anna spent the last 30 years of her life [5]fighting to have Mother's Day celebrated in the spirit that she had originally intended.

Q. 밑줄 친 1)~5)중 어법에 맞지 않는 것은?

4. There is a saying: Breakfast like a king, lunch like a prince, and dine like a pauper. This means that breakfast should be the largest meal of your day. In many countries, the biggest meal of the day is dinner. ① So why does this saying advise us to eat a large breakfast instead? The answer is in the word *breakfast* itself, which means the *breaking* of a *fast*, or a long period without eating. ② The gap between dinner and breakfast can be up to twelve hours, so the meal that breaks your fast should be healthy and wholesome. Unlike your evening meal, the food you consume for breakfast will give you energy to use while you are active during the day. ③ There is evidence that eating a big breakfast, particularly one containing whole grains and fruit, can improve your concentration and mood, and boost your energy levels. ④ Although health experts stress the importance of eating a good breakfast and having a big meal earlier in the day, not many people are changing their daily eating habits. ⑤ Most people seem to think that what they eat is more important than when they eat it.

Q. ①~⑤중 다음 문장이 들어가기에 적절한 곳은?
   In the United States, for example, about two-thirds
   of the population still has its main meal in the evening.

[실전 독해 B]　각 문항의 물음에 답하세요.

1.　The relation between parents and children today seems to have a freedom that would have been impossible with my father. Yet if freedom means the right to think one's own thoughts and to follow one's own pursuits, then no one respected and indeed insisted upon freedom more completely than he did. His sons and daughters, though he cared little enough for the higher education of women, should follow whatever profession they choose. If at one moment he rebuked a daughter sharply for smoking a cigarette, she had only to ask him if she might become a painter, and he assured her all the help he could, and kept his word. Freedom of that sort was worth thousands of cigarettes.

　　　Q. 이 글의 내용과 일치하지 않는 것은?
　　　　1) The father was strict but affectionate.
　　　　2) The father didn't like his children to go to college.
　　　　3) One of the daughters seems to have become an artist.
　　　　4) The sons and daughters were free to choose their own jobs.
　　　　5) The writer seems sympathetic to her father's view of freedom.

2.　It is true that a writer or an artist works primarily for his own time. The artistic product, like the intellectual product, of any age is the individual response of the artist to the circumstances of his time. In a sense all art is journalism.
　　ⓐ We read a book or look at a picture of the past primarily because
　　　　it has something to say to us at this present moment.
　　ⓑ Yet the greatest artists reach beyond their age to the mind of
　　　　timeless humanity.
　　ⓒ Therefore all the knowledge we acquire of the author and his age
　　　　is not of primary importance.
　　ⓓ The essential enjoyment which they give comes from a quality
　　　　that is independent of period.
It will no doubt add in some degree to the enjoyment which the simple reading or viewing gives, but it will certainly not be a substitute for that enjoyment.

　　　Q. ⓐ~ⓓ의 문장을 문맥에 맞게 배열하면?
　　　　1) ⓐ-ⓒ-ⓑ-ⓓ　　2) ⓐ-ⓓ-ⓒ-ⓑ　　3) ⓑ-ⓒ-ⓐ-ⓓ
　　　　4) ⓑ-ⓓ-ⓐ-ⓒ　　5) ⓒ-ⓐ-ⓑ-ⓓ

3. ①He could hardly _____ the injured arm at all. ②Many parents in this country want to _____ their children in the Catholic faith. ③We have no plans to _____ taxes at present. ④It would be wonderful to _____ cattle and sheep on the meadow. ⑤They managed to _____ over $5,000 through donations and other events.

    Q. ① ~ ⑤의 문장의 빈칸에 공통으로 들어갈 낱말은?

4. A well-known magazine advertised over the radio. The magazine offered a special price of $19.99 for a subscription. For $19.99, people would receive ten issues of the magazine. When some people called the magazine's toll-free number to place their orders, they gave their credit card number and then their shoe sizes. Why did they give their shoe sizes? They had misunderstood the words "ten issues." They thought they were ordering _____ _____.

    Q. 빈칸에 들어갈 각각의 낱말은?

5. One of the common arguments against having just one child is that an only child may be more spoiled than one with siblings. Many people believe a single child will not have learned to [a]initiate/negotiate with others, and respect the give-and-take involved in many relationships. Some think this may leave the child less capable of interacting well with people of his or her own age than one who has been brought up with siblings. [b]Despite/Besides these arguments, the number of parents choosing to have only one child is increasing in many parts of the world. In the United States, for example, 14 percent of women between 18 and 34 plan to have just one child, and this percentage is expected to [c]rise/raise. The same trend can be seen in other developed countries such as the U.K., Japan, and Korea.

    Q. 밑줄 친 a) ~ c)에서 문맥에 맞는 각 낱말은?

1)	initiate	Despite	rise
2)	initiate	Besides	raise
3)	initiate	Despite	raise
4)	negotiate	Besides	raise
5)	negotiate	Despite	rise

[명작 감상]   Ovid (43 B.C. ~ A.D. 17)

Metamorphoses 『변신』

Cephisus' child had reached his sixteenth year, and could be counted as at once boy and man. Many lads and many girls fell in love with him, but his soft young body housed a pride so unyielding that none of those boys and girls dared to touch him. One day, as he was driving timid deer into his nets, he was seen by that talkative nymph who cannot stay silent when another speaks, but yet has not learned to speak first herself. Her name is Echo, and she always answers back. Echo still had a body then, she was not just a voice: but although she was always chattering, her power of speech was not different from what it is now. All she could do was to repeat the last words of the many phrases that she heard....

The boy, by chance, had wandered away from his faithful band of comrades, and called out: "Is there anybody here?" Echo answered: "Here!" Narcissus stood still in astonishment, looking round in every direction, and cried at the pitch of his voice: "Come!" As he called, she called in reply. He looked behind him, and when no one appeared, cried again: "Why are you avoiding me?" But all he heard were his own words echoed back. Still he persisted, deceived by what he took to be another's voice, and said, "Come here, and let us meet!" Echo answered: "Let us meet!" Never again would she reply more willingly to any sound. To make good her words she came out of the wood and made to throw her arms round the neck she loved: but he fled from her, crying as he did so, "Away with these embraces! I would die before I would have you touch me!" Her only answer was: "I would have you touch me!"

Thus scorned, she concealed herself in the woods, hiding her shamed face in the shelter of the leaves, and ever since that day, she dwelled in lonely caves. Yet still her love remained firmly rooted in her heart, and was increased by the pain of having been rejected. Her anxious thoughts kept her awake, and made her pitifully thin. She became wrinkled and wasted; all the freshness of her beauty withered into the air. Only her voice and her bones were left, till finally her voice alone remained; for her bones, they say, were turned to stone. Since then, she hides in the woods, and, though never seen on the mountains, is heard there by all: for her voice is the only part of her that still lives.

[확인 학습] 다음 문장을 우리말로 옮기세요.

1. If freedom means the right to think one's own thoughts and to follow one's own pursuits, then no one insisted upon freedom more completely than he did.

2. It will no doubt add in some degree to the enjoyment which the simple reading or viewing gives, but it will certainly not be a substitute for that enjoyment.

3. Some think this may leave the child less capable of interacting well with people of his or her own age than one who has been brought up with siblings.

4. Many lads and many girls fell in love with him, but his soft young body housed a pride so unyielding that none of those boys and girls dared to touch him.

5. One day, as he was driving timid deer into his nets, he was seen by that talkative nymph who cannot stay silent when another speaks, but yet has not learned to speak first herself.

[words & phrases]

A1: dote 홀딱 빠지다, rear up 우뚝 솟다, deposit 놓다/두다, stun 어리벙벙하게 하다 indignant 성난

A2: ulcer 종기/궤양, irritate 속태우다, nibble 갉아먹다, nag 잔소리하다, 바가지 긁다, athlete's foot 무좀, boredom 권태, negative 부정적인 (요소), tiny 아주 작은, frustrate 좌절시키다/실망시키다

A3: origin 기원/근원, movement 운동/활동, decease 사망(하다), merchandise 상품, intend 의도하다

A4: pauper 극빈자, fast 금식(하다), wholesome 건전한, consume 소비하다, evidence 증거, contain 담다/포함하다, grain 곡식/알곡, concentrate 집중하다, boost 증대시키다, expert 노련한/전문가

B1: right 권리, pursue 추구하다, insist (up)on ~을 주장하다, profession (전문)직업, rebuke 꾸짖다

B2: product 생산물, intellectual 지적인, respond 반응하다, circumstances 상황/환경, in a sense 어떤 의미에 있어서, acquire 획득(습득)하다, in some degree 어느 정도, substitute 대체하다/대체물

B3: injure 상처를 입히다, meadow 초원, manage to (do) 그럭저럭 ~하다, donate 기부하다/기증하다

B4: advertise 광고하다, subscribe to ~을 구독하다, issue 발행(하다), order 주문(하다), toll 요금/운임

B5: argue 논쟁하다/주장하다, spoil 망쳐놓다, sibling 형제/자매, bring up ~을 키우다/양육하다,

C1: lad 소년, yield 굴복하다, timid 겁많은, talkative 수다스러운, nymph 요정, chatter 재잘대다, comrade 친구, persist 고집하다, embrace 포옹/포용(하다), scorn 경멸(하다), conceal 숨기다, shelter 은신처, dwell 거주하다, anxious 걱정하는/갈망하는, wrinkle 주름(지다), wither 시들다

[실력 점검 A] 다음 각 동사의 우리말 뜻을 쓰세요.

1. stun: 2. erupt: 3. confirm:

4. strive: 5. attain: 6. conform:

7. hasten: 8. wrinkle: 9. disinfect:

10. ignite: 11. excavate: 12. persevere:

13. intend: 14. postpone: 15. concentrate:

16. comply: 17. hibernate: 18. subscribe to:

19. draw up: 20. stem from:

[실력 점검 B] 각 항목에 대응하는 영어 단어를 찾아 쓰세요.

보기   clue, instinct, equator, volcano, stability, astrology, countenance, tomb, pauper, humidity, boredom, monument, immortality, controversial, timid, advent, secure, coherent, impartial, ultraviolet

1. 적도: 2. 본능: 3. 용모:

4. 권태: 5. 습도: 6. 불멸:

7. 화산: 8. 도래: 9. 안정성:

10. 무덤: 11. 단서: 12. 기념비:

13. 극빈자: 14. 점성술: 15. 자외선:

16. 안전한: 17. 소심한: 18. 일관된:

19. 공평한: 20. 논쟁적인:

[실력 점검 C] 빈칸에 알맞은 낱말을 쓰세요.

1. No effort has been _____ to put the idea _____ practice.

2. The cat's grey coat was beautiful _____ the purple of the cushion.

3. The news _____ he was killed in the war was a great shock to her.

4. It is only in childhood _____ books have any deep influence on us.

5. It would be all wrong for a scientist to get emotional when he describes a daffodil, and it would be all wrong for a poet _____ _____.

명시 감상

The Road Not Taken

Robert Frost

Two roads diverged in a yellow wood
And sorry I could not travel both
And be one traveler, long I stood
And looked down one as far as I could
To where it bent in the undergrowth;

Then took the other, as just as fair,
And having perhaps the better claim,
Because it was grassy and wanted wear;
Though as for that the passing there
Had worn them really about the same,

And both that morning equally lay
In leaves no step had trodden black.
Oh, I kept the first for another day!
Yet knowing how way leads on to way,
I doubted if should ever come back.

I shall be telling this with a sigh
Somewhere ages and ages hence:
Two roads diverged in a wood, and I —
I took the one less traveled by,
And that has made all the difference.

* diverge 갈리다/분기하다, undergrowth 관목/덤불, wear 닳음, 닳게 하다, tread 밟다, sigh 한숨, hence 지금부터

Unit 18   필수 동사 500

[Test 1] 다음 각 동사의 우리말 뜻을 쓰세요.

1. fix:	2. rob:	3. rub:
4. sue:	5. sob:	6. ban:
7. saw:	8. sew:	9. sow:
10. rule:	11. flee:	12. leap:
13. bear:	14. tear:	15. tend:
16. heal:	17. leak:	18. fade:
19. soar:	20. stun:	21. defy:
22. lean:	23. reap:	24. gasp:
25. quit:	26. vary:	27. wipe:
28. omit:	29. shed:	30. tame:
31. grab:	32. bury:	33. roam:
34. fold:	35. mold:	36. mend:
37. split:	38. stare:	39. cease:
40. alter:	41. store:	42. cause:
43. infer:	44. refer:	45. boast:
46. exalt:	47. exult:	48. exert:
49. utter:	50. cheat:	51. claim:
52. deter:	53. defer:	54. plead:
55. faint:	56. adapt:	57. adopt:
58. seize:	59. apply:	60. scold:
61. spoil:	62. dwell:	63. hover:
64. force:	65. evade:	66. imply:
67. order:	68. abuse:	69. frown:
70. drift:	71. float:	72. weave:
73. trace:	74. yield:	75. endow:
76. cling:	77. crash:	78. crush:
79. avert:	80. tread:	81. tempt:

82. erupt: 83. grasp: 84. dread:

85. share: 86. scare: 87. scorn:

88. carve: 89. excel: 90. decay:

91. adore: 92. adorn: 93. sweep:

94. bleed: 95. breed: 96. mourn:

97. found: 98. annoy: 99. amend:

100. state: (60~70: C⁺ / 70~80: B / 80~90: B⁺ / 90~100: A)

[정답] 출제된 동사의 "가장 흔히 쓰이는 뜻"을 정답으로 하였음.

1. 고치다/수리하다, 고정시키다   2. 빼앗다/강탈하다   3. 비비다/문지르다
4. 고소하다/소송하다   5. 울다/흐느끼다   6. 금(지)하다
7. 톱질하다   8. 꿰매다/바느질하다   9. 씨앗을 뿌리다
10. 통치하다/판결하다   11. 도망치다/달아나다   12. 뛰다/도약하다
13. 낳다/품다, 참다/견디다   14. 찢다/뜯다   15. 돌보다, ~경향이 있다
16. 고치다, 낫게 하다   17. 새다/새어나오다   18. 흐려져(사라져)가다
19. (높이) 날다/치솟다   20. 거두다/수확하다   21. 대항하다/반항하다
22. 기대다(~ on/against)   23. 아찔(어리벙벙)하게 하다   24. (숨을) 헐떡이다
25. 그만두다/중단하다   26. 변화하다/다양하다   27. 닦다/닦아내다
28. 생략하다   29. (빛을) 발하다,(눈물) 흘리다   30. 길들이다
31. 붙잡다/움켜쥐다   32. 묻다/매장하다   33. 헤매다/배회하다
34. 접다/접히다   35. 주조하다/형성하다   36. 수리하다/수선하다
37. 쪼개다/쪼개지다   38. 응시하다/노려보다(~at)   39. 그치다/멈추다
40. 바꾸다/변경하다   41. 저장하다   42. 초래하다/야기하다
43. 추론하다   44. 지칭하다, 참고하다(~ to)   45. 자랑하다(~ of)
46. 높이다/고양하다   47. 몹시 기뻐하다   48. 발휘(행사)하다
49. 말하다/발언하다   50. 속이다, 부정행위를 하다   51. 주장하다/요구하다
52. 제지하다/만류하다   53. 미루다/연기하다   54. 간청하다/변론하다
55. 기절하다/실신하다   56. 적응하다/적응시키다(~ to)   57. 채택하다/입양하다
58. 붙잡다/붙들다   59. 적용하다(~ to)/지원하다(~ for) 60. 꾸짖다/꾸중하다
61. 망치다/망쳐놓다   62. 거주하다, 숙고하다(~ on)   63. (공중에) 떠다니다
64. 강요하다/강제하다   65. 피하다/모면하다   66. 의미하다/함축하다
67. 명령하다, 주문하다   68. 욕하다, 남용하다/학대하다   69. 찡그리디/찌푸리다
70. 표류하다/떠돌다   71. 떠다니다/표류하다   72. 짜다/엮다
73. (흔적을) 밟다/추적하다   74. 생산하다, 굴복하다(~ to)   75. 주다/부여하다
76. 매달리다/달라붙다(~ to)   77. 충돌하다/무너지다   78. 으깨다/뭉개다
79. 피하다/모면하다   80. 밟다/디디다   81. 꾀다/유혹하다
82. (화산이) 분출하다   83. 잡다/쥐다, 이해하다   84. 두려워(무서워)하다,
85. 나누다/공유하다   86. 겁주다/위협하다   87. 경멸하다
88. 새기다/조각하다   89. 능가하다/탁월하다   90. 썩다/부패하다
91. 사모하다/흠모하다   92. 꾸미다/장식하다   93. 쓸다/휩쓸다
94. 피를 흘리다   95. 낳다/기르다/번식하다   96. 슬퍼하다/애도하다
97. 세우다/설립하다   98. 괴롭히다, 귀찮게 굴다   99. 수정하다/개정하다
100. 진술하다

[Test 2] 다음 각 동사의 우리말 뜻을 쓰세요.

1. erect: 2. elect: 3. grant:

4. reign: 5. sneer: 6. swear:

7. creep: 8. strive: 9. thrive:

10. stifle: 11. starve: 12. affirm:

13. retire: 14. resign: 15. wither:

16. entail: 17. invent: 18. invest:

19. linger: 20. define: 21. secure:

22. recall: 23. reveal: 24. reform:

25. reside: 26. impair: 27. impart:

28. resent: 29. assign: 30. invade:

31. adjust: 32. hinder: 33. govern:

34. object: 35. accuse: 36. expose:

37. derive: 38. banish: 39. vanish:

40. depict: 41. debate: 42. devour:

43. betray: 44. absorb: 45. modify:

46. induce: 47. reduce: 48. emerge:

49. pursue: 50. adhere: 51. assume:

52. extend: 53. expand: 54. expend:

55. supply: 56. oppose: 57. compel:

58. affect: 59. attach: 60. detach:

61. attain: 62. retain: 63. rebuke:

64. perish: 65. revise: 66. lament:

67. digest: 68. ignite: 69. ignore:

70. fasten: 71. hasten: 72. ponder:

73. notify: 74. purify: 75. occupy:

76. detect: 77. impose: 78. exceed:

79. ignite: 80. refund: 81. convey:

82. assent:

83. submit:

84. remark:

85. deride:

86. donate:

87. abound:

88. devise:

89. plunge:

90. remove:

91. forbid:

92. behold:

93. beware:

94. offend:

95. belong:

96. comply:

97. punish:

98. menace:

99. summon:

100. aspire:

(60~70: C$^+$ / 70~80: B / 80~90: B$^+$ / 90~100: A)

[정답] 출제된 동사의 "가장 흔히 쓰이는 뜻"을 정답으로 하였음.

1. (똑바로) 세우다/건립하다
2. 뽑다/선출하다
3. 주다/부여하다, 인정하다
4. 지배하다/통치하다
5. 비웃다/조소하다(~ at)
6. 맹세하다, 욕설하다
7. 기다/기어가다
8. 애쓰다/노력하다
9. 번성하다/번창하다
10. 질식시키다, 숨막히게 하다
11. 굶다/굶주리다
12. 확언하다/긍정하다
13. 은퇴하다/퇴직하다
14. 물러나다/사임하다
15. 시들다/이울다
16. 수반하다/함의하다
17. 발명하다
18. 투자하다
19. 꾸물대다/지체하다
20. 정의하다
21. 얻다/확보하다
22. 상기하다/회상하다
23. 드러내다, 게시하다
24. 개혁하다
25. 살다/거주하다
26. 손상시키다
27. 주다/나눠주다
28. 화내다/분개하다
29. 할당하다, 양도하다
30. 침입하다/침략하다
31. 적응하다/조정하다(~ to)
32. 방해하다/가로막다
33. 다스리다/통치하다
34. 반대하다/싫어하다(~ to)
35. 비난하다/기소하다
36. 노출시키다
37. 파생(유래)하다(~ from)
38. 추방하다
39. 사라지다)
40. 그리다/묘사하다
41. 토론하다
42. 삼키다, 먹어 치우다
43. 배반하다, 드러내다
44. 흡수하다
45. 고치다/수정하다
46. 권유하다, 유발하다
47. 줄(이)다/축소하다
48. 나타나다/출현하다
49. 추구하다, 추적하다
50. 고수하다/집착하다(~ to)
51. 가정하다, 떠맡다
52. 뻗(치)다, 넓히다/확장하다
53. 팽창하다/부풀다
54. 쓰다/지출하다
55. 공급하다/배급하다
56. 반대하다/대립시키다
57. 강요하다/강제하다
58. 영향을 주다, 가장하다
59. 붙이다/부착하다
60. 떼다/분리하다
61. 달성하다/도달하다
62. 보유하다/존속시키다
63. 꾸짖다/비난하다
64. 죽다/사멸하다
65. 고치다/개정하다
66. 한탄하다/개탄하다
67. 소화하다, 요약하다
68. 점화하다/발화하다
69. 무시하다/묵살하다
70. 묶다/매다/고정하다
71. 서두르다/재촉하다
72. 곰곰이 생각하다
73. 통지하다/통보하다
74. 정화하다/순화하다
75. 점령하다/차지하다
76. 탐지하다/간파하다
77. 과하다/부과하다
78. 초과하다/능가하다
79. 점화하다/발화하다
80. 환불하다/반품하다
81. 전하다/전달하다
82. 동의하다/찬성하다
83. 제출하다, 복종하다(~ to)
84. 말하다/언급하다
85. 비웃다/조소(조롱)하다
86. 기부하다/기증하다
87. 많다/풍부하다(~ in/with)
88. 고안하다/궁리하다
89. 뛰어들다/곤두박질하다
90. 없애다/제거하다
91. 금하다/금지하다
92. 보다/바라보다
93. 조심하다/경계하다(~ of)
94. (감정을) 해치다, 위반하다
95. 속하다/소속하다(~ to)
96. 응하다/따르다(~ with)
97. 벌주다/징벌하다
98. 위협하다/협박하다
99. 소환하다/호출하다
100. 열망하다/갈망하다(~ to/after)

[Test 3] 다음 각 동사의 우리말 뜻을 쓰세요.

1. falter:	2. obtain:	3. cancel:
4. assert:	5. soothe:	6. preach:
7. pierce:	8. reckon:	9. beckon:
10. resist:	11. retort:	12. refute:
13. arrest:	14. defeat:	15. thrust:
16. suffer:	17. repent:	18. prefer:
19. insult:	20. elapse:	21. lessen:
22. shiver:	23. shrink:	24. retreat:
25. desert:	26. confer:	27. seduce:
28. loathe:	29. persist:	30. remind:
31. assure:	32. devote:	33. gamble:
34. recruit:	35. impute:	36. deplete:
37. delude:	38. mingle:	39. recover:
40. outrun:	41. outlive:	42. outvote:
43. spread:	44. ascend:	45. descend:
46. instill:	47. install:	48. violate:
49. isolate:	50. inherit:	51. inhabit:
52. imitate:	53. subject:	54. specify:
55. inquire:	56. intrude:	57. neglect:
58. predict:	59. resolve:	60. revolve:
61. decline:	62. dismiss:	63. involve:
64. abolish:	65. cherish:	66. surpass:
67. capture:	68. inspect:	69. replace:
70. extract:	71. harness:	72. subside:
73. relieve:	74. release:	75. reverse:
76. discard:	77. deprive:	78. conceal:
79. collide:	80. prevent:	81. precede:

82. exploit: 83. explore: 84. explode:

85. acquire: 86. deserve: 87. improve:

88. enclose: 89. decease: 90. measure:

91. deceive: 92. pretend: 93. examine:

94. analyze: 95. confuse: 96. abandon:

97. divorce: 98. conform: 99. condemn:

100. confirm: (60~70: C$^+$ / 70~80: B / 80~90: B$^+$ / 90~100: A)

[정답] 출제된 동사의 "가장 흔히 쓰이는 뜻"을 정답으로 하였음.

1. 비틀거리다, (말을) 더덤다   2. 얻다/획득하다   3. 취소하다
4. 주장하다   5. 달래다/진정시키다   6. 설교하다
7. 꿰뚫다/꿰찌르다   8. 셈하다, 생각(간주)하다   9. 손짓으로 부르다
10. 저항하다   11. 응수하다/대꾸하다   12. 반박하다/논박하다
13. 체포하다   14. 쳐부수다/패배시키다   15. 밀어 넣다, 찔러 넣다
16. 겪다/고생하다(~ from)   17. 후회하다/참회하다(~ of) 18. 선호하다, 더 좋아하다
19. 모욕하다   20. (시간이) 경과하다   21. 줄다/줄이다
22. 떨다/전율하다   23. 움츠리다/수축하다   24. 물러서다/후퇴하다
25. 버리다/탈영하다   26. 수여하다/베풀다   27. 꾀다/유혹하다
28. 몹시 싫어하다   29. 고집하다(~ in)   30. 생각나게 하다
31. 보증하다/확실히 하다   32. 바치다/헌신하다   33. 도박하다/노름하다
34. 모집하다/충원하다   35. ~탓으로 돌리다   36. 수탈하다/고갈시키다
37. 속이다/미혹시키다   38. 섞다/뒤섞이다   39. 회복하다/되찾다
40. ~보다 빨리 달리다   41. ~보다 오래 살다   42. ~보다 많이 득표하다
43. 펴다/퍼지다   44. 오르다/올라가다   45. 내리다/내려가다
46. 주입시키다   47. 설치하다/설비하다   48. 어기다/위반하다
49. 격리하다/고립시키다   50. 상속하다/물려받다   51. 살다/거주하다
52. 모방하다/흉내내다   53. 종속시키다   54. 명시하다/상술하다
55. 묻다/문의하다   56. 끼어들다/참견하다   57. 무시하다/게을리하다
58. 예측하다   59. 결심하다, 해결하다   60. 돌다/회전하다
61. 기울다/쇠퇴하다, 거절하다 62. 해고하다, 해산시키다   63. 수반하다/연루시키다
64. 폐지하다   65. 소중히 간직하다   66. 능가하다/뛰어나다
67. 붙잡다/생포하다   68. 조사하다/검사하다   69. 대신하다/대체하다
70. 발췌하다/추출하다   71. (동력으로) 이용하다   72. 가라앉다/함몰하다
73. 구원하다, 덜다/덜어주다   74. 풀어놓다/방출하다   75. 뒤집다/거꾸로하다
76. 버리다/폐기하다   77. 빼앗다/박탈하다   78. 숨기다/감추다
79. 충돌하다   80. 예방하다/막다   81. 앞서다/선행하다
82. 개발하다, 착취하다   83. 탐험하다, 탐구하다   84. 폭발하다/폭발시키다
85. 획득하다/습득하다   86. ~할 만하다   87. 개선하다/향상시키다
88. 둘러싸다; 동봉하다   89. 죽다/사망하다   90. 재다/측정하다
91. 속이다   92. ~인 체하다   93. 검사하다/검토하다
94. 분석하다   95. 혼동하다/혼란시키다   96. 버리다/포기하다
97. 이혼하다   98. 따르다/순응하다(~ to)   99. 비난하다, 선고하다
100. 확인하다, 확실히 하다

[Test 4] 다음 각 동사의 우리말 뜻을 쓰세요.

1. fulfill: 2. shatter: 3. utilize:

4. certify: 5. qualify: 6. clarify:

7. justify: 8. dignify: 9. gratify:

10. inflict: 11. attract: 12. disturb:

13. sustain: 14. reserve: 15. suspect:

16. ascribe: 17. indulge: 18. observe:

19. deduct: 20. publish: 21. degrade:

22. contain: 23. prosper: 24. respond:

25. declare: 26. hesitate: 27. magnify:

28. nurture: 29. nourish: 30. smuggle:

31. confine: 32. contend: 33. embrace:

34. appoint: 35. compare: 36. compete:

37. agitate: 38. dictate: 39. provide:

40. refrain: 41. prevail: 42. pervade:

43. irritate: 44. irrigate: 45. undergo:

46. inspire: 47. stagger: 48. separate:

49. deliver: 50. furnish: 51. astonish:

52. pollute: 53. survive: 54. swallow:

55. operate: 56. convert: 57. collapse:

58. despise: 59. console: 60. grumble:

61. initiate: 62. instruct: 63. sentence:

64. restore: 65. migrate: 66. preserve:

67. present: 68. witness: 69. multiply:

70. forbear: 71. forsake: 72. stammer:

73. include: 74. exclude: 75. maintain:

76. destroy: 77. flourish: 78. consume:

79. discern: 80. prohibit: 81. conceive:

82. restrict:

83. subtract:

84. purchase:

85. classify:

86. dwindle:

87. prophesy:

88. confess:

89. confront:

90. complain:

91. tolerate:

92. navigate:

93. endeavor:

94. infringe:

95. immerse:

96. dominate:

97. identify:

98. meditate:

99. exchange:

100. distort:

(60~70: C⁺ / 70~80: B / 80~90: B⁺ / 90~100: A)

[정답] 출제된 동사의 "가장 흔히 쓰이는 뜻"을 정답으로 하였음.

1. 성취하다/완수하다
2. 산산이 부수다
3. 이용하다
4. 증명하다/공인하다
5. 자격을 부여하다
6. 분명히 하다(밝히다)
7. 정당화하다
8. 고귀(존엄)하게 하다
9. 충족(만족)시키다
10. 가하다/입히다
11. 끌다/매혹하다
12. 방해하다, 흩뜨리다
13. 지탱하다/유지하다
14. 예약하다/비축하다
15. 의심하다
16. ~탓으로 돌리다
17. 방종하다/탐닉하다(~ in)
18. 관찰하다, 준수하다
19. 감하다/공제하다
20. 출판하다/출간하다
21. 격하하다/타락하다
22. 담다/내포하다
23. 번영하다/번창하다
24. 반응하다/응답하다(~ to)
25. 선언하다/선포하다
26. 망설이다/주저하다
27. 확대하다
28. 키우다/양육하다
29. 기르다, 자양분을 주다
30. 밀수하다/밀항하다
31. 제한하다/가두다
32. 다투다/주장하다
33. 포옹하다/포용하다
34. 임명하다/지정하다
35. 비교하다/비유하다
36. 겨루다/경쟁하다
37. 휘젓다/동요시키다
38. 명령(지시)하다, 구술하다
39. 공급하다
40. 참다/삼가다(~ from)
41. 우세하다, 만연(유행)하다
42. 스며들다/퍼지다
43. 화나게(속타게) 하다
44. (논/밭에) 물을 대다
45. 겪다/경험하다
46. 고취하다/고무하다
47. 비틀거리다
48. 분리하다/떼어놓다
49. 구해내다, 배달하다
50. 공급하다, (가구) 비치하다
51. 놀라게 하다
52. 오염시키다
53. 생존하다/살아남다
54. 꿀꺽 삼키다
55. 작동하다, 수술하다(~ on)
56. 전환하다/개종하다
57. 붕괴하다/내려앉다
58. 멸시하다
59. 위로하다/위문하다
60. 투덜대다/불평하다
61. 시작하다/개시하다
62. 가르치다/지시하다
63. 선고하다
64. 되찾다/회복시키다
65. 이주하다/이동하다
66. 보존하다/보전하다
67. 제시(발표)하다/증정하다
68. 목격하다/증언하다
69. 곱하다/배가하다
70. 참다/억제하다
71. 저버리다/내버리다
72. 말을 더듬다
73. 포함하다/내포하다
74. 배제하다/제외하다
75. 주장하다, 유지하다
76. 파괴하다/부수다
77. 번영(번성)하다
78. 소비하다/소모하다
79. 식별하다/인식하다
80. 금(지)하다
81. 품다/생각하다(~ of)
82. 제한하다/한정하다
83. 빼다/감하다
84. 구입하다/구매하다
85. 분류하다
86. 줄(이)다/약화되다
87. 예언하다
88. 고백하다/자백하다
89. 직면하다/대면하다
90. 불평하다(~ of/about)
91. 참다/관용하다
92. 항해하다
93. 노력하다/애쓰다
94. 위반하다/침해하다
95. 담그다/몰두시키다
96. 지배하다/우세하다
97. (신원) 확인하다/동일시하다
98. 명상(숙고)하다
99. 바꾸다/교환하다
100. 비틀다/왜곡하다

[Test 5] 다음 각 동사의 우리말 뜻을 쓰세요.

1. indicate:	2. generate:	3. diagnose:
4. disclose:	5. interrupt:	6. comprise:
7. overtake:	8. overlook:	9. overcome:
10. distract:	11. decorate:	12. surround:
13. dissolve:	14. intensify:	15. encroach:
16. sprinkle:	17. proclaim:	18. postpone:
19. disperse:	20. conserve:	21. renounce:
22. dissuade:	23. persuade:	24. vanquish:
25. register:	26. traverse:	27. transport:
28. transmit:	29. translate:	30. transform:
31. cultivate:	32. captivate:	33. contradict:
34. evaluate:	35. illustrate:	36. illuminate:
37. attribute:	38. distribute:	39. contribute:
40. convince:	41. conclude:	42. emphasize:
43. associate:	44. negotiate:	45. investigate:
46. withdraw:	47. withstand:	48. undermine:
49. eliminate:	50. cooperate:	51. exaggerate:
52. intervene:	53. recognize:	54. summarize:
55. eradicate:	56. surrender:	57. degenerate:
58. fascinate:	59. submerge:	60. overwhelm:
61. advertise:	62. apologize:	63. accompany:
64. originate:	65. humiliate:	66. accumulate:
67. reproach:	68. represent:	69. emancipate:
70. recollect:	71. subscribe:	72. concentrate:
73. advocate:	74. evaporate:	75. recommend
76. reconcile:	77. undertake:	78. compensate:
79. penetrate:	80. substitute:	81. compromise:

82. outweigh: 83. persevere: 84. domesticate:

85. construct: 86. appreciate: 87. demonstrate:

88. encounter: 89. embarrass: 90. comprehend:

91. anticipate: 92. participate: 93. contemplate:

94. constitute: 95. extinguish: 96. contaminate:

97. determine: 98. distinguish: 99. manufacture:

100. stimulate: (60~70: C⁺ / 70~80: B / 80~90: B⁺ / 90~100: A)

[정답] 출제된 동사의 "가장 흔히 쓰이는 뜻"을 정답으로 하였음.

1. 가리키다/지적하다
2. 낳다/발생시키다
3. 진단하다
4. 드러내다/폭로하다
5. 방해하다/가로막다
6. 구성하다/구성되다
7. 따라잡다/추월하다
8. 간과하다/내려다보다
9. 이기다/극복하다
10. (정신/주의를) 흩뜨리다
11. 꾸미다/장식하다
12. 에워싸다/둘러싸다
13. 녹(이)다/용해시키다
14. 격렬(강렬)하게 하다
15. 침해하다/잠식하다
16. 뿌리다/흩뿌리다
17. 선언하다/공포하다
18. 미루다(연기하다)
19. 흩뜨리다/흩어지다
20. 보존하다/보호하다
21. 단념하다/포기하다
22. ~못하게 설득하다
23. ~하도록 설득하다
24. 정복하다/극복하다
25. 등록하다/기입하다
26. 횡단하다/가로지르다
27. 운송하다/수송하다
28. 전하다/전달하다
29. 번역하다/해석하다
30. 변형시키다
31. 경작하다/함양하다
32. 사로잡다/매혹하다
33. 모순되다/반박하다
34. 평가하다
35. 예증하다/설명하다
36. 밝히다/조명하다
37. ~탓으로 돌리다
38. 분배하다/배포하다
39. 기여(공헌)하다(~ to)
40. 확신(납득)시키다
41. 종결하다/결론짓다
42. 강조하다
43. 교제하다, 연상하다
44. 협상하다/교섭하다
45. 조사하다
46. 철수하다; (예금) 인출하다
47. 버티다/저항하다
48. 훼손하다/손상시키다
49. 제거하다/없애다
50. 협력하다/협동하다
51. 과장하다
52. 끼어들다/간섭하다
53. 인지하다/인식하다
54. 요약하다/개괄하다
55. 박멸하다/근절하다
56. 항복하다/굴복하다
57. 퇴보하다/타락하다
58. 매혹하다/매료시키다
59. 잠기다/잠수하다
60. 압도하다/위압하다
61. 광고하다
62. 사과하다/변명(해명)하다
63. 동반하다, 반주하다
64. 기원하다/유래하다
65. 창피(굴욕감)를 주다
66. 쌓다/축적하다
67. 꾸짖다/비난하다
68. 묘사/대표/상징하다
69. 해방시키다
70. 상기(회상)하다
71. (신문/잡지)구독하다(~ to)
72. 집중하다(~ on)
73. 옹호하다/주창하다
74. 증발하다/증발시키다
75. 추천하다
76. 화해시키다/조화시키다
77. 맡다/떠맡다
78. 보상하다/보충하다
79. 침투하다/꿰뚫다
80. 대신하다/대체하다
81. 타협하다, 더럽히다
82. ~보다 무겁다/중요하다
83. 참다/인내하다
84. 길들이다/순화시키다
85. 건설하다/건축하다
86. 감사하다/평가하다
87. 입증하다, 시위하다
88. 만나다/마주치다
89. 당황(당혹)하게 하다
90. 이해하다/파악하다
91. 고대하다/기대하다
92. 참가하다/참여하다(~ in)
93. 심사 숙고하다
94. 구성하다/조직하다
95. (불을) 끄다/멸종시키다
96. 오염시키다
97. 결심하다/결정하다
98. 구별하다/식별하다
99. 제조하다/만들다
100. 자극하다

Unit 19 필수 명사 500

[Test 1] 다음 각 명사의 우리말 뜻을 쓰세요.

1. clue:

2. fake:

3. instinct:

4. crop:

5. debt:

6. disaster:

7. flaw:

8. mine:

9. heredity:

10. soil:

11. poll:

12. illusion:

13. bias:

14. vein:

15. relative:

16. tool:

17. firm:

18. conflict:

19. role:

20. barn:

21. scissors:

22. heir:

23. cane:

24. religion:

25. fate:

26. gene:

27. aptitude:

28. scar:

29. prey:

30. obstacle:

31. fine:

32. oath:

33. sculptor:

34. fuel:

35. lead:

36. humility:

37. trap:

38. poet:

39. property:

40. epic:

41. lyric:

42. violence:

43. vice:

44. shelf:

45. courtesy:

46. cone:

47. fame:

48. prospect:

49. mess:

50. wage:

51. vocation:

52. myth:

53. moth:

54. response:

55. tomb:

56. comb:

57. evidence:

58. plow:

59. layer:

60. diameter:

61. folly:

62. peril:

63. literature:

64. tribe:

65. bribe:

66. organism:

67. verse:

68. prose:

69. contempt:

70. shift:

71. scent:

72. patience:

73. choir:

74. troop:

75. ancestor:

76. razor:

77. quest:

78. optimist:

79. labor:

80. vapor:

81. pessimist:

82. trend:

83. parrot:

84. substance:

85. adult:

86. dwarf:

87. operation:

88. favor:

89. clown:

90. insurance:

91. fraud:

92. vogue:

93. adversary:

94. globe:

95. agony:

96. colleague:

97. greed:

98. portal:

99. avalanche:

100. trait:

(60~70: C$^+$ / 70~80: B / 80~90: B$^+$ / 90~100: A)

[정답] 출제된 명사의 "가장 흔히 쓰이는 뜻"을 정답으로 하였음.

1. 단서/실마리
2. 가짜/위조품/사기꾼
3. 본능
4. 농작물/수확(물)
5. 빚/채무
6. 재난/재해
7. 흠/결함
8. 광산/지뢰
9. 유전/세습
10. 흙/토양
11. 투표/여론조사
12. 환상/착각
13. 사선/편견
14. 혈관/정맥
15. 친척
16. 연장/도구
17. 회사/상사(상회)
18. 갈등/알력/투쟁
19. 역할/배역
20. 헛간/곡간
21. 가위
22. 상속인/후계자
23. 단장/지팡이
24. 종교
25. 운명/숙명
26. 유전자
27. 적성/소질
28. 흉터/상처
29. 먹이감/희생물
30. 장애(물)/방해(물)
31. 벌금/과태료
32. 맹세/서약/선서
33. 조각가
34. 연료
35. 납
36. 겸손/겸양
37. 덫/함정/올가미
38. 시인
39. 재산/소유지/특성
40. 서사시
41. 서정시/노래(가사)
42. 폭력
43. 악/악덕
44. 선반/책꽂이
45. 예의/공손
46. 외뿔
47. 명성/평판
48. 전망/가망/예상
49. 엉망/난잡/불결
50. 임금/품삯
51. 직업/천직
52. 신화
53. 나방
54. 반응/응답
55. 묘/무덤
56. (머리)빗
57. 증거
58. 쟁기(=plough)
59. 층/켜
60. 지름/직경
61. 우둔/어리석음
62. 위험
63. 문학/문헌
64. 부족/종족
65. 뇌물
66. 유기체/생명체
67. 운문/시
68. 산문
69. 경멸
70. 교대/변경/변동
71. 냄새/향기
72. 인내(심)/참을성
73. 합창단/합창대
74. 군대/병력
75. 조상/선조
76. 면도날/면도칼
77. 탐구/탐색
78. 낙관주의자
79. 노동/근로/산고
80. 수증기
81. 비관(염세)주의자
82. 추세/동향
83. 앵무새
84. 물질
85. 어른/성인
86. 난장이
87. 수술/작동/작전
88. 호의/찬성/부탁
89. 광대/어릿광대
90. 보험
91. 사기/협잡
92. 유행
93. 적/적수
94. 구/지구
95. 고뇌/고민
96. 동료/동업자
97. 욕심/탐욕
98. 문/입구/정문
99. 눈사태/쇄도
100. 특성/특질

[Test 2] 다음 각 명사의 우리말 뜻을 쓰세요.

1. craft: 2. fever: 3. fortnight:

4. dairy: 5. shape: 6. infection:

7. grave: 8. defect: 9. suspicion:

10. trial: 11. scale: 12. sacrifice:

13. liver: 14. lungs: 15. editorial:

16. aisle: 17. fable: 18. nutrition:

19. flour: 20. beast: 21. pesticide:

22. feast: 23. client: 24. affection:

25. asset: 26. crime: 27. gratitude:

28. flesh: 29. flame: 30. authority:

31. order: 32. chaos: 33. prejudice:

34. canal: 35. epoch: 36. continent:

37. solid: 38. liquid: 39. ingenuity:

40. spear: 41. shield: 42. candidate:

43. comet: 44. planet: 45. dormitory:

46. pirate: 47. ellipse: 48. barometer:

49. origin: 50. legend: 51. biography:

52. insect: 53. famine: 54. astrology:

55. award: 56. reward: 57. astronomy:

58. treaty: 59. device: 60. multitude:

61. estate: 62. timber: 63. posterity:

64. status: 65. spouse: 66. spectator:

67. statue: 68. survey: 69. intention:

70. threat: 71. colony: 72. principle:

73. effect: 74. hazard: 75. principal:

76. infant: 77. impact: 78. slaughter:

79. defeat: 80. advent: 81. coward:

82. vanity:

83. muscle:

84. resource:

85. policy:

86. umpire:

87. addiction:

88. patent:

89. dismay:

90. petroleum:

91. notion:

92. custom:

93. geography:

94. misery:

95. magnet:

96. companion:

97. reptile:

98. mammal:

99. commodity:

100. fossil:

(60~70: C⁺ / 70~80: B / 80~90: B⁺ / 90~100: A)

[정답] 출제된 명사의 "가장 흔히 쓰이는 뜻"을 정답으로 하였음.

1. 기술/기능, 선박/항공기	2. (발)열/열병	3. 2주일간
4. 낙농업/낙농장	5. 모양/형상	6. 전염/감염
7. 무덤	8. 결함/결점	9. 의심/의혹
10. 시도/시련/재판	11. 규모/저울/비늘	12. 희생/제물
13. 간	14. 폐/허파	15. 사설/논설
16. 복도/통로	17. 우화	18. 영양/자양분
19. 밀가루	20. 짐승/야수	21. 살충제
22. 잔치/축제	23. 고객, 단골 손님	24. 애정
25. 자산/재산	26. 죄/범죄	27. 감사
28. 살/육신/살코기	29. 화염/불꽃	30. 권위(자), (pl.)당국
31. 질서/순서/명령/주문	32. 혼돈/혼란/무질서	33. 편견/선입견
34. 운하/수로	35. (새)시대/신기원	36. 대륙
37. 고체	38. 액체	39. 창의성/독창성
40. 창	41. 방패	42. (입)후보자
43. 혜성	44. 행성/혹성	45. 기숙사
46. 해적/약탈자	47. 타원	48. 기압계, 지표/척도
49. 기원/발단/유래	50. 전설	51. 전기/일대기
52. 곤충/벌레	53. 기아/기근	54. 점성술
55. 상/상금/수상	56. 보답/보상	57. 천문학
58. 조약/협정	59. 고안(물)/장치/기구	60. 많음/다수/군중
61. 토지/사유지	62. 목재/재목	63. 자손/후세/후대
64. 지위/신분	65. 배우자	66. 구경꾼/관중/관객
67. (조각)상/조상/동상	68. 조사/개관/측량	69. 의도/의향/목적
70. 위협/협박	71. 식민지	72. 원리/원칙
73. 결과/효과/영향	74. 위험(물)	75. 교장/학교장
76. 유아/아기	77. 충격	78. 살인/살육
79. 패배/패퇴	80. 도래/출현	81. 겁쟁이/비겁자
82. 공허/허영(심)	83. 근육	84. 자원/재원
85. 정책	86. 심판(원)	87. 중독
88. 특허(권)/특허품	89. 당황/경악/낙담	90. 석유
91. 개념/관념	92. 관습, (pl.)세관/관세	93. 지리(학)/지형
94. 불행/비참	95. 자석	96. 동료/친구/반려
97. 파충류	98. 포유류	99. 상품
100. 화석		

[Test 3] 다음 각 명사의 우리말 뜻을 쓰세요.

1. virtue:	2. expert:	3. stability:
4. factor:	5. harbor:	6. diversity:
7. theory:	8. temper:	9. relativity:
10. spiral:	11. vessel:	12. territory:
13. profit:	14. radius:	15. tradition:
16. saliva:	17. poison:	18. intensity:
19. wallet:	20. eclipse:	21. curiosity:
22. deceit:	23. copper:	24. molecule:
25. parcel:	26. pledge:	27. applicant:
28. lizard:	29. drawer:	30. detective:
31. victim:	32. decade:	33. sympathy:
34. access:	35. sewage:	36. antipathy:
37. refuge:	38. sermon:	39. evolution:
40. throne:	41. remedy:	42. reverence:
43. breeze:	44. weapon:	45. fragrance:
46. ladder:	47. revenge:	48. resolution:
49. textile:	50. vacuum:	51. influence:
52. corpse:	53. revenue:	54. definition:
55. thread:	56. tyranny:	57. obligation:
58. botany:	59. zoology:	60. regulation:
61. insight:	62. biology:	63. reputation:
64. rapture:	65. rupture:	66. simulation:
67. wound:	68. pension:	69. revolution:
70. dignity:	71. product:	72. mythology:
73. surgery:	74. triumph:	75. philosophy:
76. physics:	77. dynasty:	78. emergency:
79. sibling:	80. chamber:	81. conference:

82. fatigue:

83. meadow:

84. archeology:

85. suicide:

86. congress:

87. parliament:

88. surplus:

89. monarch:

90. convention:

91. content:

92. economy:

93. conscience:

94. formula:

95. symptom:

96. assumption:

97. drought:

98. geometry:

99. superstition:

100. shelter:

(60~70: C⁺ / 70~80: B / 80~90: B⁺ / 90~100: A)

[정답] 출제된 명사의 "가장 흔히 쓰이는 뜻"을 정답으로 하였음.

1. 덕/미덕
2. 전문가/숙련가
3. 안정/안정성
4. 요인/요소
5. 항구/피난처
6. 다양함/다양성
7. 이론
8. 기질/성질, 침착/평정
9. 상대성
10. 나선/나선형
11. 배/선박, 용기/그릇
12. 영토/영역
13. 이익/이윤/수익
14. 반경/반지름
15. 전통, 구전/구비
16. 침/타액
17. 독/독약
18. 격렬/강렬/강도
19. 지갑
20. 일식/월식
21. 호기심
22. 속임/사기
23. 구리
24. 분자
25. 소포/꾸러미
26. 서약/공약/저당
27. 지원자/응시자
28. 도마뱀
29. 서랍/장롱
30. 탐정/형사
31. 피해자/희생자
32. 십 년
33. 공감/동감/동정
34. 접근/진입
35. (하수) 오물/쓰레기
36. 반감/혐오
37. 피난/피신
38. 설교
39. 진화/발전
40. 왕위/왕좌
41. 구제책/치료(약)
42. 존경/경의
43. 미풍/산들바람
44. 무기
45. 향기
46. 사다리
47. 복수/앙갚음
48. 결의/결심
49. 섬유/직물
50. 진공
51. 영향/영향력
52. 시신/시체
53. 수입/소득
54. 정의/말뜻
55. 실/무명실
56. 폭정/포학
57. 의무
58. 식물학
59. 동물학
60. 규정/규칙
61. 통찰/통찰력
62. 생물학
63. 명성/평판
64. 환희/열광
65. 균열/파열/결렬
66. 모의 실험
67. 상처/부상
68. 연금/수당
69. 혁명/회전
70. 존엄(성)/위엄
71. 생산물/생산품
72. 신화
73. 수술/외과
74. 승리
75. 철학
76. 물리학
77. 왕조
78. 응급/위급(상황)
79. 형제(의)/자매(의)
80. 방/침실
81. 회의/회담
82. 피로/피곤
83. 초원/목초지
84. 고고학
85. 자살
86. (미국) 의회
87. (영국) 의회
88. 잉여/여분/과잉
89. 군주/제왕
90. 관습/인습, 회의/집회
91. (pl.)내용/목차
92. 경제/절약(검소)
93. 양심
94. 식/공식
95. 증상
96. 가정/억측, 인수/취임
97. 가뭄/결핍(부족)
98. 기하학
99. 미신
100. 숙소/피난처

[Test 4] 다음 각 명사의 우리말 뜻을 쓰세요.

1. disease:
2. fallacy:
3. fertilizer:
4. caution:
5. routine:
6. statistics:
7. account:
8. heritage:
9. currency:
10. barrier:
11. vehicle:
12. periodical:
13. ceiling:
14. funeral:
15. ingredient:
16. athlete:
17. peasant:
18. hypothesis:
19. gravity:
20. equator:
21. adolescent:
22. charity:
23. proverb:
24. temptation:
25. torture:
26. pastime:
27. descendant:
28. patient:
29. impulse:
30. submission:
31. receipt:
32. conduct:
33. pharmacist:
34. species:
35. institute:
36. institution:
37. variety:
38. anxiety:
39. enthusiasm:
40. habitat:
41. therapy:
42. antibiotic:
43. benefit:
44. premise:
45. patriotism:
46. brevity:
47. orchard:
48. conviction:
49. faculty:
50. garbage:
51. expedition:
52. feather:
53. concern:
54. laboratory:
55. finance:
56. expense:
57. benefactor:
58. dispute:
59. purpose:
60. livelihood:
61. destiny:
62. remorse:
63. likelihood:
64. surface:
65. slumber:
66. amphibian:
67. despair:
68. worship:
69. skyscraper:
70. tragedy:
71. emotion:
72. instrument:
73. harvest:
74. plumber:
75. proportion:
76. deposit:
77. alumnus:
78. conspiracy:
79. contact:
80. costume:
81. wilderness:

82. outlook: 83. mercury: 84. manuscript:

85. prophet: 86. perfume: 87. microscope:

88. parallel: 89. diagonal: 90. experiment:

91. surgeon: 92. boredom: 93. comparison:

94. security: 95. rectangle: 96. ambassador:

97. analysis: 98. aquarium: 99. masterpiece:

100. dialect: (60~70: C^+ / 70~80: B / 80~90: B^+ / 90~100: A)

[정답] 출제된 명사의 "가장 흔히 쓰이는 뜻"을 정답으로 하였음.

1. 병/질병
2. 오류/잘못
3. 비료
4. 조심/주의
5. 일과, 판에 박힌 일
6. 통계/통계학
7. 계좌/설명/중요성
8. 유산, 상속 재산
9. 화폐/통화/유통
10. 장벽/장애(물)
11. 차량/수송수단
12. 정기간행물
13. 천장/상한(선)
14. 장례(식)
15. 성분/요소/재료
16. 운동가/경기자
17. 농부/농민
18. 가설/가정
19. 엄숙함/중대함, 중력
20. 적도
21. 청소년
22. 자선/자비/사랑
23. 속담/격언
24. 유혹
25. 고문/고통
26. 오락/여흥
27. 자손/후손
28. 환자
29. 충동
30. 복종/순종
31. 수령/영수증
32. 행위/행동
33. 약사/조제사
34. 종/종류
35. 연구소/(공과)대학
36. (사회의) 제도/기관
37. 변화/다양(성)
38. 걱정/근심
39. 열성/열의
40. 서식지/거주지
41. 치료
42. 항생제
43. 혜택/이익
44. 전제/전제조건
45. 애국심
46. 간결/간략함
47. 과수원
48. 확신/신념
49. 능력/교직원
50. (음식) 쓰레기/찌꺼기
51. 탐험(대)/원정(대)
52. 깃/깃털
53. 관심/걱정
54. 실험실/실습실
55. 재정/금융/자금
56. 경비/비용
57. 은인/후원자
58. 논쟁/분쟁
59. 목적
60. 생계/살림
61. 운명/숙명
62. 후회/회한/가책
63. 가능성/가망성
64. 표면
65. 잠/선잠
66. 양서류
67. 실망/절망
68. 숭배/예배
69. 마천루, 초고층 건물
70. 비극
71. 감정/정서
72. 도구/기구/악기
73. 수확/추수
74. 배관공/배관기사
75. 비율/비례/부분(몫)
76. 예금/보증금
77. 동창생/졸업생
78. 음모/공모
79. 접촉
80. 의상/복장
81. 황야/황무지
82. 관점/견해/전망/조망
83. 수은/수은주
84. 원고/필사본
85. 예언자
86. 향기/향수
87. 현미경
88. 평행/평행선
89. 대각선/사선
90. 실험
91. 외과 의사
92. 권태/지루함
93. 비교
94. 안전/보안/방위
95. 직사각형
96. 대사/사절
97. 분석
98. 수조/수족관
99. 걸작(품)
100. 방언/사투리

[Test 5] 다음 각 명사의 우리말 뜻을 쓰세요.

1. quality: 2. quantity: 3. architect:

4. altitude: 5. attitude: 6. intestine:

7. identity: 8. disguise: 9. Antarctica:

10. facility: 11. solitude: 12. profession:

13. portrait: 14. industry: 15. alternative:

16. summit: 17. intuition: 18. inspiration:

19. dictator: 20. mischief: 21. disposition:

22. attempt: 23. souvenir: 24. destination:

25. friction: 26. fraction: 27. agriculture:

28. priority: 29. behavior: 30. gravitation:

31. validity: 32. envelope: 33. installment:

34. stimulus: 35. cemetery: 36. proposition:

37. incident: 38. accident: 39. conception:

40. majority: 41. minority: 42. vaccination:

43. contract: 44. emphasis: 45. hibernation:

46. disciple: 47. sequence: 48. catastrophe:

49. premier: 50. tendency: 51. temperance:

52. strategy: 53. ornament: 54. controversy:

55. creature: 56. specimen: 57. compliment:

58. delivery: 59. physician: 60. prescription:

61. disposal: 62. chemistry: 63. temperature:

64. disgrace: 65. landscape: 66. significance:

67. capacity: 68. ultraviolet: 69. expenditure:

70. pressure: 71. commerce: 72. environment:

73. hardship: 74. frustration: 75. meteorology:

76. ambition: 77. distinction: 78. countenance:

79. moisture: 80. monument: 81. consequence:

82. devotion: 83. confidence: 84. thermometer:

85. prudence: 86. acquisition: 87. consumption:

88. diplomat: 89. providence: 90. temperament:

91. fragment: 92. community: 93. anthropology:

94. exposure: 95. psychology: 96. independence:

97. opponent: 98. constitution: 99. circumstances:

100. velocity: (60~70: C$^+$ / 70~80: B / 80~90: B$^+$ / 90~100: A)

[정답] 출제된 명사의 "가장 흔히 쓰이는 뜻"을 정답으로 하였음.

1. 질/품질/자질	2. 양/수량	3. 건축가/설계자
4. 높이/고도	5. 태도	6. 내장/창자
7. 정체/주체성, 동일함	8. 변장/위장	9. 남극 대륙
10. 쉬움/용이함,(pl.)시설/설비	11. 고독/외로움	12. 직업/전문직
13. 초상(화)	14. 산업/근면	15. 대안, 다른 방도
16. 정상/꼭대기	17. 직관(력)/직감	18. 영감, 고무/고취
19. 독재자	20. 해/해악, 장난(기)	21. 성질/기질
22. 시도/노력	23. 기념품	24. 행선지/목적지
25. 마찰	26. 파편/조각/분수	27. 농업/농사
28. 우선/우선권	29. 행동/행실	30. 중력/인력
31. 타당성/정당성/유효성	32. 봉투	33. 할부/월부
34. 자극/자극제	35. 공동 묘지	36. 명제/제안
37. 사건	38. 사고/우연	39. 개념, 임신/수태
40. 다수	41. 소수	42. 예방 접종
43. 계약	44. 강조	45. 동면, 겨울 잠
46. 제자/사도	47. 연속/연쇄	48. 큰 재앙, 파국
49. 수상/총리	50. 경향	51. 절제/금주
52. 전략/작전	53. 장식(품)	54. 논쟁/논전
55. 생물/피조물	56. 견본/표본	57. 찬사/칭찬
58. 배달, 해산/분만	59. 내과 의사	60. 처방(전)
61. 처분/처리	62. 화학	63. 온도/기온
64. 망신/치욕	65. 경치/풍경	66. 의미/중요성
67. 능력/수용능력	68. 자외선	69. 지출/경비/비용
70. 압력/기압	71. 상업/통상/교섭	72. 환경
73. 곤란/곤경	74. 좌절(감)/실패	75. 기상학
76. 야망/야심	77. 구별/차별/탁월	78. 용모/안색/표정
79. 수분/습도	80. 기념비/기념물	81. 결과/중요성
82. 헌신/몰두	83. 자신/확신	84. 온도계/체온계
85. 신중/분별	86. 획득/습득	87. 소비
88. 외교관	89. (신의) 섭리	90. 성미/기질
91. 파편/조각	92. 공동체/지역사회	93. 인류학
94. 노출/발각/탄로	95. 심리/심리학	96. 독립/자립
97. 반대자/적/상대	98. 헌법/구성/체질	99. 주위/환경
100. 속도/속력		

Unit 20 필수 형용사 500

[Test 1] 다음 각 형용사의 우리말 뜻을 쓰세요.

1. rare:	2. ripe:	3. rash:
4. pale:	5. tiny:	6. tidy:
7. bald:	8. bold:	9. sour:
10. thin:	11. thick:	12. vital:
13. frail:	14. prior:	15. tense:
16. silly:	17. solar:	18. lunar:
19. civil:	20. loyal:	21. royal:
22. stale:	23. stout:	24. lucid:
25. fatal:	26. rural:	27. pious:
28. alert:	29. close:	30. novel:
31. lofty:	32. acute:	33. timid:
34. rusty:	35. grave:	36. urban:
37. legal:	38. sober:	39. broad:
40. utter:	41. valid:	42. vague:
43. rigid:	44. rapid:	45. aware:
46. plain:	47. hasty:	48. dense:
49. blunt:	50. moist:	51. sound:
52. strict:	53. intact:	54. weary:
55. futile:	56. ethnic:	57. urgent:
58. latent:	59. sticky:	60. supple:
61. stable:	62. secure:	63. sacred:
64. scarce:	65. placid:	66. candid:
67. verbal:	68. vulgar:	69. vacant:
70. racial:	71. brutal:	72. greedy:
73. frugal:	74. stingy:	75. shabby:
76. divine:	77. elastic:	78. prompt:
79. sturdy:	80. steady:	81. official:

82. coarse:

83. insane:

84. shrewd:

85. mortal:

86. normal:

87. solemn:

88. annual:

89. mutual:

90. mature:

91. abrupt:

92. absurd:

93. clumsy:

94. ragged:

95. rugged:

96. dogged:

97. minute:

98. modest:

99. gloomy:

100. subtle:

(60~70: C$^+$ / 70~80: B / 80~90: B$^+$ / 90~100: A)

[정답] 출제된 형용사의 "가장 흔히 쓰이는 뜻"을 정답으로 하였음.

1. 드문/진기한
2. 익은/원숙한
3. 경솔한/성급한
4. 창백한/연한/옅은
5. 작은/조그마한
6. 말쑥한/단정한
7. 대머리의
8. 대담한
9. 신/시큼한
10. 얇은/엷은/가는
11. 두꺼운/두터운/짙은
12. 활력의/중요한
13. 약한/연약한
14. 우선한/앞서의(~ to)
15. 팽팽한/긴장한
16. 어리석은
17. 태양의
18. 달의
19. 시민의/정중한
20. 충실한/충직한
21. 왕(족)의/왕립의
22. (음식이) 상한/진부한
23. 튼튼한/뚱뚱한
24. 맑은/투명한
25. 치명적/운명적
26. 시골의/전원의
27. 경건한/종교적인
28. 경계하는, 방심 않는
29. 가까운/밀접한/세밀한
30. 새로운/색다른
31. 높은/고매한
32. 예리한/날카로운
33. 소심한/겁많은
34. 녹슨, 녹이 난
35. 엄숙한/진지한
36. 도시의/도회지의
37. 법률적/합법적
38. 맑은 정신의, 술 취하지 않은
39. 넓은/폭넓은
40. 철저한/전적인
41. 타당한/유효한
42. 모호한
43. 굳은/완고한/엄격한
44. 빠른/신속한
45. 인식하는(~ of)
46. 평이한/평범한
47. 급한/서두르는
48. 짙은/조밀한
49. 무딘/무뚝뚝한
50. 습한/축축한
51. 건전한/건강한
52. 엄한/엄격한
53. 본래대로의, 손대지 않은
54. 치친/피로한
55. 헛된/무익한
56. 인종의/인종학상의
57. 긴급한/위급한
58. 잠재된, 숨어 있는
59. 들러붙는/끈적끈적한
60. 유연한/유순한
61. 안정된/견실한
62. 안전한/튼튼한
63. 신성한
64. 부족한/결핍한
65. 고요한/평온한
66. 솔직한
67. 말의/언어의
68. 속된/저속한
69. 빈, 비어 있는
70. 인종의/민족의
71. 야만적, 짐승 같은
72. 탐욕의, 욕심 많은
73. 검소한/검약한
74. 인색한, 너무 아끼는
75. 초라한/남루한
76. 신의/신성한
77. 탄력성의, 탄력 있는
78. 재빠른/즉석의
79. 억센/굳센/튼튼한
80. 꾸준한/착실한
81. 공식적/공무상의
82. 조잡한/거친
83. 미친/광기의
84. 약은/영민한
85. 죽음을 면치 못할 운명인
86. 정상적인
87. 엄숙한/장엄한
88. 일년의/매년의
89. 상호간의
90. 성숙한
91. 돌연한/갑작스러운
92. 불합리한/터무니없는
93. 서투른, 솜씨 없는
94. 텁수룩한, 누더기를 걸친
95. 험한/울퉁불퉁한
96. 끈질긴/집요한
97. 세세한/세밀한
98. 겸손한/공손한
99. 흐린/어두운/우울한
100. 미묘한/예민한

[Test 2] 다음 각 형용사의 우리말 뜻을 쓰세요.

1. fertile:	2. barren:	3. sterile:
4. hostile:	5. logical:	6. thrifty:
7. extinct:	8. remote:	9. reliable:
10. polite:	11. trivial:	12. selfish:
13. initial:	14. willful:	15. wistful:
16. native:	17. partial:	18. general:
19. fierce:	20. fragile:	21. prudent:
22. rotten:	23. typical:	24. discreet:
25. innate:	26. eternal:	27. shallow:
28. severe:	29. crucial:	30. obvious:
31. serene:	32. patient:	33. obscure:
34. tactful:	35. similar:	36. familiar:
37. formal:	38. serious:	39. extreme:
40. decent:	41. unique:	42. eminent:
43. virtual:	44. vicious:	45. virtuous:
46. frantic:	47. mental:	48. physical:
49. dismal:	50. private:	51. immune:
52. drastic:	53. dreary:	54. diverse:
55. neutral:	56. radical:	57. grateful:
58. ethical:	59. optical:	60. popular:
61. critical:	62. regular:	63. gradual:
64. intense:	65. jealous:	66. zealous:
67. elegant:	68. furious:	69. hideous:
70. curious:	71. cynical:	72. common:
73. infinite:	74. nuclear:	75. immense:
76. chronic:	77. official:	78. officious:
79. corrupt:	80. earnest:	81. sublime:

82. precise:

83. profuse:

84. animate:

85. secular:

86. solitary:

87. genuine:

88. current:

89. content:

90. constant:

91. evident:

92. anxious:

93. compact:

94. ancient:

95. arduous:

96. potential:

97. durable:

98. amiable:

99. amicable:

100. thirsty:

(60~70: C⁺ / 70~80: B / 80~90: B⁺ / 90~100: A)

[정답] 출제된 형용사의 "가장 흔히 쓰이는 뜻"을 정답으로 하였음.

1. 비옥한/풍작의
2. 메마른/불모의
3. 메마른/불모의/살균의
4. 적대적, 적개심을 품은
5. 논리적/논리상의
6. 검소한/절약하는
7. 꺼진/소멸된/멸종된
8. 먼, 먼 곳의, 외딴
9. 신뢰할 수 있는
10. 공손한, 예의 바른
11. 사소한/하찮은
12. 이기적인
13. 처음의/시작의
14. 고의적/외고집의
15. 탐내는/동경하는
16. 본래의/타고난/토착의
17. 부분적인/편파적인
18. 일반적/총체적
19. 맹렬한/격렬한
20. 깨지기(부서지기) 쉬운
21. 신중한/세심한
22. 썩은/부패한
23. 전형적인
24. 신중한, 사려 깊은
25. 본래의/선천적인
26. 영원한/영속적
27. 얕은/천박한
28. 모진/혹독한
29. 결정적인/중대한
30. 분명한/명확한
31. 고요한/잔잔한
32. 인내하는, 참을성 있는
33. 희미한/흐릿한
34. 재치 있는, 요령 있는
35. 유사한/비슷한(~ to)
36. 친숙한/익숙한
37. 형식의/격식적/공식적인
38. 심각한/진지한
39. 극도의/극단적인
40. 고상한/품위 있는
41. 유일무이한/독특한
42. 저명한/유명한
43. 사실상의/가상(허상)의
44. 사악한/악덕한
45. 미덕의/고결한
46. 광란의, 미친 듯 날뛰는
47. 정신의/정신적
48. 육체적/물리적
49. 음산한/음침한
50. 사적인/사사로운
51. 면역(성)의
52. 철저한/급격한/과감한
53. 황량한/음산한
54. 다양한/가지각색의
55. 중립의/중립적
56. 급진적/과격한
57. 감사하는(~ for)
58. 윤리적/윤리상의
59. 눈(시각)의/광학적
60. 대중적, 인기 있는
61. 비판적/비난하는/중대한
62. 규칙적인/정규적인
63. 점진적/점차적
64. 격렬한/강렬한
65. 질투하는/시샘하는
66. 열심인/열성적인
67. 우아한/고상한
68. 분노한/격노한
69. 섬뜩한/무시무시한
70. 호기심 있는, 호기심 끄는
71. 냉소적/비꼬는
72. 흔한/평범한/공통의
73. 무한한/무수한
74. (세포/원자) 핵의
75. 막대한/광대한
76. 만성적/고질적
77. 공무상의/공식적인
78. 참견하는/비공식적인
79. 부패한/타락한
80. 진지한/성실한
81. 장엄한/숭고한
82. 적확한/정밀한
83. 풍부한/아낌없는
84. 살아(생명이) 있는
85. 세속의/세속적인
86. 고독한/외로운
87. 진짜의/친필의
88. 현행의/통용되는
89. 만족하는(~ with)
90. 일정한, 변함 없는
91. 분명한/확실한
92. 걱정하는/갈망하는
93. 간결한/소형의
94. 옛날의/고대의
95. 힘든/분투하는
96. 잠재적/잠재력의
97. 내구성의, 오래 쓰는
98. 상냥한/다정한
99. 우호적인/친화적인
100. 목마른/갈증나는

[Test 3] 다음 각 형용사의 우리말 뜻을 쓰세요.

1. literal:	2. literate:	3. literary:
4. inferior:	5. superior:	6. punctual:
7. paternal:	8. maternal:	9. immortal:
10. distinct:	11. definite:	12. opposite:
13. explicit:	14. implicit:	15. cautious:
16. relative:	17. absolute:	18. slovenly:
19. ruthless:	20. reckless:	21. splendid:
22. flexible:	23. judicial:	24. judicious:
25. abstract:	26. concrete:	27. generous:
28. rational:	29. ignorant:	30. universal:
31. tropical:	32. fragrant:	33. muscular:
34. eligible:	35. habitual:	36. awkward:
37. suitable:	38. relevant:	39. dominant:
40. overdue:	41. accurate:	42. malicious:
43. precious:	44. previous:	45. enormous:
46. insolent:	47. indolent:	48. thorough:
49. vertical:	50. arrogant:	51. appalling:
52. vigilant:	53. contrary:	54. abundant:
55. tranquil:	56. inherent:	57. moderate:
58. adverse:	59. obsolete:	60. profound:
61. pathetic:	62. reserved:	63. strenuous:
64. positive:	65. negative:	66. courteous:
67. resolute:	68. frequent:	69. indignant:
70. childish:	71. ordinary:	72. imminent:
73. credible:	74. manifest:	75. numerous:
76. peculiar:	77. invisible:	78. miserable:
79. intimate:	80. pregnant:	81. conscious:

82. decisive: 83. bankrupt: 84. credulous:

85. intricate: 86. domestic: 87. audacious:

88. desolate: 89. emphatic: 90. premature:

91. obstinate: 92. stubborn: 93. horizontal:

94. inclusive: 95. exclusive: 96. composed:

97. objective: 98. subjective: 99. dependent:

100. random: (60~70: C⁺ / 70~80: B / 80~90: B⁺ / 90~100: A)

[정답] 출제된 형용사의 "가장 흔히 쓰이는 뜻"을 정답으로 하였음.

1. 문자상의, 글자 그대로의
2. 글을 아는, 읽고 쓸 수 있는
3. 문학의/문학적
4. ~보다 열등한(~ to)
5. ~보다 우월한(~ to)
6. 시간을 엄수하는
7. 부성의/아버지의
8. 모성의/어머니의
9. 불후의/불멸의
10. 뚜렷한/구별되는
11. 분명한/명확한
12. 정반대의/맞은편의
13. 명백한/명시된
14. 은연중의/암시적인
15. 신중한/조심하는
16. 비교적/상대적
17. 절대의/절대적
18. 너절한, 단정치 못한
19. 무정한/무자비한
20. 무모한, 분별 없는
21. 빛나는/찬란한
22. 유연한, 융통성 있는
23. 사법의/재판상의
24. 현명한, 분별 있는
25. 추상적
26. 구체적
27. 후한/관대한
28. 합리적/이성적
29. 무지한/모르는(~ of)
30. 보편적
31. 열대(지방)의
32. 향기로운
33. 근육의/근육질의
34. 적격의, 자격을 갖춘
35. 습관적인
36. 서투른/어색한
37. 알맞은/적절한(~ for)
38. 관련된/적절한(~ to)
39. 지배적인/우세한
40. 만기일이 지난
41. 정확한
42. 악의 있는, 심술궂은
43. 귀중한/소중한
44. 앞의/이전의
45. 엄청난/거대한
46. 거만한/무례한
47. 나태한/게으른
48. 철저한/완벽한
49. 수직의/수직적
50. 거만한/건방진
51. 끔직한/섬뜩한
52. 방심 않는, 늘 경계하는
53. 반대(거꾸로)의(~ to)
54. 많은/풍부한
55. 고요한/평온한
56. 본래의/타고난
57. 적당한/온건한
58. 불리한/거스르는
59. 낡은, 폐물이 된
60. 깊은/심오한
61. 애처로운/불쌍한
62. 과묵한, 말이 없는
63. 열심인/분투하는
64. 긍정적/적극적
65. 부정적/소극적
66. 예의 바른, 정중한
67. 결연한/확고한
68. 빈번한, 자주 일어나는
69. 성난/분개한
70. 유치한, 어린애 같은
71. 보통의/통상의
72. 절박한/임박한
73. 믿을 수 있는
74. 명백한/분명한
75. 수많은
76. 독특한/특이한
77. 눈에 보이지 않는
78. 비참한/불행한
79. 친밀한/절친한
80. 임신한
81. 의식적의/의식하는(~ of)
82. 결정적인/단호한
83. 파산한/도산한
84. 쉽사리 믿는, 잘 속는
85. 복잡한/뒤얽힌
86. 가정의/집안의/국내의
87. 대담한/뻔뻔한
88. 황량한/쓸쓸한
89. 강조의/강조하는
90. 조숙한
91. 완고한/완강한
92. 완고한/완강한
93. 수평적/수평(선)의
94. 포함한/포함하는
95. 배제하는/배타적/독점적
96. 침착한/차분한
97. 객관적
98. 주관적
99. 의존하는(~ on)
100. 임의의, 되는 대로의

[Test 4] 다음 각 형용사의 우리말 뜻을 쓰세요.

1. chaotic:	2. cunning:	3. adequate:
4. primary:	5. obscene:	6. excessive:
7. available:	8. favorable:	9. accessible:
10. artificial:	11. pictorial:	12. laborious:
13. effective:	14. efficient:	15. infectious:
16. resentful:	17. luxuriant:	18. luxurious:
19. financial:	20. incessant:	21. medieval:
22. impotent:	23. ferocious:	24. temporary:
25. desirable:	26. ingenious:	27. ingenuous:
28. deficient:	29. sufficient:	30. suspicious:
31. skeptical:	32. luminous:	33. unanimous:
34. primitive:	35. confident:	36. anonymous:
37. plentiful:	38. ludicrous:	39. competent:
40. fabulous:	41. impudent:	42. significant:
43. secluded:	44. particular:	45. substantial:
46. fictitious:	47. proficient:	48. reasonable:
49. synthetic:	50. intangible:	51. everlasting:
52. reluctant:	53. ridiculous:	54. outrageous:
55. gorgeous:	56. lukewarm:	57. prosperous:
58. elaborate:	59. negligible:	60. benevolent:
61. offensive:	62. legendary:	63. malevolent:
64. attractive:	65. disgusting:	66. unbearable:
67. desperate:	68. promising:	69. formidable:
70. tenacious:	71. intelligent:	72. intelligible:
73. nutritious:	74. prominent:	75. subsequent:
76. clockwise:	77. hospitable:	78. remarkable:
79. charitable:	80. successive:	81. omnipotent:

82. erroneous:

83. persuasive:

84. complacent:

85. inevitable:

86. monstrous:

87. economical:

88. incidental:

89. accidental:

90. provocative:

91. beneficial:

92. imaginary:

93. imaginative:

94. expensive:

95. equivalent:

96. melancholy:

97. oppressive:

98. aggressive:

99. compulsory:

100. principal:

(60~70: C⁺ / 70~80: B / 80~90: B⁺ / 90~100: A)

[정답] 출제된 형용사의 "가장 흔히 쓰이는 뜻"을 정답으로 하였음.

1. 혼돈의/무질서한
2. 교활한/교묘한
3. 알맞은/적절한
4. 주요한/일차적
5. 음란한/외설적인
6. 과도한/지나친
7. 이용(입수) 가능한
8. 유리한/호의적인
9. 접근할 수 있는
10. 인공적/인위적
11. 그림의, 그림으로 나타낸
12. 고된/힘든
13. 효과적인
14. 효율적/능률적인
15. 전염되는/전염성의
16. 화난/분개한
17. 울창한/무성한
18. 사치(호사)스러운
19. 재정적/금융상의
20. 끊임없는/부단한
21. 중세의/중세풍의
22. 무력한/무능한
23. 사나운/맹렬한
24. 임시의/일시적인
25. 바람직한
26. 창의적인/독창적인
27. 솔직한/꾸밈없는
28. 부족한/결핍한
29. 충분한
30. 의심하는/의심스러운
31. 회의적, 의심 많은
32. 빛을 내는, 빛나는
33. 만장일치의
34. 원시의/원시적
35. 확신하는, 자신이 있는
36. 익명의, 작자 미상의
37. 많은/풍부한
38. 우스운, 바보 같은
39. 유능한, 능력 있는
40. 굉장한/멋진
41. 건방진/뻔뻔스러운
42. 중요한, 의미 있는
43. 외딴/한적한
44. 특정한/개개의
45. 상당한/실질적인
46. 가공의/허구적인
47. 능숙한/능란한
48. 합리적/합당한
49. 합성의/인조의/종합적인
50. 무형의, 형태가 없는
51. 영속적/영구적
52. 꺼리는/마지못해하는
53. 우스운/어리석은
54. 격노한/격분한
55. 화려한/훌륭한
56. 미지근한/미온적인
57. 번창(번영)하는
58. 정교한/공들인
59. 하찮은, 무시할 만한
60. 자비로운/호의적인
61. 불쾌한/모욕(공격)적인
62. 전설상의/전설적인
63. 악의 있는, 심술궂은
64. 매력적인, 관심을 끄는
65. 혐오스러운
66. 참을(견딜) 수 없는
67. 필사적인/절망적인
68. 유망한, 장래가 촉망되는
69. 가공할/무서운
70. 완강한/집요한
71. 지적인/영리한
72. 이해할 수 있는
73. 영양의, 영양분이 있는
74. 현저한/저명한/돌출한
75. 연이어 일어나는
76. 시계방향으로(우로) 도는
77. 호의적인/환대하는
78. 현저한, 주목할 만한
79. 자선의/자비로운
80. 연속적인/계승하는
81. 전지전능한
82. 오류의/잘못된/틀린
83. 설득력이 있는
84. 만족한/자기만족의
85. 필연적인, 피할 수 없는
86. 괴물 같은, 끔직한
87. 검소한/절약하는
88. 부수적인/부차적인
89. 우연한/우발적인
90. 약올리는/도발적인
91. 유익한/이로운
92. 상상의/가상의
93. 상상력이 풍부한
94. 비싼/값비싼
95. 동등한/대등한(~ to)
96. 우울한/침울한
97. 압제의/억압적인
98. 공격적인/호전적인
99. 강제적인/의무적인
100. 주요한/중요한

271

[Test 5] 다음 각 형용사의 우리말 뜻을 쓰세요.

1. sensible:

2. sensitive:

3. equivocal:

4. essential:

5. notorious:

6. significant:

7. perpetual:

8. grotesque:

9. convenient:

10. obedient:

11. different:

12. indifferent:

13. identical:

14. practical:

15. practicable:

16. apparent:

17. statistical:

18. miraculous:

19. informal:

20. reversible:

21. appropriate:

22. priceless:

23. disastrous:

24. tremendous:

25. industrial:

26. industrious:

27. extravagant:

28. repetitive:

29. momentary:

30. momentous:

31. rebellious:

32. carnivorous:

33. herbivorous:

34. invariable:

35. affirmative:

36. spontaneous:

37. deliberate:

38. considerate:

39. considerable:

40. optimistic:

41. pessimistic:

42. mischievous:

43. respective:

44. painstaking:

45. fundamental:

46. redundant:

47. preliminary:

48. superstitious:

49. outspoken:

50. outstanding:

51. approximate:

52. customary:

53. competitive:

54. conventional:

55. exemplary:

56. enthusiastic:

57. controversial:

58. superficial:

59. commercial:

60. contradictory:

61. instinctive:

62. prospective:

63. simultaneous:

64. instructive:

65. sympathetic:

66. inexhaustible:

67. inquisitive:

68. affectionate:

69. extraordinary:

70. permanent:

71. confidential:

72. indispensable:

73. theoretical:

74. inconsistent:

75. conscientious:

76. impressive:

77. magnificent:

78. contemporary:

79. intentional:

80. conspicuous:

81. inconceivable:

82. destructive:

83. constructive:

84. contemptuous:

85. prestigious:

86. complicated:

87. supplementary:

88. ambiguous:

89. comparative:

90. unprecedented:

91. transparent:

92. independent:

93. compassionate:

94. progressive:

95. conservative:

96. comprehensive:

97. responsible:

98. disinterested:

99. impressionable:

100. involuntary:

(60~70: C⁺ / 70~80: B / 80~90: B⁺ / 90~100: A)

[정답] 출제된 형용사의 "가장 흔히 쓰이는 뜻"을 정답으로 하였음.

1. 분별 있는, 지각 있는
2. 민감한(~ to)
3. 모호한/애매한
4. 본질적/필수적
5. 악명 높은
6. 중요한, 의미 있는
7. 부단한/항구적인
8. 기이한/기괴한
9. 편리한
10. 복종하는/순종하는
11. 다른/상이한(~ from)
12. 무관심한(~ to)
13. 동일한/일치하는
14. 실제(상)의/실용적인
15. 실행(실천) 가능한
16. 분명한/명백한
17. 통계의/통계적
18. 기적의/기적적인
19. 비격식적/비공식적
20. 뒤집을 수 있는
21. 적합한/알맞은
22. 엄청난 값이 나가는
23. 재난의/재해의
24. 엄청난/거대한
25. 산업(공업)의/산업적
26. 근면한/부지런한
27. 사치하는/낭비하는
28. 반복적/반복하는
29. 순간의/순간적인
30. 중대한/중요한
31. 반역의/반항적인
32. 육식의/육식성의
33. 초식의/초식성의
34. 불변의/변함없는
35. 찬성의/긍정적인
36. 자발적인/자연스런
37. 고의적인/신중한
38. 자상한/배려하는(~ of)
39. 상당한, 고려할 만한
40. 낙관적/낙천적인
41. 비관적/염세적인
42. 해로운, 장난기 있는
43. 각각의/각자의
44. 힘드는/수고하는
45. 기본적/근본적인
46. 중복되는/불필요한
47. 예비의/예비적인
48. 미신의/미신적인
49. 솔직한/숨김없는
50. 뛰어난/걸출한
51. 근사한/대략적인
52. 관습적인/습관적인
53. 경쟁의/경쟁적인
54. 인습적인/전통적인
55. 모범적인/본보기의
56. 열성적인/열정적인
57. 논쟁의/논쟁적인
58. 피상적인/표면(상)의
59. 상업의/상업적
60. 모순된/모순적인
61. 본능의/본능적인
62. 유망한/예견되는
63. 동시의/동시적인
64. 교훈적인/교육적인
65. 동정적인/공감하는
66. 무진장한, 다함이 없는
67. 캐묻기 좋아하는
68. 다정한/애정어린
69. 비상한/비범한
70. 영속적/항구적인
71. 기밀(비밀)의/은밀한
72. 필수적인, 없어서는 안될
73. 이론(상)의/이론적인
74. 일관성이 없는
75. 양심의/양심적인
76. 인상적인/감동적인
77. 장대한/장려한/굉장한
78. 당대의/동시대의/현대의
79. 의도적인/고의적인
80. 현저한/두드러진
81. 생각조차 못할
82. 파괴적인/파괴하는
83. 건설적인/건설하는
84. 경멸적/경멸하는
85. 유명한, 명성이 있는
86. 복잡한/번거로운
87. 보충적/보완적인
88. 모호한, 이중적 뜻을 가진
89. 비교적/비교(상)의
90. 선례(전례)가 없는
91. 투명한/공명한
92. 독립의/독립적인(~ of)
93. 연민어린/온정적인
94. 진보적/진취적
95. 보수적/보존적
96. 포괄적인, 이해력이 있는
97. 책임이 있는(~ for)
98. 사심(사욕)이 없는
99. 감수성이 예민한
100. 무심결의, 본의 아닌

fatoz

교양 영어

정답/해설

Unit 1 품사(parts of speech)

문법 연습 A
1. lately (최근에) → late (늦은/늦게)
2. many advices → many pieces of advice
3. or → nor (either ~ or ~, neither ~ nor ~)
4. new anything → anything new (anything, something, everything, nothing 등을 수식하는 형용사는 뒤쪽에 위치)
5. was → were (committee, family, jury, audience 등은 집단 전체를 지칭할 때는 단수, 구성원 개개인들을 지칭할 때는 복수로 취급)
6. was → were
7. is → are (police, cattle, people 등은 복수로 취급)
8. couldn't hardly → could hardly (hardly는 부정의 부사)
9. kind itself → kindness itself (친절 그 자체) = very kind
10. alive → living (alive, asleep, alone, alike, afraid 등의 형용사는 명사를 수식하는 한정적 기능은 없고, 술어동사와 함께 쓰이는 서술적 기능만을 갖는다.)
11. Neither → none (둘의 경우에는 either/neither, 셋 이상의 경우에는 any/none 사용)

문법 연습 B
1. 전치사: "~외에는"
2. 형용사: "바로 그"
3. 동사: "갈망하다/열망하다"
4. 전치사: "~같은, ~처럼"
5. 명사: "동안/시간/잠시"
6. 전치사: "~에도 불구하고" (= in spite of ~)
7. 전치사: "~에 관하여" (= about ~)
8. 부사: "이리저리 (뛰어다니다)"
9. (접속)부사: "그러나/하지만"
10. (부정)대명사: "많은 것, 많은 양"
11. (종속)접속사: "일단 ~하여/하면"
12. 부사: "(의자 위에 올라가지 않고서도 전구를 갈 만큼) 충분히 (큰)"
13. (등위)접속사: "왜냐하면 ~이기 때문에" (because-절은 주절보다 선행해도 무방하지만, for-절은 주절에 뒤따라 나오며, 의미의 인과관계에 있어서도 "because"보다는 약함)
14. (종속)접속사: "비록 ~이지만" (=Though I was flattered by his attention, ~)

실전 문법 A
1. 4) (강/바다 이름, 형용사의 최상급 등에는 정관사 "the"를 붙임)
2. 4) (Cattle were ~, sit up late, a two-week vacation, something wonderful)
3. 3) (have never seen, busy answering, lonely people, near enough)

실전 문법 B
1. 2) (furniture는 수적 개념이 아닌 양적 개념)
2. 4) (the port: 詩心)
3. 3) (of +추상명사 = 형용사적 성격)

필수 어휘 A
1. (be) due to (+명사): ~때문에/(때문이다)
2. be due to (do) ~할 예정이다
3. be likely to (do) ~일 것 같다, ~일 가능성이 있다

4. be anxious to (do) ~하기를 갈망(열망)하다
5. be capable of ~할 수 있다
6. be aware of ~을 인식하다
7. be forced to (do) ~하지 않을 수 없다, 어쩔 수 없이 ~하다
8. be inclined to (do) ~하는 경향이 있다, ~하고 싶어하다
9. be acquainted with ~와 알다, 안면(면식)이 있다
10. be apt to (do) ~하기 쉽다, ~하는 경향이 있다
11. be supposed to (do) ~하기로 되어있다, ~할 것으로 상상(기대)되다
12. be willing to (do) 기꺼이 ~하다
13. be reluctant to (do) ~하기를 꺼리다/싫어하다, 마지못해 ~하다,

필수 어휘 B

1. be subject to ~에 지배를 받다, ~에 걸리기 쉽다, ~을 조건으로 하다
2. be gifted with ~을 (선천적으로/천부적으로) 타고나다
3. be prone to ~하기/걸리기 쉽다, ~하는 경향이 있다
4. be involved in ~에 연루되다/관련되다
5. be similar to ~와 유사하다/비슷하다
6. be exposed to ~에 노출되다
7. be convinced of ~을 확신하다
8. be absorbed in ~에 몰두하다
9. be suited for ~에 알맞다/어울리다/적합하다
10. be preoccupied with ~에 몰두하다/열중하다
11. be opposed to ~에 반대하다
12. be grateful for ~에 감사하다
13. be indebted to ~에게 빚지다

구문 연습

1. Narcissus는, 낮의 더위 속에서 사냥하느라 지쳐서, 이곳에 누웠다: 왜냐하면 그는 그곳의 아름다움과 샘(물)에 끌렸기 때문이었다. 그가 자신의 갈증을 풀려고 하는 동안에도, 또다시 갈증이 생겨났으며, 그가 물을 마셨을 때, 그는 자신이 본 (물에 비친) 아름다운 그림자에 매료되었다.
2. 그는 공허한(실체가 없는) 희망과 사랑에 빠졌다, 단순한 그림자를 진짜 신체로 오인하고서. 금빛 양초가 부드러운 열에 녹듯이, 아침 서리가 태양의 온기에 녹듯이, 그렇게 그는 사랑에 야위고 쇠잔해갔으며, 서서히 그 (사랑의) 불길에 소실되었다.
3. Echo가 한때 사랑했던 그 육신은 흔적도 남아있지 않았다. 그의 누이들은 그를 위해 통곡하며, 자신들의 머리카락을 잘라 동생에 대한 존경을 표했지만, 그의 시신은 어디에서도 찾을 수 없었다. 그의 시신 대신에, 그들은 노란 중심부 둘레에 하얀 꽃잎들이 원을 이루고 있는 한 송이 꽃[narcissus: 수선화]을 발견했다.

작문 연습

1. My hobby is fishing, mountaineering[climbing the mountain], listening to music, and playing the guitar.
2. Will[Could] you bring us a glass of water, two cups of coffee, and three bottles of beer?
3. She was interested not only in music and art but also in literature and philosophy.
4. It seems, nowadays, that the new drives out the old in almost all fields of life.
   Nowadays, the new seems to drive out the old in almost all fields of life.
5. The government authorities should be prepared to take care of the poor and alienated.

실전 독해 A

1. 2) (격식을 갖춘, 일반적인, 소형의/간결한, 정확한, 효과적인)
2. 3) ("정확한 글읽기"는 주어진 글의 내용이 아님)
3. 1) (글이나 단락의 전체적인 내용의 통일성을 해치는 문장을 찾아야 함)
4. 1-1) (추상적/현대적/원시적/전통적/현저한)   2-5) (아프리카 예술품이 피카소에 끼친 영향)

실전 독해 B

1. 5) (서로 다른 관점)
2. 1-③   2-4) (미국적 상징으로서의 상점들)
3. part (부품, 부분/지역, 역할, take part in ~에 참가하다, in large part 주로/대체로)
4. 4) ("Youth in Asia"를 연음으로 발음하면 "Euthanasia"와 거의 같게 들림)
5. 2) (it gets <u>so</u> cold <u>that</u> ~; making <u>it</u> impossible <u>for</u> aircraft <u>to</u> land)

확인 학습

1. 많은 연구에 의하면, 평균적인 독자는 기본적인 이해력을 잃지 않고서도 일반 독서에
   있어서 자신들의 (독서)율을 배가할 수 있다고 한다.
2. 그들이 막 그것(닭)을 죽이려고 했다, 그때 그 닭은 살려달라고 간청했다, 날도 새기 전에
   사람들을 깨워 일을 시작하게 함으로써 유익한 봉사를 했다고 탄원하면서.
3. 미국은, 사막 주민들도 마치 자신들이 온화한 대도시에 거주하는 것처럼 (꼭 그렇게) 살
   권리가 있다고 믿는 세계에서 유일한 나라이다.
4. 그것은 어떤 산의 수직면 위에 몇 개의 거대한 바위들에 의해서 형성되었는데, 그 바위들은,
   적절한 거리에서 (적당히 멀리서) 바라볼 때는, 정확히 사람의 얼굴(용모) 모습을 닮은 그런
   위치로 함께 굴러 떨어져 있었다.
5. 많은 사람들의 믿음에 의하면, 그 골짜기는 그 풍요로움의 많은 것을, 계속해서 그곳을
   비춰주고 구름을 밝혀주며 그곳의 부드러움을 햇볕 속으로 불어넣어 주고 있는 이 자애로운
   모습에 빚지고(은혜를 입고) 있었다.

실력 점검 A

1. 빚지다, 은혜를 입다	2. 건너뛰다, 대충 훑다	3. 슬퍼하다/애도하다
4. 떠다니다/표류하다	5. 일으키다/초래하다	6. 매혹하다, 황홀케 하다
7. 으깨다/뭉개다	8. 반사하다/반영하다	9. 가로막다/방해하다
10. 상속하다/물려받다	11. 고립시키다/격리하다	12. 늘리다/곱(셈)하다
13. 제출하다/복종하다(~to)	14. 해석하다/통역하다	15. 설립하다/확립하다
16. 끄다/해소하다	17. 꾸짖다/비난하다	18. 지배하다/위압하다
19. 묘사하다/대표하다	20. 이해하다/내포하다	

실력 점검 B

1. commodity	2. fossil	3. weapon
4. sacrifice	5. proverb	6. fatigue
7. tolerance	8. reward	9. peasant
10. crop	11. coward	12. originality
13. divine	14. transparent	15. substantial
16. stable	17. instructive	18. prevalent
19. fragile	20. accessible	

실력 점검 C

1. but (~외에는), but (~외에는)
2. where (=in which), on, with, on, up, away

Unit 2 주어(subject)

문법 연습 A

1. is → are (관계대명사 "that"의 선행사는 "you")
2. were → was (이 문장에서 "ten years"는 양적 개념)
3. If → Whether ("~인지 아닌지"뜻의 "if-절"은 주어로서는 사용 불가: 목적어로 쓰임)
4. make → makes ("all work and no play"는 의미상 한 묶음: "공부만하고 놀지 않는 것")
5. It is necessary (for you) to learn ~. (necessary, difficult, possible 등은 "it ~ for ~ to ~"구문)
6. are → is (주어 "a good set"은 단수)
7. know → knows (주어는 their mother: "either A or B"에서 주어는 B)
8. is → are (the Japanese, the Chinese 등은 복수 명사)
9. have → has (주어는 my brother: "A as well as B"에서 주어는 A)
10. are → is (시인인 동시에 소설가: "the poet and the novelist"나 "a poet and a novelist"는 복수)
11. is → are (a number of = many: "the number of ~"는 단수)
12. is → are (the educated = educated people)
13. seem → seems (주어는 their teacher: "not only A but also B"에서 주어는 B)
14. have → has ("many a(n) ~"은 단수 취급)

문법 연습 B

1. (Very) little ("not"의 의미를 담고 있는 대명사)
2. How life began (생명이 어떻게 시작되었나)
3. Whosoever saves a single life (하나의 생명을 구한 사람은 그 누구이든지)
4. much of the land (= Much of the land is *so* barren *that* ~: 그 땅의 많은 부분은 너무 매말라서 ~)
5. a wider law (uniting them all) (그것들 모두를 통합하는 하나의 보다 폭넓은 법칙)
6. How we dispose of ~ them (핵폐기물을 어떻게 처리할 것이며 어디에 버릴 것인가)
7. Whether or not the child eats what is put on his plate (접시 위에 놓인 것을 먹느냐 마느냐는)
8. the customs (into which we are born) (우리들이 그 속으로 태어난 관습들)
9. That secondhand smoke, like the active smoking, can cause serious health problems (that-절이 주어)
10. the presence of comforting music (어린이들이 필요로 하지만 자신들 스스로는 낳을 수 없는 평화로운 분위기/환경에 가장 도움이 되는 것이 위안을 주는 음악의 존재이다. = The presence of comforting music is most helpful to the peaceful atmosphere that the children ~ for themselves.

실전 문법 A

1. What (관계대명사 "what (~인 것/일)": 행하여진 것은 되돌릴 수 없다.)
2. there (문장의 형식상의 주어로서, 부가의문문의 주어가 됨)
3. that (중요한 것은 사람의 재산이 아니라 그 사람의 인품/됨됨이다: "It ~ that ~" 강조구문.)
4. none ("not ~ so/as ~ as ~": 대등/동등 비교 구문인 "as ~ as ~"의 부정문)
5. Nothing (아기에게 화내는 것 보다 더 우스운/어리석은 것은 없다.)
6. That (that-절이 주어: 사람이 자신은 "모든 시대의 상속자"임을 깨닫는 것이 좋다는 것)
7. There (형식상의 주어, 내용상의 주어는 "periods in history when ~.")
8. it (가주어: 진주어는 that-절: "작가가 자기 작품을 대체로 완전히 만족스럽게 바라보는 것")
9. Whether (영혼이 죽음 후에도 살아남느냐 마느냐), that (영혼이 있다는 것/사실)

실전 문법 B

1. 2) (are → is: "five hundred dollars"는 양적 개념)
2. 5) (it → they: 이 문장에서 "fish"는 단수가 아닌 복수)
3. 1) (have → has: 내용상 주어인 "much speculation"은 단수)
4. 1) (This → It: that-절을 가리키는 가주어가 필요함)
5. 3) (his → their: "the English"는 복수)
6. 2) (helps → help: "media"는 "medium"의 복수형)

필수 어휘 A

1. poverty (가난/궁핍)　　2. height (높이)　　3. depth (깊이)
4. wisdom (지혜/현명함)　5. length (길이)　　6. width (폭/너비)
7. cruelty (잔인성)　　　8. simplicity (단순함)　9. jealousy (질투/)
10. strength (힘/강도)　　11. fluency (유창함)　12. popularity (인기/대중성)
13. variety (다양성)　　　14. modesty (겸손)　　15. accuracy (정확성)
16. curiosity (호기심)　　17. solitude (고독)　　18. misery (불행/빈곤)

필수 어휘 B

1. hatred (미움/증오)　　2. obedience (복종)　　3. denial (부정/거부)
4. solution (해결)　　　5. occurrence (발생/사건)　6. attendance (참석)
7. explanation (설명)　　8. suspicion (의심)　　9. description (묘사/기술)
10. pursuit (추구/추적)　11. destruction (파괴)　12. consumption (소비)
13. negligence (태만/소홀)　14. explosion (폭발)　15. complaint (불평)
16. acquisition (획득/습득)　17. conquest (정복)　18. emphasis (강조)
19. descent (하강/혈통)　　20. discovery (발견)　21. distinction (구별/탁월)

필수 어휘 C

1. prevent (~ from ~): ~을 ~못하게 막다
2. distinguish (~ from ~): ~을 ~와 구별하다
3. explain (설명하다)
4. happen (일어나다/발생하다)
5. causes (일으키다/초래하다)
6. removed (제거하였다)
7. understand (이해하다)
8. pretends (~인 체하다/척하다)
9. appear (나타나다/출현하다 = turn up)
10. occurred (일어나다/발생하다)

구문 연습

1. 내 관심의 범위 내에서 내가 가볍게 혹은 진지하게 다루어보지 않은 주제는 거의 없다.
2. 사실 모든 문제는 그 자체로서 열린 마음으로 연구될 수 있다, 그것(그 문제)에 대해서 이미 배운 것을 모른다 해도.
3. 사람이 하는 일은 무엇이든 그 자체로서 하나의 보상일 뿐만 아니라, 결국에는 더 많이 보상을 받을 것이다; 그리고 이해할 수 있는 사람이 거의 없는 것이 바로 이점이다.
4. 언론의 자유는 지금은 당연한 일로서 받아들여지지만, 자신의 견해를 표현할 자유는 인간의 사회 생활을 위해서 필요 불가결한 것이라고 사람들을 설득하는 데에는 수 세기가 걸렸다.
5. 부모님들이 자신들의 삶을 가능한 한 충만하게 사는 것이 대단히 중요하듯이, (꼭 그처럼) 교사들과 교육자들도 그러한 (똑같은) 삶을 사는 것이 중요하다.

작문 연습

1. There must be something wrong with my computer.
   There must be some problem with my computer.
2. Excuse me, but how long does it take to walk to the subway station?
   Excuse me, but how long will it take to get to the subway station on foot?
3. It was my sister that he met in the bookstore the other day.
4. It is almost impossible for me to get up early tomorrow morning.
5. What is important is to do your best in everything you do.

실전 독해 A
1. 1-2) (증오, 질투, 자만/자존심, 욕심/탐욕, 편견)　 2. a) observation (관찰)　 b) observance (준수)
2. 1. a) sunny　 b) change　 2. 1) (긍정적으로 생각하라.)
3. 1-definition(정의)　 2-those (those who(m) ~하는 사람들, those (who is) around him 주변 사람들)
4. 1-2) (유언장)　　 2-masculine (남성의/남성적).

실전 독해 B
1. what it was like to be young (젊다는 것이 무엇 같은지: "to be young"을 가리키는 가주어 "it")
2. 1-4) (게다가/더욱이)　　 2-5) (어떤 세균들을 당신의 몸으로부터 추방하려는 반사작용)
3. 3) (연장/도구, 본능, 예/모범/본보기, 교육, 정보)
4. 2) (이 문장은 "contradictory(모순적인)" 내용이 아님)
5. 1) (to run → run: 사역 동사 "have"는 목적격 보어로서 "(to없는) 원형 부정사"를 취함)

확인 학습
1. 다른 아이를 희생시키고 한 아이를 총애하는 모습이 조금만 보여도 즉시 관찰되어 분개하게/원망하게 된다.
2. 그가 제공하는 혜택은, 일상 생활의 일에 있어서 이른 바 편안함이나 편리함과 유사한 것이라고 여겨질 수 있다; 즉, 그는 편안한 의자나 따뜻한 목욕과 같다, 피로를 풀어주고 따뜻함을 제공함에 역할을 하는.
3. 인간의 우월성은 행동은 물론 관찰에 달려있다; 어떤 재주(요령)를 행하기에 앞서 진정한 관찰을 할 수 있는 동물은 거의 없지만, 인간(존재)은 본보기에 의해서 쉽사리 이득을 본다.
4. 노인이 매일같이 빈 쪽배로 들어오는 것을 보는 것이 소년을 슬프게 만들었고, 소년은 늘 내려가서 감아놓은 줄이나 갈고리 그리고 돛대 둘레에 감겨있는 돛을 노인이 운반하는 것을 도와주었다.

실력 점검 A
1. 분개하다
2. 드러내다
3. 숨기다
4. 벌주다/징벌하다
5. 공급하다
6. 개선하다/개선되다/향상시키다
7. 그리다/묘사하다
8. 탐험하다/탐구하다
9. 줄이다/감소하다/감소시키다
10. 발명하다
11. 대신하다/대체하다
12. 비난하다/판결하다/선고하다
13. 고무하다/고취하다
14. 포획하다/포착하다
15. 분배하다/배포하다
16. 모방하다/흉내내다
17. 분류하다
18. 공식화하다, 공식으로 나타내다
19. 처분하다/처리하다
20. 제거하다/없애다

실력 점검 B
1. content
2. evidence
3. statement
4. conception
5. end
6. miracle
7. consequence
8. instrument
9. dialect
10. phenomenon
11. moisture
12. origin
13. disguise
14. species
15. superiority
16. expert
17. sufficient
18. outstanding
19. extinct
20. aggressive

실력 점검 C
1. Who(so)ever (복합 관계 대명사: "누구이든")
2. shadow(그림자),　 shade(그늘/음지)
3. carpenter(목수),　 shield(방패),　 battles(전투),　 braver(더 용감한)

Unit 3 동사(verb)

문법 연습 A

1. I had my bike stolen yesterday. (또는 My bike was stolen yesterday.)
2. rightly → right ("sound(~로 들리다)"는 불완전 자동사: 보어는 명사/형용사, 부사는 안됨)
3. We provided them with food and water. (또는 We provided food and water for them.)
4. What do you think he is going to do? (think/believe/imagine/guess/suppose 등의 동사는 의문사 바로 뒤쪽으로 삽입이 되며, 그리고 간접 의문문에서는 "주어/동사"가 도치되지 아니함)
5. That will save you a lot of trouble. ("save"는 S+V+IO(간접목적어)+DO(직접목적어)의 구조임)
6. to steal → steal, stealing (지각 동사 "notice(인지하다)"의 목적격 보어로서 to-부정사는 불가)
7. marry with → marry ("marry"는 타동사이므로 전치사 "with"는 불필요)
8. We hope (that) you will win ~. (동사 "hope"는 S+V+O+C의 구조를 취할 수 없음)
9. discuss about → discuss ("discuss"는 타동사이므로 전치사 "about"는 불필요)
10. succeeded to make → succeeded in making (succeed in ~에 성공하다)
11. did → made (make a mistake: 실수하다)
12. explained me → explained to me (동사 "explain"은 S+V+IO+DO의 구조 불가)
13. approach to → approach ("approach"는 타동사이므로 전치사 "to"는 불필요)

문법 연습 B

1. 완전 타동사 (S+V+IO+DO: 보어가 불필요한 완전동사이며, 목적어가 필요한 타동사)
2. 불완전 타동사 (S+V+O+C: 우리는 그를 바보라고 불렀다.)
3. 완전 타동사 (S+V+O: She smiled her brightest (smile): 동족 목적어는 생략)
4. 불완전 타동사 (S+V+O+C: 그들은 그 문을 초록으로 칠했다.)
5. 불완전 타동사 ((S)+V+O+C: 아무쪼록 편히 하십시오.)
6. 완전 자동사 (S+V: (여기) WS가 누워 있다.)
7. 완전 타동사 (S+V+O: "가주어/진주어" 구문: 질투하는 것은 너에게 어울리지 않는다.)
8. 불완전 자동사 (S+V+C: 이 모든 것이 (결국) 잘 될거야.)
9. 불완전 타동사 (S+V+O+C: 그는 나를 (버스 정류장에서) 계속 기다리게 했다.)
10. 불완전 자동사 (S+V+C: 그녀의 진술은 거짓임이 판명되었다.)
11. 불완전 타동사 (S+V+O+C: 그 자신의 노력이 그를 오늘날의 그로 만들었다.)
12. 불완전 타동사 (S+V+O+C: 가목적어 "it", 진목적어 "to convince him (그를 납득 시키는 것)"

실전 문법 A

1. to (prefer A to B: A를 B보다 더 좋아하다)
2. prevent (prevent ~ from ~을/가 ~못하게 하다/막다)
3. cause (초래하다/유발하다)
4. of (of+추상명사: 형용사적 성격, of complex origin: 기원이 복잡한)
5. had(=got) (have my picture taken: 내 사진을 찍다(=찍게 하다/시키다)
6. it (가목적어: 진목적어는 "for us to refuse")
7. of (deprive A of B: A에게서 B를 빼앗다/박탈하다)
8. himself (absent oneself from = be absented from = be absent from ~에 결석하다)
9. to (attribute/ascribe/impute A to B: A를 B탓으로 돌리다)
10. enable (enable ~ to (do): ~을/가 ~할 수 있도록 가능하게 하다/해주다)
11. play(=do) (play(=do) a part(=role) in ~에 역할을 하다)

실전 문법 B

1. 2) (done → made: make an effort 노력하다)
2. 2) (has made possible → has made it possible: 가목적어 "it"의 진목적어는 "to work ~ away")
3. 4) (makes → has: have an effect on ~에 영향을 주다)

4. 3) (differently → different: 불완전 자동사 "look(~로 보이다)"의 보어는 형용사)
5. 4) (provide animals a safe place → provide animals with a safe place)
6. 5) (poetically → poetic: 불완전 자동사 "sound(~로 들리다)"의 보어는 형용사)
7. 1) (enter(들어가다)는 타동사이므로 전치사 "into"는 불필요: enter into ~을 시작하다/착수하다)

필수 어휘 A

1. enrich (부유하게 하다)	2. enlarge (크게 하다)	3. shorten (짧게 하다)
4. lengthen (길게 하다)	5. strengthen (강화하다)	6. threaten (위협하다)
7. enforce (시행(강제)하다)	8. simplify (단순화하다)	9. impoverish (궁핍하게 하다)
10. embody (구현하다)	11. imprison (투옥하다)	12. endanger (위태롭게 하다)

필수 어휘 B

1. 1) (좋다/충분하다, 알맞다, 선호하다, 자양분을 주다, 대신하다/대체하다)
2. 2) (씨앗을 뿌리다, (열매) 맺다, 유지하다/간직하다, 자라다/키우다, 익다)
3. 3) (채택하다/입양하다, 거주하다, 상속하다, 버리다/폐기하다, 임명하다)
4. 5) (만들다, 덮다, 우세하다/이기다, 확인하다, ~할 만하다)
5. 4) (경향이 있다, 유혹하다, 참석하다, 의도하다, 다투다/주장하다)

필수 어휘 C

1. comprises (~으로 이루어져 있다, 구성되다/구성하다)
2. occurred (발생하다/발발하다)
3. raised (=reared) (기르다/키우다/양육하다)
4. encountered (우연히 만나다/부딪히다)
5. happen (생기다/일어나다/발생하다)
6. abolish (없애다/폐지하다)
7. deceived (속이다)
8. succeeded (성공하다)
9. prove (판명되다/입증되다)
10. refused (거절하다)

구문 연습

1. 우리에게 자연의 새로운 아름다움을 보도록 가르치는 것은 바로 예술가/미술가들이다, 그 (새로운 아름다움의) 존재에 대해서 우리는 결코 꿈에도 생각해 본 적이 없다.
2. 미래의 어떤 사회에서는 부(재산)가 인간 삶의 온당한 목적에 이르는 한낱 수단으로서 여겨지게끔 하라.
3. 인간은 평등하게 창조되었다는 사실에 나는 유념하며, 우리가 평등한 사회를 건설하기 위해서 모든 노력을 다하는 것이 우리들의 의무이자 특권이라고 나는 생각한다.
4. 어떤 물건이 우리에게 중요할수록, (그것에 대한) 우리의 소비를 줄이는 것이 더 어려우며, 그것의 가격 변화가 우리가 구매하는 (그것의) 양에 미치는 영향도 더 적다(미미하다).
5. 나는 진심으로 원한다, 내 젊은 시절 나의 독서를 지도해 줄 양식(교양)있는 누군가가 있었더라면 하고. 난 한숨짓는다, 나에게 큰 도움이 되지 않았던 책들에 내가 허비한 시간의 양을 회고해 볼 때면. 내가 가졌던(경험했던) 적은 (독서) 지도마저도 나는 어느 젊은이에게 빚지고(은혜를 입고) 있다, 내가 묵고 있던 하이델베르크의 같은 가정에 묵게 된 (젊은이).

작문 연습

1. I owe what I am to my parents. I am indebted to my parents for what I am (today).
2. The heavy rain prevented us from going to school yesterday.
3. He takes it for granted that his daughter passed the examination.
4. She found it difficult to make a good friend.
5. The computer enables us to do many(=a lot of) things rapidly(=with rapidity).

실전 독해 A

1. ② (이와 같은 상황은 하나의 역설을 낳는다.)
2. 1-2) (다양성, 부재/없음, 숭배/예배, 혼합, 조화)   2-5) (종교적 신념의 반영으로서의 예술)
3. 1-for no beast behaves so violently as man   2-5) (=Nevertheless, if a fight should ensue ~)
4. a)-5 (claim)   b)-1 (get)   c)-3 (reach)   d)-9 (owed)   e)-4 (avoid)   f-7 (keep)

실전 독해 B

1. 3) (여성: 6000명, 남성: 3000명)
2. 1-5) (말(horse)과 같은 동물들을 가리킴)   2-1) (반려 동물)
3. bill (청구서, 법안, 지폐, 벽보, 부리)
4. a)-while (반면에)   b)-much (have to do with ~와 관계가 있다)   c)-play (~ a part: 역할을 하다)
5. 5)

확인 학습

1. 왜냐하면, 국제 무역이 국가들을 더 상호의존적으로 만드는 반면, 국가들은 자신들의
   수입과 수출을 자신들이 더 독립적이 될 그런 방식으로 규제하려고 노력하기 때문이다.
2. 그럼에도 불구하고, 만약 싸움이 일어난다면, 양쪽 짐승 어느 쪽도 심하게 다치진 않을
   것이다, 왜냐하면 패자는 굴복의 자세를 취함으로써 자기 자신을 구할 것이기 때문이다.
3. 그러므로, 집단 내에서 보다 높은 직책을 갖고 있거나 집단 내에서 할 중요한 역할을 갖고
   있다고 느끼는 구성원들이 자신들의 (일을) 수행함에 있어 더 많은 자신감을 갖는다.
4. 제가 어느 여관으로 갔는데 그들은 저를 쫓아냈지요, 제가 Mairie에서 어쩔 수 없이 보여
   주었던 저의 가석방 허가서 때문에. 제가 개집으로 기어들어가니 개가 저를 물면서 저를
   몰아냈어요, 꼭 마치 자기가 사람이고 제가 누구인지를 아는 것처럼.

실력 점검 A

1. 영향을 미치다	2. 움츠리다/수축하다	3. 높이다/향상하다
4. 괴롭히다	5. 이용하다/활용하다	6. 버리다/단념하다
7. 정의하다	8. 정복하다/가라앉히다	9. 보전하다/보존하다
10. 무시하다/묵살하다	11. 발췌하다/추출하다	12. 경작하다/배양하다
13. 침입하다/간섭하다	14. 위로하다/위문하다	15. 기여하다/기부하다
16. 충돌하다	17. 배제하다/제외하다	18. 입증하다/시위하다
19. 침범하다/침해하다	20. 길들이다/순화시키다	

실력 점검 B

1. tendency	2. experiment	3. molecule
4. defeat	5. sacrifice	6. client
7. dignity	8. tribe	9. principal
10. insurance	11. dispute	12. evolution
13. latitude	14. indifference	15. architect
16. obstacle	17. flour	18. employee
19. tame	20. extraordinary	

실력 점검 C

1. for   (꾸중/비난/칭찬 등에는 전치사 "for"를 사용함)
2. into   (persuade ~into ~을 ~하도록 설득하다)
3. from   (dissuade ~ from ~을 ~못하도록 설득하다)
4. paid   (pay little attention to ~에 거의 주목하지 않다)
5. wisdom, happiest, fool

Unit 4 조동사(auxiliary) Ⅰ

문법 연습 A
1. God grants us ~! → May God grant ~!   (기도/기원의 조동사)
2. does he? → can he? (조동사나 "be"동사가 있을 때는 그것을 이용함.)
3. No, you must not. → No you need not.   ("~해야만 합니까?" "아니요, ~할 필요가 없습니다."
4. may → must   (필연: "반드시 죽는다")
5. had to be → must be (~임에 틀림이 없(었)다) ("~해야만 한다"의 뜻 일 때만 have to = must)
6. not to smoke → not smoke   ("had better" 다음에는 원형 부정사를 사용함)
7. Whatever can happen → Whatever may happen (또는 Whatever happens)
8. did it? → wasn't it? (긍정문에서는 부정문의 부가(꼬리표) 의문문 (tag question)이 요구됨)
9. must go → (may) go   (=Wherever you (may) go, ~.)
10. does → has   (완료형의 조동사 "have"를 이용함: "그의 누이 또한 그러하다.")
11. dreamed → dream   (=I little dreamed that ~.)
12. did not need to worry → need not have worried   ("걱정할 필요가 없었는데....")
13. may → can   (cannot have heard ~을 들었을 리가 없다)
14. may → might   ("산을 움직이는 것"은 가상적이므로, 가정법(가상법) 시제가 타당함)

문법 연습 B
1. They may have arrived in Seoul.
2. She cannot have gone so far.
3. He must have taken advantage of his friends.
4. She may (very) well be proud of her children.
5. He need not have met them.

실전 문법 A
1. may   (~일지도 모른다, ~일 수도 있다)
2. too   (cannot ~ too ~ 아무리 ~해도 부족하다, 지나치지 않다)
3. cannot (아팠을 리가 없다)
4. may 또는 can   ((so) that ~ may/can ~하기 위해서, ~할 수 있도록: "(오직) 칭찬받기 위해서")
5. must   (비가 내렸음에 틀림이 없다)
6. did   (강조의 조동사: 어디엔가 분명 지도를 갖고 있었는데, ~.)
7. as   (may as well ~ as ~: ~하느니 ~하는 게 더 낫다)
8. did   (강조/도치의 조동사: =I never thought that ~.)
9. does   (강조/도치의 조동사: =The sun not only gives us light, but it also ~.)
10. without   (cannot ~ without ~: ~없이는 ~할 수 없다, ~할 때마다 ~늘 ~한다)
11. well   (may well ~하는 것도 당연하다)
12. may   (=No matter what faults he may have, ~: 그가 무슨 결점을 갖고 있다 하더라도,)

실전 문법 B
1. 2) (so → too: cannot ~ too ~: 아무리 ~해도 부족하다, 지나치지 않다)
2. 2) (economical → economic: economic 경제(상)의, economical 경제적인/절약하는/검소한)
3. 2) (to decide → deciding: have difficulty/trouble ~ing: ~에 어려움/곤란을 겪다)
4. 2) ("experience"와 "undergo"는 둘 다 "겪다/경험하다"의 뜻이므로, 어느 하나는 불필요)
5. 5) (they are accustomed → (which) they are accustomed to, 또는 to which they are accustomed)
6. 3) (may → might: "해가 서쪽에서 뜨는 것"은 가상적이므로, 가정법 시제가 타당함)

필수 어휘 A
1. 1) (fix = repair 고치다/수리하다/수선하다, crash 충돌(하다))
2. 5) (influence 영향(을 미치다), spoil 망치다/망쳐놓다, adapt 적응하다/적응시키다)
3. 2) (alter 바꾸다/변경하다, arrange 정리하다/배열하다/알선하다, decorate 장식하다)

4. 5) (grasp 잡다/쥐다/이해하다, infer 추론하다, impair 손상시키다)

5. 2) (conceal = hide 숨기다, disguise 위장/변장(하다))

6. 3) (adjust 조절하다/조정하다, prosper 번창하다/번성하다)

7. 4) (emerge 나타나다/출현하다, vanish 사라지다, improve 개선하다/향상되다)

필수 어휘 B

1. understand (이해하다)

2. obtain (얻다/획득하다)

3. cancelled (취소하다)

4. resembles (닮다)

5. finish (끝내다)

6. undergone (겪다/경험하다)

7. consider (고려하다/배려하다)

8. decided, determined (결정하다/결심하다)

9. consider (= take ~ into consideration ~을 고려하다/배려하다)

10. explained (설명하다)

11. contact (접촉(하다))

구문 연습

1. 지식을 개발함에 있어 우리는 우리의 선조들과 협력해야만 한다; 그렇지 않다면 우리는, 그 분들이 도달한 곳에서가 아니라, 그 분들이 시작한 곳에서 (다시) 시작해야만 한다.

2. 아무리 강조되어도 지나치지 않듯이, 대학이란 폭넓은 시야(조망)를 형성하기 위한 것이며, 전인(온전한 사람들)을 만들기 위한 것이다; 아무도 속담에 나오는, (공부만 하고) 놀 시간이 없는 우둔한(따분한) 소년, Jack을 원치 않는다. (All work and no play makes Jack a dull boy.)

3. 지휘관의 과업이 아무리 힘들다 하더라도, 그는/지휘관은 자신의 명령에 의해 죽고 사는 부하들을 대면할 수가 없다, (자신이) 부하들에게 수행하도록 명한 그 과업 보다는 자신의 과업이 얼마나 훨씬 더 쉬운가를 느끼지 않고서는. (즉, 부하들을 대면할 때면 늘 ~ 느낀다.)

4. 문학 작품은 그 저자의 동시대인들의 마음에 닿아서 (그들의) 감정에 접해야만 한다. 만약 작가가 그렇게 할 수 없다면, 그는 자신의 원고를 금고 속으로 치워버리는 게 낫다, 자신의 작품이 살아날 (미래의) 세대가 있을지도 모른다는 희망 속에서.

작문 연습

1. Well may we do away with the death penalty. We may (very) well abolish the capital punishment.
   It is quite natural that we should abolish the capital punishment.

2. I cannot see this picture without thinking(=being reminded) of my school days.
   Whenever I see this picture, I am reminded of my school days.

3. They need not have left(=started, set out) so early in the morning.

4. He may not have attended the international conference last weekend.

5. We cannot emphasize too much the importance of natural environment and ecosystem.
   We cannot overemphasize the significance of natural environment and ecosystem.

실전 독해 A

1. 2) (발명하다, 외로운)

2. 1-1) (간단히 말하면)   2-4) ("~ is always undesirable" → "~ is not always desirable" (부분 부정))

3. 4) (실험; have+목적어+과거분사: have a new pane put in: 새 창유리를 끼우다, 끼우게 시키다)

4. 2) (성격/본질)
5. 1-from (distinguish ~ from ~을 ~와 구별하다)   2-2) (leave out ~을 빠뜨리다/생략하다 = omit)

실전 독해 B

1. a)-peoples (국민들/민족들)   b)-commodity (상품)   c)-for (자력으로)   d)-it (가목적어)
2. 1-4) (결과적으로)   2-agreement ((이 새로운 이론이 자신의 실험들과의 탁월한) 일치)
3. 5) ("벌목은 결코 하나의 새로운 현상이 아니다"는 이 글의 흐름에 맞지 않는 내용임)
4. 2) (to have → to have had: 완료 부정사: "(당시에는) 진정한 가치가 있었다고 알려져 있다")
5. ③ (어떻게 당신이 1파운드의 살을 1온스의 현금과 교환할 수 있겠는가?)

확인 학습

1. 처음부터 그 신념(확신)이 국민들과 그들의 지도자들 사이에서 증대해왔다, 정부는
    시민들이 어떤 양의 교육을 받는지를 유념할 책임이 있다는 (그 신념/확신).
2. 내 생각에는, 대부분의 성인들은 자신들의 언어를 당연하게 여기며, 어린애가 처음으로
    언어를 배울 때 그 애를 스쳐감에 틀림없는 그 외경심과 흥분됨을 거의 느끼지 못한다.
3. 흡연과 심장병이나 폐암과 같은 주요 사망 원인들 사이의 의학적 연관성 때문에, 보험
    회사들은 비흡연자들에게 보다 낮은 (보험료)율로써 20년 동안 보답해오고 있다.
4. 같은 이유로 사람들이 자신들의 현재의 낮고 원시적인 상태에 남아있는 것처럼 나에게는
    보였다; 그러나 만약 그들이 자신들을 깨우는 봄 중의 봄의 영향력을 느끼게 된다면, 그들은
    반드시 보다 높고 보다 정신적인/영묘한 삶으로 올라서게 될 것이다.

실력 점검 A

1. 굶다/굶주리다
2. 불쾌하게 하다, 위반하다
3. 애쓰다/노력하다
4. 확보하다/획득하다
5. 개혁하다
6. 더 무겁다/중요하다
7. 흡수하다
8. 없애다/폐지하다
9. 시작하다
10. 투자하다
11. 부과하다
12. 쌓다/축적하다
13. 보다/바라보다
14. 분석하다
15. 타협하다
16. 전달하다
17. 확인하다/동일시하다
18. 깊이 생각하다
19. 무시하다/게을리하다
20. 확신시키다/납득시키다

실력 점검 B

1. humility
2. maturity
3. legend
4. protest
5. territory
6. constitution
7. confidence
8. characteristic
9. suspicion
10. institution
11. awe
12. rusty
13. instruction
14. vanity
15. rational
16. deficient
17. ignorant
18. simultaneous
19. indignant
20. significant

실력 점검 C

1. use (중요한 것은 우리가 아는 것을 어떻게 이용하느냐이다; make use of ~을 이용하다.)
2. home (come home to ~에게 절실히 와 닿다; bring ~ home to ~을 ~에게 절실히 느끼게 하다)
3. reserved (보류된/예약된/예비의, 말없는/과묵한/내성적인)
4. takes (요구하다, 필요로 하다, (시간이) 걸리다)
5. bear, result (bear(=keep) ~ in mind ~을 명심하다; result in ~ 결국(결과적으로) ~이 되다

Unit 5 조동사(auxiliary) Ⅱ

문법 연습 A

1. living → live ("die"와 병렬구조: parallelism)
2. must → should ("impossible"등의 판단의 형용사에 수반되는 that-절에는 "should")
3. ought to be not allowed → ought not to be allowed ("not/never"는 부정사 앞에 위치함)
4. should come → should have come (should have p.p.: ~했어야 했는데.....)
5. be → being (be used to ~ing: ~에 익숙하다; speak to (~에게 말을 걸다)
6. should not → should (lest ~ should ~: ~할까 봐, ~하지 않도록, "lest"가 "not"의 의미를 포함)
7. takes → (should) take (요구/제안/명령/주장의 동사/명사에 수반되는 that-절에는 "should")
8. would be → (should) be (요구/제안/명령/주장의 동사/명사에 수반되는 that-절에는 "should")
9. shouldn't → wouldn't (현재/과거의 고집/의지를 나타내는 will/would: "들으려고 하지 않았다")
10. will → shall (의지미래 의문문 3인칭: "그들이 다음에는 무엇을 하도록 할까요/시킬까요?")
11. should happen → happened (요구/제안/명령/주장의 동사/명사에 수반되는 that-절의 "should"는 "~해야만 한다"는 뜻의 가정법/가상법 시제임: 직설법의 경우에는 "should"를 사용하지 않음)

문법 연습 B

1. shall (청유형(Let's ~)의 tag question(부가/꼬리표 의문문)은 "shall we?"
2. will (명령문의 tag question은 "will you?")
3. should (후회/유감의 동사/명사에 수반되는 that-절에 사용되는 조동사)
4. will (습성/경향을 나타내는 조동사: "물에 빠진 사람은 지푸라기라도 잡으려는 경향")
5. will (습성/경향: "기름은 물에 뜨는 경향")
6. would (과거의 습관을 나타내는 조동사)
7. will (의지/고집을 나타내는 조동사: "듣지 않으려고 하는 사람만큼 귀 먼 사람은 없다")
8. ought (ought to have p.p. = should have p.p. = ~했어야 했는데.....)
9. should (for fear (that) ~ should = lest ~ should ~ = ~ 할까 봐 (두려워서), ~하지 않도록)
10. should (일출을 봤어야 했는데.....: 일출을 보지 못해서 유감/후회)
11. should (요구/제안/명령/주장의 동사/명사에 수반되는 that-절의 "should")
12. used (used to (do) ~했었다, ~하곤 했다)
13. should (판단의 형용사 "important"에 수반되는 that-절의 "should"(~해야만 한다)
14. would (~하기를 원하다/의도하다 = wish to ~, intend to ~)
15. should (lest ~ should ~ = for fear (that) ~ should ~ = ~할까 봐 (두려워서), ~하지 않도록)

실전 문법 A

1. so (= ~ and Jane can, too.)
2. neither (= ~ I don't, either.)
3. would (~하기를 원하다/의도하다)
4. should ("should"는 생략 가능; move ~을 제안하다, adjourn 휴회하다/휴정하다/연기하다)
5. lest (미끄러지지 않도록, 미끄러질까봐 두려워서)
6. looking (cannot help looking around = cannot but look around 둘러보지 않을 수 없다)
7. haven't (긍정문에서는 부정문의 부가(꼬리표) 의문문을 사용함)
8. should (전화했어야 했는데.....)
9. might 또는 could (so that ~ may/can ~하기 위해서, ~할 수 있도록)

실전 문법 B

1. 3) (are required → (should) be required: "요구/제안/명령/주장"의 that-절)

2. 3) (written down it → written it down: 목적어가 대명사인 경우, 동사와 부사 사이에 위치)

3. 3) (to have not entered → not to have entered: "not/never"는 부정사의 앞에 위치

4. 5) (from their parents ~ → from those of their parents ~: "those"는 "feelings"를 받는 지시 대명사)

5. 2) (carries → (should) carry: 판단의 형용사 "essential(필수적)"에 수반되는 that-절)

6. 1) (should → would: 의지/고집을 나타내는 조동사 will/would)

7. 4) (left → (should) leave: 요구/제안/명령/주장의 동사/명사에 수반되는 that-절

8. 5) (no matter how you ~ → no matter how busy you may be = however busy you may be)

필수 어휘 A

1. 4) (애쓰다/노력하다, 배우다, 개정하다/교정하다, 얻다/획득하다, 수정하다/변경하다)

2. 1) (금하다/금지하다, 남용하다/학대하다, 피하다/회피하다, 좋아하다/찬성하다, 제한하다)

3. 3) (동의하다, 싫어하다, 거절하다, 받아들이다, 약속하다)

4. 2) (공손한/예의바른, 신중한/조심하는, 논리적, 합리적, 경제적인/검소한/절약하는)

5. 3) (극복하다, 포기하다/항복하다, 화해하다, 멈추다/만두다, 잠깐 들르다/방문하다)

6. 1) (나중의/후대의, 어린/젊은, 일차적인/주요한, 번창하는/번영하는, 선례(전례)가 없는)

필수 어휘 B

1. 3) (돌보다, 경향이 있다; 적용하다; 의지하다/호소하다; 시도하다; 따르다/순응하다)

2. 4) (드문/진귀한, 많은, 안전한, 소멸된/멸종된, 희미한/모호한/무명의)

3. 2) (축축한, 습기 있는; 비옥한/다산의; 불모의/살균한; 불모의/메마른; 열대(지방)의)

4. 3) (기대다, 참다/견디다, 준비하다/대비하다, 쓰다/소비하다, 보존하다/보전하다)

5. 1) (고객, 배우자, 형제/자매, 친척, 동료)

6. 5) (사소한, 적대적인, 관대한, 호의적인, 무관심한)

7. 1) (물리학, 생태학, 유전학, 기하학, 천문학)

구문 연습

1. 경건한 사람들이 생각하는 게 (참) 이상하다, 자신들이 노예같이 하나님께 꽃 같은 찬사를 바칠 때 하나님이 기뻐할 수 있다고 (생각하는 게).

2. 나는 하나의 애기를 들은 적이 있다, 자기 나라에서 행하는 데 익숙한 것(들)이 어떻게 다른 나라에서는 오해 받을 수 있나를 잘 보여주는 (하나의 애기를).

3. 우리는 우리 나라를 향해서 행동해야만 한다, 여성이 자신이 사랑하는 남성을 향해서 행동하듯이. 사랑하는 아내는 자신의 남편을 위해서 어떤 일이든 할 것이다, 비판해서 남편을 개선하려는 노력을 멈추는 것을 제외하고는. 우리도 똑같은 애정어리지만 날카로운, 시선을 우리 나라에 던져야만 한다.

4. 내 삼촌은 늘 희망했었다, 내가 교회로 들어가기를 (목사가 되기를), 비록 그가 알았어야 했지만, 내가 말더듬이여서 그 어떤 직업도 (목사/목회 보다) 더 알맞지 않을 수 없다는 것을. 내가 그에게 (목사가 되지) 않겠다고 말했을 때, 그는 나의 거절을 자신의 통상적인 무관심으로써 받아들였다; 하나의 제안이 있었다, 내가 공무원이 되었으면 하는 (제안).

작문 연습

1. We agreed to his suggestion that we (should) go to the movies.

2. She was very careful lest she should make mistakes in the examination.
   She was very cautious for fear (that) she should make mistakes in the examination.

3. You should not have asked him such a foolish question. (= ~ so foolish a question.)
   You ought not to have asked him such a silly question. (= ~ so silly a question.)

4. He who would be a poet must have a special interest in his mother tongue.
   One who would be a poet should have a special interest in his or her native language.
   He/One who wants/wishes/intends to be a poet must/should have a special interest in his (or her) ~.

5. He is so obstinate that he will not listen to anyone. He is so stubborn that he will not listen to anybody.

실전 독해 A
1. 2) (어떻게 반응할 것인가 = 반응하는 방법)
2. 1)
3. ④ (우리는 꼭 그만큼 공간의 법칙에도 거의 신경을 쓰지 않는다.)
4. 5) (c: she (should) keep the change: 요구/제안/명령/주장의 동사에 수반되는 that-절)
        (d: when he comes: 시간/조건의 부사절에서는 미래시제 대신에 현재시제를 사용)

실전 독해 B
1. 1-2) (요구/요청/신청)   2-2) (심각한/진지한)
2. 1-1) (means 수단, end 목적)   2-argument (논쟁/논증)
3. make up (구성하다, 생각해내다/만들어내다, 화장하다, 보충하다, 화해하다)
4. 5) (필요는 발명의 어머니)
5. 1-5)   2-4)

확인 학습
1. 시의 미덕은 말해야 하는 바를 아름답게 암시의 힘으로 말하는 것이며, 그래서 시는
    독자에게 정서적 반응을 촉발할 수 있으며 산문보다 더 강력하게 더 많은 의미를 전달할
    수 있다.
2. 어느 정도는 그 차이점들은 논쟁의 여지가 있었다; 이것은 사람들이 어떤 주어진 목적을
    달성하기 위한 수단에 관해서 (견해가) 서로 상이할 때였다. (as to ~에 관해서/대해서)
3. 그러나 그가 그것에 다가왔을 때, 그는 알았다, 물(수면)이 너무 낮아서 그가 몸을 구부리고
    뒤틀고 함에도 불구하고 그것(물)에 도달할 수 없다는 것을. (with all ~에도 불구하고)
4. 야후 종족의 하나와 교접함으로써 내가 더 많은 야후 종족의 부모가 되었다고 여기기
    시작했을 때, 나에게 극도의 수치심, 혼란, 공포(소름)가 엄습했다.
5. 첫 해 동안에는 나는 내 면전에 있는 아내나 자식들을 참을 수가 없었으며, 그들의 바로 그
    냄새는 견딜 수가 없었는데, 하물며 내가 그들과 같은 방에서 식사를 겪을 수 있었겠는가.

실력 점검 A
1. 어울리다/적합하다   2. 의미하다/함축하다   3. 참다/관용하다
4. 바꾸다/변경하다   5. 전염시키다   6. 횡단하다/가로지르다
7. 잡다/쥐다//이해하다   8. 끌다/매혹하다   9. 맞서다/직면하다
10. 맹세하다/욕설하다   11. 바치다/헌신하다   12. 비난하다/선고하다
13. 버리다/탈영하다   14. 떠맡다/가정하다   15. 꿰뚫다/침투하다
16. 노출시키다   17. 번영하다/번창하다   18. 강조하다
19. 반대하다/대항하다   20. 반성하다/숙고하다

실력 점검 B
1. contempt   2. authority   3. factor
4. therapy   5. myth   6. acquaintance
7. theft   8. prejudice   9. gravitation
10. anecdote   11. principle   12. notion
13. luxury   14. heredity   15. gene
16. conventional   17. tropical   18. complicated
19. hostile   20. inevitable

실력 점검 C
1. a, a (같은 장사를 하는 두 사람은 화합하기 어렵다; 같은 깃을 가진 새들은 함께 모인다)
2. it, between, full, until (it ~ that ~: 가주어/진주어; not ~ until ~할 때 까지는 ~않다/아니다)

Unit 6 시제(tense)

문법 연습 A

1. When did you arrive ~? ("when ~"은 명백한 과거를 의미하므로 현재완료 사용 불가)
2. We arrived in Seoul just now. 또는 We have just arrived in Seoul. ("just now"는 현재완료 불가)
3. have gone to → have been to. (1인칭/2인칭의 주어에는 "have gone to ~에 가고 없다" 사용 불가)
4. passed → have passed ("since ~"가 있으면, 주절은 현재 완료형 되어야 함)
5. waited → was waiting 또는 had been waiting
6. bought → had bought ("카메라를 구입한 것"이 시간적으로 더 앞선 시제여야 함)
7. No sooner we sat ~ → No sooner had we sat ~ 또는 We had no sooner sat ~ (~하자마자 ~하다)
8. will come → comes ("before ~"는 "시간의 부사절"이므로 미래 시제 대신에 현재 시제 사용)
9. was → had been ("그의 아버님이 돌아가신 것"이 시간적으로 더 앞선 시제여야 함)
10. will have done → have done ("when ~"은 "시간의 부사절"이므로 미래완료 대신에 현재완료)
11. Sandy will read → Sandy will have read; if she will read → if she reads ("미래의 특정 시점을 기준"으로 얘기하므로 미래 완료가 타당함; "if ~"는 "조건의 부사절"이므로 미래 대신에 현재)

문법 연습 B

1. lied, lied ("거짓말하다"는 규칙 동사)
   lay, lain (눕다, 누워 있다; ~에 있다, 놓여 있다)
   laid, laid (~을 눕히다, 놓다/두다, (알을) 낳다)
2. fell, fallen (떨어지다/추락하다, 넘어지다/쓰러지다)
   felled, felled (~을 넘어뜨리다)
3. found, found (~을 찾아내다/발견하다)
   founded, founded (~을 세우다/설립하다)
4. rose, risen (오르다/일어나다/일어서다)
   raised, raised (~을 올리다/기르다/모금하다)
5. sawed, sawn (톱질하다, 톱으로 켜다)
   sewed, sewn (꿰매다/바느질하다)
   sowed, sewn (씨를 뿌리다, 퍼트리다/유포하다)
6. wound, wound (감다/휘감다/굽이치다)
   wounded, wounded (상처를 내다, 상처를 입히다)

실전 문법 A

1. How (어떻게 지냈니?)
2. Where (어디 있었니? 어디 갔다 왔니?)
3. ago (3년 전부터)
4. is (속담/진리 등은 항상 현재 시제로 표현됨)
5. had (= I expected to have seen her ~: 그녀를 보기를 기대했었는데.....)
6. had ((먼 옛날부터 그때까지) 살았던 가장 위대한 소설가들 중의 하나였다.)
7. than (말이 떨어지자 즉각 실행된다, 즉각 실행하겠소!)
8. before 또는 when (소년들은 나를 보자마자 부리나케 달아났다)
9. before (distinguish oneself: 특출하다, 두각을 나타내다; 머지않아 두각을 나타낼 것이다)
10. since (결혼한 이래로/이후로)
11. when 또는 before (hardly/scarcely ~ when/before ~하자마자 ~하다)

실전 문법 B

1. 2) (you will be graduated → you are graduated: "by the time ~"은 "시간의 부사절")
2. 4) (will be solved → is solved: "unless ~"는 "조건의 부사절")
3. 1) (found → founded: find-founded-founded 설립하다)
4. 1) (was living → had been living: "came to know (알게 되었다)"보다 시간적으로 더 앞선 시제)
5. 1) (No sooner he closed his eyes → No sooner had he closed)
6. 5) (long before people will do → long before people do: "before ~"는 "시간의 부사절")
7. 4) (left → had left: "remembered"보다 시간적으로 더 앞선 시제가 타당함)

필수 어휘 A

1. 1) (사다/구입하다)
2. 4) (attribute/ascribe/impute A to B: A를 B탓으로 돌리다)
3. 2) (입증하다/판명되다, 지키다/준수하다/관찰하다, 조사하다, 고려하다, 미루다/연기하다)
4. 4) (겪다/고생하다, 참다/견디다, 겪다/경험하다, 이기다/극복하다, 경험하다)
5. 5) (=perilous 위험한)
6. 3) (brood over = think over = dwell on = reflect on 깊이 생각하다, 심사 숙고하다)

필수 어휘 B

1. 3) (be subject to ~에 종속되다/복종하다, ~받기/입기/걸리기 쉽다)
2. 2) (엄격한, 글자(문자) 그대로의, 자연적/자연스러운, 흔한/평범한/공통의, 보통의/통상의)
3. 2) (시골의/전원의, 도시의/도회지의, 중앙의/중심의, 혼잡한, 외딴/한적한)
4. 1) (적응하다, 채택하다/입양하다, 응답하다/대답하다, 적용하다/응용하다, 응하다/따르다)
5. 3) (dwell on/upon ~ = think over ~을 깊이 생각하다; recollect 상기하다/회상하다/기억하다)
6. 1) (상태, 무대/단계, 상/조(각)상, 지위/신분, 전략/작전; restore 복원하다/회복시키다)
7. 5) (윤리(학), 통계(학), 신학, 고고학, 인류학)

구문 연습

1. 유달리 유쾌한 작은 수다를 떤 후, 그가 가고 없을 때, 그녀는 자기 혼자 미소를 지었지만, 마음이 약간 동요되지 않는 것은 아니었다.
2. 당신이 당신의 일에 호기심을 갖게 된다면, 그 일은 단순히 하나의 일거리가 아니라 하나의 문이 될 것이다, 그 문을 통해서 당신은 삶이 당신에게 줄 수 있는 최고의 것으로 들어간다.
3. 나는 결코 대단한 관광객이었던 적은 없다. 세계의 위대한 볼거리에 너무나 많은 열정이 소진되어서 (막상) 내가 그 볼거리들을 마주할 때는 거의 감흥을 느낄 수가 없다.
4. 내가 학교에 도착하자마자 나는 소유물을 소유하는 문제를 배웠다. 나는 하루에 두 번씩 읽혀지는(발표되는) 분실물 목록을 두려워하곤 했다. 나는 창피해서 얼굴을 붉히곤 했다, 내가 잃어버린 물건들을 수거하기 위해 전교 학생들 앞에서 일어서야만 했으므로.

작문 연습

1. My grandfather has already been dead for three years. It is already three years since my grandfather died. Three years have already passed since my grandfather died. My grandfather already died three years ago.
2. How long have you lived a rural life in the country?
   How long have you led a rustic life in the countryside?
3. No sooner had she met me than she began to find fault with my friend.
   She had hardly/scarcely met me when/before she began to ~. As soon as she met me, she began to ~.
4. He heard that she had been in hospital for a week.
5. I will have climbed the mountain three times if I climb it once again.

실전 독해 A
1. 1-1) (무료로, 값싼, 엄청난 값이 나가는, 인상적인/감동적인, 상상력이 풍부한) 2-quarter
2. 3) ("get up late"를 연음으로 발음하면 "get a plate"처럼 들린다; get a start 흠칫 놀라다)
3. ③ (각각(의 능력들)이 교육을 요구한다)
4. 1-1) (삶은 불결하고 짧았다) 2-3) (더욱이)

실전 독해 B
1. 1-constitution (헌법) 2-2) (종속구/종속절이 선행할 경우, 주절의 주어를 대명사화 가능)
2. 3) (none → neither: 둘의 인 경우에는 either/neither, 셋 이상의 경우에는 any/none 사용)
3. 3) ("그는 생계를 위해서 일하지 않음에 틀림없다"는 관찰에 의한 "추론의 진술"임)
4. 5) (비극, 한계, 만족, 모순, 당황/당혹)
5. 1) (소설가는 자신의 편견에 좌우된다; at the mercy of ~에 좌우되는)

확인 학습
1. 세심하게 측정된 견제와 균형이 삽입되었다, 어느 한 분야에서의 힘(권력)의 획득이나
   집중을 막기 위해서 또한 다수의 잠재적인 통치로부터 소수의 권리를 보호할 목적으로.
2. 독서의 문제와 관련하여, 우리들의 어려움은 양의 부족으로부터 생겨나는 것이 아니라
   질의 진정한 식별로부터 생겨난다. 우리들의 처분에 놓여(맡겨져) 있는 책들의 바로 그
   가지각색의 다양함에서 우리들은 당혹감을 갖게 된다.
3. 아무리 열심히 그가 객관적이 되려고 노력한다 하더라도, 그는 자신의 특이성의 노예로
   남게 된다. 아무리 열심히 그가 치우치지 않으려고 노력한다 하더라도, 그는 편들지 않을
   수가 없다. 그는 자신의 사실들을 독자들의 주목을 사로잡는 그런 (방)식으로 정리한다.
4. 그것(그녀의 미모)에 깃든 그 매력들을 나는 예전에 본 적이 있었다; 내가 예전에 본 적이
   없었던 것은, 한때는 거만했던 그 눈의 슬퍼진 부드러운 (눈)빛이었다; 내가 예전에는 결코
   느끼지 못했던 것은, 한때는 무정했던(둔감했던) 그 손의 다정한 감촉이었다.

실력 점검 A
1. 높이다/고양시키다	2. 비틀거리다/머뭇거리다	3. 경쟁하다
4. 살다/거주하다	5. 고집하다/존속하다	6. 낳다/발생시키다
7. 비틀다/왜곡하다	8. 고발하다/비난하다	9. 주장하다/유지하다
10. 줄이다/감소시키다	11. 능가하다/뛰어나다	12. 매혹하다/매혹시키다
13. 떠받치다/유지하다	14. 경멸하다/멸시하다	15. 기대하다/고대하다
16. 기울다/거절하다	17. ~할 만하다	18. 참가하다
19. 둘러싸다/동봉하다	20. 앞서다/선행하다	

실력 점검 B
1. relative	2. cause	3. sculpture
4. revolution	5. fallacy	6. controversy
7. logic	8. reputation	9. barrier
10. torch	11. sermon	12. obstinacy
13. intuition	14. autobiography	15. opponent
16. perilous	17. ethical	18. simultaneous
19. theoretical	20. deliberate	

실력 점검 C
1. terms (in terms of ~의 관점에서/견지에서)
2. merely, undone (not merely = not only; leave ~ undone "~을 하지 않은 채로 내버려두다")
3. nature, work, when (관계 부사 "when"의 선행사는 "the time": 만약 예술/미술이 단순히
   자연의 외관에 대한 하나의 기록이라면, 가장 세밀한 모방이 가장 만족스러운 예술/미술
   작품이 될 것이며, 사진술이 회화를 대신할 시간이 빨리 다가올 것이다.)

Unit 7 부정사(infinitive)

문법 연습 A

1. to find → find   ("have(시키다)"는 사역 동사이므로 원형 부정사가 타당)
2. to lift it → to lift   (=The table is so heavy that I cannot lift it.)
3. to live → to live in   (a house to live in: (그 안에) 살 집)
4. to cry → cry   ("do nothing but"은 원형 부정사를 취함: "그 아기는 종일 울기만 한다")
5. open her mind → open her mind to   (~에게 마음을 열다)
6. to have not answered → not to have answered   ("not/never"는 부정사/동명사/분사 앞에 놓임)
7. to be wounded → to have been wounded   ("부상당한 것"이 시간적으로 앞선 사실: 완료 부정사)
8. wait → to wait; will come → comes   (~외에는 선택의 여지가 없다; "until~"은 "시간의 부사절")
9. to be seated → be seated   ("notice(알아채다/인지하다)"는 지각 동사이므로 원형 부정사가 타당)
10. clean → to clean   ("get(시키다)"은 사역 동사로 간주하지 않음)
11. enough interesting → interesting enough   ("enough"가 형용사/부사를 수식할 때는 뒤쪽에 위치)
12. staying → stay   (술어 동사 "go out"과의 병렬구조(parallelism)이므로 원형 부정사가 타당)
13. of listening → to listen   (tend to (do) = have a tendency to (do) ~하는 경향이 있다)

문법 연습 B

1. The sisters are too proud for boys to speak to.   (too ~ (for ~) to ~ = so ~ that ~ cannot ~)
2. The question was easy enough (for everybody) to answer.   (enough (for ~) to ~ = so ~ that ~ can ~)
3. She seemed to be on good terms with ~.   (주절과 종속절의 시제가 일치하면 단순 부정사 사용)
4. The old man seems to have been living ~.   (종속절의 시제가 시간적으로 앞선다면 완료 부정사)
5. I think it almost impossible to finish ~.   (주어+동사+가목적어+(목적격)보어+진목적어)
6. It would be very wise of you to consult ~.   (성격/성품의 형용사("wise") 뒤에는 "of+목적격" 사용)

실전 문법 A

1. for   (우리가 전화하는 것이 언제 당신에게 편리합니까?)
2. as   (= He was so tall that he could touch the ceiling. = He was tall enough to touch the ceiling.)
3. justice   (to do ~ justice: ~을/를 공평하게 평하자면)
4. of   (사람의 성격/성품을 나타내는 형용사("stupid")에 수반되는 "of+목적격")
5. For   ("여자들이 어린 나이에 결혼하는 것이 전적으로 나쁜 것만은 아니다.")
6. with   (keep company with ~와 사귀다/교제하다)
7. to   ("to go"의 반복 사용을 피하기 위한 대(代)부정사)
8. how   (how to (do): ~하는 방법)
9. enough   (당신 자녀들은 스스로를 돌 볼 만큼 (충분히) 나이가 들었습니까?)
10. with   (당신에게 솔직히 말하자면)
11. it   (가목적어: 진목적어는 "to make it public ~ (가능한 빨리 그것을 공표하는 것")
12. only   (to-부정사 바로 앞에 "but"이나 "only"가 오면, 흔히 "결과"를 나타내는 부사적 용법)

실전 문법 B

1. 5)   (and are not to be taken ~: not/never는 부정사 바로 앞에 위치함)
2. 3)   (they were not too proud to learn ~을 배울 수 없을 정도로 (너무) 오만한 것은 아니었다)
3. 2)   (is the ability to read: "be able to (do)"나 "ability to (do)" 등의 표현이 타당함)
4. 5)   (I felt a cold shuddering pass ~: "feel"은 지각 동사이므로 "pass"는 원형 부정사가 타당함)
5. 1)   (a pleasant place to live in: ((그 안에) 살 유쾌한 곳/장소)

6. 5) (why people start, stop or continue smoking: 동사 "start/continue" 등은 동명사나 to-부정사가
    목적어로 가능하지만, 동사 "stop"의 목적어는 명사/동명사; "to smoke" 담배 피기 위해서.

필수 어휘 A

1. illegal (불법적)   2. Immortal (영원 불멸의)   3. irregular (불규칙적)
4. infinite (무한한)   5. dishonest (부정직한)   6. infamous (악명 높은)
7. ignoble (비천한)   8. abnormal (비정상적)   9. extraordinary (비범한)
10. inability (무능력)   11.misfortune (불운)   12. malnutrition (영양 실조)

필수 어휘 B

1. 2) (신화, 우화, 소설, 전설, 전기)
2. 4) (앞/정면/전선, 해안, 경계/국경, 수직적, 수평적)
3. 4) (금지하다, 의심하다, 보호하다, 창피(굴욕감)를 주다, 격려하다)
4. 1) (해고하다, 피하다/모면하다, 없애다/제거하다, 평가하다, 가로막다/방해하다)
5. 2) (그리다/묘사하다, 배반하다/드러내다, 줄이다/감소하다, 가리키다/나타내다, 과장하다)
6. 5) (소심한/겁많은; 질투하는/시샘하는; 신중한; 거만한; 쉽사리 믿는, 잘 속아 넘어가는)
7. 3) (일반적/총체적, 관대한, 진짜의, 영리한/독창적인, 솔직한/꾸밈없는)

필수 어휘 C

1. ~은 물론,~은 말할 것도 없고 (= not to mention ~ = to say nothing of ~)
2. ~라고 말할 수는 없지만
3. ~을 희생하고서, 희생으로 하여 (= at the cost of ~)
4. ~에 좌우되는/좌우되어
5. 당황하는, 어찌할 바를 모르는
6. 흔히, 빈번히, 꽤 자주 (= fairly often = frequently)

구문 연습

1. 만약 당신의 이름이 정녕 살아남고자 한다면, 사람들의 가슴속에 살아남게 하는 것이 단지
    그들의 머리/두뇌 속에 (살아남게 하기) 보다는 훨씬 더 낫다.
2. 일단 사람들이 어떤 주어진 방식으로 배우게 되었다면, 그들이 어떤 다른 방식으로 배우는
    것이 지극히 어렵다.
3. 나는 대부분의 시간에 혼자 있는 것이 건전하다(건강에 좋다)고 알고 있다. 함께 있는 것은,
    심지어 가장 좋은 사람들과 함께 (있는 것) 조차도, 곧 피곤해지고 지치게 된다.
4. 내가 인간 영혼을 정밀 분석하는 것은 천문학자가 태양계를 다시 만드는 것 만큼이나 주제
    넘을 것이다. 내가 하고 싶은 것이라고는 하나님이 자신들을 어떤 사람으로 만들었던가를
    환자들이 이해하도록 돕는 것이다.
5. 논쟁에 있어서, 올바름 다음으로, 가장 중요한 것은, 당신의 반대자를 위한 탈출구를 남겨
    놓는 것, 그가 우아하게 당신 편으로 넘어올 수 있도록, 너무 많은 분명한 체면 손상 없이.

작문 연습

1. There are many sights to see in Kyungju, (which was) the capital (city) of the Silla dynasty.
2. You are to be back home by ten o'clock at the latest at night. You have to get home ~.
3. It seems that he was interested in Korean traditional music and (its) instruments.
    He seems to have been interested in Korean traditional music and (its) instruments.
4. She grew up to be a famous poet, and lived until the age of eighty. [= ~ until she was eighty years old.]
5. I advised them never to tell a lie to anyone. I advised them never to lie to anybody.

실전 독해 A
1. 1-it (동사 "find"의 가목적어)   2-1) ("후자 즉, 하나의 결점/허물을 잊기 위해서")
2. 4) (작가의 진정한 견해가 무엇인가를)
3. 1-5) (반대로/오히려/도리어)   2. a) social order, b) the moment
4. 4)

실전 독해 B
1. so ((just) as ~, so ~: (꼭) ~이듯이, ~도 그러하다
2. a) for   b) beating   c) should (칭찬/비난의 전치사; 분사 구문; "꾸짖었어야 했는데.....")
3. account (고려(=consideration); 설명(=explanation); 중요성(=of little importance); on no account
                결코 ~이 아닌(=never); checking/savings account 당좌/저축(예금) 계정/계좌)
4. 4) (종의 보존/보전)
5. ④ (아주 정반대이다)

확인 학습
1. (혁명이 발발하는 것은 늘 사태가 악화되고 있을 때만은 아니다.) 오히려 억압적인 통치를
    오랜 기간 동안 저항 없이 견뎌온 국민이 정부가 그 억압을 완화한다고 갑자기 알게 될 때,
    국민이 정부에 맞서 무기를 들게 되는 경우가 더 흔하다.
2. 내 삶의 온전한 확신은 이제 그 믿음에 의거한다, 외로움은, 내 자신에게나 몇몇 다른
    고독한 사람들에게 (국한되는) 드물고 진기한 하나의 현상이기는커녕, 인간 존재의
    핵심적이고도 피할 수 없는 사실이라는 믿음에 (의거한다).
3. 그는 생각했다, 어떻게 자기 옆에 누워있는 그녀가 자신의 가슴속에 그 수많은 세월 동안
    자기 (옛) 연인의 눈(동자)의 그 모습을 간직해 왔던가를, 그 연인이 그녀에게 자신은 살고
    싶지 않다고 말했을 때의 (그 눈의 그 모습을 간직해 왔던가를 그는 생각했다).

실력 점검 A
1. 새기다/조각하다   2. 슬퍼하다/슬퍼하다   3. 한탄하다/개탄하다
4. 소화하다/요약하다   5. 얻다/획득하다   6. 번영하다/번성하다
7. 비틀거리다/망설이다   8. 헤매다/배회하다   9. 품다/생각하다
10. 구해내다/배달하다   11. 관개하다, 물을 대다   12. (깜짝) 놀라게 하다
13. 고갈시키다   14. 임명하다/지정하다   15. 응축하다/압축하다
16. 빼앗다/박탈하다   17. ~인 체하다/척하다   18. 협력하다/협동하다
19. 참다/관용하다   20. 내려다보다/눈감아주다

실력 점검 B
1. gratitude   2.meadow   3. affection
4. conflict   5. privilege   6. ingredient
7. ancestor   8. contract   9. abundant
10. comet   11. fragment   12. novelty
13. organism   14. transparent   15. identical
16. substantial   17. contemporary   18. respective
19. inexhaustible   20. superficial

실력 점검 C
1. contact, otherwise (나의 장인어른/시아버님을 통해서 나는 많은 사람들과 쉽게 접촉할 수
    있었다, 그렇지 않았더라면 단지 멀리서만 알았을 (많은 사람들을).
2. lose, goes, missing (우리가 무엇을 갖고 있는지를 우리는 그것을 잃을 때까지는
    모른다는 것은 사실이다, (옛) 속담의 말처럼. 하지만 우리가 무엇을 잃고 있었는지를 그것이
    (우리에게) 도착할 때까지는 우리는 모른다는 것 또한 사실이다.)

Unit 8 동명사(gerund)

문법 연습 A
1. to wash → washing ("spend"는 "~ing"를 취함)
2. to be injured → being injured ("escape"는 동명사를 목적어로 취함)
3. see → seeing (look forward to ~ing: ~을 학수고대하다)
4. taking → to take (stop taking a rest: 휴식 취하기를 멈추다, stop to take ~: 휴식을 취하기 위해서)
5. to move → moving ("consider"는 동명사를 목적어로 취함)
6. to receive → receiving (forget to receive 받을 것을 잊다, forget receiving 받은 것을 잊다)
7. go → going (what do you say to ~ing: ~하는 것이 어때? ~하자꾸나)
8. to prepare → preparing (형용사 "busy, worth"는 "~ing"를 취함)
9. develop → developing (be opposed to ~ing: ~에 반대하다 = object to ~ing)
10. study → studying (with a view to ~ing: ~하기 위해서, ~을 바라고)
11. having not answered → not having answered (not/never는 부정사/동명사/분사 앞에 위치함)
12. to water → watering 또는 to be watered (need watering = need to be watered)
13. study → studying (devote A to B: A를 B에 바치다/헌신하다, "to"는 전치사)
14. being educated → having been educated ("(과거에) 교육받은 것"을 (현재) 자랑스러워하다)

문법 연습 B
1. He regretted not being able to help his sister. (주절의 시제와 종속절의 시제가 일치함)
2. We insisted on their(=them) being invited to the party. (insist on ~ing: ~을 주장하다)
3. There is no knowing what will happen tomorrow. (there is no ~ing: ~하는 것은 불가능하다)
4. I had great difficulty (in) finding his new office in town. (have difficulty ~ing: ~에 어려움을 겪다)
5. She was convinced of her son('s) having been innocent of the crime. (종속절이 시간적으로 더 앞섬)
6. I have no doubt of there being many youngsters at the concert. ("there"는 "being"의 (형식) 주어임)

실전 문법 A
1. telling (그는 거짓말을 할 사람이 아니다.)
2. like (feel like ~ing: ~하고 싶다, ~하고 싶은 마음이 들다)
3. while ("worth" 바로 뒤에는 흔히 명사 "while(시간/잠시)"이 온다)
4. making ("avoid(피하다)"는 명사/동명사를 목적어로 취함; make a mistake 실수하다)
5. of (it is no use ~ing = it is of no use to ~해도 소용 없다)
6. for (감사/칭찬/비난/징벌 등을 나타내는 전치사)
7. of (hard of hearing 귀가 어두운)
8. its 또는 it (날씨의 비인칭 주어 "it"의 소유격 또는 목적격)
9. On 또는 Upon (on ~ing: ~하자마자; =As soon as the clock struck nine, ~)
10. being (be taught = learn; 동물들은 가르쳐주지 않아도 해야 할 모든 일을 할 수 있다)
11. of ("동격"의 전치사; 올해 당신이 휴가를 가질 가능성이 있습니까?)
12. Besides 또는 In addition to ("~외에도"; 영리함 외에도, 친절하고 관대하며 배려심이 깊다.)

실전 문법 B
1. 2) (help → helps: "losing leaves (나뭇잎을 잃는 것)"는 단수)
2. 4) (thinking → to think: (생각하기 위해서 (멈추다))

3. 3) (of being not able → of not being able ("not, never"는 동명사/부정사/분사 앞에 위치함)
4. 1) (modify → modifying: "when it comes to ~ing" ~으로 말하자면)
5. 5) (to see → seeing: "remember to see" 볼 것을 기억하다, "remember seeing" 본 것을 기억하다)
6. 5) (to support and encourage → supporting and encouraging: "worth"는 동명사를 취함)
7. 4) (have → having: "in addition to (~외에도)"다음에는 명사/동명사가 타당함)

필수 어휘 A

1. 5) (말쑥한/단정한, 본래의/타고난, 버젓한/품위있는, 알맞은/적절한, 각각의)
2. 1) ((위험을)무릅쓰다, 간직하다/유지하다, 만들다, ~보다 더 오래 살다, 겪다/경험하다)
3. 3) (무기, 생각, (친한)사이/(교제)관계, 관세/세관, 예절/예의)
4. 4) (비옥한/다산의, 목마른/갈증나는, 최후의/궁극적, 유리한/호의적인, 온건한/보통의)
5. 4) (요청된; 예약된/보류된/예비의; 가능한; 이용 가능한, 이용할 수 있는; 접근하기 쉬운)
6. 2) (덫/함정/올가미, 단서/실마리, 범(죄)인, 사건들, 상황/환경)

필수 어휘 B

1. 4) (점원/사원/서기, 마당/법정, 고객, 회사/상회, (전문) 직업)
2. 3) (끝/종결, 결과, 목적, 태도, 결론)
3. 1) (깊은/심오한, 분명한/명백한, 분명한/명확한, 철저한/면밀한, 얕은/피상적인)
4. 4) (섞다, 채우다, 대신하다, 오염시키다, 조사하다; lead 납, mercury 수은)
5. 5) (즐기다, 설명하다, 비난하다/비판하다, 요약하다, 이해하다)
6. 2) (벌다, 저축하다, 모금하다, 기부하다/기증하다, 축적하다; lay(=put) by(=aside))
7. 1) (이용하다/사용하다, 받다, 개선하다/향상시키다, 보존하다, 보상하다/보충하다)

구문 연습

1. 재활용은 제품/생산품을 재차 사용하는 방법을 찾는 것을 의미한다. 재활용 운동의 표어는 "줄여라, 재사용하라, 재활용하라[재순환시켜라]"이다.
2. 표절은 저작권 침해의 가장 흔한 방식중의 하나이다. 다른 사람의 작품을 표절한다는 것은 그것을 자기 자신의 것인 양 속여넘기는 것을 의미한다.
3. 사람들이 나무를 베어내는 것에 대해서는 새로운 것은 없다. 나무를 베어내는 어떤 이유들이 있는 반면, 지구상의 생명(체)에 대한 치명적인 결과들도 또한 있다.
4. 인간 정신이 새로운 가치를 발명할 힘을 갖지 못하는 것은, 새로운 원색을 상상할 힘을 갖지 못하거나, 또는, 참으로, 새로운 태양과 그 태양이 운행할 새로운 하늘을 창조할 힘을 갖지 못하는 것과 같다. (A is no more B than C is D: A 가 B 아닌 것은 C 가 D 아닌 것과 같다)
5. 열린[개방적인] 마음은 나름대로 대단히 좋긴 하지만, 어떤 것을 마음속에 간직하거나 혹은 배척하는 것이 불가능할 정도로 열려있어서는[개방적이어서는] 안된다. 열린 마음도 때로는 그 문을 닫을 수 있어야만 한다, 그렇지 않으면 다소 (찬) 바람이 새어 들어올 지도 모른다.

작문 연습

1. What is worth doing is worth doing well. Whatever is worth doing at all is worth doing well.
2. The child came/went near to being bitten by the dog. The child nearly/narrowly escaped being bitten ~.
3. It goes without saying that health is above wealth. It is needless to say that ~.
4. He spent the whole night reading the novel (which/that) she (had) lent (to) him.
5. She had no difficulty (in) making herself understood in English.

실전 독해 A

1. 5)
2. 1-that ("part(역할)"의 반복 사용을 피하는 대명사) 2-3) (배타적/독점적) 3- absence (不在)
3. 4) (그러나 대부분의 멸종은 이제 인간의 간섭에 의해서 초래된다.)
4. 3)

실전 독해 B

1. 1-where (=in which) 2-as they are (사물들이 존재하는 (모습) 그대로)
2. 1-5) (반면에, 이와 반대로, 또 (다른) 한편으로는) 2-4) (더군다나) 3-5) (=besides ~외에도)
3. 3)
4. 2) (has been built: (400년 동안) 건설되어왔다)
5. 1) (인간은 원숭이로부터 진화되었다)

확인 학습

1. 육아에 관하여 남성들이 하는 역할에 대한 사회의 변화하는 견해[태도] 외에도, 사회 과학자들은 또한 자녀의 복지와 발달에 대해 아버지가 하는 기여를 재검토하고 있다.
2. 미학적으로 즐거운[만족스러운] 것에 대한 자기 자신의 인식은 물론, 문화적 역사적 영향들이 자신이 예술이라고 믿는 것에 하나의 역할을 한다.
3. 다윈의 진화론에 대한 도전들은 성서적인 창조론자들과 관련되어 있다, 인간은 원숭이로부터 진화되었다고 배우고 있는 교실로부터 자기 자녀들을 정기적으로 떼어놓는 (창조론자들)
4. 싸이키[프시케]는 이러한 설득에 최대한 저항했지만, 그 설득들은 그녀의 마음에 영향을 미치지 않을 수 없었으며, 자기 자매들이 가고 났을 때, 그들의 말과 그녀 자신의 호기심은 너무나 강력해서 그녀는 저항할 수가 없었다.

실력 점검 A

1. 추적하다/쫓아가다
2. 그리다/묘사하다
3. 강요하다/강제하다
4. 멈추다/그만두다
5. 주다/부여하다
6. 숨기다
7. 기르다/양육하다
8. 먹어치우다/삼켜버리다
9. 강화하다/보강하다
10. 꾸물대다/지체하다
11. 정당화하다
12. 당혹하게 하다
13. 묶다/매다/고정하다
14. 수반하다/연루시키다
15. 궁금하게 하다
16. 사라지다/없어지다
17. 가리키다/나타내다
18. 동반하다/반주하다
19. 가두다/제한하다
20. 말을 더듬다

실력 점검 B

1. lead
2. gift
3. formula
4. adult
5. commodity
6. inhabitant
7. benefit
8. affliction
9. infant
10. regulation
11. continent
12. ingenuity
13. colony
14. anonymous
15. eminent
16. vague
17. crucial
18. involuntary
19. absurd
20. decent

실력 점검 C

1. distinguished, discouraged (distinguish oneself: 뛰어나다/특출하다, on account of ~때문에: 학교에서 두각을 나타내지 못한 사람들은 그것 때문에 낙담할 필요가 없다.)
2. reflecting, few, where, purpose (대부분의 사람들은 거울이다, 그 시대의 분위기와 정서를 반영하는 (거울); 창문인 사람은 거의 없다, 문제[분쟁]가 곪는 어두운 구석에 영향을 미치는 빛을 가져다 주는 (창문). 교육의 온전한 목적은 거울을 창문으로 변화시키는 것이다.)

Unit 9 분사(participle)

문법 연습 A

1. lying
2. dying
3. dyeing
4. stopping
5. admitting
6. preferring
7. picnicking
8. mimicking
9. escaping

문법 연습 B

1. comparing → compared   (be compared with ~와 비교되다)
2. the died → the dead   ((죽어가는 사람들과) 죽은 사람들)
3. While waiting → While I was waiting   (주절의 주어와 상이한 분사구문의 주어는 생략 불가)
4. Dressing → Dressed   (be dressed in ~을 입고 있다)
5. amusing → amused   (amuse 즐겁게/흥겹게 하다, be amused 즐겁다/흥겹다)
6. folding → folded   (수동[피동]의 뜻이므로 과거분사가 타당함)
7. We speaking strictly → Strictly speaking   (일반주어가 생략된 비인칭[무인칭] 독립분사구문)
8. Being → It being   (주절의 주어와 상이한 분사구문의 주어 "it(날씨)"는 생략 불가)
9. locating → located   (locate ~에 위치를 정하다, be located ~에 위치하다)
10. pleasant → pleased   ("pleasant"는 "즐거운/유쾌한" 사물을 표현할 때 쓰임)
11. Having not read → Not having read   (not/never는 부정사/동명사/분사 앞에 위치함)

문법 연습 C

1. When[While] I was walking along the street, ~.
2. The boy picked up a stone, and he threw it ~.
3. The rock, if[when] it is seen from a distance, looks like ~.
4. If she had been born in America, ~.
5. Though he had lived in China for a year, ~.

실전 문법 A

1. done   (당신이 (남들에게) 대접받고자 하는 대로 남들에게 (대접)하라.)
2. understood   (make oneself understood 자신의 생각을 (남들에게) 이해시키다)
3. with   (그는 그곳에 서있었다, 두 손을 호주머니에 넣고서)
4. Taken   (take ~ by surprise ~을 습격하다; 습격을 당해서 그들은 어찌할 바를 몰랐다.)
5. There   (형식주어 "there": 이용 가능한 버스가 없어서, 우리는 택시를 타야만 했다.)
6. rolling   (구르는 돌에는 이끼가 끼지 않는다는 속담이 있다.)
7. Brought   (bring up ~을 키우다/양육하다; 좋은 가정에서 자라서, 그는 친절하고 젊잖다.)
8. taken   (=Taking all things into account 모든 것을 고려한다면, 모든 것을 고려할 때)
9. taken   (take a picture 사진 찍다, have[get] one's picture taken 사진 찍게 하다/시키다)
10. being   (= ~, and the earth is one of them. 두 어절을 연결하는 접속사가 없을 때는 분사구문)

실전 문법 B

1. 5)   ((which/that are) joined together 함께 결합된)
2. 4)   (a smallpox, a disease resulting 결과된 질병인 천연두; result from ~으로부터 결과되다)
3. 4)   (and generate electricity; "to control ~, (to) provide ~, and (to) generate ~"는 병렬구조)
4. 1)   (When I was a child: 주절의 주어와 상이한 종속절[분사구문]의 주어는 생략 불가)
5. 1)   (Now considered ~ =Though she is now considered ~ 지금은 (주요 시인으로) 여겨지지만)
6. 5)   (to have his music performed 자신의 음악을 공연되게 하는 것, 공연되게 시키는 것)
7. 4)   (and being excited about the mysteries; excite 흥분시키다, be excited 흥분하다)

필수 어휘 A

1. 3) (유용한, 불합리한, 중요한/결정적인, 복잡한/뒤얽힌, 효과적인)
2. 2) (성급한, 조심하는, 걱정하는, 예의 바른, 우스운/어리석은)
3. 2) (느린, 서투른/어색한, ~을 할 수 없는, 걱정하는/염려하는, 친숙하지 못한
4. 1) (= well-to-do; 부유한/풍부한, 유명한, 감사하는, 바람직한, 편안한/안락한)
5. 5) (지친/피곤한, 겁먹은/무서워하는, 들뜬/흥분한, 깜짝 놀란, 당황한/당혹한)
6. 4) (엄격한, 없는/분실한/실종된, 의심스러운, 불가능한, 유리한/호의적인)
7. 3) (잃다, 대신하다, 버리다/포기하다, 드러내다/누설하다/폭로하다, 참다/견디다)
8. 3) (입증하다/증명하다, 예측하다, 제외하다/배제하다, 이기다/극복하다, 결심하다)

필수 어휘 B

1. never (결코 ~이 아닌)
2. almost (거의)
3. omitted (빠뜨리다/생략하다)
4. stopped (=ceased 멈추다/그만두다)
5. respect (존경하다)
6. despise (멸시하다)
7. participate (참가하다)
8. replace (대신하다/대체하다)
9. visit (=stop by 방문하다, 잠깐 들르다)
10. anticipating (기대하다/학수고대하다)

구문 연습

1. 그 남자는 그 소녀들 앞에 앉아 있었는데, 그의 먼지투성이의 얼굴은 나이를 가늠할 수
    없었으며, 자신에게 맞지 않는 수수한 갈색 양복을 입고 있었다.
2. 호주머니는 물건들을 집어넣기에 자연스런 곳이라고 확신하고서, 나는 늘 호주머니를
    다양한 물건들로 가득 채웠다.
3. "대중" 음악과 "고전" 음악 사이의 구분은 꽤 분명히 정의되어왔다, 어느 한쪽 영역에서
    활동하는 사람들은 다른 영역을 거의 침해하지 않았는데, 오늘날보다 더욱 그러한 적은
    결코 없었다.
4. 당나귀는, 사자의 가죽을 쓰고서, 주변을 어슬렁거리며 자신이 만나는 모든 동물들을
    놀라게 했다. 여우를 보고서, 그는 또한 놀라게 하려고 했다. 그러나 여우는, (예전에) 그의
    목소리를 들은 적이 있었으므로, 말했다, "나 역시 놀랐을거야, 만약 네가 우는 소리를 내가
    들은 적이 없었다면."

작문 연습

1. The accused, found guilty of murder[homicide], was sentenced to life[lifelong] imprisonment.
2. It was a fine day in spring[springtime], (with) little butterflies flying in the flowerbed.
3. Taking all things into account, he does not seem (to be) so bad.
    All things taken into consideration, he does not seem to be such a bad man.
4. Written in plain English, the book is not so difficult to read.
5. The deceased was a great scholar (who was) respected by many students and colleagues.

실전 독해 A

1. 4) (젊음/청춘)
2. 1-1) (작동하다, 잘 되어가다, 효과[효험]가 있다)   2-4) (과학적 이론을 무시하였다)

3. 1-cannot (=can't)   2-4)   3-few (cannot be overemphasized 아무리 강조되어도 부족하다;
    for all ~ = with all ~ 에도 불구하고; "의지만 있다면 더 잘 할 수 없는 사람은 거의 없다.")
4. 2)

실전 독해 B

1. 2) (富의 상대성)
2. 1-3) (상당히[상당한 정도로] 다르다)   2-subjective (주관적인)
3. place (out of place 부적절한, place ~을 놓다/두다, take the place of ~을 대신하다, take place
            일어나다/발생하다/개최되다, take one's place ~을 대신하다)
4. 3) (Not only do they provide ~ = They not only provide ~)
5. 1-4) (= for example)   2-⑤ (사실은 정반대이다)

확인 학습

1. 그것[젊음]은 그 상실을 그가 진실로 슬프고도 은밀한 기쁨으로 환영하는 (그러한) 것이며,
    그가 결코 기꺼이 두 번 다시는 살고 싶지 않은 (그러한) 것이다, 설령 그것이 어떤 마술에
    의해서 그에게 회복될 수 있다 하더라도.
2. 예술과 과학 둘 다 진리의 추구에 관여하는 반면에, 한편으로 예술가에 의해서 동원되는
    과정과 방법들은 다른 한편 과학자에 의해서 동원되는 과정과 방법들과는 상당히 다르다.
3. 고고학자들의 노력이 성경의 옳음을 증명하는 데로 향하는 것이 아닌 것은, 그것은 필요
    하지도 가능하지도 않지만, 하나님을 믿는 것이 과학적으로 입증될 수 없는 것과 마찬가지.
4. 어떤 사람들은 태어날 때 풍부히 부여 받았다; 그러나 자신들의 이점에도 불구하고, 그들은
    성공적인 적응을 성취하지 못한다. 또 다른 사람들은 재능을 덜 타고났지만, 성공하려는
    강한 의지를 갖고 있어서 대단히 높이에까지 오른다, 왜냐하면 그들은 자신들이 부여 받은
    것들을 가장 잘 활용해왔기 때문이다.

실력 점검 A

1. 기르다/양육하다   2. 줄다/줄이다   3. 광고하다/선전하다
4. 가하다/입히디   5. 유래하다/파생하다   6. 예증하다/도해하다
7. 탐지하다/간파하다   8. 주다/부여하다   9. 구성하다/조직하다
10. 살다/거주하다   11. 배반하다/드러내다   12. 결심하다/결정하다
13. 보증하다/증명하다   14. 나타나다/출현하다   15. 조사하다/연구하다
16. 회복하다/복원하다   17. 소비하다/소모하다   18. 보충하다/보완하다
19. 담다/내포하다   20. 간섭하다/방해하다

실력 점검 B

1. perspiration   2. comb   3. status
4. disgust   5. perfume   6. catastrophe
7. summit   8. manuscript   9. trait
10. forgery   11. compliment   12. contradiction
13. throne   14. appearance   15. spectator
16. compass   17. frugal   18. elaborate
19. prospective   20. indispensable

실력 점검 C

1. good (be as good as one's word 자신의 약속을 지키다)
2. Whether, while (공간 여행이든 시간 여행이든, 그것을 가치 있게 만들기 위해서는 ~)
3. as, proud (우리들의 타고난 열정 중에서 자존심[자만심]만큼 정복하기[억제하기] 어려운
            것은 없다. 설령 내가 그것을 완전히 극복했다고 생각할 수 있다 하더라도,
            나는 아마도 나의 겸손함을 자랑[자만]하고 있을 것이다.)

Unit 10 관계사(relative)

문법 연습 A

1. whom I spoke → of whom I spoke 또는 (whom) I spoke of (speak of~에 대해서 말하다
2. in which coal miners inhabit → (which) coal miners inhabit ("inhabit(살다/거주하다)"는 타동사)
3. that → as ("the same ~ that ~"은 동일 물건, 즉 잃어버린 바로 그 시계를 말한다)
4. by which → in which 또는 how
5. that → what (그가 그녀에게 말한 것)
6. Whoever that violates → Whoever violates (=Anyone who violates ~)
7. whomever → whoever ("told a lie"의 주어로서 복합 관계 대명사 주격이 타당함)
8. which → where(=in which) ("stay"는 자동사이므로 관계부사가 타당함)
9. that → who (관계대명사 "that"는 계속적 용법에 사용불가하며, 전치사와의 결합도 불가함)
10. whom → who ("came of ~"의 주어이므로 주격이 타당함; "she believed"은 삽입된 구절임)
11. who are → who is (관계대명사 "who"의 선행사 "the only one of the students"는 단수)
12. but none of whom → none of whom 또는 but none of them (관계대명사 = 접속사+대명사)

문법 연습 B

1. The newcomer, who is smart and handsome, is from Korea.
2. She was married to a man who I thought was very wealthy.
3. He was absent from school, which I didn't know.
4. She is reciting a poem whose title [the title of which, of which the title] I cannot remember.
5. The day will come when you will really understand your parents.
6. They went to their uncle's in Seoul, where they stayed for a month.
7. I was surprised at the great fluency with which he spoke English.

실전 문법 A

1. what 또는 as (3이 12에 대한 관계는 5가 20에 대한 관계와 같다.)
2. as (such ~ as ~: 그는 우리 모두가 칭송하는 꼭 그런 선생님이시다.)
3. but (자기 자신을 사랑하지 않는 부모는 없다. = ~ that[who] do not love their children.)
4. whatever (누가 뭐라고 하든 Sam은 태생이 영국인이다.)
5. which (앞 어절의 전체 또는 일부를 가리키는[선행사로 하는] 관계 대명사 "which")
6. as (동등 비교구문 "as ~ as ~": 우리들은 필요한 만큼의 돈을 모금해야 한다.)
7. whose (그 모양이 공 같은 물체는 구라고 불린다; = the shape of which = of which the shape)
8. why (선행사 "the reason"은 생략됨: 이것이 내가 그들과 어울리고 싶지 않은 이유다.)
9. whoever 또는 whosoever (=anyone who likes him: 자기를 좋아하는 사람은 누구든지)
10. what (그녀는 과거의 그녀가 아니다: what she used to be = what she was = 과거의 그녀)
11. which (명사 "idea"를 수식하는 관계 형용사: 그 생각[공공 소유(권)]에 나는 반대한다.
12. what (= what is still better, ~ 더욱 좋은 것은, 대단히 교훈적이다.)

실전 문법 B

1. 4) (for whoever keeps up ~: 그 누구든 인간 존엄성과 독립심을 고양하는 사람들에 대해서는)
2. 3) (who he thought deserved: "he thought"는 삽입, 동사 "deserved"의 주어가 되는 관계대명사)
3. 5) ((which/that) we dread or long for: 타동사 "dread or long for"의 목적어로서의 관계 대명사)
4. 4) (where[=at which] an increase in temperature is imminent~: 온도[기온]의 증가가 임박한 지점)
5. 2) (which[that] slopes gently away: 완만하게 경사져 내려가는 (대양 밑바닥의 부분)

6. 4) (by which behavior changes: 그 과정에 의해서 행동이 변화된다)

7. 4) (what he was trying to mean: 그가 의미하려고 하는 것, 그가 무엇을 의미하려고 하는지)

필수 어휘 A

1. cock	2. goddess	3. heroine
4. duchess	5. (bride)groom	6. Widower
7. wizard	8. waitress	9. niece

필수 어휘 B

1. oxen	2. dice	3. mice
4. thieves	5. crises	6. stimuli
7. sheep	8. formulae	9. menservants
10. have-nots	11. passers-by	12. phenomena

필수 어휘 C

1. 2) (명성, 평판)

2. 1) (과묵한, 말이 없는)

3. 2) (솔직한)

4. 5) (만족하는)

5. 1) (주된, 주요한)

6. 4) (보유하다, 유지하다)

7. 3) (지키다, 준수하다)

8. 1) (부리나케 달아나다)

구문 연습

1. 잘못할까 봐 너무나 신중하게 두려워해서 어떤 일도 감히 거의 하지 못하는 사람들이 있다.

2. 소위[이른바] 높은 생활수준은, 다분히, 근육적인 에너지[활동]를 피하고 감각적인[관능적인] 즐거움을 증가시키기 위한 제도[장치]에 있다.

3. 기나긴 측정되지 아니한 시간의 맥박이 모든 것을 움직인다. 그것[시간의 맥박]이 밝힐 수 없는 미지의 것은 아무 것도 없으며, (또한) 한번 알려진 것이 (또다시) 미지의 것이 될 수 없는 것도 아무 것도 없다.

4. 사람들이 컴퓨터 기술로써 상호작용[상호교감]하는 매체 공간인 가상 공간은, 건강한 인간 삶을 해치고 새로운 범죄를 발생시키며 가진 자와 못 가진 자 사이의 간극을 넓힐 상당한 위험성이 있다.

5. 내 젊음의 최고의 부분을, 내가 공부하고 명상하며 때로는 유유자적할 기회를 가졌어야 했을 그 중대한 4년을, 나는 고달픈 환경에서 앞서가기 위한 힘든, 실용적인 작은 재주를 익히는데 다 보냈다.

작문 연습

1. One[He] who is not diligent cannot succeed in anything. Those who are not industrious cannot succeed ~.

2. The time has come when all of us should advocate liberty[freedom] and justice and put them into practice.

3. An individual is to the nation what[as] a cell is to the body.

4. What I really wish[want] to do is to make a trip to Europe with you.

5. Wherever you (may) go, you will not find such a comfortable place as home.
   No matter where you (may) go, you will not (be able to) find a comfortable place like home.

실전 독해 A

1. 1) (the most complete and healthy sleep: 명사를 수식하는 형용사의 최상급에는 정관사를 붙임)
2. 1-5) (환경과 경험)   2-2) ("일란성"확률(1/300)의 2~3배)
3. right (권리: 스스로 결정할 권리, 죽음에 처해질 권리)
4. 1-2) (좋다/충분하다)   2-3) (~외에는, ~을 제외하고)   3-4) (청소년기의 수줍음)

실전 독해 B

1. 1-what[=as] (사실들이 과학자에 대한 관계는 낱말들이 시인에 대한 관계와 같다.)   2-5)
2. ① (그리고 당신은 줄[대기 순번]에서 당신의 위치를 알고 있다.)
3. 1) (Oil has been substituted for coal: replace A with[by] B = substitute B for A (A를 B로 대체하다))
4. 4) (획일성이 클수록 그것을 완화할 수 있는 차별성에 대한 탐색은 더 열렬해진다)
5. 5) (ⓒ의 첫 낱말 "Yes"에 현혹되지 말 것)

확인 학습

1. 아마도 풀밭이나 건초 위에서, 한 그루의 나무에 의해 뜨거운 태양으로부터 그늘져서, 잠자는 것만큼 절묘한 고독감은 없을 것이다.
2. 사실들의 모음이 과학이 아닌 것은 낱말들의 모음 즉, 사전이 시가 아닌 것과 같다. 자신의 사실들의 둘레에 과학자는 하나의 논리적 모형이나 이론을 짠다[엮는다], 그 사실들에 질서와 의미를 부여할 (논리적 모형이나 이론).
3. 또 다른 사람들은 꼭 그만큼 강력하게 주장한다, 고통과 다른 사람들에게 방해가 되는 삶에 직면하고 있는 환자들은 삶을 연장하는 치료들과 약물들을 계속할지 말지를 스스로 결정할 권리가 있다고

실력 점검 A

1. 쪼개다/쪼개지다
2. 사라져가다/희미해지다
3. 얕보다/멸시하다
4. 낳다/기르다/양육하다
5. 내쫓다/추방하다
6. 알아보다/인지하다
7. 전염시키다/감염시키다
8. 조심하다/경계하다
9. 격려하다, 용기를 북돋우다
10. 조정하다/조절하다
11. 설교하다/전도하다
12. 창피를 주다, 굴욕감을 주다
13. 달래다/진정시키다
14. 소중히 하다/간직하다
15. 질식시키다/질식하다
16. 우세하다/풍미하다
17. 부수다/파괴하다
18. 대신하다/대체하다
19. 침입하다/침범하다
20. 통합하다/융합하다

실력 점검 B

1. twilight
2. descendant
3. stimulus
4. epoch
5. virtue
6. installment
7. orbit
8. folly
9. asset
10. conference
11. dormitory
12. puberty
13. ladder
14. reptile
15. laboratory
16. neutral
17. comprehensive
18. mutual
19. intact
20. unprecedented

실력 점검 C

1. regardless (regardless of ~ = without regard to ~에 관계없이: 사회적 신분에 관계없이)
2. as (not so much A as B = not A so much as B: A라기 보다는 B)
3. bring (come home to ~에게 절실히 와 닿다, bring ~ home to ~을 ~에게 절실히 와 닿게 하다)
4. out (out of ~으로(써); 재료를 나타냄: What did he make it out of?)
5. over, universal (음악은 시보다 큰 이점, 모든 민족에게 공통인 보편적 언어라는 점에서.)

Unit 11 연결사(connective)

문법 연습 A

1. 요청하다; 안부를 묻다
2. (~에 놓여) 있다; (~으로) 이루어져 있다
3. 적용되다; 지원하다/응시하다
4. 성공하다; 계승하다/상속하다
5. 주목하다/경청하다; 돌보다/보살피다
6. (~을 ~에) 비유하다; (~을 ~와) 비교하다
7. 돌보다/보살피다; 닮다/본받다
8. 열망하다, (걱정하다); 걱정하다/염려하다
9. 홀로/혼자서; 자력으로, 혼자 힘으로
10. 제 정신이 아닌; 무심코, 저도 모르게
11. ~때문이다; (~할) 예정이다
12. (~에게) 감사하다; 어쩔 수 없이 ~하다
13. 중요치 않은; 결코 ~이 아닌
14. 일어나다/일어서다; 도망치다/달아나다
15. 확실히/틀림없이; 전혀 불가능한
16. 관계하다/관련되다; 걱정하다/염려하다

문법 연습 B

1. at (식사 중; at sea 항해 중, at school 수업 중)
2. of (=very valuable fossils 매우 귀중한 화석)
3. of (같은 나이/또래의)
4. with (도구: 가위로(써) 자르시겠어요?)
5. by (내 손을 잡았다)
6. to (음악에 맞춰)
7. on (내 등을 가볍게 쳤다)
8. To (내가 놀랍게도)
9. of (암으로 죽다)
10. for (mistake A for B: A를 B로 오인하다)
11. on (lie on one's back 위로 보고 눕다)
12. at (목전에/가까이에)
13. for (10달러 주고 샀다)
14. between (행간을[숨은 뜻을 파악하며] 읽다)
15. against 또는 on (벽에 기대다)
16. against (그 계획에 반대니 찬성이니?)
17. out (그 복사기는 고장이다)
18. with (내 차에 무언가 문제가 있다)
19. with (=confidently 자신 있게)
20. for (=considering: 나이에 비해서)

실전 문법 A

1. but (~외에는: 용감한자 외에는 누구도 미인을 치지할 수 없다.)
2. With (David가 (가고) 없으니, 우리들은 (이제) 공간이 더 많다.)
3. for (snowboarding으로 말하자면, 그가 최고다.)
4. With 또는 For (그의 학식에도 불구하고, 그는 가장 단순한[바보 같은] 사람이다)
5. beyond (사회적 상황이 몰라보게 변했다.)
6. because (단지 부자이기 때문에 그 사람이 행복하다고 당신은 말할 수 없다.)
7. or (즉, 환언하면, 바꿔 말하면: 식물학 즉, 식물들에 대한 연구/공부)
8. as (=though they would laugh, ~: 그들이 웃곤 했지만, ~)
9. that (now that ~ = since ~: ~이므로)
10. as (as to ~ = about ~: "as to"는 흔히 명사절 앞에 놓인다)
11. so ((just) as A is B, so C is D: (꼭) A가 B이듯이, (그처럼) C가 D이다)
12. for (물론 나는 동의했다, 왜냐하면 누가 그런 멋진 제안을 거절하겠는가?)
13. of (동격: =She had no intention that she would spend her whole life ~.)

실전 문법 B

1. 2) (prefer A to B: A를 B보다 더 좋아하다; A is preferable to B: A가 B보다 차라리 더 낫다)
2. 4) (전치사 "like" 뒤에는 어구가 오며, 접속사 "as" 다음에는 어절이 오는 것이 타당함)
3. 4) (동격의 접속사 "that": the idea that all men have equal rights ~.)
4. 3) (or that Canada is on the equator: 등위 접속사 "and, but, or" 다음의 "that"은 생략 불가)
5. 5) (on our hands and knees 손과 무릎으로 기어서: 버팀목을 나타내는 전치사 "on")
6. 5) (until he succeeds ~: 시간/조건의 부사절에서는 미래 시제 대신에 현재 시제를 사용함)

필수 어휘 A

1. 2) (~을 제외하고: 가장 예외적인 경우를 제외하고)
2. 4) (=for all ~ = in spite of ~ = despite ~에도 불구하고: 폭넓게 받아들여짐에도 불구하고)
3. 1) (go blind 눈이 멀다, 장님이 되다)
4. 2) (drive ~ mad ~를 미치게 하다, 골나게 하다)
5. 3) (=brittle: 유효한/타당한, 미묘한/절묘한, 부서지기[깨지기] 쉬운, 사소한/하찮은, 투명한)
6. 2) (상속인/후계자, 내용/내용물, 기념품, 주거/거주/주택, 명성/평판)
7. 4) (단서/실마리, 특성, 방법, 증상, 조건/상태)
8. 5) (길/방법/방식, 장벽/장애(물), 결정, 고난/곤경, 대안)

필수 어휘 B

1. 되는대로/임의로/무작위로
2. 십중팔구(=probably)
3. 담당[담임]하는 (그녀는 유치원을 담당한다/담임한다)
4. 당분간(=for the present)
5. ~을 위해 (=arguing for argument's sake 논쟁을 위한 논쟁; art for art's sake 예술을 위한 예술)
6. ~와 다름없는/진배없는 (안경이 없으면 그녀는 눈먼 것과 다름없다.)
7. 위험한, 위태로운, 문제가 되어 (건강과 안전이라는 기본적인 문제가 위태롭다.)
8. ~의 면전에서 (그는 내 친구들 면전에서 나를 모욕했다.)
9. 나로서는, 나에 관한 한 (as far as I know 내가 아는 한)
10. ~의 관점에서/견지에서 (우리는 아주 부유 하지만, 행복의 관점에서는 그렇지 않다.)

구문 연습

1. 아무리 사소(한 행동이라) 하더라도, 일련의 결과를 낳지 않는 행동이란 없다, 아무리 작더라도 그림자를 드리우지 않는 머리카락이 없듯이.
2. 우리가 추위를 경험했기 대문에 따뜻함의 진가를 알듯이, 증오의 감정을 갖는 것이 어떠한가를 우리가 알기 때문에 사랑이 무엇을 의미하는지를 더욱 더 절실히 인식한다.
3. 점점 더 많은 여성들이 직업을 갖게 됨으로써, 가족의 소득을 증가하기 위해서든 자신을 위한 경력을 쌓기 위해서든, 가족의 전통적 형태가 더욱 더 많이 변화된다.
4. 자신의 "인생 철학"에 관한 강의나 설교를 하는 사람을 우리는 주목해서는 안 된다, 그 사람이 자신의 아내, 자신의 자식들, 자신의 이웃사람들, 자신의 친구들, 그리고 자신의 적들을 어떻게 다루는지를 우리가 정확히 알 때까지는.

작문 연습

1. (Just) as the moon moves around the earth, so the earth moves around the sun.
2. The student came to me quietly and fell on his knees without saying a word.
3. The landscape[scenery] was so beautiful that I wished to stay there forever.
4. It was not until he met her that he came to know what love was.
   He did not come to know what love was until he met her.
5. I meet him not because I like him but because I don't dislike him.

실전 독해 A

1. 1-2) (apart from ~ 은 별개로 하고)   2-4) ((if it is) rightly pursued: 올바르게 추구된다면)
2. 1)
3. 2)
4. 1: a) in b) others c) but d) in   2: tastes and habits of the people who are to occupy the room

실전 독해 B

1. 5) (협상하고 타협하는 방법을 아는 것)
2. 4) (입자, 재배열하다, 실험들)
3. put on (입다/쓰다/걸치다, 켜다/틀다, 마련하다/공연하다, ~하는 체하다/가장하다, 늘리다)
4. 2) (어떤 식품이나 의약에 사용하기 위한 동물 (신체) 부위들에 대한 수요)
5. 5) (to picture → picturing: have difficulty[trouble] ~ing: ~하는 데 어려움을 겪다)

확인 학습

1. 대부분의 시간에는 당신은 당신의 몸 속에서 무슨 일이 일어나고 있는지를 인식하지 못한다. 대체로 당신이 알아채는 것은 몸이 아프거나 고통을 느낄 때뿐이다.
2. 그러나 이 모든 것들과는 별개인 것이, 그것들도 바람직하지만, 여행 그 자체의 즐거움이다. 이것은 어떤 이들에게는 주된[주요한], 또 다른 이들에게는 적어도 하나의 중요한 동기이다.
3. 그것은 아마도 부분적으로는 많은 주택들이 건축주(인)들의 습관에 친숙하지 못한 사람들에 의해서 건축되고 장식된다는(사실 때문이다.
4. 그는 어떤 성취의 희망도 없이 하나의 천체를 사랑하는 것이 자신의 운명이라고 여겼으며, 이러한 통찰로부터 그는 극기[체념]와 자신을 향상시키고 순화시킬 고요한, 충실한 고통에 대한 전체적인[완전한] 철학을 구축했다.

실력 점검 A

1. 높이 날다/치솟다
2. 발휘하다/휘두르다
3. 찬성하다/승인하다
4. 미루다/연기하다
5. 꾀다/유혹하다
6. 포옹하다/포용하다
7. 꾸짖다/비난하다
8. 점령하다/차지하다
9. 협상하다/교섭하다
10. 산산이 부수다
11. 개발하다/착취하다
12. 우연히 만나다/마주치다
13. 간청하다/탄원하다
14. 수정하다/변경하다
15. 더럽히다/오염시키다
16. 선언하다/선포하다
17. 다투다/주장하다
18. 수용하다/숙박시키다
19. 억제하다/구속하다
20. 타협하다/절충하다

실력 점검 B

1. divorce
2. famine
3. insult
4. analysis
5. digestion
6. torture
7. ceiling
8. pursuit
9. banquet
10. obligation
11. fertilizer
12. spectator
13. diplomat
14. prestigious
15. terrestrial
16. modest
17. obscure
18. inherent
19. disinterested
20. courteous

실력 점검 C

1. touch (get in touch[contact] with ~와 접촉하다/연락하다)
2. civilized, course, accustomed, as, recent, lain
(현재, 가장 문명화된 나라들에서는, 언론의 자유는 하나의 당연한 일로서 받아들여지며 완벽히 단순한 일인 것처럼 보인다. 우리들은 그것에 너무나 익숙해져 있어 그것을 천부의 권리로 여긴다. 그러나 이 권리는 단지 아주 최근에야 획득되었으며, 그것의 획득에 이르는 그 길은 피의 호수들을 통해 놓여[뻗어/펼쳐져] 왔다.)

Unit 12 지시사(demonstrative)

문법 연습 A

1. another → the other (손은 두 개)
2. so did she → so has she (be동사/have동사/조동사 등이 없을 때만 do/does/did를 도입함)
3. so I should be → so should I be (주어와 (조)동사가 도치되어야 함)
4. the others → others ("some"이 불특정이므로, "others"도 불특정이어야 함)
5. who → whom ("hates"의 목적어: 내 누이가 싫어하는 사람을 내 형[동생]은 좋아하는 경향)
6. very → so (so ~ that ~: 너무나 ~해서 ~하다)
7. Japan → that of Japan (동일한 명사(the climate)의 반복 사용을 피하는 지시 대명사)
8. others → the others (한 쪽이 "three"로 특정되어 있으므로, 다른 한 쪽도 특정되어야 함)
9. None → Neither (둘인 경우에는 neither/either 사용, 셋 이상인 경우에는 none/any 사용)
10. such → so (과거분사 "written"을 수식하기 위해서는 지시 형용사가 아닌 지시 부사가 타당)
11. North Korea → that of North Korea ("the population"의 반복 사용을 피하는 지시 대명사)
12. the one → one (둘인 경우에는 "one, the other" 사용, "the one, the other"은 전자/후자[후자/전자])

문법 연습 B

1. others (어떤 이들은 그것이 사실이라고 하고, 또 다른 이들은 사실이 아니라고 한다.)
2. another (또 다른 것 하나 보여주세요.)
3. such ("as to ~"나 "that-절"의 내용을 가리키는 지시 형용사)
4. another (말하는 것과 행하는 것은 아주 별개의 문제다.)
5. so (that-절의 내용을 가리키는 지시 부사)
6. so (창문 또한/역시 닫혀있었다.)
7. neither (그의 형[동생] 또한/역시 불어를 못한다.)
8. as ("so"는 "as to ~"나 "that-절"의 내용을 가리키는 지시 부사)
9. those (those (who are) around them: 그들 주변[주위]에 있는 사람들)
10. such (그것은 그 자체로서는 하나의 합의[협정/협약]가 아니지만, ~)
11. that (단수 명사("the temperature")의 반복 사용을 피하는 지시 대명사)
12. those (복수 명사("the ears")의 반복 사용을 피하는 지시 대명사)
13. so (=Tom is such a honest student that his teacher is proud of him.)

실전 문법 A

1. such (변변치는 않지만)
2. another (듣는 것과 보는 것은 아주 별개의 문제다.)
3. Such (뉴턴 같은 과학자는 인류사에 드물다.)
4. so (인간은 상징 없이는 오래 기억할 수 없게 (그렇게) 만들어져 있다.)
5. such (그들의 식품[음식물]은 필요한 비타민들을 얻을 수 없는 그러한 것이었다.)
6. that, those (그의 옷은 신사의 옷이지만 그의 예절은 광대의 예절이란다.)
7. this, that (후자(육체)는 인간의 활동성에 관계하고, 전자(정신)는 창의성에 관계한다.)
8. former (또는 one), latter (또는 other) (노동과 절제[금주]는 두 명의 가장 좋은 내과 의사이다. 전자는 식욕을 돋우고, 후자는 방종[탐닉]을 과도하지 않게 한다.)

실전 문법 B

1. 2) (such ~ that ~: 명사("wings and tails")를 수식할 때는 "so"가 아닌 "such"가 타당함)
2. 1) (so ~ that ~: The sun is *so* much hotter than the earth *that* ~.)
3. 5) (~ differs from *that* of other species: "the evolution"의 반복 사용을 피하는 지시 대명사)

4. 4) (and *the other* is published ~: 둘의 경우에는 "one, the other"을 사용함)
5. 1) (so ~ that ~: She was *so* surprised ~ *that* she had to hide ~.)
6. 2) (*of which* the public has *imperfect knowledge*: "그 문제에 대한 불완전한 지식": 대중이
         불완전한 지식을 갖고 있는 어떤 문제에 있어서는, 대중의 견해[여론]도 똑같이 잘
         모르는 개인의 견해만큼이나 틀릴 가능성이 있다.)
7. 5) (and *those* who ~: "the people"의 반복 사용을 피하는 지시 대명사)

필수 어휘 A

1. 2) (해보다/시도하다, 시작하다, 거절하다/퇴짜놓다, 요구하다, 미루다/연기하다)
2. 1) (직면하다/대면하다, 피하다/회피하다, 받아들이다, 개혁하다, 이기다/극복하다)
3. 1) (=세밀한/세세한: 작은, 정확한, 사소한/하찮은, 특정한/특유한/구체적인, 중요한)
4. 3) (찾아내다/발견하다, 증명하다/입증하다, 주장하다, 기소하다/고발하다, 의심하다)
5. 1) (물러나다/퇴각하다, ~보다 오래 살다, 보호하다, 내려가다/하강하다, 분리하다)
6. 2) (피하다/회피하다, 저항하다/견디다, 준비하다, 동면하다, 떠맡다)
7. 3) (=공평한, 치우치지 않은: 불합리한, 적대적인, 중립적인, 다정한, 일관된)
8. 3) (정신/혼령, 유행, 방법/방식, 모방, 훈련/훈육/규율)

필수 어휘 B

1. (별로) 중요치 않다
2. 가슴에 와 닿았다, 분명히 이해되다.
3. ~을 공유하다, 공통점으로 갖다.
4. 방해되다, 훼방을 놓다
5. ~에 의지하다/의존하다
6. ~와 관계가 있다, 관계를 맺다
7. ~을 마음대로 (집어)먹다/마시다
8. 수지 (타산)를 맞추다
9. 최대한 이용하다/활용하다
10. 그런대로 때우다, (대용품으로) 임시 변통하다

구문 연습

1. 진보[발전]는 인간의 이성과 인간의 본능 사이의 끝없는 전투의 점진적인 결과인데,
    그 전투에서는 전자[이성]가 느리지만 확실히 (후자[본능]를) 이긴다.
2. 원시인이 먹었던 식품에 가까운 자연[천연] 식품이 인간의 소화에 가장 적합할 것
    같다는 확고한 믿음을 우리는 갖고 있다.
3. 언어는 너무나 우리들의 일상 활동의 일부분이어서 우리는 그것을 눈 깜박임이나 숨쉬기와
    같은 자동적이고 자연적인 행동으로 여기게 되는지도 모른다.
4. 그 누구도, 아무리 박식하다 하더라도, 자기 사회의 관습과 제도를 안전하게 판단해서
    간단히 처리할[결말을 내릴] 만큼 (그런) 완전한 이해에 도달 할 수는 없다.
5. 행동이 말보다 더 정직하게 말해준다; 우리가 사람들의 비 언어적인 행동으로부터 끌어내는
    추론들이 그들이 자신들에 대해서 얘기하는 것에 우리가 기반하는 추론들보다 더 안전하다.

작문 연습

1. To like is one thing, and to love is (quite) another. To like and to love are one thing another.
    It is one thing to like, and (it is) quite another to love.
2. The cultural tradition of Korea is very[quite] different from that of Japan or China.
3. Some people look upon life as a blessing, and others as a curse. Some people regard[consider] life ~.
4. His love for her was such that he wrote a letter to her almost every day.
5. There is a widespread conspiracy to conceal the former and to reveal and exaggerate the latter.

실전 독해 A
1. 3) (우선/우선권, 해결/해결책, 봉급[임금] 지불 수표, 세대, 좌절/좌절감)
2. 1-1) (대처하다, 숙고하다, 발생하다, 이용하다, 최대한 활용하다)   2-3)
3. 1-less (덜 뚜렷해진다)   2-② (이것은 논리적이다: "~ must be extremely ancient"가 힌트)
4. 2)

실전 독해 B
1. 2) (재능, 근면/산업, 적성, 야망, 개성)
2. a)-10 (사치)   b)-2 (곡물)   c)-4 (붕괴)   d)-5 (소송)   e)-7 (악덕)
   f)-3 (건강)   g)-8 (평화)   h)-wishes (소망)   i)-cost (비용/손실/희생)
3. 2) (believe → disbelieve)
4. 3) (마찬가지로, 아프리카를 유럽의 식민지들로 쪼갠 19세기 동안 유럽에서 그어진
   (경계)선들은 많은 상이한 문화들을 담고 있는 몇몇 국가들을 낳았으며, 또한
   통합된 문화들을 분리된 국가들로 잔인하게 쪼개었다.)
5. 5) (what my problem was: 간접의문문에서는 주어/동사가 도치되지 아니함)

확인 학습
1. 불행히도, 우리가 산업화가 될수록 우리는 식물과의 직접적인 접촉으로부터 더욱
   멀어지며, 우리들의 식물학 지식은 더욱 흐릿해진다.
2. 이 잘못된 생각[신조]이 우리들 안에 강화되어서 마침내 우리의 눈이 흐려지고
   우리의 마음이 둔화된다, 만약 그렇지 않다면 우리의 일상적인 주변[환경]으로부터
   우리가 경험할 수도 있는 그 모든 멋진 심오한 즐거움에 (둔화된다).
3. 모든 사람은 농사[경작]에 대해서 예외적인 존경심과, 이것이 자기 종족의 본래의
   직업이라는 느낌, 자신이 그것을 당분간 다른 사람의 손에 위임하게 만드는 어떤
   사정[상황]에 의해서 자기 자신이 그것으로부터 면제될 뿐이라는 느낌을 갖고 있다.
4. 만약 그가 자신을 농부에게 추천하는 어떤 기술, 농부가 그에게 옥수수로 교환해주는
   어떤 생산품을 갖고 있지 않다면, 그는 스스로 농부들 사이의 자신의 마땅한 자리로
   돌아가야만 한다.

실력 점검 A
1. 제지하다/만류하다   2. (공중에) 떠다니다   3. 토하다/게우다
4. 지니다/보유하다   5. 번영하다/번창하다   6. 버리다/폐기하다
7. 놀라다, 놀라게 하다   8. 모집하다/충원하다   9. 집행하다/처형하다
10. 주장하다/단언하다   11. 속타게[짜증나게] 하다   12. 꺾다/좌절시키다
13. 기르다, 자양분을 주다   14. 폭발하다/폭발시키다   15. 누르다/압도하다
16. 품다/생각하다   17. 이기다/극복하다   18. 만들다/제조하다
19. 추천하다/천거하다   20. 인정하다/자인하다

실력 점검 B
1. pressure   2. violence   3. capacity
4. offspring   5. prosperity   6. preference
7. heritage   8. tension   9. precaution
10. fortune   11. incident   12. candidate
13. destination   14. spouse   15. mammal
16. innate   17. rational   18. exclusive
19. desperate   20. alert

실력 점검 C
1. such, what (모든 문제는 그 자체로서 연구될 수 있다 ~.)
2. Somebody, Anybody, Nobody, Somebody, Everybody, Nobody ("공동 책임은 무책임")

Unit 13 태(voice)

문법 연습 A

1. The woman was heard to call her daughter.
2. What is this flower called in English?
3. Such a serious question has never been answered (by anyone).
4. 1) Pre-school education was not paid any attention to by the government.
   2) No attention was paid to pre-school education by the government.
5. 1) It was said that he would arrive in Seoul at ten in the morning.
   2) He was said to arrive in Seoul at ten in the morning.
6. 1) It is not believed that she was accused of assault and battery.
   2) She is not believed to have been accused of assault and battery.

문법 연습 B

1. from (화학적 변화)
2. of (물리적 변화)
3. for (유명하다, 알려져 있다)
4. by (식별되다/판단되다)
5. to (~와 약혼하다)
6. in (~에 종사하다)
7. of (~을 소유하고 있다)
8. with (=be obsessed with ~에 사로잡혀 있다)
9. with [by] (~으로 대체되다)
10. for (~대신에 대체되다)
11. into (얼어서 ~이 되다)
12. with (=be satisfied with ~에 만족하다)
13. into (쪼개지다, 나누어지다)
14. to (=be condemned to ~에 선고되다)
15. of (~을 빼앗기다/박탈당하다)
16. of (~을 빼앗기다/강탈당하다)
17. in (~에 몰두하다/열중하다)
18. of (~을 통고 받다, 통지 받다)
19. with (~에 직면하다)
20. with (~으로 붐비다/혼잡하다)

실전 문법 A

1. 2) (=What he said was taken no notice of.: "resemble"은 수동태 불가; take no notice of ~을 주목하지 않다; be known to ~; They are said to have stayed ~; It resulted from some ~)
2. 5) (make a fool of ~을 놀리다, 바보 취급하다: Let it not be regarded ~; listen to → be listened to; speak ill of ~을 욕하다 → be ill spoken of; The general is reported to have been killed ~)

실전 문법 B

1. 1) (to be ranked as a masterpiece 걸작품으로 평가 받기 위해서는)
2. 4) (though it once was considered ~ 그것[침술]이 예전에는[한때는] ~로 여겨졌지만)
3. 5) (even to be created 심지어 창조되어야 (한다))
4. 4) (has now disappeared: "disappear(사라지다)"는 자동사이므로 수동태 불가)
5. 2) (we were told that ~라는 말을 들었다)
6. 1) (The students were offered ~을 제공받았다)
7. 1) (A man (who was) asked to define ~을 정의하도록 요청 받은 사람)

필수 어휘 A

1. 2) (deal in ~을 장사하다/취급하다: 수확하다, 거래하다, 생산하다, 교환하다, 경작하다)
2. 1) (참다/견디다, 부인하다/부정하다, 받아들이다, ~할 만하다, 자극하다)
3. 2) (운명, 결과, 목적, 재난/재해, 장애/장애물)
4. 5) (드문/진귀한, 안정된, 무한한, 엄청난/막대한, 하찮은(무시할 만한))

5. 1) (달아나다/도망치다, 응시하다, 웃다/비웃다, 사라지자, 놀라다)
6. 1) (멈추다/그만두다, 떠나다, 고치다/수리하다, 취소하다, 미루다/연기하다)
7. 4) (좋아하다, 애쓰다/노력하다, 갈망하다, 결심하다/결정하다, 의도하다)
8. 3) (자라다/키우다, 담다, 소진하다(다 써버리다=use up), 줄이다/감소하다, 황폐시키다)

필수 어휘 B

1. compensate (보상하다/보충하다)
2. composed (be made up of ~ = be composed of ~ = consist of ~으로 구성되어 있다)
3. tolerate (=bear=stand 참다/견디다/관용하다)
4. stayed (=lodged 묵다/머물다/투숙하다)
5. started (시작하다/착수하다)
6. intentionally (=purposely = by design 고의로, 의도적으로)
7. forever (=for ever 영구히/영원히)
8. occasionally (=sometimes = at times = (every) now and then 가끔/때때로)
9. heavily (=in torrents 억수같이)

구문 연습

1. 생활과 책은 적절한 비율로 흔들어 (섞어서) 섭취되어야 한다. 도서관에서만 자란 소년은 책벌레가 되며, 들판에서만 자란 소년은 흙벌레[지렁이]가 된다.
2. 현미경은 급속히 개량되어 왔다, 19세기 초반에 보다 나은 렌즈들이 도입된 이래, 그래서 이제 미세한 사물들을 직경[지름] 2000배 이상으로 확대하는 것이 가능하다.
3. 서양에서의 삶의 의미는 "행복의 추구"보다 더 높은[고매한] 어떤 것으로 여겨지지 않게 되었다, 헌법에 의해 엄숙히 보장되어 온 목표(인 "행복의 추구").
4. 만약 당신이 (지금) 하고 있는 일들에 흥미가 있다면, 그것은 당신이 특정한 종류의 일들에 타고난 흥미를 갖고서 태어났기 때문이 아니라, 당신이 그 일들을 하는데 흥미를 갖게 되었기 때문이다. [come to (do) = get to (do) = learn to (do) ~하게 되다]

작문 연습

1. The bank was robbed of hundreds of thousands of dollars last night.
2. On my way home, I was caught in a shower and drenched to the skin.
3. Don't you know (that) what is done cannot[=can never] be undone?
4. It is said that his uncle was missing during the Korean War.
    His uncle is said to have been missing during the Korean War.
5. The puppy was being taken good care of by the next-door neighbor.
    Good care was being taken of the puppy by the next-door neighbor.
    [The next-door neighbor was taking good care of the puppy.]

실전 독해 A

1. 1-5) 2-which (앞 어절의 전체 또는 일부분을 가리키는 관계 대명사: 여기서는 "daily washing dries out the skin and hair"를 가리킴)
2. 4) (모든 이는 가르치는 사람이 될 잠재력을 가지고 있다.)
3. 1) (그러므로 과학은 다양성의 통일성으로의 축도[정리]로서 정의될 수 있다.)
4. 2) (우리가 익숙한 풍습이나 관습과는 다른 모든 풍습과 관습에는 두려움과 혐오감을 갖고서 바라보는 것이 아마도 타고난[자연스런] 인간의 충동일 것이다.
5. 1) (이 글의 주제인 hurricane의 "power"와는 맞지 않는 문장임)

실전 독해 B

1. 1: a) are ("are carrying about"의 대동사)   b) do ("enjoy"의 대동사)
   2: ④ (세상을 운영하는 데 필수적인 모든 장비/채비)
   3: 3)
2. take ((시간이) 걸리다, 필요로 하다, 가지고 가다, 받아들이다, 고려하다/거론하다)
3. 4) (Oxonian: Oxford 대학생)
4. 3) (~ is not interested 흥미[관심]가 없다)

확인 학습

1. 여성들이 자신들의 것이 될 수 있고 또한 되어야만 하는 사회적 지위와 권리를 획득하지 못하게 함에 있어 호주머니가 해온 역할을 아무도 조사한 적이 없다.
2. 과학은 끝없이 다양한 자연의 현상들을 설명하려고 노력한다, 특정 사건들의 독특함을 무시하고, 그것들이 공유하는 점에 집중하여 마침내 어떤 종류의 "법칙"을 추상함으로써.
3. Hester Prynne이 감옥에서 나왔을 때보다 더 귀부인[숙녀] 같아 보인 적이 결코 없었다, 그 용어("ladylike")의 옛날 해석[의미]에 있어서,
4. 아기를 자신의 가슴에 꼭 껴안는 것이 그녀의 첫 충동인 것 같았다; 모성애의 충동에 의해서라기 보다는 그렇게 함으로서 어떤 표식을 숨길 수 있다는 충동, 그 표식은 수놓아 그녀의 가슴에 부착되어 있었다. [not so much A as B: A라기 보다는 B]

실력 점검 A

1. 꾸미다/장식하다	2. 주입하다/주입시키다	3. 방해하다/훼방하다
4. 시들다/쇠약해지다	5. 해치다/손상하다	6. 위협하다/협박하다
7. 기뻐하다/즐거워하다	8. 방해하다/어지럽히다	9. (~의) 탓으로 돌리다
10. 살다/서식하다	11. 돌다/회전하다	12. 수[자수]놓다
13. 없애다/제거하다	14. 규정하다/규제하다	15. 복잡하게 하다
16. 빠지다/탐닉하다	17. 밀수하다/밀항하다	18. 구별하다/차별하다
19. 내리다/하강하다	20. 낳다/발생시키다	

실력 점검 B

1. substance	2. proverb	3. allowance
4. drawer	5. symptom	6. inconvenience
7. prey	8. drought	9. detergent
10. garment	11. chimney	12. obesity
13. prophecy	14. equation	15. amphibian
16. competent	17. tranquil	18. confidential
19. distinct	20. instructive	

실력 점검 C

1. cost (=expense: 그 군주는 많은 생명을 희생시키고 그 계획을 실행했다.)
2. place (사장님은 John의 대신에 누구를 승진시킬까를 생각 중이었다.)
3. such, customs, generations, history (지시사 "such"는 "as to ~"를 가리킴: 그 어떤 사람도, 아무리 총명하거나 박식하다 하더라도, 자기 사회의 관습과 제도를 안전하게 판단해서 간단히 처리할 만큼 (그러한) 완전한 이해에 도달할 수는 없다, 왜냐하면 이것들은 역사의 실험실에서 수세기의 실험을 거친 여러 세대의 지혜이기 때문이다.)

Unit 14 법(mood)

문법 연습 A

1. stop → stopped 또는 should stop
2. go → went   (=I wish you went home right away.)
3. was → were
4. worked → had worked
5. read → had read
6. can → could
7. will → would   (take A for B: A를 B로 여기다)
8. are → were
9. is → were
10. as if she once was ~ → as if she had once been ~
11. would have been → had been
12. may → might   (=If it had not been for ~이 없었더라면)
13. were not killed → had not been killed   (복합 가정법)

문법 연습 B

1. if   (what if ~하면 어쩌지? 어떻게 될까?)
2. could   ("could have come" 혹은 "had come")
3. had   (= Oh, if I had listened to my parents then!)
4. or   (조심해라, 그렇지 않으면 머리를 부딪힐 것이다.)
5. were   (만약 전쟁이 발발한다면, ~)
6. and   (하루만 더 지나면, (그러면) 휴가[방학]는 끝날 것이다.)
7. were   (모든 어린이들이 집에 갈 시간이다.)
8. were   (그녀는 마치 산에 걸려 넘어지는 것처럼 느꼈다.)
9. were   (만약 내가 당신의 입장[처지]에 있다면)
10. if   (대개/보통, 늘/항상은 아니지만, 우리는 "cannot"을 한 낱말로 쓴다.)
11. without   (=if it had not been for his leadership 그의 지도력이 없었다면)
12. otherwise   (그렇지 않았다면 나는 그것을 하지 않았을거야.)
13. Were   (=if it were not for ~= without ~= but for ~이 없다면)

실전 문법 A

1. otherwise   (다른, 그렇지 않은: "wise"와 운(rhyme)을 맞춘 경쾌한 표현)
2. But   (but for ~ = without ~ = If it were not for ~, If it had not been for ~이 없(었)다면)
3. were   (as it were = so to speak 말하자면/이를테면)
4. Be   (=Even if it may be so humble, ~ = However humble it may be, ~)
5. Had   (=If I had met you before, ~ 예전에 내가 당신을 만난 적이 있었더라면, ~)
6. unless   (= ~ if we had not found him.)
7. should   (주관적 판단/감정의 형용사에 수반되는 that-절의 가정법 시제)
8. should (생략 가능)   (요구/제안/명령/주장의 동사에 수반되는 that-절의 가정법 시제)
9. be   (=should be: 요구/제안/명령/주장의 동사에 수반되는 that-절의 "should"는 생략 가능)

실전 문법 B

1. 3)   (I had had someone: ((내 젊은 시절에)누군가가 있었더라면(하고 지금 원한다.))
2. 4)   (and were blind: 가정법에서는 "was"은 사용 불가)
3. 2)   (that you should realize: 판단의 형용사에 수반되는 that-절 사용되는 가정법 시제)
4. 4)   (she had not spoken: 그 말이 자신의 입술을 떠나자마자 그런 식으로 말하지 않았더라면
하고 그녀는 은밀히[속으로] 원했다: scarcely[hardly] ~ before[when] ~하자마자 ~하다)
5. 1)   (If Kevin had been: 특정한 뜻이 없는 "would"는 가정법의 조건절에서는 사용되지 않음)

6. 4) (as if the world were: "as if ~"는 구어체에서는 직설법도 많이 씀(=as if the world is ~))
7. 3) (that they (should) attend: 요구/제안/명령/주장의 동사에 수반되는 that-절의 가정법 동사)
8. 2) (were not high but low: 가정법 과거 시제(if ~ were ~, ~ would be ~)가 되어야 타당함)

필수 어휘 A

1. virtue (미덕)	2. quantity (양)	3. failure (실패)
4. prose (산문)	5. tragedy (비극)	6. descendant (자손/후손)
7. import (수입/수입하다)	8. pessimist (비관주의자)	9. employee (고용인/종업원)
10. rural, rustic (시골의)	11. artificial (인공적/인위적)	12. abstract (추상적)
13. innocent (결백한/무죄의)	14. domestic (국내의/가정의)	15. positive (긍정적/적극적)
16. barren (메마른/불모의)	17. superior (우월한)	18. paternal (아버지의/부성의)
19. physical (육체적/신체적)	20. spiritual (정신적)	21. subjective (주관적)
22. horizontal (수평적)	23. relative (상대적/비교적)	24. decrease (감소/감소하다)
25. subtract (빼다/감하다)	26. multiply (곱(셈)하다)	27. consume (소비하다)
28. descend (내리다/내려가다)	29. exclude (제외(배제)하다)	30. destroy (부수다/파괴하다)

필수 어휘 B

1. 3) (몇 시에 만날래?)
2. 1) (저장하다, 이용하다, 구제하다/덜다/경감하다, 개선하다/향상시키다, 이해하다)
3. 5) (단정한/깔끔한, 소심한/겁많은, 신중한/조심하는, 민감한, 감수성이 예민한)
4. 4) (상호간의, 윤리적, 사적인/개인적인, 가정의/가사의, 여성의/여성적인)
5. 1) (패배, 장애/장애물, 승리, 전략, 퇴각/철수)
6. 5) (신화, 우화, 기념품, 기념비/기념물, 걸작/명작)
7. 2) (추한 신축 건물들이 중세의 건물들을 대신했다/대체했다.)
8. 2) (부모님께 얼마나 많은 은혜를 입고 있는지가 그에게 절실히 와 닿았다.)

구문 연습

1. 과학의 다양한 분야들 사이에서의 현재의 협동 정신은 많은 발견들을 이룩해왔다,
    그렇지 않았더라면 이룩되지 못했을 지도 모를 (많은 발견들을).
2. (충분히) 심하게 압박을 받는다면, 대부분의 사람들은 거의 확실히 인정[자인]할 것이다,
    정치적 자유—즉, 자유롭게 말하고 반대하는 행동을 할 권리—는 실질적인 필요라기
    보다는 (오히려) 하나의 고귀한 이상임을 (인정[자인]할 것이다).
3. 다양한 발명들이 없었더라도 산업은 느린 발전을 계속했을 지도 모른다—회사들은 더
    커지고, 거래[무역]은 더 널리 퍼져나가며, 노동의 분화(분업)은 더 세밀해졌을 것이다
    —그러나 산업 혁명은 없었을 것이다.
4. 만약 내가 지금 알고 있는 것을 그때에 알았더라면 나의 20대와 30대에 나는 무엇을
    다르게 했을까? 한 가지는, 나는 더 많이 웃었을 것이고, 더 적게 슬퍼했을 것이다. 나는
    더 일찍 이해했을 것이다, 모든 상실이 다 영원한 것도 아니고 잃어버린 어떤 것들은
    간직할 가치가 없었다는 것을.

작문 연습

1. I wish (that) my son were a doctor working for the hospital.
2. If the sun were to rise in the west, what would happen to us?
3. Without oxygen and hydrogen, no drop of water could be formed.
    If it were not for oxygen and hydrogen, no drop of water could be formed.
4. If he had worked hard in his youth, he could now live in comfort.
    Had he worked hard in his youth, he could now live a comfortable life.
5. Would I have become a better writer if I had devoted my whole life to literature?

실전 독해 A

1. 3) (작가, 학자, 교사, 역사가, 철학자)
2. 1-2) (친구/일행) 2-to determine who will be his friends 3-1) (우정은 이성을 초월한다)
3. 3) (서식지/거주지, 본능, 폭력, 협력/협동, 환경)
4. 1-1) (the sky (should) be blue) 2-4) (좋은 예술가는 상투적인 생각과 개념을 기꺼이 포기한다)

실전 독해 B

1. 5) (Ms. Wallace를 추천하는 글임)
2. 1-3) 2-4) (다 써버리다, 키우다/양육하다, 초래하다, 찾아내다/생각해내다, 따라잡다)
3. 3) ("neuron"에 관한 이 문장은 글의의 전체적인 통일성을 해치고 있음)
4. 4) (하나의 적극적 과정으로서의 독서)
5. 5) (그 문은 당신에게 잘못된 신호를 주고 있다.)

확인 학습

1. 당신이 고결해서 고결한 친구를 원한다는 이유로 당신이 당신의 친구를 선택한다면,
   상업적인 이유로 당신의 친구를 선택하는 경우보다 진정한 우정에 더 가깝지는 않다.
2. 우리들이 그 존재에 대해서 결코 꿈도 꾸지 못했던 자연의 새로운 아름다움을 우리에게
   보도록 가르치는 것은 바로 그들[예술가/미술가들]이다.
3. 그는 너무나 자기 자신에게 열중해왔고 은둔 생활을 영위해와서, 집주인 여자는 말할 것도
   없고, 어느 누구도 만나기를 두려워하였다.
4. 계단에 멈춰서 그와는 전혀 관계도 없는 따분한 헛소리를 듣고, 그 모든 집요한 지불
   요구를 듣고, 그 모든 으름장과 불평을 듣고서 그럴듯한 변명을 생각해내고 거짓말을
   해야만 하는 것 보다는 차라리 – 아니! 생쥐처럼 조용히 아래층으로 미끄러져 (내려가) 어느
   누구에게도 눈에 뛰지 않게 벗어나는 것이 천 배는 더 낫지.

실력 점검 A

1. 통치하다/판결하다
2. 새다/새어나오다
3. 설치하다/가설하다
4. 붙잡다/움켜잡다
5. (~으로) 여기다/간주하다
6. 자격을 부여하다
7. 변호하다/간청하다
8. 금하다/억제하다
9. 손짓하다/신호하다
10. 할당하다/부여하다
11. 권유하다/야기하다
12. 평가하다, 값을 구하다
13. 뒤쫓다/추구하다
14. 투표에서 이기다
15. 따라잡다/추월하다
16. 둘러싸다/동봉하다
17. 증발하다/증발시키다
18. 훼손하다/손상시키다
19. 소환하다/호출하다
20. 위협하다/협박하다

실력 점검 B

1. disaster
2. impulse
3. agriculture
4. routine
5. labor
6. consciousness
7. altitude
8. figure
9. conviction
10. refuge
11. dairy
12. acquisition
13. victim
14. funeral
15. harsh
16. thirsty
17. abstract
18. bankrupt
19. tranquil
20. redundant

실력 점검 C

1. well (~ as well: ~또한)
2. With (또는 For), such (그가 자신의 아버지로부터 물려받은 그 큰 재산에도 불구하고,
   그는 너무나 높은 인격의 사람이어서 소박한[검소한] 삶을 살았다.)
3. too, without (cannot ~ too ~: 아무리 ~해도 부족하다[지나치지 않다], get along 잘 지내다)

Unit 15 화법(narration)

문법 연습 A

1. said to → told
2. where were his wife and children → where his wife and children were
3. last night → the night before 또는 the previous night
4. saw → had seen, ago → before
5. was → is (진리는 항상 현재 시제로 표현함)
6. that → if 또는 whether (~인지 아닌지)
7. was → is (속담/격언은 항상 현재 시제로 표현함)
8. had been invented → was invented (역사적 사실은 항상 과거 시제로 표현함)
9. if he was a bird → if he *were* a bird (가정법 시제는 변환되지 않음)
10. and he couldn't ~ → and *that* he couldn't ~ (and, but, or 다음의 접속사 "that"은 생략 불가)

문법 연습 B

1. He said (that) it was three years since my father had died.
2. She asked me if(=whether) I had seen her brother the day before (=the previous day).
3. The captain told(=ordered) his men to keep an eye on the prisoners.
4. She asked him to show her the way to the church.
5. He asked her not to forget to see him there the next(=following) day.
6. She asked me where I had been, and suggested that we (should) go out for lunch.
7. He exclaimed that she was a very lovely girl, and said that he wished she were his girlfriend.
   He exclaimed what a lovely girl she was, and said that he wished she were his girlfriend.
8. She told him that she had liked him very much, but that she hadn't loved him at all.

실전 문법 A

1. 5) (she hung up the phone: hang-hanged-hanged 목매달다, 교수형에 처하다)
2. 1) (From their beginnings: "newspaper comics (신문 만화들)"가 복수형임에 유의)
3. 4) (it is very difficult for them to learn: learn to (do) = come to (do) = get to (do) ~하게 되다)
4. 3) (would he be able: 강조된 어구/어절이 문장 첫머리에 놓일 경우, 주어/동사가 도치됨)
5. 5) (until new leaves appear: 시간/조건의 부사절에서는 미래 시제 대신에 현재 시제 사용)
6. 2) (some of my friends have: 앞 어절이 완료형이므로 "have"를 대동사로 채택해야 함)

실전 문법 B

1. 1) (I was taking a shower: 문장의 의미상 과거 진행형이 되어야 타당함)
2. 4) (a primary concern of literary critics: literate 글을 아는, 읽고 쓸 수 있는, literary 문학의)
3. 4) (lay in the coastal area: lie-lay-lain(~에) 놓여있다, lay-laid-laid(~을) 놓다/두다/낳다)
4. 2) (is that the subway train: "The reason is because ~"도 점차 쓰이는 경향이 있음)
5. 3) (is the basic foodstuff: 문장의 주어인 "plankton"이 단수 명사임에 유의)
6. 2) (that his son (should) spend ~: 요구/제안/명령/주장의 that-절의 가정법 시제)

필수 어휘 A

1. 3) (make sense 이해되다, 합당하다, 이치에 맞다, make sense of ~을 이해하다)
2. 2) (지폐/청구서, 수표(=cheque), 신용/외상, 잔돈/거스름돈, 계좌/계정)

3. 1) (빚/채무, 명성, 허영/허영심, 무질서/장애, 질문/의문)
4. 2) (have no idea (~에 대해) 전혀 모르다)
5. 5) (have a good command of ~을 잘 구사하다)

필수 어휘 B
1. 2) (의미하다/함축하다, 비난하다, 후회하다, 용서하다/변명하다, 관계하다)
2. 3) (재능 있는, 품위 있는, 유명한/저명한, 희미한/이름없는, 영리한/창의적인)
3. 1) (숙련된/능숙한, 흥분된, 기쁜/즐거운, 놀란, 만족한)
4. 1) (모호한, 논리적, 분명한/명확한, 추상적, 복잡한)
5. 3) (영향을 주다, 참다/견디다, 줄이다/축소하다, 숨기다, 없애다/제거하다)
6. 5) (믿음, 이론, 태도, 원리/원칙, 개념)
7. 4) (끝내다/마치다, 계속하다, 수행하다/공연하다, 운동하다/훈련하다, 노력하다)
8. 2) (최근의/최신의: out-of-date 낡은/구식의)

구문 연습
1. 누군가가 아리스토텔레스를 비난했단다, 사악한 사람에게 너무 자비로웠다고. "나는 정말 그 사람에게 자비로웠소," 그는 대답했다, "그러나 그의 사악함에는 자비롭지 않았소."
2. 양 한 마리가 서투르게 털을 깎이고 있었다. "만약 당신이 원하는 게 나의 (양)털이라면," 그 양은 말했다, "너무 바싹 깎지는 마시오. 만약 당신이 추구하는 게 나의 살(코기)라면 나를 곧장 죽이시오. 조금씩 조금씩 죽어가도록 나를 고문하지는 마시오."
3. "Shaw씨," 어떤 기자가 물었다, "만약 당신이 당신의 삶을 다시 살아서 당신이 알고 있는 어떤 사람이나 역사상의 어떤 인물이 될 수 있다면, 당신은 누가 되고 싶습니까?" "나는 선택하고 싶소," Shaw가 응답했다, "George Bernard Shaw가 될 수 있었지만 결코 되지 못한 그 사람이 되기를."
4. 한번은 내가 전화상으로 아빠가 어떠시냐고 물어봤을 때, 불쑥 엄마 말씀이, "너네 아빠가 좀 이상한 것 같아. 아무 것도 켜놓지/걸치지(on) 않고 거실에 앉아 계셔." "아무 것도 안 걸치고/켜놓고?" 나는 반복했다, 걱정이 되어서. "그래," 엄마가 응답하셨다, "TV도 끄고, 라디오도 끄고, 컴퓨터도 껐단다.

작문 연습
1. She asked me if(=whether) I had seen (a) deer in the woods.
2. He said to me, "Is there anything new in today's newspaper?"
3. He told me that his mother had died a few years before.
4. He said to her, "What do you say to playing gold this weekend?"
5. My homeroom teacher said (that) heaven helps those who help themselves.

실전 독해 A
1. 1) (욕심/탐욕, 부/재산, 허영/허영심, 이기심, 유혹)
2. 1-2)   2-1)
3. sense (사려/분별력, 지각하다/알아채다, 감/느낌, 뜻/의미, 감각/오감)
4. ③ (우리들은 그것에만 의존하지는 않는다.)
5. 1-None (그 누구도 그것 없이 지낼 수 있을 만큼 (그렇게) 부유하지는 않다.)
    2-as those who have none left to give (줄 것이 아무것도 남겨져 있지 않은 사람들만큼 ~)

실전 독해 B

1. 5) (무는 刼도 때로는 물린다.)
2. 2) (방심/명함(얼 빠짐)/건망증: absent-minded = inattentive, forgetful, preoccupied)
3. 5) (가정법 과거: who *would* care about the new year if it *were* in mid July?)
4. 4) (만약 내가 남들에게 빚진[은혜를 입고 있는] 그 모든 것을 설명할 수 있다면,
   내 자신의 것은 단지 조금 밖에 없을 것이다. give an account of ~을 설명하다)
5. 1-4) 2-5) (현명한, 예의 바른, 정직한, 겸손한, 총명한/명석한)

확인 학습

1. 사람들이 자신들에 관해서 제공하는 정보가 거짓일 수 있다는 사실이 그 정보는
   결코 신뢰할 수 없다는 것을 함의[뜻]하지는 않는다.
2. 그 누구도 그것(미소)없이 지낼 수 있을 만큼 (그렇게) 부유하지는 않다; 그들은
   그것의 혜택 때문에 더욱 부유하다. 줄 것이 아무 것도 남겨져 있지 않은 사람들만큼
   미소를 필요로 하는 사람은 없다.
3. 그녀는 자신의 실수를 알아채지 못했다, 아기의 왼발을 (빨래)줄에 핀으로 꽂을 때
   그 아기가 울 때 까지, 말리기 위해서 아기를 마당에 걸어놓을 때에.
4. 길가 여관에서 우연히 만나는 어느 집단의 사람들도 그들, Oblonsky 가족과 그 하인들,
   보다는 더 많은 것을 공유하고 있었을 것이다.
5. 아마도 그는 자신의 비행을 아내에게 숨김에 있어 더 성공적이었을 것이다, 만약 그가
   그 발각이 그녀에게 미칠 영향을 어렴풋이 느꼈더라면.

실력 점검 A

1. 저장하다/보관하다
2. 추론하다/추리하다
3. 의심하다, 낌새를 느끼다
4. 숨막히게 하다
5. 더럽히다/변색시키다
6. 격노케 하다
7. (나누어) 주다
8. 확장하다/팽창하다
9. 자극하다/북돋우다
10. 뒤집다, 거꾸로 하다
11. 속이다/기만하다
12. 횡령하다/착복하다
13. 면제하다
14. 검사하다/검토하다
15. 초월하다
16. 바꾸다/전환하다
17. 버티다/저항하다
18. 감사하다/평가하다/인식하다
19. 재다/측정하다
20. 과장하다

실력 점검 B

1. planet
2. insect
3. patience
4. faculty
5. defect
6. despair
7. oath
8. expenditure
9. device
10. well
11. opportunity
12. celebrity
13. velocity
14. priority
15. insight
16. prophet
17. criminal
18. perpetual
19. odious
20. inconsistent

실력 점검 C

1. appear, visible (if it were not for dust ~: 먼지가 없다면 하늘은 절대적으로 검게 보일 것이며,
   별들은 심지어 대낮에도 눈에 보일 것이다.)
2. effect, still, affect (have an effect on ~ = affect = influence ~에게 영향을 미치다: 모든 사람은,
   아무리 하찮은 사람이라도, 누군가 딴 사람에게 영향을 미친다, 돌 하나가
   고요한 물속에 던져질 때 잔 물결을 내보내는 것 처럼. 다른 사람들에게
   이런 저런 식으로 영향을 미치지 않는 사람은 없다.)

Unit 16 비교(comparison)

문법 연습 A

1. than → to   (prefer A to B: A를 B보다 선호하다)
2. prettier → the prettier   ("of the two"로 한정되므로 비교급에서도 정관사를 붙임)
3. wiser → more wise   (하나의 대상 내부에서의 다른 측면의 비교)
4. better → the better   ("for ~"로 한정되므로 비교급에서도 정관사를 붙임)
5. father → further   ("거리"의 개념이 아닌 "정도"의 개념임)
6. later → latter   (시간적 개념이라기 보다는 순서적 개념: "그녀 인생의 후반부")
7. the most dangerous → most dangerous   (명사를 수식하지 않는 형용사의 최상급)
8. very → much 또는 far, even, still, a lot   (비교급을 강조하는 부사들)
9. brightest → the brightest   (the brightest (student): 명사를 수식하는 형용사의 최상급)
10. last → latest   (순서적 개념이 아닌 시간적 개념: "가장 최신(최근)의 것")
11. superior as → superior to   (~보다 우월한 ↔ inferior to ~보다 열등한)
12. girls → girl   (비교급에서는 "any other + 단수명사"를 사용함)
13. old → older   (grow older = get older 더 늙어 가다, 나이가 더 들다)

문법 연습 B

1. to   (=She is senor to my sister by two years. ↔ junior to ~보다 연하의)
2. the   (사람은 많이 가질수록 더 많이 원한다.)
3. many   (열 명의 사람들이 열 명의 유령들처럼 모여들었다.)
4. far   (as far as ~만큼 멀리: 그들은 지하철역까지 갔다)
5. less   (much less = still less: 걸을 수 조차 없는데, 하물며 뛸 수야.)
6. many   (3시간이 3분같이 지나갔다.)
7. better   (know better than to (do) ~할 만큼 바보가 아니다)
8. without   (그녀는 작별 인사 조차 없이 떠났다.)
9. as   (그는 과학자라기 보다는 기술자다.)
10. as   (배수는 동등비교 "as ~ as" 앞에 위치함.)
11. less   (너의 어머니는 나의 어머니보다 훨씬 덜 늙어 보인다.)
12. many   (우리는 열 장의 표가 있지만, 열 장 더 필요할 것이다.)
13. the   (of the two, for, because 등으로 한정될 때는 비교급에서도 정관사 사용)

실전 문법 A

Mt. Baekdu is the highest mountain in the Korean peninsula.
= Mt. Baekdu is the highest of all the mountains in the Korean peninsula.
= Mt. Baekdu is higher than any other mountain in the Korean peninsula.
= No (other) mountain in the Korean peninsula is higher than Mt. Baekdu.
= No (other) mountain in the Korean peninsula is so(=as) high as Mt. Baekdu.

실전 문법 B

1. 3)   (as essential an activity: "as, so, too, how, however" 바로 뒤에는 형용사/부사가 온다)
2. 4)   (to a phrase or sentence: prefer A to B)
3. 5)   (is determined by his or her height: A is no more B than C is D)
4. 4)   (I had expected: 그런 곳에서 만나리라고 내가 결코 기대하지 못했던 사람")
5. 4)   (because the poles are closer: 극지방이 (적도보다) 지구의 중심에 더 가깝기 때문에)
6. 5)   (exactly what making a thing means 간접 의문문은 주어/동사가 도치되지 아니함)
7. 4)   (still less = much less: 앞 어절이 부정문임에 유의; learn ~ by heart ~을 암기하다)
8. 2)   (as any other communication device: "as ~ as ~" 동등 비교 구문)
9. 2)   (the less detail it can show: 지도가 감당하는 영역이 넓을수록 덜 상세함)

필수 어휘 A

1. 역사적인(획기적인), 역사에 남는; 역사의(역사상의), (역)사적인
2. 경제의(경제상의); 경제적인(실속 있는), 검소한, 절약하는
3. 확실한, 믿을[신뢰할] 수 있는; 쉽사리 믿는, 잘 속아넘어가는
4. 상상의/가상의; 상상력이 풍부한
5. 산업의/산업적; 근면한/부지런한
6. 비교되는(with), 필적하는(to); 비교적/상대적, 비교(상)의
7. 존경하는, 경의를 표하는; 존경할 만한, 존경할 수 있는
8. 인상적인, 감동적인; 감수성이 예민한, 감동을 잘하는
9. 순간의/순간적인; 중대한/중요한
10. 바람직한, 갖고 싶은; ~을 바라는, 원하는
11. 분별 있는, 느낄 수 있는; ~에 민감한, 예민한
12. 상당한, 고려할 만한; ~을 고려하는/배려하는, 잘 생각해 주는

필수 어휘 B

1. 4) (~보다 빛나다: 질식시키다, 칭송하다, 속이다, 능가하다, 따라잡다)
2. 5) (알다, 받아들이다, 상상하다, 깨닫다/인식하다, 이해하다)
3. 1) (게으른/나태한, 화난/성난, 겸손한, 조심하는/주의하는, 거만한)
4. 5) (높은, 적절한, 자연적, 적당한/온화한/보통의, 일정한/불변의)
5. 2) (잉여: 위기, 초과/과다, 공급, 수요, 부족)
6. 3) (부정어의 앞에서 "거의": *next to* nothing, *nest to* impossible)
7. 2) (as often as not = fairly often, more often than not = usually)

구문 연습

1. 질투하는 사람은 남들에게서 그들의 이점을 빼앗는데, 그것은 그에게는 똑같은
   이점을 자기 스스로 확보하는 만큼이나 바람직하다.
2. 언어에 있어 원시성의 문제를 우리가 고려하면[생각하면] 할수록, 어떤 언어를
   열등하다든가 원시적이라고 부르는 것은 합리적이지 못한 것처럼 보인다.
3. 당신이 당신 자신을 험담하는 말을 할 때만큼 사람들이 당신을 쉽사리 믿어주는 때는
   없으며, 그들이 당신 말을 곧이곧대로 받아들일 때만큼 당신이 많이 속상할 때도 없다.
4. (아직) 많은 것이 발견되어야[밝혀져야] 한다, 무엇이 어떤 사람들은 다른 사람들보다
   더 영리하고, 더 유능하며, 더 큰 응용력을 갖게 하는지에 관해서.
5. 그 어떤 문화나 문명에 있어서 최우위에 있어야만 하는 것은 철학이지 과학이 아니다,
   왜냐하면 단순히 그것[철학]이 답변할 수 있는 문제들이 더 중요하기 때문에. 분명한
   것은 우리가 더 많은 과학을 소유할수록 우리는 철학을 더 많이 필요로 한다는 점이다,
   왜냐하면 우리가 더 많은 힘을 가질수록 우리는 방향을 더 많이 필요로 하기 때문이다.

작문 연습

1. The more you enjoy smoking and drinking, the more difficult it becomes to stop them.
2. The public library has more than three times as many books as we have.
3. Frankly speaking, he is not so much a real artist as a mere imitator.
   To be frank with you, he is not a real artist so much as a mere imitator.
4. As we gets older, we come to realize that life is worth living.
5. Dokdo is no more a Japanese island than Daemado is a Korean island.
   Dokdo is not a Japanese island any more than Daemado is a Korean island.

실전 독해 A

1. 1-as ("as ~as ~" 동등 비교 구문: "~에 관심이 없는 만큼이나 ~에도 관심이 없다")
   2-1) (keep ~ from ~ = prevent ~ from ~: "죽음에 대한 생각처럼 숙고하지 못하게 되는")
2. 5) (~ *so* well known *that* ~; *without* capital letter (대문자 없이 (소문자로), 즉 일반 명사로)
3. 3) (= Nothing is so beautiful *that* does *not* betray ~을 드러내지 않을 만큼 아름다운 것은 없다.)
4. 4) ("자신[자아]에 대한 혐오감으로부터 샘솟는[솟아나는] 고통들이 파괴하는 것처럼")
5. 5) (자연 과학이 사회 과학 보다 훨씬 더 많은 발전을 해왔다.)

실전 독해 B

1. 1-5) 2-(the idea of) group loyalty (집단 충성심: pack mentality 집단[패거리] 정신) 3-3)
2. 2)
3. as, conservative (사람들은 일반적으로 진보적이라기 보다는 보수적.)
4. 4) (= any task [that/which] a computer is asked to do must be spelled out ~.)

확인 학습

1. 대다수의 사람들은 일반적인 자연의 작용[활동]에 관심이 없다, 그들이 자기 자신의 몸 속에서 일어나는 과정[작용]에 관심이 없는 만큼이나.
2. 가까이서 보면, 그것들의 매력은 사라지고 본래의[내재적인] 추함만 남는다. 면밀히 조사해 보면 얼마간 결점[결함]을 드러내지 않을 정도로 (그렇게) 아름다운 것은 아무 것도 없다.
3. 컴퓨터 프로그래밍에 관한 스쳐가는 지식이나마 있는 사람이라면, 하나의 기계가 평이한 영어의 중의성[다의성]을 이해하게 될 가능성은 (거의) 놀라움에 가깝다.
4. 나의 아버님의 상속 재산은, 15명의 자식들 사이에 나누어진 매우 작은 땅[소유지]의 단지 1/15이었는데, 거의 없는 것이나 마찬가지였으며, 아버님은 생계를 위해서 전적으로 시계 제조공의 직업에 의존하셨는데, 그것에 아버님은 대단한 숙련공이셨다.

실력 점검 A

1. 돌보다, 경향이 있다
2. 크게 기뻐하다
3. 열망하다/갈망하다
4. 발전하다/진화하다
5. 칭찬하다/감탄하다
6. 숨쉬다/호흡하다
7. 초과하다, 도를 넘다
8. 포함하다/포함시키다
9. 땀을 흘리다
10. 뛰어들다, 던져 넣다
11. 조사하다/검사하다
12. 놀라게 하다
13. 주다/수여하다
14. 위협하다/협박하다
15. 구성하다, 구성되어 있다
16. 간청하다/애원하다
17. 삼키다/들이켜다
18. 물러나다/인출하다
19. 회상하다/상기하다
20. 밝히다/조명하다

실력 점검 B

1. harvest
2. statistics
3. appetite
4. germ
5. fuel
6. prospect
7. immigrant
8. villain
9. colleague
10. anxiety
11. emergency
12. editorial
13. reaction
14. illegal
15. temporary
16. urgent
17. stubborn
18. supplementary
19. archive
20. periodical

실력 점검 C

1. mightier (might 힘, mighty 힘센/강력한: "文이 武보다 강하다고 정말 믿니?")
2. scarcely, itself (scarcely[hardly] ~ before[when] ~ : ~하자마자 ~하다; paradox 역설)
3. about, significance, physical (bring about ~을 초래하다; 중요성; 신체의/육체적)

Unit 17 문체(style)

문법 연습 A

1. stay and help → to stay and help
2. where you live → address
3. neither be happy in the city ~ → be happy neither in the city ~
4. but what he does → but by what he does
5. who is admired by all of us → whom all of us admire
6. that he invented dynamite → his invention of dynamite
7. a strong desire that he wishes to be ~ → a strong desire to be ~
8. the people of the country → of the people of the country
9. at any time or even now → at any time

문법 연습 B

1. Who is it that is going to take care of the children?
2. It is their freedom and independence that they are fight for.
    (=It is for their freedom and independence that they are fighting.)
3. It was not until after the First World War that women gained the vote.

문법 연습 C

1. Down came the rain with a clap of thunder.
2. So angry was my teacher that he didn't know what to do.
3. Never did he think that she was about to go on stage again.
4. Not until after the First World War did women gain the vote.

실전 문법 A

1. very (바로 그 밑바닥)
2. whatever (그 어떤 화제[논제]라도)
3. ever (소년 시절 이래로/이후로 줄곧)
4. earth (대체/도대체: on earth = in the world)
5. right (지금 당장은)
6. very (바로 그 생각)
7. ever (지금껏 쓰여진: ~ which have ever been written.)
8. whatever (그 어떤 과학적 증거도)
9. oneself 또는 himself (자기 스스로는 완벽히 정상적이라고 여기는 것)

실전 문법 B

1. 1) (It is in the joint ~: 뼈의 움직임이 일어나는 것은 인체의 관절에서이다.)
2. 3) (did Charles Ives receive ~: 자신의 작품에 대해서 어느 정도 인정을 받다.)
3. 5) (of ill health and early death in our society: "parallelism"에 유의할 것.)
4. 2) (have people begun to realize: 문두에 도치/강조된 어구/어절이 있음에 유의.)
5. 5) (on any other sense: "parallelism"에 유의 할 것)
6. 3) (collecting stamps: "parallelism"에 유의할 것.)
7. 4) (what he saw, heard and felt: 능동태/수동태의 혼용: 표현의 일관성에 유의.)
8. 3) (yet so feeble is our observation: "so ~ that ~": "그러나 관찰력이 너무나 미약해서 ~")

필수 어휘 A

1. 1) (perish 죽다/멸망하다/사라지다)
2. 4) (prudent = careful, cautious 신중한, 세심한, 조심성 있는)
3. 3) (objective = purpose, aim, goal 목적/목표)
4. 2) (abrupt 돌연한/갑작스러운)
5. 3) (humility 겸손/겸양)
6. 5) (neglect 무시하다/간과하다, negligible 무시할 만한, 하찮은, 사소한)

필수 어휘 B

1. 1) (loathe 질색하다, 몹시 싫어하다)
2. 5) (grumble 불평하다/투덜대다)
3. 2) (humiliate 창피를 주다, 굴욕감을 주다)
4. 4) (yield 생산하다/산출하다, yield to ~에게 양보하다/양도하다/굴복하다)
5. 5) (priceless 대단히 귀중한, 돈으로 살 수 없는)
6. 4) (refer to ~ 관계하다/관련하다, 참고하다/조회하다, 언급하다/인용하다)
7. 1) (avail oneself of ~을 이용하다/사용하다, 받아들이다)

구문 연습

1. 옳은 순간에 옳은 친구를 만나는 사람은 행운이며, 옳은 순간에 옳은 적을 만나는 사람 또한 행운이다.
2. 삶의 아름다움은 중요한 것이 아니라고 감히 주장할 사람은 거의 없을 거라고 나는 생각하지만, 대부분의 문명인들은 마치 그것이 아무 것도 아닌 양 행동한다.
3. 오늘날 문제[의문]시 되는 것은 "자유"나 "민주주의" 같은 말에 부착된 가치들이다.
4. 인간의 언어와 동물의 의사소통의 형태[형식] 사이의 간극[격차]이 너무나 커서 그것[격차]은 진화론적인 설명을 (제공)하기가 가장 어려운 인간의 특성으로 남아있다.
5. 심각한 에너지 부족과 극심한 오염이 일상 생활을 방해하기 시작할 때 까지는 아니었다, 우리가 지구의 자원들에 대한 우리의 무책임한 사용을 문제시하고 자연을 이용됨은 물론 보호될 힘으로 보기 시작한 것은. (= ~이 일상 생활을 방해하기 시작해서야 비로소, 우리는 ~을 문제시하고 자연을 ~힘으로 보기 시작했다.)

작문 연습

1. It was the day before yesterday that I happened to meet the young man on the street.
2. Little did she dream that she would fall in love with him.
3. Let's think about the theory of relativity and its application to our life.
4. So harmonious were the temple and the valley that the scenery was a work of art.
   (The temple and the valley were so harmonious that the scenery was a work of art.)
5. Among the causes of the diminution of our intelligence is the last half a century of television watching.
   (The last half a century of television watching is among the causes of the diminution of our intelligence.)

실전 독해 A

1. 1)
2. 1-4)   2-4)
3. 2) ((should) be set aside: 제안("made the suggestion") 동사의 that-절의 조동사 "should")
4. ⑤ (예를 들면, 미국에서는 인구의 약 2/3가 아직도 주된 식사를 저녁에 갖는다.)

실전 독해 B

1. 2) (딸/여자들의 고등 교육[대학 교육]에 대해 별로 좋아하지 않았을 뿐이다.)
2. 4) (글의 순서를 파악할 때는 정관사, 대명사, 접속(부)사 등에 특히 유의할 것.)
3. raise (~을 올리다/세우다/일으키다, 기르다/키우다/재배하다, 모금하다/조달하다)
4. tennis shoes ("ten issues(열 개의 발행판/호)"를 연음으로 발음하면 거의 같게 들림.)
5. 5) (시작하다/협상하다, ~에도 불구하고/~외에도, 오르다(증가하다)/~을 올리다)

확인 학습

1. 만약 자유가 자기 자신의 생각을 생각하고 자기 자신의 추구하는 바를 따를 권리를 의미한다면, 그 분이 그랬던 것 보다 더 완전하게 자유를 주장한 사람은 없다.
2. 그것은 확실히 어느 정도 단순한 독서나 관람이 가져다 주는 즐거움을 증가시키겠지만, 그것이 분명히 그 즐거움의 대체물은 아닐 것이다.
3. 이것이 그 어린이를, 형제 자매와 함께 양육된 어린이 보다, 자기 또래의 사람들과 교통하는 능력을 저하시킬 수 있다고 어떤 이들은 생각한다.
4. 많은 소년 소녀들이 그와 사랑에 빠졌지만, 그의 부드러운 젊은 몸은 너무나 단호한 자존심을 담고 있어서 그 소년 소녀들의 어느 누구도 감히 그와 접촉하지 못했다.
5. 어느 날, 겁 많은 양들을 우리 속으로 몰아넣고 있었을 대, 그는 그 말 많은 요정의 눈에 띄게 되었는데, 그 요정은 다른 이가 말할 때는 조용히 있을 수가 없으나 아직 자신이 먼저 말하는 법은 배우지 못했다.

실력 점검 A

1. 아찔(어리벙벙)하게 하다
2. 내뿜다/분출하다
3. 확인하다, 확실히 하다
4. 애쓰다/노력하다
5. 달성하다/도달하다
6. 따르다/순응하다(~ to)
7. 서두르다/재촉하다
8. 주름(살)이 지다
9. 소독하다/살균하다
10. 점화하다/발화하다
11. 파내다/발굴하다
12. 참다/견디다/버티다
13. 의도하다/작정하다
14. 미루다/연기하다
15. 집중하다/집결하다(~ on)
16. 따르다/응하다(~ with)
17. 동면하다/피한하다
18. ~을 구독하다, ~에 기명하다
19. ~을 작성하다/입안하다
20. 생기다/유래하다

실력 점검 B

1. equator
2. instinct
3. countenance
4. boredom
5. humidity
6. immortality
7. volcano
8. advent
9. stability
10. tomb
11. clue
12. monument
13. pauper
14. astrology
15. ultraviolet
16. secure
17. timid
18. coherent
19. impartial
20. controversial

실력 점검 C

1. made, in[into] (make an effort 노력하다, put ~ in/into practice ~을 실행하다/실천하다)
2. against (대조/대비/배경: *against* the blue sky ~을 배경으로, ~에 대조되어/대비되어)
3. that (동격의 that-절: "그가 전쟁에서 사망했다는 소식 ~")
4. that ("it is ~ that ~" 강조 구문: 강조되는 부분은 "only in childhood")
5. not to (代부정사: ~ for a poet *not to* (get emotional when he describes a daffodil.))

Writing Checklist

01. About them sentence fragments.

     토막 문장을 만들지 말 것.

02. Verbs *has* to agree with their subjects.

     동사는 주어와 일치할 것.

03. Try *to* not ever *split* infinitives.

     분리 부정사를 쓰지 말 것.

04. Between you and *I*, case is important.

     격(格)의 사용에 유의 할 것.

05. When *dangling*, watch your participles.

     현수(懸垂)분사에 유의할 것.

06. Avoid clichés like the *plague*.

     상투적인 어구를 피할 것.

07. Use your apostrophe's correctly.

     어포스트러피를 올바르게 사용할 것.

08. Do*n't* use *no* double negatives.

     이중 부정을 쓰지 말 것.

09. Don't use commas, that aren't necessary.

     코머를 불필요하게 사용하지 말 것.

10. Proofread *you* writing.

     쓴 글은 교정을 볼 것.